THE
INTERNATIONAL UNIVERSITY SERIES
IN
PSYCHOLOGY

Edited by
CARL MURCHISON, Ph.D.
Professor of Psychology and Director of the
Psychological Laboratories in Clark University

THE
INTERNATIONAL UNIVERSITY SERIES

Directed by
CARL MURCHISON, Ph.D.

Professor of Psychology and Director of the
Psychological Laboratories in Clark University,
Director of the Clark University Press

THE INTERNATIONAL UNIVERSITY SERIES IN BIOLOGICAL SCIENCE

EDITED BY HERBERT SPENCER JENNINGS, Ph.D., Sc.D., LL.D.

Henry Walters Professor of Zoology and
Director of the Biological Laboratory in The
Johns Hopkins University

THE INTERNATIONAL UNIVERSITY SERIES IN CULTURE AND SOCIETY

EDITED BY CLARK WISSLER, Ph.D.

Professor of Anthropology in the Institute of
Psychology, Yale University, and Curator in
Anthropology, American Museum of Natural
History

THE INTERNATIONAL UNIVERSITY SERIES IN DIPLOMACY AND INTERNATIONAL RELATIONS

EDITED BY GEORGE HUBBARD BLAKESLEE, Ph.D., L.H.D.

Professor of History and International Relations
in Clark University

THE INTERNATIONAL UNIVERSITY SERIES IN ECONOMICS

THE INTERNATIONAL UNIVERSITY SERIES IN GEOGRAPHY

EDITED BY WALLACE WALTER ATWOOD, Ph.D.

President of Clark University and Director of
the Graduate School of Geography

THE INTERNATIONAL UNIVERSITY SERIES IN HISTORY

THE INTERNATIONAL UNIVERSITY SERIES IN PSYCHOLOGY

EDITED BY CARL MURCHISON, Ph.D.

Professor of Psychology and Director of the
Psychological Laboratories in Clark University

PSYCHOLOGIES OF 1925

THE
INTERNATIONAL UNIVERSITY SERIES
IN
PSYCHOLOGY
Edited by
CARL MURCHISON, Ph.D.
Professor of Psychology and Director of the
Psychological Laboratories in Clark University

PSYCHOLOGIES OF 1925
By Madison Bentley, Knight Dunlap, Walter S. Hunter,
Kurt Koffka, Wolfgang Köhler, William McDougall, Mor-
ton Prince, John B. Watson and Robert S. Woodworth.

CRIMINAL INTELLIGENCE
By Carl Murchison, Ph.D., Professor of Psychology and
Director of the Psychological Laboratories in Clark Uni-
versity.

THE CASE FOR AND AGAINST PSYCHICAL BELIEF
By Sir Oliver Lodge, Sir Arthur Conan Doyle, Frederick
Bligh Bond, L. R. G. Crandon, Mary Austin, Margaret
Deland, William McDougall, Hans Driesch, Walter Frank-
lin Prince, F. C. S. Schiller, John E. Coover, Gardner
Murphy, Joseph Jastrow, and Harry Houdini.

VOLUMES IN PRESS
THE COMMON-SENSE OF DREAMS
By Henry J. Watt, Ph.D., Late Lecturer in Psychology in
the University of Glasgow, and Consulting Psychologist to
the Glasgow Royal Asylum. Author of "The Psychology
of Sound."

FEELINGS AND EMOTIONS: THE WITTENBERG
SYMPOSIUM
By A. Adler, F. Aveling, V. Bechterev, M. Bentley, G. S.
Brett, K. Bühler, W. B. Cannon, H. A. Carr, Ed.
Claparède, K. Dunlap, R. H. Gault, D. W. Gruehn, L. B.
Hoisington, D. T. Howard, E. Jaensch, P. Janet, J. Jas-
trow, C. Jörgensen, D. Katz, F. Kiesow, F. Krüger, H. S.
Langfeld, W. McDougall, H. Piéron, W. B. Pillsbury, M.
Prince, C. E. Seashore, C. E. Spearman, W. Stern, G. M.
Stratton. M. F. Washburn, A. P. Weiss, R. S. Woodworth.

THE INTERNATIONAL UNIVERSITY SERIES IN PSYCHOLOGY

I
PSYCHOLOGIES OF 1925
POWELL LECTURES IN PSYCHOLOGICAL THEORY
Third Edition

By

MADISON BENTLEY, Ph.D.
University of Illinois

KNIGHT DUNLAP, Ph.D.
The Johns Hopkins University

WALTER S. HUNTER, Ph.D.
Clark University

KURT KOFFKA, Ph.D.
University of Giessen

WOLFGANG KÖHLER, Ph.D.
University of Berlin

WILLIAM McDOUGALL, Sc.D., F.R.S.
Harvard University

MORTON PRINCE, M.D.
Harvard University

JOHN B. WATSON, Ph.D.
The Johns Hopkins University

ROBERT S. WOODWORTH, Ph.D.
Columbia University

Edited by
CARL MURCHISON, Ph.D.
Clark University

WORCESTER, MASSACHUSETTS
CLARK UNIVERSITY PRESS
LONDON: HUMPHREY MILFORD
OXFORD UNIVERSITY PRESS
1928

First Edition, May, 1926
Second Edition, February, 1927
Third Edition, January, 1928

PRINTED IN THE UNITED STATES OF AMERICA

PREFACE TO THE THIRD EDITION

It has become necessary to issue a third edition of this book. No actual changes have been made in the text, except the elimination of certain errors that had been overlooked during the preparation of the second edition.

CARL MURCHISON

CLARK UNIVERSITY
WORCESTER, MASSACHUSETTS
January 10, 1928

PREFACE TO THE SECOND EDITION

The first edition of *Psychologies of 1925* is almost exhausted at the end of eight months from publication. We have decided to issue a second edition in order that several typographical errors may be corrected, and in order that the series may always be obtainable. It is now practically certain that the *Psychologies of 1930* will be issued early in the spring of 1930. The *Psychologies of 1930* will comprise a second cross-section of contemporary theoretical psychology, much more comprehensive than the *Psychologies of 1925,* and will also comprise expert surveys of the various fields of psychology. As the series increases at five-year intervals, it will be our task to see that each cross-section is more comprehensive than the preceding, and that all issues are available at all times for comparative purposes.

CARL MURCHISON

CLARK UNIVERSITY
WORCESTER, MASSACHUSETTS
February 1, 1926

PREFACE TO THE FIRST EDITION

Having, during certain stages in my own student days, experienced something of the futility resulting from unadmitted fundamental differences in theoretical presuppositions, I have grown more and more convinced that experimental methods are largely instances of the more or less systematic theories of the experimenter. Practically any publication from the Cornell Psychological Laboratory carries a majority of the ear-marks of Structuralism. One would look in vain for those ear-marks in any scientific article from Watson, Hunter, or Lashley,—for the ear-marks of Behaviorism attract attention there. Any scientific publication from Berlin these days establishes once more the *Gestalt Theorie*. The pedagogical danger here is caused by the tendency of each of these theoretical groups to think of its rivals in terms of caricature, and so to describe them to the public and to young students. The result is that theoretical tradition becomes established in certain educational communities, and students are born structuralists or behaviorists just as one may be born a democrat or a presbyterian.

Upon mentioning these matters to my father-in-law, Dr. Elmer Ellsworth Powell, I found him already thinking of the same difficulties. Shortly afterwards he made a financial gift to Clark University, initiating a series known as the Powell Lectures in Psychological Theory. The men who have lectured in this series are admitted by all psychologists to be true leaders in the theoretical provinces herein described.

ix

We have here a genuine cross-section of contemporary theoretical psychology. Here are the norms with which future psychologies can be compared. Here are the principles which are up-to-date through the year 1925. We at Clark hope that it is the beginning of a series of cross-sections appearing at five or ten-year intervals. If such proves to be the case, it is to be hoped that in the future the various *fields* of psychology may also be represented.

CARL MURCHISON

CLARK UNIVERSITY
WORCESTER, MASSACHUSETTS
February 1, 1926

TABLE OF CONTENTS

TABLE OF ILLUSTRATIONS

PART I

Schools of Behaviorism

John B. Watson

CHAPTER I

WHAT THE NURSERY HAS TO SAY ABOUT INSTINCTS*

By John B. Watson

I. General Considerations

Introduction: In this brief course of lectures I wish to talk about how man is equipped to behave at birth—a subject that touches the very heart of human psychology.

When the array of facts about any subject is not very complete, it is only human nature to announce a thesis, that is, state what one is going to try to prove and then try to prove it by a logical argument. I am in that position tonight. I have not the full set of facts about the so-called "instinctive" nature of man—I do not know who has; hence, please look upon these lectures both as logical presentations of what facts there are in the case and as a thesis which I am trying to defend. I shall present my thesis first.

The Thesis Presented

Man is an animal born with certain definite types of structure. Having that kind of structure, he is forced to respond to stimuli at birth in certain ways (for example: breathing, heart beat, sneezing, and the like; a fairly full list I shall give you later on). This repertoire of responses is in general the same for each of us. Yet there exists a certain amount of variation in each—the variation is probably merely proportional to the variation there is in structure (including in structure, of course, chemical constitution). It is the same repertoire now that it was when the *genus homo* first appeared many millions of years ago. Let us' call this group of reactions, man's *unlearned behavior*.

In this relatively simple list of human responses there is none corresponding to what is called an "instinct" by present-day psychologists and biologists. There are then for us no instincts—we no longer need the term in psychology. Everything we have been in the habit of calling an "instinct" today is a result largely of training—belonging to man's *learned behavior*.

*Powell Lecture in Psychological Theory at Clark University, January 16, 1925.

As a corollary from this, I wish to draw the conclusion that there is no such thing as an inheritance of *capacity, talent, temperament, mental constitution* and *characteristics.* These things again depend on training that goes on mainly in the cradle. The behaviorist would *not* say: "He inherits his father's capacity or talent for being a fine swordsman." He would say: "This child certainly has his father's slender build of body, the same type of eyes. His build is wonderfully like his father's. He, too, has the build of a swordsman." And he would go on to say: "—and his father is very fond of him. He put a tiny sword into his hand when he was a year of age, and in all their walks he talks sword play, attack and defense, the code of duelling and the like." A certain type of structure, plus early training—*slanting*—accounts for adult performance.

The Argument In Its Defence

Let me start by saying that man to the behaviorist is a *whole animal. When he reacts he reacts with each and every part of his body.* Sometimes he reacts more strongly with one group of muscles and glands than with another. We then say he is doing something. We have named many of these acts— such as breathing, sleeping, crawling, walking, running, fighting, crying, etc. But please do not forget that each of these named acts involves the whole body.

We must begin, too, to think of man as a mammal—a primate —a two-legged animal with two arms and two delicate, mobile hands; as an animal that has a nine months embryonic life, a long helpless infancy, a slow developing childhood, eight years of adolescence and a total life span of some three score years and ten.

We find this animal living in the tropics almost without shelter; going naked; living upon easily caught animals and upon fruit and herbs that require no cultivation. We find him in temperate regions, but dwelling here in well-built, steam-heated houses. We find the male always heavily clad even in summer, wearing a hat upon his head—the only naturally protected part of his body. We find the female of this species dressed in the scantiest of clothes. We find the male working frantically (the female rarely) at almost every kind of vocation, from digging holes in the ground, damming up water like beavers, to building tall buildings of steel and concrete. Again we find man in arctic regions, clad in furs, eating fatty foods and living in houses built of snow and ice.

Everywhere we find man, we find him doing the strangest things, displaying the most divergent manners and customs. In Africa we find the blacks eating one another; in China we find men eating mainly rice and throwing it towards the mouth with dainty chopsticks. In other countries we find man using a metal knife and fork. So widely different is the adult behavior of the primitive Australian bushmen from that of the dwellers in internal China, and both of these groups differ so widely in behavior from the cultivated Englishman, that the question is forced upon us—*Do all members of the genus homo, wherever they are found in biological history, start at birth with the same group of responses, and are these responses aroused by the same set of stimuli?* Put in another way, is the *unlearned*, birth equipment of man, which you have been in the habit of calling *instincts*, the same wherever he is found, be it in Africa or in Boston, be it in the year six million B. C. or in 1925 A. D., whether born in the cotton fields of the South, in the Mayflower or beneath the silken purple quilts of European royalty?

The Genetic Psychologists' Answer

The genetic psychologist—the student best qualified to answer this question—hates to be faced with it because his data are limited. But since he is forced to answer, he can give his honest conviction. His answer is, "Yes, within the limits of individual variation, man is born with the same general set of responses (let us wait before we call them instincts, though) regardless of the station of his parents, regardless of the geological age in which he was born and regardless of the geographical zone in which he was born."

But you say, is there nothing in heredity—is there nothing in eugenics—is there no advantage in being born an "F. F. V." —has there been no *progress* in human evolution? Let us examine a few of the questions you are now bursting to utter.

Certainly black parents will bear black children if the line is pure (except possibly once in a million years or so when a sport or "mutant" is born which theoretically may be white, yellow or red). Certainly the yellow-skinned Chinese parents will bear yellow-skinned offspring. Certainly Caucasian parents will bear white children. But these differences are relatively slight. They are due among other things to differences in the amount and kind of pigments in the skin. I defy anyone to take these infants at birth, study their behavior, and mark off differences in behavior that will characterize white from

black, and white or black from yellow. There will be differences in behavior but the burden of proof is upon the individual,
be he biologist or eugenist, who claims that these racial differences are greater than the individual differences.

Again you say, "How about children born from parents who
have large hands, with short stiff fingers, with extra fingers
or toes? It can be shown that children from these parents
inherit these peculiarities of structure." Our answer is: "Yes,
thousands of variations are laid down in the germ plasm and
will always appear (other factors being equal) in the offspring."
Other inheritances are color of hair, color of eyes, texture
of skin, Albinism (very light individuals with little or no pig-
ment in hair and eyes—vision always being defective). The
biologist, knowing the makeup of the parents and grandparents,
can predict many of even the finer structural characteristics
of the offspring.

So let us hasten to admit—yes, there are heritable differences
in form, in structure. Some people are born with long, slender
fingers, with delicate throat structure; some are born tall, large,
of prize-fighter build; others with delicate skin and eye coloring. These differences are in the germ plasm and are handed
down from parent to child. More questionable are the inheritance of such things as the early or late graying of hair,
the early loss of hair, the span of life, the bearing of twins,
and the like. Many of these questions have already been answered by the biologists and many others are in the process
of being answered. But do not let these undoubted facts of
inheritance lead you astray as they have some of the biologists.
The mere presence of these structures tell us not one thing
about function. This has been the source of a great deal of
confusion in the subject we have under consideration tonight.
Much of our structure laid down in heredity would never
come to light, would never show in function, unless the organism were put in a certain environment, subjected to certain
stimuli and forced to undergo training. Our hereditary structure lies ready to be shaped in a thousand different ways—
the same structure mind you—depending on the way in which
the child is brought up. To convince yourself, measure the
right arm of the blacksmith, look at the pictures of strong men
in our terrible magazines devoted to physical culture. Or turn
to the poor bent back of the ancient bookkeeper. They are
structurally shaped (within limits) by the kinds of lives they
lead.

Are 'Mental' Traits Inherited?

But every one admits this about bone and tendons and muscles—"How about mental traits? Do you mean to say that great talent is not inherited? That criminal tendencies are not inherited? Surely we can prove that these things can be inherited." This was the older idea, the idea which grew up before we knew as much about what early shaping throughout infant life will do as we know now. The question is often put in specific form: "Look at the musicians who are the sons of musicians; look at Wesley Smith, the son of the great economist, John Smith—surely a chip off the old block if ever there was one." You already know the behaviorist's way of answering these questions. You know he recognizes no such thing as mental traits, dispositions or tendencies. Hence, to him, there is no sense to the question of the inheritance of talent as the question is ordinarily raised.

Wesley Smith early in life was thrown into an environment that fairly reeked with economic, political and social questions. His attachment for his father was strong. The path he took was a very natural one. He went into that life for the same reason that your son becomes a lawyer, a doctor or a politician. If the father is a shoemaker, a saloon keeper or a street cleaner, or engaged in any other non-socially recognized occupation, the son does not follow so easily in the father's footsteps, but that is another story. Why did Wesley Smith succeed in reaching eminence when so many sons who have famous fathers fail to attain equal eminence? Was it because this particular son inherited his father's talent? There may be a thousand reasons, not one of which lends any color to the view that Wesley Smith inherited the "talent" of his father. Suppose John Smith had had three sons who by hypothesis all had equal abilities and all began to work upon economics at the age of six months.[1] One was beloved by his father. He followed in his father's footsteps and, due to his father's tutorship, this son overtook and finally surpassed his father. Two years after the birth of Wesley, the second son was born, but the father was taken up with the elder son. The second son was beloved by the mother who now got less of her husband's time, so she devoted her time to the second son. The second son could not follow so closely in the footsteps of his father; he was influenced naturally by what his mother was doing.

---

[1] And by this statement we do not mean that their genetic constitution is identical.

He early gave up his economic studies, entered society and ultimately became a "lounge lizard." The third son, born two years later, was unwanted. The father was taken up with the eldest son, the mother with the second son. The third son was also put to work upon economics, but receiving little parental care, he drifted daily towards the servants' quarters. An unscrupulous maid taught him to masturbate at three. At twelve the chauffeur made a homosexual out of him. Later, falling in with neighborhood thieves, he became a pickpocket, then a stool-pigeon and finally a drug fiend. He died in an insane asylum of paresis. There was nothing wrong with the heredity of any one of these sons. All by hypothesis had equal chances at birth. All could have been the fathers of fine, healthy sons if their respective wives had been of good stock (except possibly for the third son *after* he contracted syphilis).

You will probably say that I am flying in the face of the known facts of eugenics and experimental evolution—that the geneticists have proven that many of the behavior characteristics of the parents are handed down to the offspring—they will cite mathematical ability, musical ability, and many, many other types. My reply is that the geneticists are working under the banner of the old "faculty" psychology. One need not give very much weight to any of their present conclusions. Before the evening is over I hope to show you that there are no "faculties" and no stereotyped patterns of behavior which deserve the name either of "talent" or "instinct."

Differences in Structure and Differences in Early Training Will Account for All Differences in Later Behavior

A while ago I said that, granting individual variation in structure, we could find no real proof that man's unlearned repertoire of acts has differed through the ages or that he has ever been either more or less capable of putting on complex training than in 1925. The fact that there are marked individual variations in structure among men has been known since biology began. But we have never sufficiently utilized it in analyzing man's behavior. Tonight I want to utilize still another fact only recently brought out by the behaviorists and other students of animal psychology, namely, that *habit formation starts in all probability in embryonic life, and that even in the human young, environment shapes behavior so quickly that all of the older ideas about what types of behavior are inherited and what are learned break down.* Grant variations in structure at birth and rapid habit formation from birth, and you have a basis for explaining many of the so-called facts of inheritance of "mental" characteristics. Let us take up these two points:

(1) *Human Beings Differ in the Way They are Put Together*

Those of you who have physiological training have a good idea of the complexity of the material that goes into the human body.   You realize the fact that there must be variation in the way these complicated tissues are put together. We have just brought out the fact that some human beings are born with long fingers, some with short; some with long arm and leg bones, some with short; some with hard bones, and some with soft; some with over-developed glands; some with poorly functioning glands. Again you know that we can identify human beings by differences in their finger prints. No two human beings have ever had the same finger prints, yet you can mark off man's hand and foot prints from the tracks of all other animals. No two human beings have bones exactly alike, yet any good comparative anatomist can pick out a human bone (and there are over 200 of them) from the bones of every other mammal. If so simple a thing as the markings on the fingers differ in every individual, you have absolute proof that general behavior will and must be different. They crawl differently, cry differently, differ in the frequency with which defaecation and urination occur, differ in early vocal efforts, in requirements for food, in the speed and rapidity with which they use their hands—even identical twins show these differences—because they differ structurally and differ slightly in their chemical makeup. They differ likewise in the finer details of sense organ equipment, in the details of brain and cord structure, in the heart and circulatory mechanisms and in the length, breadth, thickness and flexibility of the striped muscular systems.

Yet with all of these structural differences "a man's a man for a' that"—all are made up of the same material and have the same general architectural plan regardless of habits.

(2) *Differences In Early Training Make Men Still More Different*

There are then admittedly these slight but significant differences in structure between one human being and every other human being. Differences in early training are even more marked. I will not stop now to give much proof of this—

the next two lectures will furnish it abundantly. We now know that conditioned reflexes start in the human child at birth (and possibly before)—we know that there is no such thing as giving two children, even belonging to the same family, the same training. A doting young married couple have twins—a boy and a girl—they are dressed alike and fed alike. But the father pets and fondles the girl, surrounds her with love; the mother treats the boys in the same way, but the father wants the boy to follow in his own footsteps. He is stern with him—he can't help shaping the boy his way. The mother wants the girl to be modest and maidenly. Soon they show great differences in behavior. They receive different training from infancy. The next children are born. Now the father is more taken up with affairs—he has to work harder. The mother is more taken up with social duties; servants are brought in. The younger children have brothers and sisters; they are brought up in a wholly different world. One child falls ill. Strict training is abandoned; all rules are off with a sickly child. Again, one child gets badly frightened—becomes conditioned—shows fear at everything; he becomes timid and his regular course of boyish activity is interfered with. Indeed we may take an actual case. Two girls, aged nine, live in adjoining houses. They have the "same" training (mothers are close friends and bring up children according to the same rules). One day they took a walk. The girl on the left looked at the street and saw only street activity, the one on the right looked towards the houses and saw a man exposing his sex organs. The girl on the right was considerably troubled and disturbed and reached equanimity only after months of discussion with her parents.

In this audience I am sure I do not need to multiply instances of early differences in training and conditioning.

The Conclusion We Draw

How will these two things explain the so-called facts of inheritance of talent or mental characteristics. Let us take a hypothetical case. Here are two boys, one aged 7, the other 6. The father is a pianist of great talent, the mother an artist working in oil, a portrait painter of note. The father has strong, large hands but with long, flexible fingers (it is a myth that all artists have long, tapering, finely formed fingers). The older son has the same type of hand. The father loves his first born, the mother the younger. Then the process of "creating he them in his own image" begins.

The world is brought up on the basis largely of shaping the young you are attached to as you yourself have been shaped. Well, in this case the older becomes a wonderful pianist, the younger an indifferent artist. So much for different training or different slanting in youth. But what about different structure? Please note this: The younger son, under ordinary conditions, could not have been trained into a pianist. His fingers were not long enough and the muscular arrangement of the hand was not flexible enough. But even here we should be cautious—the piano is a standard instrument—a certain finger span and a certain hand, wrist and finger strength are needed. But suppose the father had been fond of the younger child and said, "I want him to be a pianist and I am going to try an experiment—his fingers are short—he'll never have a flexible hand, so I'll build him a piano. I'll make the keys narrow so that even with his short fingers his span will be sufficient, and I'll make different leverage for the keys so that no particular strength or even flexibility will be needed." Who knows?—the younger son under these conditions might have become the world's greatest pianist.

Such factors, especially those on the training side, have been wholly neglected in the study of inheritance. We have not the facts to build up statistics on the inheritance of special types of behavior, and until the facts have been brought out by the study of the human young, all data on the evolution of different forms of human behavior and eugenics must be accepted with the greatest caution.

Our conclusion, then, is that we have no real evidence of the inheritance of traits. I would feel perfectly confident in the ultimately favorable outcome of careful upbringing of a *healthy, well-formed baby* born of a long line of crooks, murderers, thieves and prostitutes. Who has any evidence to the contrary? Many, many thousands of children yearly, born from moral households and steadfast parents, become wayward, steal or become prostitutes, through one mishap or another of nurture. Many more thousands of sons and daughters of the wicked grow up to be wicked because they couldn't grow up any other way in such surroundings. But let one adopted child who has a bad ancestry go wrong and it is used as incontestible evidence for the inheritance of moral turpitude and criminal tendencies. As a matter of fact, there has not been a double handful of cases in the whole of our civilization where records have been carefully enough kept for us to draw any such conclusions—mental testers, Lombroso, and all other students of criminality to the contrary notwithstanding. All of us know that adopted children are never brought up as one's own. One cannot use statistics gained from observations in charitable institutions and orphan asylums. All one needs to do to discount such statistics is to go there and work for a while, and I say this without trying to belittle the work of such organizations.

I should like to go one step further tonight and say, "Give me a dozen healthy infants, well-formed, and my own specified world to bring them up in and I'll guarantee to take any one at random and train him to become any type of specialist I might select—a doctor, lawyer, artist, merchant-chief and, yes, even into beggar-man and thief, regardless of his talents, penchants, tendencies, abilities, vocations and race of his ancestors." I am going beyond my facts and I admit it, but so have the advocates of the contrary and they have been doing it for many thousands of years. Please note that when this experiment is made I am to be allowed to specify the way they are to be brought up and the type of world they have to live in.

Where there are structural defects that are inherited, as apparently is the case in certain glandular diseases, in "mental" defectives, where there is intra-uterine infection as in syphilis and in gonorrhea, troublesome behavior of one kind or another may develop early and rapidly. But some of these children haven't the structural possibilities to be trained—as when fundamental connections in body and brain are lacking. Again, where there are structural defects more easily observed as in deformities, loss of digits, extra digits, etc., there is social inferiority—competition on equal grounds is denied. The same is true when inferior races are brought up along with superior races. We have no sure evidence of inferiority in the negro race. Educate a white child and a negro child in the same school—bring them up in the same family (theoretically without difference) and yet when society begins to exert its crushing might, the negro cannot compete.[1]

The truth is society does not like to face facts. Pride of

---

[1] I say nothing here on the inheritance of acquired behavior characteristics. The evidence in biology is all against it. An infant descended from a long line of blacksmith ancestors starts with approximately the same puny upper right arm girth as his original blacksmith forbear—and with one no larger than his own left arm.

race has been strong, hence our Mayflower ancestry—our Daughters of the Revolution. We like to boast of our ancestry. It sets us apart. We like to think it takes three generations to make a gentleman (sometimes a lot longer!) and that we have more than three behind us. Again, on the other hand, the belief in the inheritance of tendencies and traits saves us from blame in the training of our young. The mother says when her son goes wrong—"Look at his father or his grandfather (whichever one she hates). What could you expect with that ancestry on his father's side?" And the father, when the girl shows wayward tendencies—"What can you expect? Her mother has always let every man she came in contact with make love to her." If these tendencies are inherited we can't be much blamed for it. Traits in the older psychologies are god-given and if my boy or girl goes wrong, I as a parent can't be blamed.

The behaviorist has an axe to grind, you say, by being so emphatic? Yes, he has—he would like to see the presuppositions and assumptions that are blocking us in our efforts to spend millions of dollars and years of patient research on infant psychology removed because then, and only then, can we build up a real psychology of mankind.

Are There Any Instincts?

Let us, then, forever lay the ghost of inheritance of aptitudes, of "mental" characteristics, of special abilities (not based upon favorable structure such as throat formation in singing, hand in playing, structurally sound eyes, ears, etc.) and take up the more general question of what the world has been in the habit of calling instincts.

It is not easy to answer this question. Up to the advent of the behaviorist, man was supposed to be a creature of many complicated instincts. A group of older writers, under the sway of the newly created theories of Darwin, vied with one another in finding new and perfect instincts in both man and animals. William James made a careful selection from among these asserted instincts and gave man the following list: *Climbing, imitation, emulation and rivalry, pugnacity, anger, resentment, sympathy, hunting, fear, appropriation, acquisitiveness, kleptomania, constructiveness, play, curiosity, sociability, shyness, cleanliness, modesty, shame, love, jealousy, parental love.* James claims that no other mammal, not even the monkey, can lay claim to so large a list.

The behaviorist finds himself wholly unable to agree with James and the other psychologists who claim that man has unlearned activities of these complicated kinds. But you who are here tonight have been brought up on James or possibly even on a worse diet, and it will be hard to dislodge his teaching. You say, "James says an instinct is 'a tendency to act in such a way as to bring about certain ends without having foresight of those ends.' Surely this formulation fits a lot of the early behavior of children and young animals." You think you understand it, anyway. At first it looks convincing. But when you test it out in terms of your own observations on young animals and children, you find that you have not a scientific definition but a metaphysical assumption. You get lost in the sophistry of 'foresight' and 'end.'

I don't blame you for being confused. No subject in psychology today is more written about than the so-called instincts. In the past three years more than a hundred articles have been written about instincts. The articles in general are of the armchair variety written by men who have never watched the whole life history of animals and the early childhood of the human young. Philosophy will never answer any questions about instincts. The questions asked are factual ones—to be answered only by genetic observation. Let me hasten to add that the behaviorist's knowledge of instinct also suffers from lack of observed facts but you cannot accuse him of going beyond natural science in his inferences. Before attempting to answer the question "What is an instinct?" let us take a little journey into mechanics. Possibly we may find that we do not need the term after all.

A Lesson From the Boomerang

I have in my hand a hardwood stick. If I throw it forward and upward it goes a certain distance and drops to the ground. I retrieve the stick, put it in hot water, bend it at a certain angle, throw it out again—it goes outward, revolving as it goes for a short distance, turns to the right and then drops down. Again I retrieve the stick, reshape it slightly and make its edges convex. I call it a boomerang. Again I throw it upward and outward. Again it goes forward revolving as it goes. Suddenly it turns, comes back and gracefully and kindly falls at my feet. It is still a stick, still made of the same material, but it has been shaped differently. *Has the boomerang an instinct to return to the hand of the thrower?* No? Well, why does it return? Because it is made in such a way that when it is thrown upward and outward with a given force it must return (parallelogram of forces). Let me call attention to the fact here that all well made and well thrown boomerangs will return to or near to the thrower's feet, but no two will follow exactly the same forward pathway or the same return pathway, even if shot mechanically with the same application of force and at the same elevation; yet they are all called boomerangs. This example may be a little unusual to you. Let us take one a little easier. Most of us have rolled dice now and again. Take a die, load it in a certain way, roll it, and the face bearing "six" will always come up when the die is thrown. Why? The die must roll that way because of the way it was constructed. Again take a toy soldier. Mount it on a semi-circular loaded rubber base. No matter how you throw this soldier, he will always bob upright, oscillate a bit, then come to a steady vertical position. *Has the rubber soldier an instinct to stand erect?*

Notice that not until the boomerang, the toy soldier and the die are hurled into space do they exhibit their peculiarities of motion. Change their form or their structure, or alter the material out of which they are made (make them of iron instead of wood or rubber) and their characteristic motion may markedly change. But man is made up of certain kinds of material—put together in certain ways. If he is hurled into action (as a result of stimulation) may he not exhibit movement (in advance of training) just as peculiar as (but no more mysterious than) that of the boomerang?[1]

Concept Of Instinct No Longer Needed In Psychology

This brings us to our central thought tonight. If the boomerang has no instinct (aptitude, capacity, tendency, trait, etc.) to return to the hand of the thrower; if we need no mysterious way of accounting for the motion of the boomerang; if the laws of physics will account for its motions—cannot psychology see in this a much needed lesson in simplicity? Can

[1]You will argue that in mechanics action and reaction are equal—that the boomerang is hit with a force equal to so many ergs and that just that many ergs are used up in returning to the hand of the thrower (including the heat loss to the air) but that when I touch a man with a hair and he jumps two feet high, the reaction is out of all proportion to the energy in the stimulus. The reply is that in man the energy used in the reaction was stored. In dynamics you find the same thing when a match touches off a powder blast or a breeze blows from a cliff a rocking boulder that destroys a house in the valley.

it not dispense with instincts? Can we not say, "Man is built of certain materials put together in certain complex ways, and *as a corollary of the way he is put together and of the material out of which he is made—he must act [until learning has re-shaped him] as he does act?"*

But you say: "That gives your whole argument away—you admit he does a lot of things at birth which he is forced to do by his structure—this is just what I mean by *instinct."* My answer is that we must now go to the facts. We can no longer postpone a visit to the nursery. I think you will find there, in the two or three years we shall study the infant and child, *little that will encourage you to keep sacred James' list of instincts.*

II. LABORATORY STUDIES ON THE GENESIS OF BEHAVIOR

During the past 25 years the students of animal behavior have been gathering a sound body of facts about the young of nearly every species of animal except that of man. We have lived with young monkeys, we have watched the growth of young rats, rabbits, guinea pigs, and birds of many species. We have watched them develop daily in our laboratories from the moment of birth to maturity. To check our laboratory results we have watched many of them grow up in their own native habitat—in a natural environment.

These studies have enabled us to reach a fair understanding of both the *unlearned* and *learned* equipment of many species of animals. They have taught us that no one by watching the performance of the adult can determine what part of a com-plicated series of acts belongs in the *unlearned* category and what part belongs in the category of the *learned.* Best of all, they have given us a method that we can apply to the study of the human young. Finally, animal studies have taught us that it is not safe to generalize from the data we gather on one species as to what will be true in another species. For example, the guinea pig is born with a heavy coat of fur and with a very complete set of motor responses. It becomes practically independent of the mother at three days of age. The white rat, on the other hand, is born in a very immature state, has a long period of infancy; it becomes independent of the mother only at the end of thirty days. Such a wide divergence of birth equipment in two animal species so closely related (both rodents) proves how unsafe it is to generalize on the basis of infra-human animal studies as to what the unlearned equipment of man is.

Resistance to the Study of the Human Young

Until very recently we have had no reliable data on what happens during the first few years of human infancy and childhood. Indeed there has been very great resistance to studying the behavior of the human young. Society is in the habit of seeing them starve by hundreds, of seeing them grow up in dives and slums, without getting particularly wrought up about it. But let the hardy behaviorist attempt an experimental study of the infant or even begin systematic observation, and criticism begins at once. When experiments and observations are made in the maternity wards of hospitals there is naturally also considerable misunderstanding of the behaviorist's aims. The child is not sick, the behaviorist is not advancing clinical methods—therefore what good are such studies? Again, when the parents who have children under observation learn of it they become excited. They are ignorant of what you are doing and you have great difficulty in making them understand what you are doing. These difficulties at first confronted us in our work at the Johns Hopkins Hospital but, thanks to the broad-mindedness of Dr. J. Whitridge Williams, Dean of the Johns Hopkins Medical School, and of Dr. John Howland, physician-in-chief of the Harriet Lane Hospital, a satisfactory condition for study was finally arranged. It was arranged in such a way that psychological examination of the infants became a part of the regular routine of the care of all infants born in the hospital. I mention this because if any of you ever attempt to make such studies you will be confronted, until the work has become more generally accepted, with a similar set of difficulties.

Studying the Behavior of the Human Infant

No one should attempt to make studies upon the infant until he has had considerable training in physiology and in animal psychology. *He should have practical training in the nursery of the hospital where the work is to be done.* In this way he can learn what is safe to do with a baby and what is not. Before recording observations he should watch a few deliveries. By watching deliveries he will speedily learn that the human infant can stand considerable *necessary* hard usage without breaking under the strain!

What We Know About Intra-Uterine Behavior

Our knowledge of the intra-uterine life of the human young is a very meagre indeed. Intra-uterine life begins with the fertilization of the ovum. Birth occurs usually at the end of the tenth lunar month (280 days) thereafter. The heart of the foetus begins to beat around the 18th to 20th week, occasionally as early as the 14th week. The heart rate of the foetus is very rapid—120-140 beats to the minute. Movement of the striped muscular system of the foetus begins at the end of the 4th lunar month. There is some evidence that the stomach glands begin to function at the end of the 5th month. There is apparently very little support to the view that defaecation and urination occur *in utero*.

The position of the foetus in the uterus is not without significance since it affects the movements and posture of the infant for a considerable time after birth. Dr. J. Whitridge Williams describes the intra-uterine position of the foetus as follows: "Irrespective of the relation which it may bear to the mother, the foetus in the later months of pregnancy assumes a characteristic posture, which is described as its *attitude* or *habitus;* and, as a general rule, it may be said to form an ovoid mass, which roughly corresponds with the shape of the uterine cavity. Thus, it is folded or bent upon itself in such a way that the back becomes markedly convex, the head is sharply flexed so that the chin is almost in contact with the breast, the thighs are flexed over the abdomen, the legs are bent at the knee-joints, and the arches of the feet rest upon the anterior surfaces of the legs. The arms are usually crossed over the thorax or are parallel to the sides, while the umbilical cord lies in the space between them and the lower extremities. This attitude is usually retained throughout pregnancy, though it is frequently modified somewhat by the movements of the extremities, and in rare instances the head may become extended, when a totally different posture is assumed. The characteristic attitude results partly from the mode of growth of the foetus, and partly from a process of accommodation between it and the outlines of the uterine cavity." (Obstetrics, p. 180). The extent to which slight differences in the intra-uterine position of the foetus may possibly later influence or even determine right and left handedness of the individual is not known. Attention is called to the fact that the liver is on the right side in about 80% of the observed cases. Whether this large organ may swing the foetus slightly so that the right side is constantly under less restraint than the left is not known. If this is true, the infants with the liver on the right side should be right-handed from birth. My records on hundreds of infants prove that this is not the case.

In general we get our best information on foetal structures ready to function by study of infants prematurely born. At six months (lunar) the infant may draw a few gasping breaths and make a few abortive movements. It never lives. From the 7th month on to full term, infants may live. At birth they display the usual birth equipment. This proves that from the beginning of the 7th month many structures exist in the foetus ready to function as soon as the appropriate stimulus is applied: *e. g.* breathing as soon as the air strikes the lungs; complete and independent circulation and purification of the blood as soon as the umbilical cord is severed; independent metabolism showing that visceral system is ready to function, etc.

The Birth Equipment of the Human Young

Almost daily observation of several hundred infants from birth through the first thirty days of infancy and of a smaller number through the first years of childhood has given us the following set of (rough) facts on unlearned responses:[1]

Sneezing: This apparently can begin in a full-fledged way from birth. Sometimes it appears even before the so-called birth cry is given. It is one of the responses that stays in the activity stream throughout life (see p. 35); habit factors apparently affect it very little indeed. No experiments so far have ever been made to see if the mere sight of the pepper box may not after a sufficient number of conditioning experiments call out sneezing. The normal intra-organic stimulus calling out sneezing is not very well defined. Sometimes it occurs when the baby is taken from a cooler room into an overheated room. With some babies carrying them out into the sunshine apparently will produce sneezing.

Hiccoughing: This usually does not begin at birth but can be noticed in children from 7 days of age on with great ease. Over 50 cases have been observed carefully. The earliest noted case of hiccoughing was six hours after birth. So far as is known, this response is rarely conditioned under the ordinary conditions of life. The stimulus most commonly calling it out apparently is the pressure on the diaphragm coming from a full stomach.

Crying: The so-called birth cry takes place at the establish-

---

[1]Mrs. Margaret Gray Blanton, working in the psychological laboratory of the Johns Hopkins Hospital has given us our best data upon this subject (Psychological Review, Vol. 24, p. 456).

ment of respiration. The lungs are not inflated until the stimulus of the air is present. As the air strikes the lungs and mucous membranes of the upper alimentary tract, the mechanism of breathing is gradually established. To establish breathing the infant has sometimes to be plunged into icy water. Coincident with the plunge into the icy water, the cry appears. It usually appears during the vigorous rubbing and slapping of the infant's back and buttocks—a method invariably employed to establish respiration. The birth cry itself differs markedly in different infants.

Hunger will bring out crying, noxious stimuli such as rough handling, circumcision or the lancing and care of boils will bring out cries' even in extremely young infants. When the baby suspends itself with either hand crying is usually elicited.

Crying as such very shortly becomes conditioned. The child quickly learns that it can control the responses of nurse, parents and attendants by the cry, and uses it as a weapon ever thereafter. Crying in infants is not always accompanied by tears, although tears can sometimes be observed as soon as ten minutes after birth. Owing to the almost universal practice now of putting silver nitrate into the eyes shortly after birth, the normal appearance of tears is hard to determine. Tears have been observed usually, though, on a great many babies from the fourth day on. Tears, in all probability, are also conditioned very quickly, since they are a much more effective means of controlling the movements of nurses and parents than dry crying.

Numerous experiments have been carried out to see whether the crying of one infant in a nursery will serve as a stimulus to set off the rest of the children in the nursery. Our results are entirely negative. In order to more thoroughly control the conditions, we made phonographic records of a lusty crier. We would then reproduce this sound very close to the ear of, first, a sleeping infant, then a wakeful but quiet infant. The results again were wholly negative. Hunger contractions and noxious stimuli (also loud sounds) are unquestionably the unconditioned stimuli which call out crying.

Colic, bringing a set of noxious stimuli, may and usually does call out a cry and apparently one slightly different from other types. This is due to the pressure in the abdominal cavity caused by the formation of gas. The full set of muscles used in the hunger cry is thus not available for the colic cry. The cries of infants are so different that at night in a nursery of 25 it does not take very long to be able to name the child which is crying regardless of its location in the nursery.

Erection of Penis: This can occur at birth and from that time on throughout life. The complete set of stimuli calling out this response is not known. Apparently radiant heat, warm water, stroking of the sex organs, possibly pressure from the urine, are the main factors operative at birth. This, of course, is conditioned later on in life through visual stimulation and the like. The stimulus to the later appearing orgasm is possibly different. Short rhythmical contacts as in coition and in masturbation lead to the orgasm (and after puberty to its attendant ejaculation). Probably the orgasm itself both in men and women can be hastened or slowed through stimulus substitutions (through words, sounds, etc.—a factor of the utmost sociological importance).

At what age tumescence becomes a conditioned response is not known. Masturbation (a better term with infants is manipulation of the penis or vagina respectively) can occur at almost any age. The earliest case I have personally observed was a girl around one year of age (it often begins much earlier). The infant was sitting up in the bathtub and in reaching for the soap accidentally touched the external opening of the vagina with her finger. The search for the soap stopped, stroking of the vagina began and a smile overspread the face. Neither in the case of infant boys nor of infant girls have I seen masturbation carried to the point where the orgasm takes place (it must be remembered that the orgasm can occur without ejaculation in the male before the age of puberty is reached). Apparently a great many of the muscular responses later to be used in the sex act, such as pushing, climbing, stroking, are ready to function in the male at least at a very much earlier age than we are accustomed to think. In one observed case which came into the clinic, a boy of 3½ years of age would mount his mother or nurse, whichever one happened to be sleeping with him. Erection would take place and he would manipulate and bite her breast; then clasping and sex movements similar to those of adults would ensue. In this case the mother, who was separated from her husband, had deliberately attempted to build up this reaction in her child.

Voiding of Urine: This occurs from birth. The unconditioned stimulus is unquestionably intra-organic due to the pressure of the fluid in the bladder. Conditioning of the act of urination can begin as early as the second week. Usually, however, conditioning at this age requires almost infinite patience. Anywhere from the third month on, the infant can be conditioned easily by a little care. If the infant is observed closely at intervals of a half hour or so, it will occasionally be found dry. When this occurs, place it upon the chamber. If the bladder is quite full, the increased pressure which comes from putting the infant in a sitting position will be stimulus enough to release the act. After repeated trials the conditioned response is perfected. Young children can be so thoroughly conditioned in this act that the responses can be called without awakening them.

Defaecation: This mechanism seems to be perfect from birth and in all probability the mechanism was perfected several weeks before birth. The stimulus probably is pressure in the lower colon. Pressing a clinical thermometer into the anus from birth often brings about the passage of faeces.

Defaecation can also be conditioned at a very early age. One of the methods of course is to introduce a glycerine or soap suppository at the time the infant is placed upon the chamber After considerable repetition of this routine, contact with the chamber will be sufficient to call out the response.

Early Eye Movements: Infants from birth when lying flat on their backs in a dark room with their heads held horizontally will slowly turn their eyes towards a faint light. Movements of the eyes are not very well co-ordinated at birth, but "cross eyes" are not nearly so prevalent as most people seem to believe. Right and left co-ordinated movements of the eyes are the first to appear. Upward and downward movements of the eyes come at a slightly later period. Still later on a light can be followed when revolved in a circle over the baby's face.

As is well known, habit factors almost immediately begin to enter into fixation and other eye responses. I have already brought out the fact that movements both of the lids and of the pupils can be conditioned.

Smiling: Smiling is due in all probability at first to the presence of kinaesthetic and tactual stimuli. It appears as early as the fourth day. It can most often be seen after a full feeding. Light touches on parts of the body, blowing upon the body, touching the sex organs and sensitive zones of the skin are the unconditioned stimuli that will produce smiling. Tickling under the chin and a gentle jogging and rocking of the infant will often bring out smiling.

Smiling is the response in which conditioning factors begin to appear as early as the thirtieth day. Mrs. Mary Cover Jones has made an extensive study of smiling. In a large group of children she found that conditioned smiling—that is, smiling when the experimenter smiles or says babyish words to the infant (both auditory and visual factors)—begins to appear at around the thirtieth day. In her total study of 185 cases, the latest age at which the conditioned smile first appeared was eighty days.

Manual Responses: By manual responses hereafter in these lectures let us mean different movements of the head, neck, legs, trunk, toes, as well as of the arms, hands and fingers.

Turning the Head: A great many infants at birth, if placed stomach down with chin on the mattress, can swing their heads to right or left and lift their heads from the mattress. We have noticed these reactions from thirty minutes of age on. On one occasion fifteen babies were tested one at a time in succession. All except one could make these head reactions.

Holding up Head when the Infant is held in Upright Position: This seems to vary with the development of the head and neck musculature. Some newborn infants can support their heads for a few seconds. The infant is held in the experimenter's lap with stomach and back supported. There seems to be a rapid improvement in this response due apparently to the development of structure rather than to training factors. The head can be held up in most infants from the sixth month on.

Hand Movements at Birth: Marked hand movements in many children can be observed even at birth, such as closing the hand, opening it, spreading the fingers, stretching the fingers with one or both hands at the same time. Usually in these hand movements the thumb is folded inside the palm and takes no part in hand response. It does not begin to participate in the movements of the hand until a much later period—around the 100th day. I shall speak of grasping, which is also present at birth, later on (p. 25).

Arm Movements: The slightest stimulation of the skin anywhere will usually bring out marked arm, wrist, hand and shoulder responses. Apparently kinaesthetic and organic stimuli may bring out these responses as well as tactual, auditory and visual stimuli. The arms can be thrown up to the

face and even as far as the top of the head and down to the
legs. Usually, however, the first movements of the arms, no
matter where the stimulus is applied, is towards the chest and
head (probably a remnant of the intra-uterine habit). One
of the most characteristic ways of producing violent movements of arms and hands is to hold the nose. In a very few
seconds one or the other or both arms fly upward until the
hand actually comes in contact with the hand of the experimenter. If one hand is held, the other hand will go up just
the same.

Leg and Foot Movements: Kicking is one of the most pronounced movements to be seen at birth. It can be brought out
by touching the soles of the feet, by stimulation with hot or
cold air, by contact with the skin and directly through kinaesthetic stimulation. One characteristic ways of producing
leg and foot movements is to pinch the skin over the knee. If
the left leg is held out straight and the knee cap pinched, the
right foot comes up and in contact with the experimenter's
fingers. When the inside of the right knee is pinched, the
left leg goes up and strikes the experimenter's fingers. This will
appear perfectly at birth. Sometimes it takes only a few seconds for the foot to be brought up as far as the experimenter's
fingers.

Trunk, Leg, Foot and Toe Movements: When an infant
is suspending itself with either right or left hand, marked
"climbing" motions in the trunk and hips are noticeable.
There seems to be a wave of contraction pulling the trunk
and legs upward followed by a relaxation period, then another
wave of contraction sets in. Tickling of the foot, stimulating
the foot with hot water, will produce marked movements in
foot and toes. Usually if the bottom of the foot is stimulated
with a match stick, the characteristic Babinski reflex appears
in nearly all infants. This is a variable reflex. The usual
pattern is an upward jump of the great toe (extension) and
a drawing down of the other toes (flexion). Occasionally
the Babinski takes the form merely of "fanning," that is,
spreading of all the toes. The Babinski reflex usually disappears around the end of the first year although it may continue longer even in normal children. Infants cannot suspend
themselves with their toes. A wire or other small round object placed under the toes will often produce flexion, that is,
a closing of the toes, but the slightest pressure will release the
rod or wire.

Many infants almost from birth can turn over from face to back when placed naked lying on the stomach on an unyielding surface. Mrs. Blanton describes one case as follows: Subject T, at seven days of age, turned repeatedly from face to back when not impeded by clothing. Placed face downward on an unyielding surface, her arms outstretched in line with her body, she would immediately start crying. Relaxing and contracting of the muscles of the legs, arms, abdomen and back are natural accompaniments of crying. During the act she pulled her knees under her and contracted her muscles generally, then relaxed them. Gradually, owing to the unequal activity of the two sides of the body, she would finally come to lie nearer to the one side of the body—a final spasm of muscular effort would put her over. In one case it took ten minutes to effect the turn and nine separate spasms.

Picture here all of the hundreds of partial responses called out in the general larger act of turning over. Here again, habit very quickly sets in and the response becomes sharper and sharper with the dropping away of many of the part reactions. It takes many weeks and months to turn over quickly and with a minimum of muscular effort.

Feeding Responses: Touching the face of a hungry baby at the corners of the mouth or on the cheek or on the chin will cause quick, jerky head movements which result in bringing the mouth near the source of stimulation. This has been observed many, many times from five hours of age onward. The lip or sucking reflex is another characteristic response. Tapping slightly with the tip of the finger below or above the corner of the mouth of a sleeping baby may bring the lips and tongue almost immediately into the nursing position. Suckling as such varies tremendously in young infants. It can be demonstrated in practically every infant within the first hour after birth. Occasionally when there is marked injury during birth suckling is retarded. The feeding response as such includes sucking, tongue, lip and cheek movements and swallowing. With most newborn infants this mechanism, unless there is birth injury (or possibly when the parents are "feeble-minded") is fairly perfect.

The whole group of feeding responses is most easy to condition. Conditioning can be most easily observed in a bottle fed baby. Even before reaching (occurring around the 120th day) the infant will get extremely active in its bodily "squirmings" the instant the bottle is shown. After reaching has developed, the mere sight of the bottle will carry out the lustiest kind of bodily movements and crying begins immediately. So sensitive do infants become to the visual stimulus of the bottle that if it is shown from 12 to 15 feet away, the response begins to appear. There are many, many other conditioned factors in connection with feeding which I wish I had time to go into —negative reactions to food, food tantrums and the like. Most of these, so far as I can judge, are purely conditioned responses.

Crawling: Crawling is an indeterminate kind of response. Many infants never crawl at all, and all of them exhibit different behavior in crawling. After many experiments I am inclined to believe that crawling comes largely as a result of a habit formation. When the infant is placed on its stomach, the contact and kinaesthetic stimuli bring out very general bodily activity. Oftentimes one side of the body is more active than the opposite side; circular (circus) motions result. In one 9 months infant turning in a circle resulted for days but no forward progress could be observed. In this gradual twisting and turning of the body, the child sometimes moves right, sometimes left, sometimes forward, indeed, and sometimes backward. If, in these movements, it mangages to reach and manipulate some object, we have practically a situation like that of the hungry rat in a maze that has food at its center. A habit of crawling toward objects results. It probably could always be taught if teaching were regularly instituted with the milk bottle as the stimulus. Our daily test is conducted as follows. The naked infant is placed on the carpet. His legs are extended and a mark is set at the furthest reach of the toes. Then a nursing bottle or lump of sugar (previously conditioning him on sugar so that he will struggle for it) is put just out of reach of the hands. Five minutes is enough for the test. Sometimes at the end of the test if crawling does not appear an electric heater is placed a few feet behind him. This merely hastens general bodily activity.

Standing and Walking: The whole complex mechanism of standing upright, first with support, then without support, then walking, then running, then jumping, is a very slowly developing one. The start of the whole mechanism seems to lie in the development of the so-called "extensor thrust." The extensor thrust is not usually present during the first few months of infancy. Some months after birth if the infant is gradually lifted up by the arms to nearly a standing position with a part of its feet in contact with the floor at all times, there comes, as weight falls on the feet, a stiffening of the muscles of both legs. Soon after the appearance of this reflex, the child begins to attempt to pull itself up. Between 7 and 8 months of age many infants can pull themselves up with very little help and can support themselves in a standing position holding on to some object for a short space of time. After this feat has been accomplished, the next stage in the general process is walking around holding on to an object. The final stage is the first step alone. The first step alone occurs at very variable times, depending upon the weight of the baby, its general health, whether or not it has had serious mishaps through falling (conditioning and the like). Often the first step is taken at 1 year of age and sometimes slightly earlier. In the most completely observed case in my records the first step was taken at the end of 11 months and 3 days. After the first step is taken, the remainder of the act has to be learned just as the youths learns to "balance" himself in bicycle riding, swimming, skating and tight rope walking. Two factors seem to go hand in hand in the development of this mechanism. One is the actual growth of the body tissue, the other is habit formation. The act can be hastened by coaching (positive conditioning); it can be markedly retarded at almost any of these stages if the infant falls and injures itself (negative conditioning).

Vocal Behavior: The early sounds made by infants and the conditioning and organization of these sounds into words and speech habits need a longer treatment than we can give them tonight. I don't think I shall have to work hard to get you to believe every word is a conditioned response.

Swimming: Swimming is very largely a process of learning. By the time the child first attempts to swim, the well organized habits of using arms, legs, hands and trunk are well established. "Balancing," breathing, removal of fear, etc., are the remaining important factors.

When the newborn infant is placed in water at body temperature with head only supported above the water, almost no general response is called out. If plunged into cold water violent general body response is called out but no movements *even approximating* swimming appear.

Grasping: With few exceptions infants at birth can support their full weight with either right or left hands. The method we use in testing them is to place a small rod about the diameter of a pencil in one or the other hand closing the fingers on the rod. This stimulus causes the grasping reflex to appear. It usually starts crying at the same time. Then fingers and hands clamp tightly on the rod. During the reaction the infant can be completely lifted from the pillow upon which it lies. An assistant places her two hands below the infant ready to catch it as it falls back to the pillow. The length of time the infant can support itself varies all the way from a fraction of a second to more than a minute. The time in a given case may vary considerably on different days.

The reaction is almost invariable from birth until it begins to disappear around the 120th day. The time of disappearance of this response varies considerably—in observed cases from 80 days to well over 150 days. There seems to be a continuance of the reflex in defective infants long after the normal period of disappearance.

Prematurely born infants of 7 and 8 months exhibit the reflex in a normal manner. Infants born without cerebral hemispheres exhibit the same reaction: in one observed case this was tested from birth to death 18 days later.

How much more than their own weight the infants can support has never been tested out but we have made these tests when the infants were fully clothed and sometimes slightly weighted.

This primitive reaction of course finally disappears from the stream of activity never to reappear. It gives place to the *habit* of handling and *manipulation*.

Blinking: Any newborn infant will close the lids when the eye (cornea) is touched or when a current of air strikes the eye. But no infant at birth will "blink" when a shadow rapidly crosses the eye as when a pencil or piece of paper is passed rapidly across the whole field of vision. The earliest reaction I have noted occurred on the 65th day. Mrs. Mary Cover Jones noted the reaction in one infant at 40 days.

It apparently appears quite suddenly—it is at first easily "fatigued" and is quite variable. Even up to the age of 80 days some infants will not blink every time the stimulus is applied. Usually at 100 days the infant will blink whenever the stimulus is applied if at least one minute is allowed between stimulations. This reaction stays in the activity stream until death. We cannot prove it yet but this reaction looks to us very much like a conditioned visual eyelid response, as follows:

$$(U)S\ldots\ldots\ldots\ldots(U)R$$
Contact with cornea   blink

but objects which touch the eye often cast a shadow, hence

$$(C)S\ldots\ldots\ldots\ldots(U)R$$
Shadow   blink

If this reasoning is correct, blinking at a shadow is not an *unlearned* response.

Handedness: We have already pointed out the possibility of handedness being due to the long enforced intra-uterine position of the child (really a habit). Studies of handedness can be made from birth on in several different ways.

1. Measurements of right and left anatomical structures, such as width of right and left wrist, palm, length of forearm, etc. The measurements have been made, with specially devised instruments, upon several hundred children. The results show that there is no significant difference in the right and left measurements. The average error of the measurement is greater than the observed difference.

2. By recording the time of suspension (see grasping) with left and right hand. Care is taken in all such tests to begin work with the right hand on one day and with the left hand on the following day. Chart I (left two columns) shows that there is no constancy in time of suspension from day to day.

3. By recording approximately the total amount of work done with right and left hands for a given period of time. For this work we use an especially devised work adder. This in principle is an escapement wheel that works in such a way that no matter how the baby slashes its arms about, it turns the wheel always in one direction. As the wheel revolves, it winds up a small lead weight attached to the wheel by a cord. Of course there is a separate instrument in use for each hand. At the beginning of the work period, the two weights are let down until they just touch the table top. The hands of the baby are then attached. His slashing movements begin to wind the ball up. Usually the baby lies naked on his back, unstimulated by the observer. At the end of five minutes there the baby is taken out of the apparatus and the height in inches of the two weights above the table top is measured.

Again when we face the records obtained in this way we find little significant difference between the work of the two hands.

Chart I[1]

Showing daily record of results on the two hands:

Age in Days	Time of suspension [in seconds]		Work done on adders [in inches]	
	Right	Left	Right	Left
1	1.2	5.6	16.16	13.75
2	2.2	3.0	25.00	15.00
3	.6	1.4	37.50	36.25
4	.6	1.4	12.00	15.00
5	1.2	1.0	15.00	27.00
6	1.0	1.6	17.16	16.00
7	.6	3.2	21.25	29.37
8	1.0	2.2	24.16	18.37
9	1.8	1.8	17.25	13.00
10	1.4	.6	28.00	9.00
Average	1.16	2.08	21.34	19.27

Longer with right 3   More work with right 7
Longer with left 6   More work with left 3
Equal 1   Equal 0

Chart I (right two columns) gives the record of one infant for the first ten days of its life. The table as a whole shows both the results obtained from the work adder and from suspension. Note that the average time of suspension for J. was with right hand 1.16 seconds; for the left 2.08 seconds. The average work done (average height weight was wound up) with right hand was 21.34 inches; with left hand 19.27 inches. On 3 days he suspended himself longer with right hand: on 6 days with left hand; on 1 day the time of suspension was equal. Note, too, that he wound the weight up faster with right hand on 7 days and with left 3 days.

Thus we see how handedness varies during the first few days of infancy. No dependence can be placed in the records of one child. We give one record here simply to show the type of results to expect. When a distribution curve is made by plotting a large number of such records, no significant difference can be found between the hands, either when time of suspension is charted or when total work done on work adders is charted. Evidently habit (or some other hitherto undetermined structural factor) must come in to stabilize it.

4. *Testing handedness by presenting objects after the act of reaching has been established*: At the age of approximately

[1]Subject J.

120 days you can begin to get the baby to reach for a stick or gaudily striped peppermint candy. You must first positively condition him to the candy. This can be done long before the habit of reaching is established by visually stimulating the infant with the stick of candy and then putting the candy in the mouth or else putting it in the baby's hands. If the latter is done the baby puts the candy in its mouth. Usually by the 160th day the infant will reach readily for the candy as soon as it is exhibited. The infant is then ready to test for handedness.

In all, I have worked with about 20 babies during this interesting period. In making the test, the baby is held in the mother's lap so that both hands are equally free. The experimenter stands in front of the baby and extends the candy slowly towards the baby at the level of its eyes, using care to advance on a line between the two hands. When the candy gets just within reach (and usually not much before) the two hands get active, then one or the other or both are lifted and advanced towards the candy. The hand touching it first is noted.

The results of all our tests of this nature, extending from the age of 150 days to one year, show no steady and uniform handedness. Some days the right is used more often, some days the left.

The Conclusion We Draw

Our whole group of results on handedness leads us to believe that there is no fixed differentiation of response in either hand until social usage begins to establish handedness. Society soon thereafter steps in and says, "Thou shalt use thy right hand." Pressure promptly begins. "Shake hands with your right hand, Willy." We hold the infant so that it will wave "bye bye" with the right hand. *We force it to eat with the right hand. This in itself is a potent enough conditioning factor to account for handedness.* But you say, "Why is society right handed?" This probably goes back to primitive days. One old theory often advanced is probably the true one. The heart is on the left side. It was easy enough for our most primitive ancestors to *learn* that the men who carried their shields with the left hand and jabbed or hurled their spears with the right were the ones who most often came back bearing their shields rather than being borne upon them. If there is any truth in this it is easy enough to see why our primitive ancestors began to teach their young to be right handed.

Long before the shield was put aside, the day of manuscripts and books had come; and long before that, the strolling bards and minstrels had orally crystallized the tradition. The strong right arm has become a part of our legends of the hero. All of our implements—candle snuffers, scissors and the like—were and are made for right handed people.

If handedness is a habit socially instilled, should we or should we not change over the left handers—those hardy souls who have resisted social pressure? I am firmly convinced that if the job is done early enough and wisely enough, not the slightest harm results. I should want to do it before language develops very much. If I had the time I would attempt to prove tonight that from the beginning we begin *to verbalize our acts*—that is put acts into words and *vice versa*. Now changing over a left handed, talking child suddenly into a right handed child is likely to reduce the child to a 6 months infant. By interfering constantly with his acts you break down his manual habits, and at the same time *you may simultaneously interfere with speech* (since the word and the manual act are simultaneously conditioned). In other words, while he is relearning he will fumble not only with his hands but also with his speech. The child is reduced to sheer infancy again. The unorganized (emotional) visceral control of the body as a whole again became predominant. It takes wiser handling to change the child over at this age than the average parent or teacher is prepared to give.

The main problem is, I believe, settled: handedness is not an "instinct." It is possibly not even structurally determined. It is socially conditioned. But why we have 5% of out and out left handers and from 10-15% who are mixtures—e. g. using right hand to throw a ball, write or eat, but the left hand to guide an axe or hoe, etc.—is not known.[1]

---

[1] There are several factors which must be noted and followed through. Thumb, fingers and hand sucking are present in infants and often unless very wisely handled last into late childhood. Usually but not always one or the other hand is fairly steadily used. One would expect the hand not used in thumb sucking to become quickly more facile in the manipulation of objects.

Again sometimes for months the infant reaching the standing stage holds on with one or the other hand—possibly indeed with the better trained, stronger hand! During this period the other hand is left free. It may overtake or even surpass the hand slowed up from non-use. Statistical studies upon adults and questionnaires will never throw any light upon the problem.

Summary of Unlearned Equipment

Although our studies of man's birth equipment have only begun, we can get a fair picture of the type of activity to be seen and of the method of studying this equipment by what I have said tonight.

At birth or soon thereafter we find nearly all of the so-called clinical neurological signs or reflexes established, such as the reaction of the pupil to light, the patellar reflex and many others.

We find the birth cry followed forever afterward by breathing, the heartbeat and all circulatory phenomena, such as vasomotor constriction (decrease in diameter of vessels) and dilatation, pulse beat, etc. Beginning with the alimentary tract we find sucking, tongue movements, and swallowing. We find hunger contractions, digestion, necessitating glandular reactions in the whole alimentary tract and elimination (defaecation, urination, sweat). The acts of smiling, sneezing and hiccoughing belong in part at least to the alimentary canal system. We find also erection of the penis.

We find general movements of the trunk, head and neck best observed, so far as the trunk is concerned, when the infant suspends himself with the hands. Rhythmical "climbing" movements then appear. We can see the trunk at work in breathing, when the infant cries, during defaecation and urination, when turning over or when the head is raised or turned.

We find the arms, wrist, hands and fingers in almost ceaseless activity (the thumb rarely taking part until later). In this activity especially are to be noted: grasping, opening and closing hands repeatedly, "slashing" about of the whole arm, putting hand or fingers into mouth, throwing arm and fingers to face when nose is held.

We find the legs, ankles, foot and fingers in almost ceaseless movement except in sleep and even during sleep if external (and internal) stimuli are present. The knee can be bent, leg moved at hip, ankle turned, toes spread, etc. If the bottom of the foot is touched, there is a characteristic movement of the toes (Babinski reflex) ; if the left knee is pinched the right foot is brought up to the point of stimulation and *vice versa.*

Other activities appear at a later stage—such as blinking, reaching, handling, handedness, crawling, standing, sitting up, walking, running, jumping. *In the great majority of these later activities it is difficult to say how much of the act as a whole is due to training or conditioning. A considerable part is unquestionably due to the growth changes in structure, and the rest is due to training and conditioning.*

What Has Become of Instincts?

Are we not ready to admit that the whole concept of instinct is thus academic and meaningless? Even from the earliest moment we find habit factors present—present even in many acts so apparently simple that we used to call them physiological reflexes. Now turn to James' list of instincts or turn to any other list of instincts. The infant is a graduate student in the subject of *learned responses* (he is multitudinously conditioned) by the time behavior such as James describes—imitation, rivalry, cleanliness and the other forms he lists—can be observed.

Actual observation thus makes it impossible for us any longer to entertain the concept of instinct. We have seen that every act has a genetic history. Is not the only correct scientific procedure then to single out for study whatever act is in question and to watch and record its life history?

Take smiling. It begins at birth—aroused by intra-organic stimulation and by contact. Quickly it becomes conditioned; the sight of the mother calls it out, then vocal stimuli, finally pictures, then words and then life situations either viewed, told or read about. Naturally what we laugh at, whom we laugh at and with whom we laugh are determined by our whole life history of special conditionings. No theory is required to explain it—only a systematic observation of genetic facts. All the elaborate pages the Freudians have written on humor and laughter are just so much chaff which will be blown aside as observation brings out the facts.

Again take manipulation. It starts at 120 days and becomes smooth, sharp and facile at 6 months. It can be built up in a thousand ways, depending upon the time allowed for it, the toys the infant plays with, whether the infant is hurt by any of its toys, whether it is frightened by loud sounds often at the time it is handling its toys. To argue for a so-called "constructive building instinct" apart from early training factors is to leave the world of facts.

Again there is a similar printed collection of meaningless material in educative propaganda—taking the form of "let the child develop its own inward nature." Other phrases expressive of this mystical inner life of bents and instincts are "self-realization," "self-expression," "untutored life" (of the savage, for example), the "brute instincts," "man's baser self," "elemental facts," etc. Such writers as Albert Payson Terhune, Jack London, Rex Beach and Edgar Rice Burroughs, owe the response they call out from their public to the organization laid down by social traditions (especially through taboos upon sex), aided and supported by the misconceptions of the psychologists themselves.

In order that you may more easily grasp one of the central principles of behaviorism—viz. that all complex behavior is a growth or development out of simple resources, I want to introduce here the notion of "activity stream."

The Activity Stream as a Substitute for James' "Stream of Consciousness"

Most of you are familiar with William James' classic chapter on the stream of consciousness. We have all loved that chapter. Today it seems as much out of touch with modern psychology as the stage coach would be on New York's Fifth Avenue. The stage coach was picturesque but it has given place to a more effective means of transportation. Tonight I want to give you something in place of James' classical contribution; less picturesque but more adequate to the facts.

We have passed in review many of the known facts on the early behavior of the human infant. Let us draw a diagram to represent the whole increasing complexity of man's organization. This picture will be very incomplete for several reasons. In the first place we have room on the chart to show only a few of those activities. In the second place our studies are not complete enough to draw an adequate chart even if we had the space, and finally we will not have the time to take up in these lectures man's visceral and emotional equipment, his manual habits and his language habits.

In spite of these handicaps, though, try to think of a complete life chart—of the ceaseless stream of activity beginning when the egg is fertilized and ever becoming more complex as age increases. Some of the unlearned acts we perform are shortlived—they stay in the stream only a little time—such, for example, as suckling, unlearned grasping (as opposed to learned grasping and manipulation), extension of the great toe (Babinski), etc., then disappear forever from the stream. Try to think of others beginning later in life, e. g. blinking, menstruation, ejaculation, etc., and remaining in the stream— blinking until death; menstruation until, say, 45-55 years, then disappearing; the act of ejaculation remaining on the chart of the male until the 70th-80th years or even longer.

But try hardest of all to think of each unlearned act as becoming conditioned shortly after birth—even our respiration and circulation. Try to remember, too, that the unlearned movements of arms, hands, trunks, legs, feet and toes become organized quickly into our stabilized habits, some of which remain in the stream throughout life, others staying in only a short time and then disappearing forever. For example, our 2-year habits must give place to 3 and 4-year habits.

I should like to spend a whole evening upon this chart of human activity. It gives you quickly in graphic form the whole scope of psychology. Every problem the behaviorist works upon has some kind of setting in this stream of definite, tangible, actually observable happenings. It gives you, too, the fundamental point of view of the behaviorist—viz. that in order to understand man you have to understand the life history of his activities. It shows, too, most convincingly that psychology is a natural science—a definite part of biology.

In our next two lectures we will see whether at the hands of the behaviorist the case for human emotions fares better than that of instincts.

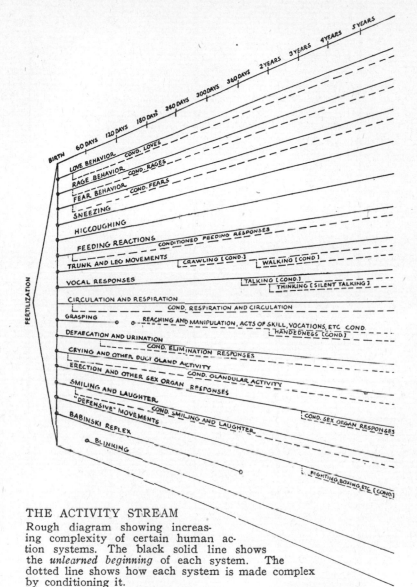

THE ACTIVITY STREAM

Rough diagram showing increasing complexity of certain human action systems. The black solid line shows the *unlearned beginning* of each system. The dotted line shows how each system is made complex by conditioning it.

Some of the systems apparently are not modified. They exist in the stream throughout life without increasing complexity. The chart is neither complete nor accurate. Until more thorough genetic work has been done, a chart of this kind cannot be used as a measuring rod of what to expect of infants of different ages.

CHAPTER II

EXPERIMENTAL STUDIES ON THE GROWTH OF THE EMOTIONS*

By John B. Watson

In my last lecture I told you that the current psychological view of instincts is not in harmony with the experimental findings of the behaviorist. Can the case for the present conception of emotions be made out any better? Probably no subject, unless it be that of instinct, has been more written about than emotions. Indeed the awe-inspiring number of volumes and papers and journals produced by Freudians and post-Freudians in the last 20 years would fill a good-sized room. And yet the behaviorist, as he reads through this great mass of literature cannot but feel in it a lack of any central scientific viewpoint. Not until his own genetic studies, started less than ten years ago, began to bear fruit, did it become apparent to the behaviorist that he could simplify the problems of emotion and apply objective experimental methods to their solution.

The Behaviorist's Approach to the Problems of Emotion

During the past 10 years the behaviorist has approached the problem of emotions from a new angle. In accordance with his usual procedure, he decided, before beginning work himself, to consign to the waste basket the work of his predecessors and to start the problem over again. His observation of adults told him rapidly that mature individuals, both men and women, display a wide group of reactions which go under the general name of emotional. The negro down South whines and trembles at the darkness which comes with a total eclipse of the sun, often falling on his knees and crying out, begging the Deity to forgive him for his sins. These same negroes show fear in passing through graveyards at night. They show "awe" and "reverence" for charms and relics. They will not burn wood which has been struck by lightning. In rural communities adults and children collect around the home as soon as dusk begins to fall. They often rationalize it by saying that they will get the "misery" from the night air. Situations of the

---

*Powell Lecture in Psychological Theory at Clark University, January 17, 1925.

most ordinary kinds judged from our more sophisticated stand-point arouse the strongest kinds of emotional reactions in them.

But let us be even more specific and bring the matter closer home. Here is the list of things a 3-year-old youngster in New York fears: Darkness, all rabbits, rats, dogs, fish, frogs, insects, mechanical animal toys. This infant may be playing excitedly with blocks. When a rabbit or other animal is introduced, all constructive activity ceases. He crowds towards one corner of his pen and begins to cry out, "Take it away, take it away." Another child examined the same day shows a different set. Another may show no fear reactions.

The more the behaviorist goes about examining the sets of reactions of adults, *the more he finds that the world of objects and situations surrounding people brings out more complex reactions that the efficient use or manipulation of the object or situation would call for.* In other words, the object seems to be 'charged,' seems to bring out thousands of accessory bodily reactions which the laws of efficient habit do not call for. I can illustrate this by the negro's rabbit foot. For us the rabbit foot is something to be cut off from the carcass of the animal and thrown away. One might toss it to one's dog as a part of his food. But to many of the negroes the rabbit foot is not an object to be reacted to in this simple way. It is dried, polished, put into the pocket, cared for and guarded jealously. He examines it now and then; when in trouble he calls upon it for guidance and aid, and in general reacts to it not as to a rabbit's foot but in the same way as a religious man reacts to a Deity.

Civilization to some extent has stripped from man these superfluous reactions to objects and situations, but many still persist, especially in the realm of religion. Bread is something to be eaten when hungry. Wine is something to be drunk with meals or on festive occasions. But these simple objects when fed to the individual at church under the guise of communion, call out kneeling, prayer, bowing of the head, closing of the eyes, and a whole mass of other verbal and bodily responses. The bones and relics of the saints may call out in devout religious individuals a different but entirely homologous (from the standpoint of religion) set of reaction to those the rabbit foot calls out in the negro. The behaviorist even goes further and investigates his colleague's everyday behavior. He finds that a noise in the basement at night may reduce his nextdoor neighbors to reactions quite infantile; that many of them are shocked when the Lord's name is "taken in vain," giving as a rationalization that it is irreverent, that punishment will be visited upon the individual so misbehaving. He finds many of them walking away from dogs and horses, even though they have to turn back or cross the street to avoid coming near them. He finds men and women picking out impossible mates without being able to rationalize the act at all in any way. In other words, if we were to take all of life's objects and situations into the laboratory and were to work out a physiologically sound and scientific way of reacting to them (experimental ethics may approach this some day) and call these forms the norm or standard, and were then to examine the man's everyday behavior in the light of such norms, we would find divergence from them the rule. Divergence takes the form of accessory reactions, slowed reactions, non-reactions (paralysis), blocked reactions, negative reactions, reactions not sanctioned by society (stealing, murder, etc.), reactions belonging to other stimuli (substitute).[1] It seems fair to call all of this group *emotional* without further defining the word at the present time.

Now as you know, we haven't physiologically standardized norms of reactions as yet. There is some approach to it. Progress in physical sciences has done much towards standardizing

---

[1]Examples:

Of accessory reactions: The subject does the task quickly and correctly but he becomes pale, he may even cry, urinate or defaecate, his mouth glands may become inactive. He reacts steadily and correctly in spite of his emotional state. Other examples of accessory reaction are whistling, talking, singing while at work.

Of slowed reactions: He does the act but his reaction time is increased—he may fumble and drop his work, or react with too much or too little energy. Response to questions comes slowly or very rapidly.

Of negative reactions: He may show fear at food—push it away or run away from it himself. Instead of the ordinary reactions to dog or horse, the subject may walk away from them. Phobias belong in this group.

Of reaction not sanctioned by society: The subject may in "heat of anger," for example, commit murder, injure property. I have in mind here all acts which the law punishes but where it tempers justice with mercy because of emotional factors.

Of reactions belonging to other stimuli: All homosexual reactions: all sex attacks by sons upon their mothers; all sex reactions to fetishes, etc. Emotional responses of parents to children masquerading under the guise of natural affection.

There are of course, legions of responses we call "emotional," that cannot be listed under any one of these headings.

our way of reacting to day and night, the seasons, the weather. We no longer react to a tree struck by lightning as accursed. We no longer think that we have any advantage over our enemy when we come in possession of his nail parings, hair and excrement.   We no longer react to the blue of the heavens above as a kingdom in which super-mundane beings dwell (at least some of us hardy souls do not!).   We no longer react to distant and almost invisible mountains as being the homes of gnomes and fairies.   Science, geography and travel have standardized our responses.   Our reactions to foods are becoming standardized through the work of the food chemist.   We no longer think of any particular form of food as being "clean" or "unclean."   We think of it now as fulfilling or not fulfilling definite bodily requirements.

Our social reactions, however, remain unstandardized. There is even no historical guide.   Professor Sumner, of Yale, has well pointed this out.   According to him, every conceivable kind of social reaction has at one time or another been considered the "normal" and unemotional way of acting.   One woman could have many husbands; one man many wives; the offspring could be killed in times of famine; human flesh could be eaten; sacrifice of offspring could be made to appease Deities; you could lend your wife to your neighbor or guest; the wife was acting properly when she burned herself on the pyre that consumed her husband's body.

Our social reactions are not standardized any better today. Think of our 1925 accessory responses when we are in the presence of our parents, in front of our social leaders.   Think of our hero worship, our veneration of the intellectual giant, the author, the artist, the church!   Think of the way we behave in crowds, at masked parties (Ku Klux as well as social)—at football and baseball games, at elections, in religious revivals (conversions, antics of the holy rollers, etc.), in grief at the loss of loved objects and people.   We have a host of words to cover these accessory reactions—reverence, love of family, of God, of church, of country; respect, adulation, awe, enthusiasm. When in the presence of many of these emotional stimuli we act like infants.

How the Behaviorist Works: The complicated nature of all these adult responses makes it hopeless for the behaviorist to begin his study of emotion upon adults.   He has to study emotional behavior genetically.

Suppose we start with three-year-olds—we will go out into

the highways and byways and collect them, and then let us go to the mansions of the rich. We bring them into our laboratory. We put them face to face with certain situations. Suppose we first let a boy go alone into a well lighted playroom and begin to play with his toys. Suddenly we release a boa constrictor or some other animal. Next we may take him to a dark room and suddenly start a miniature bonfire with newspapers. I cannot take time tonight to tell you all of the stage settings used by the behaviorist in experiments of this type. As you can see we can set the stage so that we can duplicate almost any kind of life situation.

But after testing him alone in all these situations we must test him again when an adult, possibly father or mother, is with him—when another child of his own age and sex is nearby, when another child of the opposite sex accompanies him, when groups of children are present.

In order to get a picture of his emotional behavior, we have to test separation from mother. We have to test him with different and uncustomary foods, with strange people to feed him, with strange nurses to bathe him, clothe him and put him to bed. We must rob him of his toys, of things he is playing with. We must let a bigger boy or girl bully him, we must put him in high places, on ledges (making injury impossible however), on the backs of ponies or dogs.

I am giving you a picture of how we work just to convince you of its simplicity, naturalness and accuracy—that there is a wide field for objective experimentation.

Brief Summary of Results of Such Tests

One of the sad things we find by such tests is that even at three years of age many (but not all) of the children are shot through with all kinds of useless and actually harmful reactions which go under the general name *emotional*.

They are afraid in many situations.[1] They are shy in dozens of others. They go into tantrums at being bathed or dressed. They go into tantrums when given certain foods—or when a new nurse feeds them. They go into crying fits when the

---

[1]Mrs. Mary Cover Jones reports that in the work with the older children at the Heckscher Foundation, the frog, especially when it suddenly jumps, is the most potent stimulus of all in bringing out fear reactions. The most pronounced reactions were called out from the children by an animal when it was come upon suddenly. For this reason the smaller animals were often left around the room concealed in boxes. General manipulation of objects in the room lead the child sooner or later to the sudden uncovering of the animal.

mother leaves them. They hide behind their mother's dress. They become shy and silent when visitors come. A characteristic picture is to have one hand in the mouth and the other grasping the mother's dress. One fights every child that comes near. He is called a bully, a ruffian, sadistic. Another cries and runs away if a child half his size threatens him. His parents call him a coward and his playmates make him the scapegoat.

Whence Arise These Varied Forms of Emotional Response?

A child three years of age is very young. Must we conclude that emotional reactions are hereditary? Is there an hereditary pattern of love, of fear, rage, shame, shyness, humor, anger, jealousy, timidity, awe, reverence, admiration, cruelty? Or are these just *words* to describe general types of behavior without implying anything as to their origin. Historically they have been considered hereditary in origin. To answer the question scientifically, we need new methods of experimentation.

EXPERIMENTS UPON THE ORIGIN AND GROWTH OF EMOTIONAL REACTIONS

In our experimental work we early reached the conclusion that young children taken at random from homes both of the poor and of the well-to-do, do not make good subjects for the study of the origin of emotions. Their emotional behavior is too complex. Fortunately we have been able to study a number of strong healthy children belonging to wet nurses in hospitals, and other children brought up in the home under the eye of the experimenters. Several of these children were observed from approximately birth through the first year, others through the second year and two or three children through the third year. Tonight I wish to give you an account of these studies.

In putting these hospital reared children through emotional situations we usually had the older ones sit in a small infant's chair. If the infant was very small—too young to sit up—we allowed it to sit in the lap of the mother or that of an attendant.

Reactions to Animals (a) in the Laboratory: We first took the children to the laboratory and put them through the routine of tests with various animals. We had the laboratory so arranged that they could be tested in the open room, alone; with an attendant; with the mother. They were tested in the dark room, the walls of which were painted black. This room was bare of furniture. It offered an unusual situation in itself. In the dark room we had conditions so arranged that we could turn on a light behind the infant's head or illuminate the room with the light in front of and above the infant. The infants were always tested one at a time. The following group of situations was usually presented:

First, a lively black cat invariably affectionately aggressive, was shown. The cat never ceased its purring. It climbed over and walked around the infant many times during the course of each test, rubbing its body against the infant in the usual feline way. So many false notions have grown up around the response of infants to furry animals that we were surprised ourselves to see these youngsters *positive always* in their behavior to this proverbial 'black cat.' Reaching out to touch the cat's fur, eyes and nose was the invariable response.

A rabbit was always presented. This, likewise, in every case called out manipulatory responses and nothing else. Catching the ears of the animal in one hand and attempting to put it in its mouth was one of the favorite responses.

Another furry animal invariably used was the white rat. This, possibly on account of its size and whiteness, rarely called out continued fixation of the eyes of the infant. When, however, the animal was fixated, reaching occurred.

Airedale dogs, large and small, were also presented. The dogs were also very friendly. The dogs rarely called out the amount of manipulatory response that an animal the size of the cat and rabbit called out. Not even when the children were tested with these animals in the dark room, either in full illumination or with a dim light behind their heads, was any fear response evoked.

These tests on children not emotionally conditioned proved to us conclusively that the classical illustrations of hereditary responses to furry objects and animals are just old wives' tales.

Next a feathery animal was used, usually a pigeon. The pigeon was presented first in a paper bag. This was a rather unusual situation even for an adult. The bird struggled and in struggling would move the bag around the couch. Oftentimes it would coo. While the pigeon was rattling and moving the paper bag about, the child rarely reached for the bag. The moment, however, the pigeon was taken into the experimenter's hands, the usual manipulatory responses were called forth. We have even had the pigeon moving and flapping its wings near the baby's face. This can be done easily by holding the pigeon by its feet, head down. Under these conditions even an adult will sometimes dodge and flinch a bit. When the wings fanned the infant's eyes, blinking was usually called out. Hesitation in response and failure to reach occurred. When the bird quieted down, reaching began.

Another form of test which we have often made under these same conditions, was the lighting of a small newspaper bonfire both out in the open room and in the dark room. In several cases when the paper first caught fire, the infant reached eagerly toward the flame and had to be restrained. As soon, however, as the flame became hot, reaching and manipulatory responses died down. At such times the infant may sit with hands partly up in a position that looks almost like the start of the shading reaction that the adult uses when coming too close to a fire. There isn't much question that this type of habit would have developed if the experiment had been repeated often. It probably is entirely similar to the reaction animals and humans make to the sun. When the sun gets too hot and they are not active they move into whatever shade is available.

(b) *To animals in Zoological Parks*: On several occasions hospital reared children, and home reared children whose emotional history was known, have been taken to zoological parks —always as a first experience. The children under observation were not pronounced in any of their reactions in the zoological park. Every effort was made to give them a good presentation of those animals which apparently have played considerable part in the biological history of the human. For example, a great deal of time was spent in the primates' house. Considerable time was spent also in the rooms where reptiles, frogs, turtles and snakes were kept. In such tests I have never got the slightest negative reaction to frogs and snakes, although the jumping frog, where children have been conditioned, is an extremely strong stimulus in bringing out fear responses as will be shown in the next chapter.

In the summer of 1924, I took my own two children to the Bronx Zoological Park. The older child, B, was a boy 2½ years of age. The younger child, J, was a boy 7 months of age. The younger child was without conditioned emotional fear responses. The older child had been conditioned but in a known way. For example, the first time he was taken into water up over his neck, he showed fear (I am sure that the so-called fear of the water is the same type of response that we get from loss of support). Before his trip to the Park he had seen horses, dogs, cats, pigeons, English sparrows, sea gulls, toads, worms, caterpillars and butterflies. He had developed no negative responses to any of these animals except the dog. Once a dog had attacked him and thereafter he was partly conditioned to dogs, but this fear had not transferred to other animals or to woolly toys or mechanical animals. In everyday life he began immediately to play with every animal (other than the dog) as soon as it came within his ken. Much to the distress of his mother, he would often bring to her worms and caterpillars of every description. Even to the hoptoad he showed not the slightest negative response.

In going to the Bronx Zoological Park, we had to take a ferry and this was his first experience on a large boat. Before this trip he had been in a canoe with me several times. The first time I took him out in the canoe, it was a little rough and the canoe was a tippy one. I got him out about 300 yards. A small wave struck us and he stiffened up a bit and said, "Daddy, too much water." I then took him closer in and paddled around the shore line for awhile. All fear responses to the canoe disappeared, although even now he sits pretty close and pretty tight when out in it. Shortly after his first trip in the canoe, he took the trip in question to the Zoological Park. On the ferry almost the same type of behavior developed. We got about half way over. He was leaning down and looking at the passage of the water. Suddenly he looked up and said, "Mama, too much water; Billy not afraid." But his general behavior belied his words somewhat.

In the Zoological Park he showed a tremendous eagerness to go after every animal he saw and we took him religiously to every cage, pen and yard. The animals that brought out his greatest reluctance to leave were a pair of chimpanzees. They were having a gorgeous time. They were carrying armfuls of hay up the chains of the swing. After getting to the seat they tried to slip the hay underneath them. Then suddenly they would swing down and catch each others hands, drop and hit the floor with a bang.

The animals calling out the most excited verbal response were the elephants; and next came the gaudily colored tropical birds. Every reaction to every animal was positive.

The behavior of the 7-months old baby was that of resigned boredom throughout the whole afternoon. Not once was any response shown, either positive or negative. Now and then the set fixation of the eyes was noticed. The birds seemed to bring out the most prolonged fixation.

We think that we have carried these experiments far enough on infants, the genesis of whose emotional behavior we know, to uphold our main contention that when fear responses occur in the presence of all objects and situations such as we have described they are always conditioned.

Are we to conclude from this work that in infants there are no *unlearned* reactions of a kind that might give us a starting point for building up emotional behavior?

Evidence for Three Types of Unlearned Beginnings of Emotional Reactions

I feel reasonably sure that there are three different forms of response that can be called out at birth by three sets of stimuli. Don't misunderstand me if I call these responses "fear," "rage" and love." Let me hasten to assure you that while I use the words fear, rage and love, I want you to strip them of all their old connotations. Please look upon the reactions we designate by them just as you look upon breathing, heart beat, grasping and other unlearned responses studied in the last chapter.

The facts follow.

Fear. Our work upon infants, especially those without cerebral hemispheres, where the reaction is more pronounced, early taught us that loud sounds almost invariably produced a marked reaction in infants from the very moment of birth. For example, the striking of a steel bar with a hammer will call out a jump, a start, a respiratory pause, followed by more rapid breathing with marked vasomotor changes, sudden closure of the eye, clutching of hands, puckering of lips. Then occur, depending upon the age of the infant, crying, falling down, crawling, walking or running away. I have never made a very systematic study of the range of sound stimuli that will call out fear responses. Not every type of sound will do it. Some extremely low pitched, rumbling noises will not call them out, nor will the very high tones of the Galton whistle. In the half sleeping infant of 2 or 3 days of age I have called them out repeatedly by suddenly crinkling a half of a newspaper near its ear, and by making a loud, shrill, hissing sound with the lips. Pure tones, such as those obtained from the tuning fork at any rate, are not very effective in calling them out. Considerably more work must be done upon the nature

of the auditory stimulus as well as upon the separate part reactions in the response before the whole stimulus-response
picture is complete.[1]

The other stimulus calling out this same fear reaction is
loss of support—*especially when the body is not set to com-
pensate for it.* It can best be observed in newborns just when
they are falling asleep. If dropped then, or if the blanket
upon which they lie is suddenly jerked, pulling the infant along
with it, the response invariably occurs.

In infants only a few hours old this fear reaction is quickly
"fatigued." In other words, if the same sound or the same kind
of loss of support stimulus is frequently applied, you can
often call out the reaction only once. After a few moments'
rest those same stimuli are again effective.

Even in the case of the adult human and higher mammals,
loss of support when the individual is not set for it, calls out
a strong fear reaction. If we have to walk across a slender
plank, naturally as we approach it the muscles of the body
are all set for it, but if we cross a bridge which remains perfectly steady until the middle has been reached and then suddenly begins to give way, our response is very marked. When
this happens in the case of a horse, one can with difficulty
get him to cross bridges again. There are many horses in the
country bridge shy. I am sure the same principle is operative
when a child is rapidly let out into deep water for the first
time. The buoyancy of the water actually throws him off his
balance. Even when the water is warm there is a catching
of the breath, clutching with the hands and crying.

Rage. Have you ever had the never to be forgotten experience, when proudly walking across a crowded street holding
your two-year-old daughter's hand, of having her suddenly
pull you in some other direction? And when you quickly and
sharply jerked her back and exerted steady pressure on her
arm to keep her straight did she then suddenly stiffen, begin
to scream at the top of her voice and lie down stiff as a ram-
rod in the middle of the street, yelling with wide open mouth
until she became blue in the face, and continuing to yell until

---

[1] I have found only one child out of many hundreds worked with
in whom a fear response cannot be called out by loud sounds. She
is well developed, well nourished, and normal in every way. There
were no fear reactions to any other stimuli. The nearest approach
to fear I saw was at the sight and sound of an opening and closing
umbrella. I have no explanation to offer for this exception.

she could make no further sound? If you have not, any picture of rage behavior must appear lifeless to you.

Possibly you have seen the large village bully take some child, down him and hold his arms and legs so closely to his body that the child could not even struggle. Have you watched the youngster stiffen and yell until he became blue in the face?

Did you ever notice the sudden changes that come into the faces of men when they are jostled and suddenly and unduly crowded in the street cars and railway trains? *Hampering of bodily movement* brings out the series of responses we call rage. This can be observed from the moment of birth but more easily in infants 10 to 15 days of age. When the head is held lightly between the hands; when the arms are pressed to the sides; and when the legs are held tightly together, rage behavior begins. The unlearned behavior elements in rage behavior have never been completely catalogued. Some of the elements, however, are easily observed, such as the stiffening of the whole body, the free slashing movements of hands, arms and legs, and the holding of the breath. There is no crying at first, then the mouth is opened to the fullest extent and the breath is held until the face appears blue. These states can be brought on without the pressure in any case being severe enough to produce the slightest injury to the child. The experiments are discontinued the moment the slightest blueness appears in the skin. All children can be thrown into such a state and the reactions will continue until the irritating situation is relieved, and sometimes for a considerable period thereafter. We have had this state brought out when the arms are held upward by a cord to which is attached a lead ball not exceeding an ounce in weight. The constant hampering of the arms produced by even this slight weight is sufficient to bring out the response. When the child is lying on its back it can occasionally be brought out by pressing on each side of the head with cotton wool. In many cases this state can be observed quite easily when the mother or nurse has to dress the child somewhat roughly or hurriedly.

Love. The study of this emotion in the infant is beset with a great many difficulties on the conventional side. Our observations consequently have been incidental rather than directly experimental. The stimulus to *love responses* apparently is stroking of the skin, tickling, gentle rocking, patting. The responses are especially easy to bring out by the stimulation of what, for lack of a better term, we may call the erogenous zones, such as the nipples, the lips and the sex organs. The response in an infant depends upon its state; when crying the crying will cease and a smile begin. Gurgling and cooing appear. Violent movements of arms and trunk with pronounced laughter occur in even 6-8 months old infants when tickled. It is thus seen that we use the term "love" in a much broader sense than it is popularly used. The responses we intend to mark off here are those popularly called "affectionate," "good natured," "kindly," etc. The term "love" embraces all of these as well as the responses we see in adults between the sexes. They all have a common origin.

Are There Other Unlearned Responses of These Three General Types?

Whether these three types of response are all that have an hereditary background we are not sure. Whether or not there are other stimuli which will call out these responses we must also leave in doubt.[1] If our observations are in any way complete, it would seem that emotional reactions are quite simple in the infant and the stimuli which call them out quite few in number.

These reactions which we have agreed, then, to call fear, rage and love, are at first quite indefinite. Much work remains to be done to see what the various part reactions are in each and how much they differ. They are certainly not the complicated kinds of emotional reaction we see later on in life, but at least I believe *they form the nucleus out of which all future emotional reactions arise.* So quickly do they become conditioned, as we shall show later, that it gives a wrong impression to call them hereditary modes of response. It is probably better just to keep the actual facts of observation thus: (Ordinarily called Fear:)

(U)S...................(U)R

Loss of support   Checking of breathing, "jump"
Loud sounds   or start of whole body, crying, often defaecation and urination (and many others not worked out experimentally. Probably the largest group of part reactions are visceral).

---

[1] For example, I am uncertain what the relationship is between the fear reactions we have been describing and the reactions called out by very hot objects, ice cold water, and other noxious stimuli.

(Ordinarily called Rage:)

                    (U)S.....................(U)R

| Restraint of bodily movement. | Stiffening of whole body, screaming, temporary cessation of breathing, reddening of face changing to blueness of face, etc. It is obvious that while there are general over responses, the greatest concentration of movement is in the visceral field. Blood tests of infants so manhandled show that that there is an increase in blood sugar. This means probably an increase in the secretion of the adrenal glands—release of increased output of adrenalin. |

(Ordinarily called Love:)

                    (U)S.....................(U)R

| Stroking skin and sex organs, rocking, riding on foot, etc. | Cessation of crying; gurgling, cooing and many others not determined. That visceral factors predominate is shown by changes in circulation and respiration, erection of penis, etc. |

If we think of these *unlearned* (so-called emotional) responses in the terms of these simple formulae, we cannot go very far wrong.

How Our Emotional Life Becomes Complicated

How can we square these observations with those which show the enormous complexity in the emotional life of the adult? We know that hundreds of children are afraid of the dark, we know that many women are afraid of snakes, mice and insects, and that emotions are attached to many ordinary objects of almost daily use. Fears become attached to persons and to places and to general situations, such as the woods, the water, etc. In the same way the number of objects and situations which can call out rage and love become enormously increased. Rage and love at first are not produced by the mere sight of an object. We know that later on in life the mere sight of persons may call out both of these primitive emotions. How do such "attachments" grow up? How can objects which at first do not call out emotions come later to call them out and thus greatly increase the richness as well as the dangers of our emotional life?

Since 1918 we have been at work upon this problem. We were rather loath at first to conduct such experiments, but the need of this kind of study was so great that we finally decided to experiment upon the possibility of building up fears in the infant and then later to study practical methods for removing them. We chose as our first subject Albert B, an infant weighing twenty-one pounds, at eleven months of age. Albert was the son of one of the wet nurses in the Harriet Lane Hospital. He had lived his whole life in the hospital. He was a wonderfully "good" baby. In all the months we worked with him we never saw him cry until after our experiments were made!

Before turning to the experiments by means of which we built up emotional responses in the laboratory, it is necessary for you to recall all that I tried to tell you on the conditioning of reflexes. I am going to assume that you know that when you establish a conditioned reaction, you must have a fundamental stimulus to start with which will call out the response in question. Your next step is to get some other stimulus to call it out. For example, if your purpose is to make the arm and hand jerk away every time a buzzer sounds, you must use the electric shock or other noxious stimulus each time the electric buzzer is sounded. Shortly, as you know, the arm will begin to jump away when the buzzer is sounded just as it jumps away when the electric shock is given. We already know now that there is an unconditioned or fundamental stimulus which will call out the fear reaction quickly and easily. It is a loud sound. We determined to use this just as we use the electric shock in experiments on the conditioned motor and glandular reflexes.

Our first experiment with Albert had for its object the conditioning of a fear response to a white rat. We first showed by repeated tests that nothing but loud sounds and removal of support would bring out fear response in this child. Everything coming within twelve inches of him was reached for and manipulated. His reaction, however, to a loud sound was characteristic of what occurs with most children. A steel bar about one inch in diameter and three feet long, when struck with a carpenter's hammer produced the most marked kind of reaction.

Our laboratory notes[1] showing the progress in establishing a conditioned emotional response are given here in full:

Eleven months, 3 days old. (1) White rat which he played with for weeks was suddenly taken from the basket (the usual routine) and presented to Albert. He began to reach for rat with left hand. Just as his hand touched the animal the bar was struck immediately behind his head. The infant jumped violently and fell forward, burying his face in the mattress. He did not cry, however.

(2) Just as his right hand touched the rat the bar was again struck. Again the infant jumped violently, fell forward and began to whimper.

On account of his disturbed condition no further tests were made for one week.

Eleven months, ten days old. (1) Rat presented suddenly without sound. There was steady fixation but no tendency at first to reach for it. The rat was then placed nearer, whereupon tentative reaching movements began with the right hand. When the rat nosed the infant's left hand the hand was immediately withdrawn. He started to reach for the head of the animal with the forefinger of his left hand but withdrew it suddenly before contact. It is thus seen that the two joint stimulations given last week were not without effect. He was tested with his blocks immediately afterwards to see if they shared in the process of conditioning. He began immediately to pick them up, dropping them and pounding them, etc. In the remainder of the tests the blocks were given frequently to quiet him and to test his general emotional state. They were always removed from sight when the process of conditioning was under way.

(2) Combined stimulation with rat and sound. Started, then fell over immediately to right side. No crying.

(3) Combined stimulation. Fell to right side and rested on hands with head turned from rat. No crying.

(4) Combined stimulation. Same reaction.

(5) Rat suddenly presented alone. Puckered face, whimpered and withdrew body sharply to left.

(6) Combined stimulation. Fell over immediately to right side and began to whimper.

(7) Combined stimulation. Started violently and cried, but did not fall over.

(8) Rat alone. The instant the rat was shown the baby began to cry. Almost instantly he turned sharply to the left, fell over, raised himself on all fours and began to crawl away so rapidly that he was caught with difficulty before he reached the edge of the mattress.

Surely this proof of the conditioned origin of a fear response puts us on a natural science grounds in our study of emotional behavior. It is a far more prolific goose for laying

---

[1] See the original paper by Rosalie Rayner and John B. Watson, *Scientific Monthly*, 1921, p. 493.

golden eggs than is James' barren verbal formulation. It yields an explanatory principle that will account for the enormous complexity in the emotional behavior of adults. We no longer in accounting for such behavior have to fall back upon heredity.

The Spread or Transfer of Conditioned Responses

Before the above experiment on the rat was made, Albert had been playing for weeks with rabbits, pigeons, fur muffs, the hair of the attendants and false faces. What effect will conditioning him upon the rat have upon his response to these animals and other objects when next he sees them? To test this we made no further experiments upon him for five days. That is, during this five day period he was not allowed to see any of the above objects. At the end of the 6th day we again tested him first with the rat to see if the conditioned fear response to it had carried over. Our notes are as follows:

Eleven months, fifteen days old.

(1) Tested first with blocks. He reached readily for them, playing with them as usual. This shows that there has been no general transfer to the room, table, blocks, etc.

(2) Rat alone. Whimpered immediately, withdrew right hand and turned head and trunk away.

(3) Blocks again offered. Played readily with them, smiling and gurgling.

(4) Rat alone. Leaned over to the left side as far away from the rat as possible, then fell over, getting up on all fours and scurrying away as rapidly as possible.

(5) Blocks again offered. Reached immediately for them, smiling and laughing as before.

This shows that the conditioned response was carried over the five day period. Next we presented in order a rabbit, a dog, a sealskin coat, cotton wool, human hair and a false face:

(6) Rabbit alone. A rabbit was suddenly placed on the mattress in front of him. The reaction was pronounced. Negative responses began at once. He leaned as far away from the animal as possible, whimpered, then burst into tears. When the rabbit was placed in contact with him he buried his face in the mattress, then got up on all fours and crawled away, crying as he went. This was a most convincing test.

(7) The blocks were next given to him, after an interval. He played with them as before. It was observed by four people that he played far more energetically with them than ever before. The blocks were raised high over his head and slammed down with a great deal of force.

(8) Dog alone. The dog did not produce as violent a reaction as the rabbit. The moment fixation of the eyes occurred the child shrank back and as the animal came nearer he attempted to get on all fours but did not cry at first. As soon as the dog passed out

of his range of vision he became quiet. The dog was then made
to approach the infant's head (he was lying down at the moment).
Albert straightened up immediately, fell over to the opposite side
and turned his head away. He then began to cry.

(9) Blocks were again presented. He began immediately to play
with them.

(10) Fur coat (seal). Withdrew immediately to the left side and
began to fret. Coat put close to him on the left side, he turned
immediately, began to cry and tried to crawl away on all fours.

(11) Cotton wool. The wool was presented in a paper package.
At the ends the cotton was not covered by the paper. It was placed
first on his feet. He kicked it away but did not touch it with his
hands. When his hand was laid on the wool he immediately withdrew it but did not show the shock that the animals or fur coat
produced in him. He then began to play with the paper, avoiding
contact with the wool itself. Before the hour was up, however, he
lost some of his negativism to the wool.

(12) Just in play W. who had made the experiments, put his head
down to see if Albert would play with his hair. Albert was completely negative. The other two observers did the same thing. He
began immediately to play with their hair. A Santa Claus mask
was then brought and presented to Albert. He was again pro-
nouncedly negative, although on all previous occasions he had played
with it.

Our notes thus give a convincing proof of spread or transfer.

We have here further proof in these transfers that conditioned emotional responses are exactly like other conditioned
responses. If we condition a man or lower animal by regular
conditioned reflex methods, say, to a tone A of a given pitch,
almost any other tone will at first call out the response. By
continuing the experiment—say by always feeding when tone
A is sounded but never when any other tone is sounded—you
soon get the animal to the point where it will respond only
to A. This would be a differential conditioned response.

I am sure that in these cases of transfer or spread of conditioned emotional responses the same factors are at work.

I believe, although I have never tried the experiments, that
we could set up just as sharp a differential reaction in the
emotional field as we can in any other. I mean by this merely
that if the experiment was long continued we could bring the
fear reaction out sharply whenever the rat was shown but
never when any other furry object was shown. If this were
the case, we should have a differential conditioned emotional
response. This seems to be what happens in real life. Most
of us in infancy and in early youth are in the undifferentiated
emotional state. Many adults, especially women, remain in
it. All primitive peoples remain in it (superstitions, etc.).
But educated adults by the long training they get in manipu-

lating objects, handling animals, working with electricity, etc., reach the second or differentiated stage of the conditioned emotional reaction.

There is thus, if my reasoning is correct, a thoroughly sound way of accounting for transferred emotional responses—and for the Freudian's so-called "free-floating affects." When conditioned emotional responses are first set up, a wide range of stimuli (in this case all hairy objects) physically similar will at first call out the response and so far as we know will continue to call it out unless experimental steps (or a very fortunate series of environmental settings) are taken to bring the undifferentiated conditioned response up to the differentiated stage. *In the differentiated stage only the object or situation you were conditioned upon originally will call out the response.*

SUMMARY

We must see that there is just as little evidence for a wholesale inheritance of those complicated patterns of response commonly called *emotional* as there is for the inheritance of those called *instinctive*.

Possibly a better way to describe our findings is to say that in working over the whole field of the human infant's reaction to stimuli, we find that certain types of stimuli—loud sounds and removal of support—produce a certain general type of response, namely, momentary checking of breath, a start of the whole body, crying, marked visceral responses, etc.; that another type of stimulus, holding or restraint, produces crying with wide open mouth, prolonged holding of breath, marked changes in circulation and other visceral changes; that a third stimulus, stroking the skin, especially in the sex areas, produces smiling, changes in respiration, cessation of crying, cooing, gurgling, erection and other visceral changes. Attention is called to the fact that responses to these stimuli are not mutually exclusive —many of the part reactions are the same.

These unconditioned stimuli with their relatively simple unconditioned responses are our starting points in building up those complicated conditioned, habit patterns we later call our emotions. In other words, emotional reactions are built in an order like most of our other reaction patterns. Not only do we get an increase in the number of stimuli calling out the response (substitution) through direct conditioning and through transfers (thus enormously widening the stimulus range), but also we get marked additions to and modifications of the responses themselves.

Another set of factors increasing the complexity of our emotional life must be taken into account. The same object (for example a person) can become a substitute stimulus for a fear response in one situation and a little later a substitute stimulus for a love response in another, or even for a rage response. The increasing complexity brought about by these factors soon gives us an emotional organization sufficiently complicated to satisfy even the novelist and the poet.

I am loath to close tonight until I have introduced, parenthetically at least, one additional thought. The thought is that notwithstanding the fact that in all emotional responses there are overt factors such as the movement of the eyes and the arms and the legs and the trunk, *visceral and glandular factors predominate.* The "cold sweat" of fear, the "bursting heart," "the bowed head" in apathy and grief, the "exuberance of youth," the "palpitating heart" of the swain or maiden, are more than mere literary expressions, they are bits of genuine observations.

I want to develop the thesis sometime that society has never been able to get hold of these implicit concealed visceral and glandular reactions of ours, or else it would have schooled them in us, for, as you know, society has a great propensity for regulating all of our reactions. Hence most of our adult overt reactions—our speech, the movements of our arms, legs and trunk—are schooled and habitized. Owing to their concealed nature, however, society cannot get hold of visceral behavior to lay down rules and regulations for its integration. It follows as a corollary from this that we have no names, no words with which to describe these reactions. They remain unverbalized. One can describe in well chosen words every act of two boxers, two fencers, and can criticize each individual detail of their responses, because there are verbal manuals of procedure and practice in the performance of these skillful acts. But what Hoyle has laid down the rules by which the separate movements of our viscera and glands must take place when in the presence of our lady love?

Because, then, of the fact that we have never verbalized these responses, a good many things happen to us *that we cannot talk about. We have never learned how to talk about them. There are no words for them.* The theory of the unverbalized in human behavior gives us a natural science way

of explaining many things the Freudians now call "unconscious complexes," "suppressed wishes" and the like.   In other
words, we can now come back to natural science in our study
of emotional behavior.   Our emotional life grows and develops
like our other *sets of habits*.   But do our emotional habits
once implanted suffer from disuse?   Can they be put away
and outgrown like our manual and verbal habits?   Until very
recently we had no facts to guide us in answering these questions.   Some are now available.   In my next lecture I shall
attempt to present them.

CHAPTER III

RECENT EXPERIMENTS ON HOW WE LOSE AND CHANGE OUR EMOTIONAL EQUIPMENT*

By John B. Watson

The experiments I reported at the close of my last lecture were completed in 1920. Until the fall of 1923 no further experiments were undertaken. Finding that emotional responses could be built in with great readiness, we were all the more eager to see whether they could be broken down, and if so by what methods. No further tests could be made upon Albert B., the youngster in whom the conditioned responses had been built up, because he was shortly afterwards adopted by an out-of-town family. It was just at this time that my own work at Hopkins was interrupted.

The matter of further experimentation rested until the fall of 1923. At that time a sum of money was granted by the Laura Spelman Rockefeller Memorial to the Institute of Educational Research of Teachers' College, a part of which was used for continuing the study of the emotional life of children. We found a place for work—the Heckscher Foundation. Approximately 70 children are kept there ranging in age from 3 months to 7 years. It was not an ideal place for our experimental work because we were not allowed full control of the children and because of the frequency with which work had to be stopped on account of unavoidable epidemics of one kind or another. In spite of these handicaps much work was done. While I spent considerable time there as consultant and helped to plan the work, Mrs. Mary Cover Jones conducted all of the experiments and wrote up all of the results.[1]

Tonight I wish to give you an account of this work.

The Different Methods Used in Attempting to Eliminate Fear Responses

Locating the Conditioned Fear Responses in Children:—A number of children of different ages were put through a group of situations designed to bring out fear responses if any

---

*Powell Lecture in Psychological Theory at Clark University, January 17, 1925.

[1]Partial report on this work has already appeared. See The Elimination of Children's Fears, by Mary Cover Jones. J. Exper. Psychol., 1924, p. 382.

were present. As has already been mentioned, children brought up in the home show fear reactions. These we have every reason to believe are conditioned. By passing each individual through these situations we were able not only to locate the children possessing the most pronounced conditioned fear reactions but also to locate the objects (and the general situations) that called out those reactions.

We worked here of course under one disadvantage. We did not know the genetic history of their fear responses. Hence we did not know whether a given fear reaction when observed was directly conditioned or merely transferred. This is always a handicap—an especially hard one in this work as I shall show you later.

Elimination of Fear Responses Through Disuse:—Having located a child with a fear response and the stimulus calling it out, our next step was to attempt to remove it.

It has commonly been supposed that the mere removal of the stimulus for a sufficient length of time will cause the child or adult to "forget his fear." All of us have heard the expressions "Just keep him away from it and he'll outgrow it. He will forget all about it." Laboratory tests were made to determine the efficacy of this method. I quote from Mrs. Jones' laboratory notes:

Case 1.—Rose D. Age 21 months. General situation: sitting in playpen with other children none of whom showed specific fears. A rabbit was introduced from behind a screen.
Jan. 19. At sight of the rabbit, Rose burst into tears, her crying lessened when the experimenter picked up the rabbit, but again increased when the rabbit was put back on the floor. At the removal of the rabbit she quieted down, accepted a cracker, and presently returned to her blocks.
Feb. 5. After 2 weeks the situation was repeated. She cried and trembled upon seeing the rabbit. E. (the experimenter) sat on the floor between Rose and the rabbit; she continued to cry for several minutes. E. tried to divert her attention with the peg-board; she finally stopped crying, but continued to watch the rabbit and would not attempt to play.
Case 8.—Bobby G. Age 30 months.
Dec. 6. Bobby showed a slight fear response when a rat was presented in a box. He looked at it from a distance of several feet, drew back and cried. A 3-day period of training followed bringing Bobby to the point where he tolerated a rat in the pen in which he was playing, and even touched it without overt fear indications. No further stimulation with the rat occurred until
Jan. 30. After nearly two months of no experience with the specific stimulus, Bobby was again brought into the laboratory. While he was playing in the pen, E. appeared, with a rat in her hand. Bobby jumped up, ran outside the pen, and cried. The rat

having been returned to its box, Bobby ran to E., held her hand, and showed marked disturbance.

Case 33.—Eleanor J. Age 21 months.

Jan. 17. While playing in the pen, a frog was introduced from behind her. She watched, came nearer, and finally touched it. The frog jumped. She withdrew and when later presented with the frog, shook her head and pushed the experimenter's hand away violently.

Mar. 26. After two months of no further experience with animals, Eleanor was taken to the laboratory and offered the frog. When the frog hopped she drew back, ran from the pen and cried.

These tests and many others similar in character incline us to believe that the *method of disuse in the case of emotional disturbance is not as effective as is commonly supposed.* It is admitted, however, that the tests were not extended over a long enough time to yield complete evidence.

Method of Verbal Organization

Most of the subjects in the Heckscher Foundation were under 4 years of age and the possibility of verbally organizing the children about the objects that called out fear responses was very limited. Naturally nothing can be accomplished by the use of this method until the child has a fairly wide language organization. One satisfactory subject—Jean E., a girl in her 5th year, however, was found sufficiently well organized to use in an extended test. At the initial presentation of the rabbit, marked fear responses were shown. The rabbit was not shown again for some time, but ten minutes daily conversation was given her on the subject of rabbits. The experimenter introduced such devices as the picture book of Peter Rabbit, toy rabbits and rabbits modeled from plasticeone. Brief stories about rabbits were told. During the telling of these stories, she would say "Where is your rabbit?" or "Show me a rabbit"; and once she said "I touched your rabbit and stroked it and never cried" (which was not true). At the end of one week of verbal organization, the rabbit was shown again. *Her reaction was practically the same as the first encounter.* She jumped up from her play and retreated. When coaxed she touched the rabbit while the experimenter held it, but when the animal was put down on the floor she sobbed "Put it away—take it." Verbal organization when not connected with actual manual adjustments to the animal had little effect in removing her fear responses.

Method of Frequent Application of Stimulus

While experiments with this method have not been extended, the results have not been very hopeful. The routine adopted in applying this method is to have the animal calling out the fear reaction brought in many times each day. While in some cases no actual negative responses were made, this was the only form of improvement noted—no *positive* reactions developed from the use of this method. In some cases a summation effect rather than an adjustment was obtained.

Method of Introducing Social Factors

Most of us are familiar both in the school and on the playground with what happens among groups of children. If one shows fear at any object to which the group does not show fear, the one showing fear is made a scapegoat and is called a "fraidy cat." We attempted to use this social factor in the case of some of the children. One case is given here in detail:

Case 41.—Arthur G. Age 4 years.
Arthur was shown the frogs in an aquarium, no other children being present. He cried, said "they bite," and ran out of the playpen. Later, however, he was brought into the room with four other boys; he swaggered up to the aquarium, pressing ahead of the others who were with him. When one of his companions picked up a frog and turned to him with it, he screamed and fled; at this he was chased and made fun of, but with naturally no lessening of the fear on this particular occasion.

This is probably one of the most unsafe methods in common use for eliminating fears. It tends to breed negative reactions not only to the animal feared but to society as a whole.

Where milder social methods are used, ordinarily called social imitation, better results are obtained. Mrs. Jones gives two cases which I quote:

Case. 8.—Bobby G. Age 30 months.
Bobby was playing in the pen with Mary and Laurel. The rabbit was introduced in a basket. Bobby cried "No, no," and motioned for the experimenter to remove it. The two girls, however, ran up readily enough, looked in at the rabbit and talked excitedly. Bobby became promptly interested, said "What? Me see," and ran forward, his curiosity and assertiveness in the social situation overmastering other impulses.

Case 54.—Vincent W. Age 21 months.
Jan. 19 Vincent showed no fear of the rabbit, even when it was pushed against his hands or face. His only response was to laugh and reach for the rabbit's fur. On the same day he was taken into the pen with Rosey, who cried at the sight of the rabbit. Vincent immediately developed a fear response; in the ordinary playroom situation he would pay no attention to her crying, but in connection with the rabbit, her distress had a marked suggestion value. The **fear** transferred in this way persisted for over **two weeks**.

Feb. 6. Eli and Herbert were in the play-pen with the rabbit. When Vincent was brought in, he remained cautiously standing at some distance. Eli led Vincent over to the rabbit, and induced him to touch the animal. Vincent laughed.

As will be noted, however, there are difficulties in the way of the use of this method. Occasionally the children showing no fear to the object become conditioned by the behavior of the child showing fear reactions to the object.

While all of these methods are suggestive and while none of them has been worked out to a final conclusion, none seems especially fruitful or free from danger.

The Method of Re-Conditioning or Un-Conditioning

The most successful method so far discovered for use in removing fears is the method of *unconditioning* or reconditioning. Reconditioning would be a little more satisfactory word to use except for the fact that it has been used by the physical culturists in various types of health propaganda. Unconditioning seems the only other available word.

I wish to go into the details of one case where unconditioning was attempted because it illustrates not only the method used but the various difficulties one is likely to encounter in such work.

Peter was an active eager child of approximately 3 years of age.[1] This child was well adjusted to ordinary life situations except for his fear organization. He was afraid of white rats, rabbits, fur coats, feathers, cotton wool, frogs, fish and mechanical toys. From the description of his fears, you might well think that Peter was merely Albert B. of the last lecture grown up. Only you must remember that Peter's fears were "home grown," not experimentally produced as were Albert's. Peter's fears, though, were much more pronounced as the following description will show:

Peter was put in a crib in a play room and immediately became absorbed in his toys. A white rat was introduced into the crib from behind. (The experimenter was behind a screen.) At the sight of the rat, Peter screamed and fell flat on his back in a paroxysm of fear. The stimulus was removed, and Peter was taken out of the crib and put into a chair. Barbara, a girl of two, was brought to the crib and the white rat introduced as before. She exhibited no fear but picked the rat up in her hand. Peter sat quietly watching Barbara and the rat. A string of beads belonging to Peter had been left in

---

[1] A full report on Peter is given by Mrs. Jones in the December, 1924, number of the *Pedagogical Seminary*.

the crib. Whenever the rat touched a part of the string, he would say "my beads" in a complaining voice, although he made no objections when Barbara touched them. Invited to get down from the chair, he shook his head, fear not yet subsided. Twenty-five minutes elapsed before he was ready to play about freely.

The next day his reactions to the following situations and objects were noted:

Play room and crib	Selected toys, got into crib without protest.
White ball rolled in	Picked it up and held it.
Fur rug hung over crib	Cried until it was removed.
Fur coat hung over crib	Cried until it was removed.
Cotton	Whimpered, withdrew, cried.
Hat with feathers	Cried.
White toy rabbit of rough cloth	Neither negative nor positive reaction.
Wooden doll	Neither negative nor positive reaction.

Training for removal of these fears in Peter was first begun by utilizing social factors as discussed on p. 62. There was considerable improvement, but before retraining was completed the child fell ill with scarlet fever and had to go to a hospital for a period of two months. When coming back from the hospital a large barking dog attacked him and the nurse just as they entered a taxicab. Both the nurse and Peter were terribly frightened. Peter lay back in the taxi ill and exhausted. After allowing a few days for recovery he was taken to the laboratory and again tested with animals. *His fear reactions to all the animals had returned in exaggerated form.* We determined then to use another type of procedure— that of direct unconditioning. We did not have control over his meals, but we secured permission to give him his mid-afternoon lunch consisting of crackers and a glass of milk. We seated him at a small table in a high chair. The lunch was served in a room about forty feet long. Just as he began to eat his lunch, the rabbit was displayed in a wire cage of wide mesh. We displayed it on the first day *just far enough away not to disturb his eating*. This point was then marked. The next day the rabbit was brought closer and closer until disturbance was first barely noticed. This place was marked. The third and succeeding days the same routine was maintained. Finally the rabbit could be placed upon the table— then in Peter's lap. Next tolerance changed to positive reaction. Finally he would eat with one hand and play with the rabbit with the other, a proof that his *viscera were retrained along with his hands!*

After having broken down his fear reactions to the rabbit— the animal calling out fear responses of the most exaggerated kinds—we were next interested in seeing what his reactions would be to other furry animals and furry objects. *Fear responses to cotton, the fur coat, and feathers* were entirely gone. He looked at them and handled them and then turned to other things. He would even pick up the fur rug and bring it to the experimenter.

The reaction to white rats was greatly improved—it had at least reached the tolerance stage but did not call out any very excited positive manipulation. He would pick up the small tin boxes containing rats and frogs and carry them around the room.

He was then tested in an entirely new animal situation. A mouse which he had not hitherto seen was handed to him together with a tangled mass of earthworms. His reaction was at first partly negative but this gave way in a few minutes to positive response to the worms and undisturbed watching of the mouse.

We suffer here as always in working with home grown fears by not knowing the primary situation upon which the child was conditioned (conditioned reflex of the 1st order). Possibly if we had had information upon this point and had unconditioned him on his primary fear, all of the "transferred" responses would have evaporated at once. Not until we have had more experience with building up a primary fear, noting the transfers and then unconditioning for the primary, will we be working upon sure ground in this interesting field. It is just possible that there may be certain reaction differences (intensity) between the primary conditioned response, (1st order), the secondarily conditioned responses (2nd and succeeding orders) and the various transferred responses. If this is true, then we might be able to tell, by presenting widely varying situations to children whose emotional history is unknown, just which one any given child was originally conditioned upon.

The whole field of emotions, when thus experimentally approached, is a very thrilling one and one which opens up real vistas of practical application in the home and in the school— even in everyday life.

At any rate we have now seen grow up under our very eyes the experimental genesis of a fear response and at least one case where the fear response was uprooted by a safe experimental method. If fear can be handled in this way, why not all other forms of emotional organization connected with rage (tantrums) and love? I believe firmly that they can be. In other words, emotional organization is subject to exactly the same laws as other habits, both as to origin, as we have already pointed out, and as to decline.

The method we have sketched has a serious drawback, mainly because we did not have control over all the meals of the child. (By the way, never start an experiment upon a child or infant unless you have full control). Probably if the child has been stroked, petted, and rocked (sexual stimulation) just as the fear object was presented, unconditioning might have taken place much more rapidly.

Incomplete and unsatisfactory as is this preliminary report upon the work of unconditioning, there are at present no further facts. We must leave the subject of conditioning and unconditioning of emotional reactions until we can work upon a larger number of infants and work with them under better conditions of control.

Home Factors Leading to Emotional Conditioning of Children

Is is conceivable that some day we may be able to bring up the human young through infancy and childhood without crying or showing fear reactions except when in the presence of the unconditioned stimuli (pain, noxious stimuli, loud sounds, etc.) calling out these responses. Since these unconditioned stimuli are rarely present, children ought practically never to cry. And yet look at them—morning, noon and night they are at it! An infant has an honest right to cry when it has colic, when its diaper pin is sticking into its tender flesh, and to whimper a bit when hungry, when its gets its head in between the slats of the bed, or falls down between the mattress and the side of the bed, or when the cat scratches it, or its bodily tissue is otherwise injured, or when loud sounds and loss of support assail it. But on no other occasion is the cry justifiable. This means that owing to our unsatisfactory training methods in the home, we spoil the emotional make-up of each child as rapidly as the twig can be bent.

What Situations Make the Child Cry?

In line with this thought, Mrs. Jones followed around a group of nine children from the time they first waked up in the morning until they were fast asleep at night. Every cry was noted, every laugh observed. The duration of laughing and crying was noted and the time of day it occurred and, most carefully of all, the general situations calling out these reactions were recorded and the after effects crying and laughing had upon subsequent behavior. Children in the group ranged from 16 months to 3 years of age. These children were tested in the Heckscher Foundation, but they were living there temporarily. They had been brought up in the home. One month after the first set of observations was made another set was undertaken. The results of these observations have never been published by Mrs. Jones, but she has given me the main facts which I now present.

The situations calling out cries are listed in the order of the number of cries elicited, as follows:

1. Having to sit on the toilet chair.
2. Having property taken away.
3. Having the face washed.
4. Being left alone in a room.
5. Having the adult leave the room.
6. Working at something which won't pan out.
7. Failure to get adults or other children to play with them, or look at them and talk to them.
8. Being dressed.
9. Failure to get adults to pick them up.
10. Being undressed.
11. Being bathed.
12. Having the nose wiped.

These are only twelve of the most usual situations calling out such responses. More than 100 situations called out weeping or whining. Many of the responses to these situations can be looked upon as unconditioned or conditioned rage responses, for example: (1) sitting on the toilet chair, (2) having property taken away, (3) having its face washed, (6) working at something that won't pan out, (10) being undressed, (11) being bathed, (12) having the nose wiped. On the other hand, (5) having the adult leave the room, (7) failure to get adults to play with them, and (9) failure to get adults to pick them up—would seem to belong more in the love conditioned responses approaching somewhat the grief situation where the object or person to whom the attachment is formed is removed or else will not exhibit the customary responses (as where "love" has grown cold). Mrs. Jones states that there

were a number of cases, too, where fears of both the conditioned and the unconditioned type, were responsible for a
good deal of crying—for example, when the children were
made to stand on the top of the slides, sliding down the slide,
standing on the tables. Possibly (4) and (5) of the above
classification may have elements of the fear response in them.

In making a study of this kind, it should be always borne
in mind that crying may be due to organic factors, such as
sleepiness, hunger, colic, and the like. Mrs. Jones found that
the largest number of cries (probably) due to intra-organic
causes occurred between 9 and 11 o'clock in the morning. As
a result of this finding, the institution placed its rest hours
before lunch instead of after lunch, with two rest periods
for the very young children. This considerably lessened the
amount of crying and disturbed behavior due to intra-organic
factors.

What Makes Children Laugh?

The situations which call out laughter and smiling were
recorded in the same way. The common causes of laughter are,
in order, as follows:

1. Being played with (playfully dressed, tickled, etc.).
2. Running, chasing, romping with other children.
3. Playing with toys (a ball was particularly effective).
4. Teasing other children.
5. Watching other children at play.
6. Making attempts which resulted in adjustment (e. g.
    getting parts of toys or apparatus to fit together or
    work).
7. Making sounds, more or less musical, at the piano,
    with a mouth organ, singing, pounding, etc.

In all 85 situations were listed calling out laughter and smiling. *Tickling, playfully dressing, gentle bathing, romping* with
other children, *teasing* (but always where there was a chance
at a "comeback"—probably a learned response sexually based
since the comeback involved being gently handled, pummeled
and tickled) were the most frequent situations eliciting laughter. It is hardly possible to attempt to discuss here to what
extent these smiling reactions were unconditioned and to what
extent conditioned. Attention is called to the fact that depending on the way the situations are manipulated and upon the
intra-organic condition of the youngsters, the same stimuli can
at one time bring laughter and at another time bring out crying, for example, although cries predominated in the bathroom

when their faces were being washed or when they were being bathed, it was always possible to produce a laugh.   On one occasion the introduction of a mouth organ altered the whole tenor of the room, changing distress into laughter.   Where the youngsters are just being dressed by the ordinary procedure, that is, being pulled, twisted and turned, crying nearly always results, and where dressing is playfully done, smiles and laughter instead of crying are the responses.   Attention should be called to the fact, however, that we can very easily overdo the matter of amusing the child when it is doing the things it has to do.   I have seen children, spoiled in this way, undergo torture when a new nurse is called in who does not or will not yield to their demand to be amused while being bathed, put to bed, dressed or fed.

While our results again are very incomplete, we have gone far enough to show that it is very easy to substitute for a great many of the situations in the home which now call out crying, situations that will call out smiling (and generally laughter) instead, which, in moderation is unquestionably better so far as concerns the general metabolic state of the organism. Furthermore, when we have gone far enough to show by continual watching what the sticking points are in the child's environment, we can rebuild his environment and thereby keep an unfavorable organization from developing.

Should We Implant Negative Responses in Our Children?

There is a certain amount of sentimentality going the pedagogical rounds in this country to the effect that no negative reactions should ever be forced on the child.   I have never been very much in favor of this propaganda.   In fact, I believe that certain negative responses should be scientifically implanted as a matter of protection to the organism.   I don't see any other way out of it.   I think, though, we should make a distinction between conditioned fear responses and mere negative responses. Negative responses conditioned upon the original (unconditioned) fear stimuli always apparently involve vast changes in the viscera—possibly always disruptive to normal metabolism.   Conditioned rage responses, while not necessarily negative in character (they include the positive responses in fighting, attack, etc.) apparently do the same thing.   I have the simple facts in view here which Cannon has brought out, that in fear and rage behavior, digestion and absorption are often completely interfered with—food is left in the stomach to ferment and to form a breeding ground for bacteria and for setting free toxic products. So there is some justice in the view that fear and rage behavior is in general harmful to the organism (yet the race possibly could not have survived if it had not reacted negatively to loud sounds and loss of support and had not struggled when movement was hampered). Love behavior, on the other hand, seems to heighten metabolism. Digestion and absoption apparently take place more rapidly. Questioning of husbands and wives leads to the disclosure of the fact that after normal sex intercourse hunger contractions begin in the stomach and food is very frequently sought.

But to come back to negative reactions. It is at least an opinion of mine that where negative responses are built into manual behavior (conditioned)—such as withdrawal of hands, legs, body, etc., by the use of faint noxious stimuli, there is little involvement of the viscera. To make myself clear, let me cite a case: I can build in negative behavior to a snake in two ways. Just as I show the snake I can make a terrible noise and cause the child to fall down and cry out completely terror stricken. Soon the mere sight of the snake will have the same effect. Or I can present the snake several times and each time as the infant reaches for it I can tap its fingers with a pencil and gradually establish the negative reaction without shock. I have not tried this with a snake, but I have with the candle. A child can be conditioned by a severe burn with one stimulation, but this involves always a severe reaction. By presenting the candle flame many times and each time letting it just heat the finger enough to produce withdrawal of the hand, a negative conditioned response can be built up without the severe features of shock. Building in negative responses without shock requires time, however.

I cannot tonight dwell too long upon the interesting psychological and social factors involved in the building in of negative reactions.

May I just say dogmatically that our civilization is built upon "don't" and taboos of many kinds. Individuals living adjustedly in it must learn to heed them. Since the negative responses must be built in they should be built in as sanely as possible without involving strong emotional reactions. Children and adolescents must not play in the street, run in front of automobiles, play with strange dogs and cats, run up and stand under the feet of horses, point firearms at people, run any chance of catching venereal diseases or having illegitimate children; they must not do thousands of other things that I might mention. I am not saying that all the negative reactions demanded by society are ethically right (and when I say ethically I mean the new experimental ethics that does not exist today). I don't know whether many of the taboos now adhered to are ultimately good for the organism. I am merely saying that society exists—it is a fact, and if we live under it we must draw back when social customs say draw back, or we must get our adult hands slapped. There is, of course, an ever increasing number of people in the world whose hands are tough and who do many tabooed things and take the social chastisement that inevitably follows. This means of course that social trial and error experimentation is becoming possible —the smoking of women, now tolerated in all restaurants and hotels and even in nearly every home, is a good example. As long as society rules every act through its agencies (such as political systems, church, family) no learning, no trying out of new social responses is possible. In the last 20 years we have seen marked changes in the social status of women, marked weakening of marriage ties, marked diminution in thoroughness of control of political parties (to wit, the overthrow of practically all monarchies), a marked weakening of the church's hold upon genuinely educated people, the lessening of taboos upon sex. The danger, of course, comes now from too rapid lessening of control, too superficial trials of new forms of behavior, and from the acceptance of new methods without sufficient trial.

Use of Corporal Punishment in Building in Negative Responses

The question of corporal punishment in the bringing up of children at home and at school comes up periodically for discussion. I believe our experiments almost settle the problem. Punishment is a word which ought never to have crept into our language.

Whipping or beating the body is a custom as old as the race. Even our modern views on the punishment of criminals and children have as their basis the old religious masochistic practices of the church. Punishment in the biblical sense of "an eye for an eye and a tooth for a tooth" honeycombs our whole social and religious life.

Certainly punishment of children is not a scientific method. As parents, teachers and jurists, we are or ought to be interested only in setting up ways of acting in the individual that square with group behavior. You have already grasped the notion that the behaviorist is a strict determinist—*the child*

*or adult has to do what he does do. The only way he can
be made to act differently is first to untrain him and then to
retrain him.* Both children and adults do do things which
do not correspond with the standards of behavior set up by
the home or by the group. This deviation from social standards is due to the fact that the home and the group have not
sufficently trained the individual during the formative period.
Since the formative period is coextensive with life, social
training should be continuous throughout life. It is our own
fault, then, that individuals (other than defectives and psychopaths) go "wrong," that is, deviate from set standards of
behavior—and by "our own fault" I mean the fault of the
parent, the teacher and every other member of the group;
we have neglected and are neglecting our opportunities.

But to return to the question of whipping and beating.
There is no excuse for whipping or beating!

First, because very often the deviating act occurs many hours
before father or mother come home to engage in the act of
chastising. Conditioned responses are not built up by this
unscientific procedure. The idea that a child's future bad behavior will be prevented by giving him a licking in the evening
for something he did in the morning is ridiculous. Equally
ridiculous from the standpoint of preventing crime, is our
legal and judicial method of punishment which allows a crime
to be committed in one year and punishment administered a
year or two later—if at all.

Second, whipping is used more often than not to serve as
an emotional outlet (sadistic) for parent or teacher.

Third, often when the beating occurs immediately after the
act (the only time for it if it is to take place at all) it is not and
cannot be regulated according to any scientific dosage. It is
either too mild, therefore not a strong enough stimulus to establish the conditioned negative response; or too severe, thus
stirring up unnecessarily the whole visceral system of the child;
or the deviating act does not occur frequently enough, with
attendant punishment, to meet the scientific conditions for
setting up a negative response; or, finally, it is repeated so
frequently that all effect is lost—habituation comes in, leading
possibly to the psychopathological condition known as "maso-
chism," a condition in which the individual responds positively
(sexually) to noxious stimuli.

How, then, are we to build in the negative responses which
I said above are necessary to build in? I thoroughly believe in

rapping a child's fingers when it puts them in its mouth, when it constantly fingers its sex organs, when it reaches up and pulls down glass dishes and trays, or turns on gas cocks or water hydrants, etc., *provided the child is caught in the act and the parent can administer the rap at once in a thoroughly objective way*—just as objectively as the behaviorist administers the faint electric shock when building up a negative or withdrawal response to any given object. Society, both the group and the immediate parents, uses the verbal "don't" to older children in place of the rap. It will of course always have to use "don't" but I hope some time we can rearrange the environment so that less and less negative reactions will have to be built in in both child and adult.

One bad feature in the whole system of the building in of negative responses is the fact that the parent becomes involved in the situation—I mean by that becomes a part of the punishment system. The child grows up to "hate" the person who has most often to administer the beating—usually the father. I hope some time to try out the experiment of having a table top electrically wired in such a way that if a child reaches for a glass or a delicate vase it will be punished, whereas if it reaches for its toys or other things it is allowed to play with, it can get them without being electrically shocked. *In other words, I should like to make the objects and situations of life build in their own negative reactions.*

Present Methods of Punishment for Crime are Relics of the Dark Ages

What we have said about punishment in the rearing of children holds equally well for adults in the field of crime. Since in my opinion only the sick or psychopaths (insane) or untrained (socially untrained) individuals commit crimes, society should be interested in just two things: (1) Seeing that the insane or psychopathic individuals are made well if possible, and if not, placed in well run (non-political) institutions where no harm can come to them and where they can do no harm to other members of the group. In other words, the fate of those individuals should be in medical (psychiatric) hands. The question as to whether the hopelessly insane should be etherized has of course been raised time and time again. There can be no reasons against it except exaggerated sentiment and mediaeval religious mandates. (2) Seeing that the socially untrained individuals, not insane or psychopathological, are placed where they can be trained, sent to school, made to learn, regardless of their age, a trade, made to put on culture, made to become social. Furthermore, during this period they should be placed where they cannot harm other members of the group. Such education and training may take ten to fifteen years or even longer. Failing to put on the training necessary to fit them to again enter society, they should be restrained always, and made to earn their daily bread, in vast manufacturing and agricultural institutions, escape from which is impossible. Naturally, no human being—criminal or otherwise—should be deprived of air, sunshine, food, exercise and other physiological factors necessary to optimum living conditions. On the other hand, strenuous work sixteen hours per day will hurt no one. Individuals put aside thus for additional training should of course be kept in the hands of the behaviorists.

Naturally such a view does away completely with criminal law (but not with policing). It does away naturally with the criminal lawyer and with legal (criminal) precedent, and with courts for the trial of criminals. Many jurists of note agree substantially with this view. But until all law books are burned in some great upheaval of nature and until all lawyers and jurists suddenly decide to become behaviorists, I never expect to see the present retaliation or punishment theory (a religious theory) of handling the *deviant* give place to a scientific theory based upon what we know of the establishing and breaking down of conditioned and emotional responses.

What Are Some of the Most Important Forms of Built-in Emotional Behavior?

In addition to the various forms of emotional behavior both learned and unlearned that we have discussed in this and the preceding lecture, there are several other types which interest the behaviorist very greatly. These are *jealousy* and *shame*. So far the behaviorist has had very little opportunity to make any study of them. I believe that both jealousy and shame are built in.

Other forms of emotional behavior, popularly known as sorrow, grief, resentment, anger, reverence, awe, justice, mercy, seem to the behaviorist to be quite simple. He believes them to be vast super-structures built upon the very simple types of unlearned behavior that we have already abundantly discussed.

Jealousy and shame, however, require considerable further study. So far I have not had opportunity to observe the first appearance of shame and its genetic growth. I am inclined to think that shame is in some way connected with the first overt masturbation that involves the orgasm. The stimulus is the manipulation of the sex organs, the final responses are heightened blood pressure, superficial dilatation of the capillaries of the skin known as flushing, among many others. Almost from infancy the child is taught not to masturbate or is punished if it masturbates. Consequently any situation, verbal or otherwise, connected with the touching of the sex organs or reference to the sex organs may condition the blushing and bowing of the head which nearly always takes place in masturbation. This, however, is purely speculative and I must lay it aside here for future observation.

I have recently made some observations and experiments upon jealousy.

Jealousy: Ask any group of individuals what they mean by jealousy—what the stimulus is that produces it, what the pattern of the response is, and you only get the vaguest, most unserviceable kind of replies. Ask these same individuals what the unlearned (unconditioned) stimulus is that calls out the response; ask them what the unlearned (unconditioned) response pattern is? To both questions you get unscientific answers. Most individuals say, "Oh, jealousy is a pure instinct." If we diagram thus

$$S \qquad\qquad\qquad\qquad R$$
$$? \qquad\qquad\qquad\qquad ?$$

we have to put a question mark under both stimulus and response.

And yet jealousy is one of the most powerful factors in the organization of present day individuals. It is recognized by the courts as one of the strongest of "motives" leading to action. Robberies and murders are committed because of it; careers are both made and unmade because of it; marital quarrels, separations and divorces are probably more frequently to be traced to it than to any other single cause. Its almost universal permeation through the whole action stream of all individuals has lead to the view that it is an inborn instinct. And yet the moment you begin to observe people and try to determine what kinds of situations call out jealous behavior and what the details of that behavior are, you see that the situations are highly complex (social) and that the reactions are all highly organized (learned). This in itself should make us doubt its hereditary origin. Let us watch people for awhile to see if their behavior will not throw light upon the situations and the responses.

What Situations Call Out Jealous Behavior?

In the first place, as we have said, the situation is always a social one—it involves people. What people? *Always the person who calls out our conditioned love responses.* This may be the mother, father, or brother, sister or sweetheart, wife or husband, etc. The person may be of the same or the opposite sex. The wife-husband situation is second only to the sweetheart one for calling out violent responses. This brief examination helps us somewhat in our understanding of jealousy. The situation is always a substitutive one, that is conditioned. It involves the person calling out conditioned love responses. This generalization, if true, takes it out of the class of inherited forms of behavior at once.

What are the Responses?

The responses in adults are legion. I have taken notes on a great many cases among both children and adults. To vary our procedure let us take the responses of an adult first. *Case A.* A is a "very jealous husband," married two years to a beautiful young woman only slightly younger. They go out frequently on parties. If this wife (1) dances a little close to her partner, (2) if she sits out a dance to talk to a man and talks in a low tone to him, (3) if in a moment of gaiety she kisses another man in the open light of the room before everyone, (4) if she goes out even with other women to lunch or tea or to shop, (5) if she invites her own group of friends for a party at home—then jealous behavior is exhibited. Such stimuli bring out the responses (1) refusal to talk or dance with his wife, (2) increased tension of all his muscles, mouth shuts tightly, eyes seem to grow smaller, jaw "hardens." He next withdraws himself from other people in the room. His face becomes flushed, then black. *This behavior may and usually does persist for days after the affair is started. He will talk to no one about the affair. Meditation is impossible.* The jealous state seems to have run itself down or out. The wife herself by no amount of assurance of love, of innocence, by no system of apology or obeisance can do anything towards hastening recovery. Yet his wife is devoted to him and has never been even in the slightest measure unfaithful, as he himself admits verbally when not in the jealous state. In a person less well bred, less well schooled, it is easy to see that his behavior might become overt—he might blacken his wife's eye or if there were a real male aggressor, might attack or murder him.

Take the child's jealous behavior next. The first sign of jealousy was noted in child B at about two years of age. It shows whenever the mother embraces the father, clings to him, kisses him. At two and one-half years of age this child who had never been made the "scapegoat," who had always been allowed to be present and even welcomed into the family love-making, begins to attack the father whenever the mother embraces the father. He (1) pulls at his coat, (2) cries out "my mamma," (3) pushes his father away and crowds in between them. If the kissing continues, the child's reaction state becomes very marked and intense. Always in the morning—Sundays especially, when he comes into the bedroom before his parents are up—he is taken up and welcomed and made much of by both. And yet at two and three-fourths years of age he would say to his father, "you going to office, dada?"—or else give the direct command, "you go to office, dada." At three years of age this boy was sent with his infant brother to his grandmother's, in charge of a nurse. He was separated from his mother for one month. During this time his strong attachment for his mother weakened. When the parents visited the child (then thirty-seven months of age) no jealous behavior was exhibited when they made love in front of him. When the parents clung together for a considerable time, to see if jealous behavior would finally occur, he merely ran up and hugged first one and then the other. This test was repeated for four days with the same results.

The father then seeing that the old situation failed to call it out, tried next attacking the mother, striking her on the body and head and shaking her from side to side. She on her part simulated crying, but fought back. The youngster stood this for a few minutes, then started in for his father tooth and nail and would not let up until the fight was over. He cried, kicked, tugged at his father's leg and struck with his hand.

Next the father remained passive while the mother attacked him. She inadvertently punched below the belt, causing the father to double up in no simulated way. Nevertheless, the youngster started his attack on his father again and continued it even after he was *hors de combat*. By this time the youngster was genuinely disturbed and the experiment had to be discontinued. The next day, however, no jealous behavior was exhibited when mother and father embraced.

How Early Does this Form of Jealousy against one or the other Parent Occur?

To further test the genesis of this type of jealous behavior, a test was made upon an eleven months old infant boy. This infant was well nourished and wholly without conditioned fears, yet there was a strong attachment for the mother, but none for the father who often spanked his hand when he attempted to suck his thumb and otherwise broke in upon his quiet by trying various types of experiments. At eleven months he could crawl quickly and for considerable distances.

When father and mother violently embraced, the youngster could not be made to keep his eyes on his parents. Love making between them was nothing in his young life. This was tested again and again. There was no tendency to crawl towards them, much less to crawl in between them. Jealousy was absent.

Next the father and mother attacked one another. The floor was carpeted and the noise of the blows and the low whimper of the mother (or the father in turn) was not very loud. The fight immediately stopped his crawling about, brought prolonged fixation—always of the mother and never of the father. As it continued, he whimpered and cried out aloud several times but made no effort to enter the fight on either side. The noises, shaking of the floor, and the sight of the parents' faces—which offered the same visual stimulus to him when he himself got slapped and was made to cry, were sufficiently complex stimuli to call out the observed behavior. His behavior was of the fear type partly visually conditioned. There was apparently no jealousy behavior in this infant, either when its parents made love or when either parent attacked the other. Eleven months seems to be too tender an age for jealousy to appear.

Does Jealousy Appear Suddenly when an Only Child Has to Face His Infant Brother?

Many Freudians insist that the beginning of jealousy behavior very often dates back in the life of the child to the appearance of a brother or a sister. They claim that it starts practically full-blown even though the child in question is a year or less than a year of age. And yet, so far as I know, no Freudian has ever attempted to put his theories to practical experimental test.

During my own observations on the origin of jealousy, I have had one favorable opportunity to observe the behavior of an only child when he received his newborn brother. B, whose jealous behavior directed against his father I have just told you about, was two and one-fourth years of age when the event occurred. He had formed a very strong attachment to his mother and to his own regular nurse. He had no organized reactions toward any youngster under a year of age. The mother had been absent in the hospital for two weeks. B was taken care of by his regular nurse during these two weeks. The day the mother returned, his own nurse kept B busy in his room playing until the conditions for the test were all set. The test was made at noon in a well-lighted sitting room. The mother was sitting nursing the baby, with her breast exposed. B had not seen the mother during the two weeks. In addition to the mother with her infant, there were present a trained nurse new to B, a grandmother, and the father. B was allowed to walk down the steps alone and into the room. Everyone had been instructed to remain absolutely quiet and to make the situation as natural as possible. B walked into the room and up to his mother, leaned on her knee and said, "How do, Mama." He did not attempt to kiss her or hug her. He did not notice the breast, or the baby for thirty seconds. Then he saw the baby. He said, "Little baby." Then he took the baby's hands and gently patted them, rubbed its head and its face and began to say, "That baby, that baby." Then he kissed it without any prompting. He was very gentle and tender in all of his responses. The trained nurse, who was unknown to him, took up the new baby. He reacted against this, at least verbally, saying, "Mama take baby." Thus the baby was reacted to really as a part of the mother situation and the first element of jealousy response was directed against the person who took something away from his mother (hampered his mother's movements). Surely this was as typically an un-Freudian reaction as could be imagined. This was the first sign of a jealousy response. But the response was positive for the infant and not against it—notwithstanding the fact that the brother was usurping his place on his mother's lap.

Then the new baby was taken by its nurse to its room and

put to bed. B tagged along, too. When he came back, the father said, "How do you like Jimmie?" And he said, "Like Jimmie—Jimmie sleeping." He did not notice at any time the exposed breast of the mother and really paid very little attention to the mother except when the nurse tried to take the baby away. During the whole setting, he reacted positively to the baby for only two minutes and then turned to other things.

The following day, B had to give up his own room which contained most of his toys, books, and the like, in preparation for the new baby. He was told that Jimmie had to have his room for a while. *This situation called out only the most eager positive response in helping to push and pull all of his own furniture to the new room.* He slept in the new room that night and every night until the trained nurse left. There was never the slightest sign of resentment, jealousy, etc., in his behavior directed against the new baby at any time.

The behavior of these two children has been under constant observation for one year now. Never has there been the slightest sign of jealousy. The three-year-old today is just as kind and considerate to the one-year-old infant as he was on his first introduction. Not even when nurse, mother or father takes the infant up and pets it is there any jealousy. Once a new nurse almost succeeded in establishing it by attempting to control the older child by saying: "You are a naughty boy. Jimmie is a nice boy—I love him." For just a few days jealousy threatened, but the discharge of the nurse saved the situation.

Although there is no attachment pronounced enough to cause any disturbance of his daily routine, if the younger child is not around, the older youngster takes the part of the one-year-old if mother or father attempts to chastise the youngster by spanking its hand. The moment the younger infant cries, the three-year-old will actually attack either one or both parents, saying "Jimmie good boy; you mustn't make Jimmie cry."

Can We Draw Any Conclusions About Jealousy?

So far our experiments on jealousy are merely preliminary. If any generalization at all can be made, it would seem to take the following form: Jealousy is a bit of behavior whose stimulus is a (conditioned) love stimulus the response to which is rage—but a pattern of rage containing possibly the original visceral components but in addition parts of many habit patterns, (fighting, boxing, shooting, talking, etc.). We may use this diagram to hold our facts together:

(C) S...................(U&C) R

Sight (or sound) of loved object being tampered or interfered with.	*Stiffening of whole body,* clenching of hands, reddening and then blackening of face—pronounced breathing, fighting, verbal recrimination, etc.

Naturally this is reduced to the barest schematism. The response may take many forms and the stimulus may consist of far more subtle factors than I have noted here, but I believe we are on the right track in trying to formulate jealousy in these terms.

May I say in conclusion that the behaviorist in spite of his seeming dogmatism would like to inject a word of caution about his own views? All of his conclusions on the origin and growth of emotional life are based now upon too few cases and too few experiments. This will be remedied in the near future. More and more students are at work upon emotional behavior using behavioristic methods. No sane person can ever again use the old introspective method with which James and his immediate followers came so near wrecking this most thrilling part of psychology.

Walter S. Hunter

CHAPTER IV

PSYCHOLOGY AND ANTHROPONOMY*

By Walter S. Hunter

Psychology for many years has been a discipline to intrigue the layman's fancy. It has stood for the scientist's attack upon the most subtle and experiment-defying portion of the universe, the mind. As the psychologist has extended his methods of study from sensation to memory and finally to the complex processes of thought, he has applauded his own progress so vigorously that he has almost converted his scientific colleagues to the belief that psychology knows what it is about. And yet dogging the heels of this successful science, there has always been an irritable congeries of dissenters, philosophers who have never thought highly of a scientific analysis of the conscious aspect of the universe, spiritualists, psychic researchers, and Freudians, who object to the petty laboratory problems in terms of which the psychologist outlines his field and who resent deeply and religiously the tendency in psychology to eliminate the purposeful activity of mind. Into this field of dispute, where the mind-body problem casts its shadow over the formulation of points of view and the interpretation of experimental findings, and where scientific psychology concerns itself with the analysis of experience into elements and attributes, a new and refreshing influence has come. This influence is that of behaviorism or, as I prefer to say, the influence of anthroponomy. I use the term anthroponomy for the science of human behavior, and the term anthroponomist I shall use as synonymous with behaviorist. These terms are new and therefore distracting, and yet they have the great merit of reminding us constantly that our problem is the study of man. The term behavior is too general to indicate precisely our field of investigation, and the term behaviorism suffers as a designation for a total science exactly because it is an "ism." The more detailed meaning of our new term will appear as our discussion proceeds.

It will be my purpose in this lecture to compare for you the respective merits of psychology and anthroponomy, to show you certain aspects of the two modes of attack upon the problem of human nature, and thereby to formulate for you specif-

*Powell Lecture in Psychological Theory at Clark University, March 11, 1926.

ically the anthroponomist's attitude toward certain of the persistent problems of psychology. This endeavor we shall prosecute upon a theoretical rather than upon an experimental level for the problems which concern us bear more upon the fundamental issues of the science than upon matters of fact which are only to be settled by observation and experiment. A certain amount of confusion has already been introduced into the discussions conducted by the psychologists and the behaviorists by the failure to keep disputes over problems of fact out of the consideration of the respective theoretical points of view. Thus Watson has denied the existence of centrally aroused neural processes to the great dismay of the students of immediate experience. And these latter have seized upon Watson's denial of instincts and individual differences as particularly atrocious bits of evidence showing the untenability of the behaviorist's position. These problems are only to be settled by observation and experiment and are quite irrelevant to the fundamental differences between the students of immediate experience and the anthroponomists. It is my desire, as we proceed, to place a few of the fundamental principles of anthroponomy before you in such a manner that you may be able to discriminate between the fundamental and the incidental issues in the controversy which at the present time seems to dominate the study of human nature.

There are two methods of approach to the study of human nature. One is the indirect, or psychological method, and the other is the direct, or anthroponomical, method. The psychologist believes that human nature can best be understood by studying not the human animal itself but by studying the environment in which this organism moves. To study the organism would be to encroach upon the field of his fellow scientist, the biologist, unless the human organism were studied as an object in the environment of still another human organism. The environment, studied by the psychologist, lies not only *without* the animal but also *within* it. The psychologist's task is complete when he has, first, exhaustively described the total environing situation with reference to its least discriminable aspects, when he has, second, synthesized these aspects into such complex processes as trees, melodies, food-tastes, tickle, itch, and heat in the stomach, which seem to the layman to be the essential components of the environment which he calls Nature, and when he has, third, subsumed these complex processes under his fundamental categories of sensation, perception, attention, imagination, memory, thinking, and will. The anthroponomist has a different method. He sees man working in the fields, bathing in the surf, and pursuing his intricate way in the great cities of Earth. "How wonderful is my opportunity," say the anthroponomist, "to investigate this complex organism and to add, to the knowledge which the biologist and the sociologist have, further definite information concerning those very fundamental and characteristic aspects of human nature, *viz.*, language behavior (whether verbal or non-verbal), learning, and inter-stimulation and response. Theoretically I am willing to admit the possibility of understanding human nature by the indirect method of studying not man but the environment, because obviously man is the kind of a creature that can live in this earthly environment, and he must, therefore, possess certain sensory, neural, and muscular equipment correlated with environmental conditions. My method of procedure, however, will be to describe and analyse man's organic behavior itself with only such references to the environment as shall be necessary for this purpose. I am not like my fellow scientist, the psychologist, who would understand man by cataloging all of the discriminable colors, tones, pressures, feelings, Gestalten, etc., in the universe. When I study human nature, I do so directly by observing man's changing behavior."

In order to carry forward systematically the comparison of these two sciences, psychology and anthroponomy, it is necessary to single out certain important problems as the chief foci of interest. These problems are as follows:

(1) What is the subject matter and goal of the science?
(2) What are the chief methods employed?
(3) What are the results, or products, of the science?

Let us begin with the problem of the subject matter and goal of the two sciences under consideration. Both psychology and anthroponomy take as their goal the understanding of some aspect of the human individual, leaving other aspects or portions to such sciences as anatomy, physiology, and bio-chemistry. The aspect of man which the psychologist studies is that which is termed mental, or psychical, or experiential. Thus Bentley[1] says that psychology "seeks to describe and to understand experience and the activities of the total organism in which experience plays an essential part." And again he says[2] with reference to psychosomatic functions, "Always mental resources and always bodily resources of the organism are

---

[1]Bentley, Madison. The field of psychology. New York, 1924, p. 15.
[2]*Ibid*, p. 19.

called into use for carrying out these functional performances. That is why the psychologist calls them 'psychosomatic' functions, thus distinguishing them from the purely bodily or 'somatic' functions, such as the growth of bone and the operations of enzymes and ferments." You cannot, of course, fail to see the implication in this latter statement that the somatic processes which have no accompanying psychic aspect lie beyond the domain of the psychologist.

If we now ask what experience is, and experience is environment, we are confronted by the psychologist's distinction between an experience and a physical object or between the science of psychology and the science of physics. This distinction is stated by Wundt, Titchener and Bentley, as that between an object which exists independently of human experience and an object which exists only as experienced. Let us again consult Bentley on this point. "The objects and events of physics and of the rest are regarded *as if they outlasted the experiencing of them and continued as independent of the act of apprehension* . . . Animals, the earth's strata, the ocean's substance, the planet's course, and the electron's oscillations are one and all regarded as if ordered, arranged, and preserved in existence wholly apart from the experiencing organism which discerns them. But what shall we say of the objects and the operations of the psychologist? We shall say of these that they *are* only when they are-in-experience."[3] In psychology, "When we proceed to the examination of our tones and noises, ... ; of our lights, colors, colds, warmths, sweets, sours, and the like, we must take care that we do not slip from *experiencing* to the things *experienced*, to noisy cities, to tuneful voices, to sunlight and shadows, to the chill of the night, the warmth of the noon, and so on to the other *independent objects*."[4] ". . . . when I say that I listened last night to an orchestra composed of violins, 'cellos, double basses, wood-winds, brasses, and the rest, it is obvious that I am attempting a rough analytic description of the orchestra and not of anything connected with my organism. It scarcely seems possible that such things as books and violins should be mistaken for the furnishings of the mind; but this is precisely the first error that the beginner drops into in his quest for component qualities."[5]

[3]*Ibid*, pp. 31-2.
[4]*Ibid*, p. 35.
[5]*Ibid*, p. 36.

Let me give one more quotation from Bentley with reference to "images" and to "sensations" from within the organism: " . . . . a moment's reflection will make it obvious to the reader that 'myself imagined as walking' or 'myself remembered as walking' is just as much an object of the physical order as 'myself now perceived as walking'. . . . . We all do say in the vernacular that an object which we remember or think about is only a 'mental object'; but there we only mean that the object is not at the moment present to the senses. It is no more 'mental' than the book now in your hand is 'mental.' "[6] "Many persons think that, when they announce such an interesting fact as palpitation and trembling in sudden fear or the dryness of the throat in continued thirst, they have observed and reported psychologically. They are mistaken. This is one of the nine hundred and ninety-nine *wrong* ways of analysis! . . . . But although they may come to be known through processes of experience (a group of pressures of alternating intensities, in the one case; a complex of warmth and dull massive pressure, in the other), the palpitation and the dryness are no more mental than the heart and the throat themselves are mental."[7]

I have quoted thus at length from one of the leading students of experience with much malice aforethought. I have presented these quotations in order that you might have an experientialist's own statement of the subject matter of his science before I proceeded to comment upon it. I think that one great reason for the continued, although apparently waning, popularity of psychology, lies in the belief that psychologists are conducting Cook's tours of experience. On these tours the traveler expects to see all things that the eyes can see, hear all that ears can hear, meet all memories, emotions, visceral strains, and other events that are found in the psychic world. This belief is not limited to the layman. It is also shared by many psychologists (those who believe that emotion, hunger, and pain in the leg are mental phenomena) to say nothing of the Gestalt psychologists who think that the patterns of figure and ground are matters of experience. But it does not devolve upon my shoulders to resolve these controversies among the psychologists! It is my responsibility rather to make clear the anthroponomist's position on this question of what is to be done with the "physical" environment as described by Bentley. Perhaps no other single question has so puzzled those

---

[6]*Ibid*, p. 38.
[7]*Ibid*, p. 38-9.

who have sought to understand or to criticize the behavioristic positions. However, I must not pass on to this phase of the exposition of behaviorism until I am more certain that you have understood the points involved in my quotations from Bentley.

Psychologists may be divided roughly into two camps on the basis of their treatment of meaning. One camp, represented by the Wundtian tradition, excludes meaning from observable mental phenomena. The other camp, represented by such diverse tendencies as are present in the image-less thought psychologists, the functionalists, the purposivists, and the Gestalt psychologists, includes meaning. The result is that the Wundtians, speaking through Bentley, would say that the meaning-users are describing physical objects; and the meaning-users retort that the Wundtians are dealing with non-existent artifacts. As for me, I almost agree with both schools! I think nothing could be more barren than the Wundt-Titchener-Bentley psychology. It does not describe concrete things seen, heard, or felt as these exist in the inner, *i.e.*, the sub-cutaneous, environment. Nor does it give us a description of something mental which actually exists. And, if I agree that the Wundtian psychology is barren, I also agree that the other psychologists are not describing conscious processes, experience, when they describe books, pains, hungers, tastes, colors, and melodies. Perhaps these phenomena are more properly labeled physical, but in any case they are the constituents of the inner and outer environments as viewed by common-sense. Both groups of psychologists are seeking to understand a phase of human nature by the indirect route of environment. Bentley and the other Wundtians abstract qualities, intensities, durations, and clearnesses (sometimes adding other attributes, sometimes dropping one or more) from the environment and call the material selected experience. The users of meaning take concrete objects from the environment and call these experience. If this is the path followed by the psychologists in attempting to throw light upon the nature of man, what is to be said of that followed by the students of behavior, the anthroponomists?

The anthroponomist does not deny the existence of the common-sense environment. He refuses, however, to be diverted from the direct study of man into the recording of environmental peculiarities. If you were to ask an anthroponomist to describe a certain room in the Clark laboratory, he would respond as follows: "The walls of the room are pale blue, the ceiling is white, and the floors are brown. A large grey-toned rug is upon the floor. The furniture is of a golden color; it is heavy and hard. Upon entering this room in the morning, a stale odor is easily detected, and one is at times disgusted by this odor." It must not be assumed that I am the only student of behavior who would admit the existence of such an internal and external environment as I have just described. Would anyone venture to suggest that Weiss would deny hearing the tuning forks with which he has worked, or that Lashley would refuse to say that he had seen and touched the brains of white rats? If you will turn to an article written by Carr[8] in 1912, you will find that Watson is definitely on record as having seen environmental objects of the after-image type. Let me quote some extracts from Carr's account: "After serving as a subject in a test involving considerable eye fatigue, Professor Watson was engaged in carefully and steadily observing one of the writer's eyes throughout several periods of five to six minutes duration each. The room was pitch dark with the exception that the observed eye was illumined by a minature electric flashlight . . . .

"After one of these observations, the flashlight was turned off for a period of rest. Shortly afterwards there developed in the darkness an extremely vivid and realistic positive after-image of the eye . . . . All of the minor details of coloring and marking came out distinctly . . . . Just before the lights were turned on an added tinge of reality was produced" when the phantom eye actually winked.

"Professor Watson has had considerable practice in the observation of after-images and is, apparently, more than ordinarily sensitive to the phenomenon."

If these statements are not sufficient for you, a brief inspection of the writings of any behavorist will convince you that he is neither blind, deaf, anosmic, ageusic, or anaesthetic. He lives, and admits quite frankly that he lives, in the same world of objects and events which the psychologist and the layman alike acknowledge. Let us, therefore, hear no more from the psychologist that his opponent denies the existence of these things.

One of the objects in the environment which the anthroponomist sees, hears, feels, and smells is called *homo sapiens,* man. The various members of this species differ in height, weight, color, cleanliness, race, religion, etc., etc., just as rocks differ

[8]Carr, H. A. Some novel experiences. Psych. Rev., 1912, 19, 60-61.

in size, weight, density, chemical constitution, age, location, commercial value, etc. The anthroponomist takes man as his experimental material just as the other scientists select other objects in the environment for their experimental material. Now neither the anthroponomist, the psychologist, the chemist, the physicist, nor the biologist can tell you what a man or a rock is, for like all events in the world each is in some way unique. Various hypotheses have been proposed, but it is too early to separate those which are susceptible to scientific verification from those which are not. Bentley says that the rocks and the men which I see are physical objects. The meaning-users say these objects are experiences and therefore mental. But neither of the terms is really an answer to the question. They are merely names used in order to include or exclude certain phenomena from the science. You must never forget that, when the psychologists accuse the behaviorists of denying the existence of a part of the world, the psychologists ignore certain facts: (1) that the behaviorist only denies that any one has shown the psychic, mental, character of the environment; and (2) that the behaviorist himself has offered at least three hypotheses concerning the nature of this environment. These three hypotheses are as follows: First, the electron-proton hypothesis of Weiss.[9] Weiss accepts—and note that Bentley must follow, too, if he is logical—the most recent advances in physics and chemistry which go to show that objects in our environment are electron-proton aggregations. Stones, tables, books, storms, silver, and gold are ultimately electric charges. And so likewise is the human animal and the aggregations of human animals which make up society. If the phenomenon of a storage battery is a matter of electrons and protons, so is the phenomenon of family life— unless the physicists are all wrong, or unless there is something in family life which is not an object in the external or internal environment. Personally, I think that Weiss is undoubtedly correct. I see no immediate way or need, however, to apply this principle to *change* our experimentation. All of our anthroponomical experimentation is in harmony with this theory. This, furthermore, is exactly the case in physics. Many problems in that science are attacked and solved without involving in any specific way the electron-proton conception of the nature of the universe. Even in physics it is still per-

---

[9] Weiss, A. P. A theoretical basis of human behavior. Columbus, Ohio, 1925.

missible to speak of steel and carbon and to make studies upon these substances without directly involving the question of the nature of the atom. The psychologist should, therefore, not reproach Weiss if the latter continues speaking of bio-social responses instead of attempting to state the molecular activities which make up these responses.

The second hypothesis concerning the nature of the environment is that of Lashley.[10] Lashley speaks of the environment as consciousness, conscious content, or quality, following an old tradition of the psychologist, and consciousness for him is "a complex integration and succession of bodily activities which are closely related to or involve the verbal and gestural mechanisms and hence most frequently come to social expression." Lashley also stresses the ultimate physico-chemical nature of these bodily integrations.

The third hypothesis concerning the nature of environmental objects is my own.[11] In a series of articles, I have recently elaborated the hypothesis that red, sweet, salt, emotion, books, trees, and storms are all cases of a particular stimulus-response relationship. This particular bit of behavior is the irreversible SP-LR relationship. (The letters stand for sensory process and language response.) The present lecture is hardly the place to offer you a resumé of these papers. It will perhaps be worth our while, however, to give a brief explanation of the hypothesis inasmuch as it bears specifically upon our present problem, the subject matter of the science of psychology and anthroponomy, as well as upon the problem of the nature of the methods used in these disciplines.

Let us apply our hypothesis to the case where new environmental objects make their appearance as this occurs when hitherto undifferentiated overtones of a clang are "reported" by the subject. "The beginner in the psychology laboratory does not hear these overtones, although physics can demonstrate that correlated vibrations exist in the stimulus. The subject is not 'conscious' of the tones,—at least he makes no verbal report of their presence and for scientific purposes he is said

---

[10]Lashley, K. S. The behavioristic interpretation of consciousness, I and II. Psychol. Rev., 1923, 30, 237 and 329.

[11]Hunter, W. S. The problem of consciousness. Psychol. Rev., 1924, 31, 1-31.
       The symbolic process. *Ibid*, 1924, 31, 478-497.
       The subject's report. *Ibid*, 1925, 32, 153-170.
       General anthroponomy and its systematic problems. Amer. Jour. Psychol., 1925, 36, 286-302.

to be unaware of them. The experimenter now presents the vibration frequency of the first overtone (*SP*) by itself. This stimulus elicits response *LR*. *SP* is then presented as a part of a complex stimulus in order to see whether or not the same response, *LR*, will now appear. If it does not, the training is continued. *Just as soon as the verbal response, LR, is made to the complex stimulus, just so soon does the subjectivist say that the 'consciousness of the overtone' is present* . . . Why do we not say that *LR* is the subjectivist's 'consciousness' and not merely a criterion of its presence? Because *LR*, if it is to be rated as 'conscious,' must in its turn have a language response conditioned to it and so be the beginning part of [an *SP-LR*] situation. Only in the irreversible situation do we have 'consciousness.' It now becomes a fertile field of experimentation to determine what stimulus aspects may be determiners of language responses and not merely of non-language responses. The irreversible relationships between these stimulus aspects and the language responses will then be 'states of consciousness.'

"We have chosen the two cases of the lower limen of sensitivity and the discrimination of component aspects of a complex situation, as the most vital aspects of adult human nature upon which to base our formulation, for a very definite reason. If it were possible we should follow the truly genetic method in the establishment of our thesis as well as in its application. There are, however, no well established facts concerning the 'consciousness' of infants and children, so that we must of necessity test our conception upon adults. When, however, we examine that situation at this age level, it is found that the phenomenon termed 'consciousness,' although very generally conceded to exist, is very complex and has a long history in the individual's lifetime. We must therefore select for analysis the most definite, least ambiguous, and most experimentally inviting of the instances where 'consciousness' is extended or where new 'consciousness' arises. Having arrived at our formulation upon this basis, its adequacy—and, therefore, its truth—can be tested by examining its harmony with certain accepted data gathered from adults, children and infra-human animals and by observing the extent and vitality of the experimental implications of the conception.

"In the two fundamental cases of conscious limen with which we have dealt, nothing has been found which does not come under our formulation. These cases, while convincing, may nevertheless not be thought crucial. If so, then the critical case for the formulation is the following: Can a receptor which does not normally condition 'consciousness' be made to do so? Stated from our point of view as a matter for scientific verification: Can activity in a receptor which does not normally condition a language response be made to do so by training? To be sure we have almost shown that this is possible to a limited degree, for the so-called subliminal receptor activities do not normally condition language activities. Perhaps the really crucial case comes with receptors all of whose activities psychology now treats as permanently subliminal to 'consciousness.' Can the receptors in the viscera which do not condition 'sensation' be made to do so by training? Only positive results can be crucial, *for the everyday training of the subject may have resulted in connecting with language responses all of the different kinds of receptors which it is possible to connect.* All that training may be able to do may be of the order discussed above. This, however, is a matter for experiment and not for theory to decide.[12-13]

Such are the anthroponomists' hypotheses concerning the nature of environmental objects, hypotheses which are mutually supporting and not antagonistic one to the other. Let us turn now to a consideration of the subject matter of the science as this problem concerns the classification of the sciences of psychology and anthroponomy, on the one hand, and the sciences of physics, chemistry, mathematics, and biology, on the other hand.

I have said that the environmental object, selected for study by the anthroponomist, is man. And yet the anthroponomist does not attempt to study all phases of man. Anthroponomy is the science of the behavior of the human organism as a whole. The problems of this science necessarily cover a wide range.

---

[12]Psychol. Rev., 1924, 31, pp. 15-17.

[13]Watson misinterprets this hypothesis when he says in "Behaviorism," Peoples Institute Publishing Co., 1925, p. 111, "Professor Walter S. Hunter in his superhuman efforts to straddle the gulf that divides behaviorism from introspectionism uses the verb 'to be' in a .... mystical way when he says certain types of bodily response ARE consciousness." The hypothesis which I have sketched seeks to state the nature of the observable fact which the psychologists have called consciousness. This is no more mystical than saying that the voice of God as heard in the thunder storm is merely a series of air-waves produced by the sudden coming together of great masses of air. Nor is it more mystical than Watson's own identification of emotion with pattern reactions which terminate within the body.

Some are shared with the related sciences of sociology, physiology, neurology, physics, chemistry and mathematics, while other problems are studied little if at all outside of anthroponomy. These latter problems concern the characteristics which most specifically define human nature, *viz.*, the learning and use of new forms of response, language behavior, and social behavior, which latter we call the behavior of inter-stimulation and response. Anthroponomy thus takes its place among the sciences which study *specific* objects in the environment. Here also belong such disciplines as botany which studies plants, geology which specializes upon the inorganic structure of the earth, and physiology, where the functional activities of the various structures of the body become the subject matter for investigation. In contrast to this group of sciences, which is characterized by the study of *specific* environmental objects, stands the group specializing upon those fundamental and *general* characteristics which are thought to be essential to all environmental objects. Here belong at present only mathematics, physics, and chemistry. Chemistry and physics analyze, synthesize, weigh, and measure men, rats, rocks, gases, light, and other objects in search of the fundamental general properties of nature. Mathematics seeks to write formulæ for all processes whether they occur in the rat or in light. Geology, however, focuses its efforts upon the earth, and in attempting to solve this problem, it draws upon any science that offers the slightest help. Physics, chemistry, and mathematics are geology's most useful assistants, because in solving general problems of nature, they have incidentally solved many of the geologist's own problems. The science of anthroponomy, we have said, belongs in the group with geology, physiology, botany and the other specific sciences. Man's learned behavior, his language responses, and his social activities are events in nature, in the environment, and as such they are partially illuminated by the general laws of mathematics, physics, and chemistry. This illumination, to be sure, is less than is desirable, but this is true in the relation of each science of organic processes to the group of general sciences.

I think we can now see the purport of those hypotheses concerning the nature of the environment which the students of human behavior have offered. Weiss's statement that such objects as white rats, red cows, tones, pains, and marital behavior are electron-proton combinations is merely the recognition that, if the contemporary general sciences of mathematics, physics, and chemistry are correct, we may ultimately write the results of anthroponomy in terms of mathematical formulæ. Lashley's hypothesis and my own deal less with the future and more with the present. They, therefore, seek to state environmental happenings in relation to man's action system when this latter is viewed as another object in the common-sense environment.

Let us now return to the subject of psychology and see where its adherents would place it in relation to the other sciences. Titchener says that psychology and physics deal with the same world of experience, but from two very different points of view. Psychology studies the world with man left in it, *i.e.,* it studies experience as dependent upon the nervous system, whereas physics studies experience as though existing independently of the nervous system. Psychology should, therefore, be classified with the general sciences as a discipline laying bare the general traits of mind, where mind is defined as "the sum-total of human experience considered as dependent upon a nervous system."[14] If we substitute the terms inner and outer environment for experience, the statement then reads: psychology studies the total environment viewed as existing only at the moment when it affects the (human) nervous system, whereas physics studies the total environment viewed as existing beyond the moment when it affects the (human) nervous system. I have read statements of this point of view for many years, and I will confess that for a goodly portion of that time the statements seemed just and reasonable. I no longer think so. The statements now seem vague and full of doubtful implications even as a description of psychology. *The reasonable aspect of the statement seems to me to come from the tacit recognition of the stimulus-response relationship which exists between the total environment and the human organism.*

So far I have yet to see psychologists engaged in studying thermometers, stones, water, oxygen, or the relation of acceleration to time in a falling body. And on the other hand, I have yet to read a physicist's account of the learning process. "Ah, but," you say, "there is no reason why the psychologist may not study the one group of phenomena and the physicist the other." And I answer: When the psychologists begin to study the thermometers and other objects mentioned, except as stimuli determining man's behavior, their days will be even more definitely numbered than they are at present, for it will

[14]Titchener, E. B. Textbook of psychology. New York, 1910, p. 16.

no longer be so easy to convince us that this is the way to understand man. From the point of view which we are now considering, if I put a thermometer into a vessel and observe the consequent rise of the mercury, I am said to perform a physical experiment. On the other hand, if I put a pneumograph on a human subject and observe the changes in breathing while the subject does silent arithmetic, the psychologist claims the experiment. Why? Neither is a study of experience viewed as dependent upon the human nervous system. So far as the physicist is concerned, to revert to our above question, of course he may study the learning process since his is a general science of the fundamental laws of the environment, but he can study the learning process only as dependent upon the human nervous system because much of the learning process occurs there. Not even the physicist can describe the learning process as it might be independently of the "experiencing organism," *i. e.,* the organism reacting to stimuli. But again you interrupt me to point out that the nervous system to be considered from Titchener's standpoint is not the one in which the learning-modifications occur, but the one possessed by the observer who is making the study. Can not the physicist, theoretically at least, be expected to describe the fundamental changes in the organism which are involved in learning and would this description not be held valid even for an isolated man on an island in the Pacific Ocean? How happy I am that you raised this question! Of course the physicist may solve this problem, but Titchener cannot incorporate such significant data into his science, whereas anthroponomy has a place waiting for just such results. What Titchener means by "dependent upon the nervous system" is something quite subtle and not at all the crude fact that practically all relations between man and his environment ("experience") are mediated by a nervous system. This is where the concept of "conscious" processes slips into his psychology. "Experience viewed as dependent upon a nervous system" means, in fact, for him experience as observed and as conscious. As Titchener says: "We assume that everybody knows, at first hand, what human experience is, and we then seek to mark off the two aspects of this experience which are dealt with respectively by physics and psychology. Any further definition of the subject-matter of psychology is impossible. Unless one knows, by experience itself, what experience is, one can no more give a meaning to the term 'mind' than a stone can give a meaning to the term 'matter.' "[15]

---

[15]*Ibid*, p. 9.

Even anthroponomy might be defined as a study of the environment with man left in, but we should want to place the emphasis upon man and not upon the environment. And we should not find it necessary to introduce any form of the conscious.[16]

We are thus brought back to the starting point of this lecture. Psychology is an indirect method of studying man, while anthroponomy is a direct method. The baffling questions concerning the nervous system which we have discussed above belong, therefore, to psychology. They are not involved in anthroponomy, for anthroponomy is a specific science of man and not a general science of the mental aspect of a psychophysical world or of psychosomatic processes.

Let us turn now to the second problem which we are to consider: What are the chief methods employed by the two sciences? Psychology has two methods of gathering data. One is individualistic, and the other is social. One is held to be less, and the other more scientifically fruitful. The first, or individualistic, method is utilized whenever one person undertakes to observe experience and build a science upon these observations. This method has given rise to the old armchair variety of psychology, and yet the method has never been repudiated as is evidenced by such a statement as this from Calkins: "The method has obvious advantages. It makes no especial conditions of time and place; it requires no mechanical adjunct; it demands no difficult search for suitable material; at any moment, in all surroundings, with no external outfit, one may study the rich material provided by every imaginable experience. In an extreme sense, all is grist that comes to the psychologist's mill."[17] *That the method has not been repudiated is due to the fact that the data gathered by it form the basis for the interpretation of the results secured by the social method.* Remember

---

[16]The discussion of the subject matter of psychology has been based upon the views of the Wundtians because they have stated their position on conscious processes, or experience, more clearly and specifically than others. All psychologists study conscious processes, but many of them mix the processes up with behavior in such an inextricable way that their writings do not offer clearcut statements concerning experience. The fundamental criticisms which we have directed against psychology are aimed at all psychologies, because all psychologies have in common the indirect method of studying man however much they may differ in the extent to which they also use behavioristic data.

[17]Calkins, M. W. A first book in psychology. New York, 1914, p. 7.

that the psychologist says: "We assume that everybody knows, at first hand, what experience is . . . . Unless one knows . . . . one can no more give meaning to the term 'mind' than a stone can give meaning to the term 'matter.'"

The second, or social, method of psychology is utilized wherever an experimenter utilizes subjects other than himself. Let me illustrate this method in a simple way. First, I take one blue paper disc and one black paper disc. These I mount upon the spindle of a rotating wheel in the proportion of three blue to one black. The wheel is set in rapid rotation, and my subjects are called in one at a time. I point to the discs and say, "What color quality is that?" Each subject responds in turn. "A dark, poorly saturated blue." If I change the proportion of blue and black, my subjects report differently. These are the observable facts upon which both psychologists and anthroponomists can agree, and yet notice how different are the interpretations placed upon these facts. The anthroponomist says in a very matter of fact way, "It looks as though the behavior of your subjects was controlled by a change in the visual stimulus, when your instructions remained constant. This suggests to me that man reacts to blue light of various intensities. It might now be well to state the visual stimulus in physical terms of wave length and energy in order that we may know more exactly just what the visual stimulus is and thereby help some one else in his efforts to repeat our observation." The psychologist interprets the experiment as follows: "Each subject has an immediate experience of color quality, intensity, and saturation. This inference is justified because we are all men and because I know that under the same conditions I have these experiences and use the same words to describe them. Let us by all means get the physical measurements suggested in order that later observers may be certain to get this rare experience." This interpretation by the psychologist makes us more certain than ever that the task which he has undertaken is that of describing the total environment as it appears to man and not that of describing some fundamental aspect of man himself. "But," you say, "if I know the complete description of the inner and outer environment as experienced by each man, can I not draw important conclusions concerning man?" Oh, the sly psychologist! This is another of the plausible arguments by which he seeks to convert the unwary! How can he know the experience of another subject? Philosophy, psychological definition, and poetry have closed that door to us. Listen to the way in which the poet formulates the situation:

"Yes: in the sea of life enisl'd,
With echoing straits between us thrown,
Dotting the shoreless watery wild,
We mortal millions live *alone*.
The islands feel the enclasping flow,
And then their endless bounds they know.

*　　　*　　　*　　　*

"A God, a God their severance rul'd;
And bade betwixt their shores to be
The unplumb'd, salt, estranging sea."

And, then, if the psychologist wants to draw conclusions concerning man, why does he not study man directly without all this effort at reconstructing the environment as seen by another? Perhaps at one time in my lecture you thought it might be fascinating to go with a friend on a Cook's tour, conducted by a psychologist, through the realm of experience, there to try all things at least once and to learn how many wonderful melodies could be played upon the human organism. Alas, there is no chance, for you must see the world yourself. The world as seen by others is closed to you!

The science of psychology is built upon inferences concerning the environment. These inferences are drawn from the observable facts gathered by the social method of that science. Against this method, and, therefore, against this science, I raise these objections: (1) An *unnecessary* and an *impossible* task is undertaken in attempting to reconstruct the environment as it appears to adult man, to children, and to animals. (2) The genetic point of approach, which has already proved valuable in understanding nature, requires that our investigation of man begin with the simpler stimulus-response problems and extend to the more complex ones later when we have mastered our technique. (3) The psychologist limits himself to observing the language responses of his subjects because this behavior is bound up so closely with the discriminable aspects of the environment. These language responses are admittedly late in appearance in the animal world, and yet the psychologist utilizes the language responses of adult members of European cultures in his hypothetical reconstruction of the environment not only of man but of all animals. By thus limiting himself to the language situation, the psychologist omits much that is valuable in understanding both man and

the environment.   (4) The psychologist persistently violates
one of the great canons of science when *he fails to harmonize
his problem to be investigated with the methods to be employed.*

This last point I consider of the very greatest importance
for the revision of psychological science.   I must, therefore,
comment upon it at some length.   Let us revert, first, to the
experiment with the blue and the black discs.   The psychological problem is this: How does the *experience* of blueness
change with the alteration of the relative proportions of blue
and black on the color wheel?   The experimental method involves *stimulating* the subject auditorily with instructions and
visually with the colored discs.   The subject's report is then
recorded as it is manifested in *behavior.*   The psychologist
draws his conclusions in terms of *experience,* whereas I submit that the only conclusion justified is that the subject
behaves in a certain manner when stimulated in a certain way.

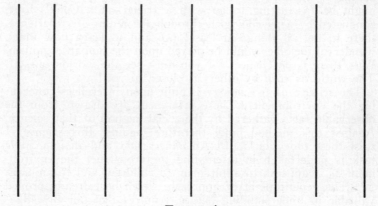

FIGURE 1

We may again illustrate the criticism by an experiment as
conducted by the Gestalt psychologists.   The problem is how
does the subject see the lines of Figure 1.   The method of
solving this apparently simple problem is as before.   The subject is brought into the room.   I stimulate his eyes with the
lines of Figure 1 and give him auditory instructions.   As a
result the subject says, "I see four groups of two lines each.
At one moment the line on the right stands alone, and at
another moment the line on the left is without a partner."
The Gestalt psychologist now concludes that the subject has

an experience of groups, or of figure and ground. The behaviorist would say that, when stimulated in this manner, the subject responds in at least two different ways. In neither of these experiments, however, would the behaviorist rest content with formulating his problem merely in such a manner that the method available would bear upon the problem formulated. In each case he would further insist upon checking up his results using some other form of behavior than the verbal response of the subject.

Suppose we turn now from the external to the internal environment. Let the psychologist again state his problem. This time it will be as follows: What is the influence of the simple affective processes upon the knee-jerk?[18] (Or the problem might have been, how many affective qualities are there? In this case, the method would differ from what we are about to describe, but the same type of criticism would be applicable.) The method selected involves the use of an apparatus for eliciting the knee-jerk and of certain "indifferent, pleasant, and unpleasant" words. When the subject's eyes are stimulated by the words and when he is stimulated auditorily in the proper way, he says, "Pleasant." We now proceed to apply the visual stimuli simultaneously with the tap on the patellar tendon. The results recorded indicate the magnitude of the knee-jerk under the several conditions. The psychologist thereupon concludes that pleasantness and unpleasantness did or did not affect the response in question.

Had a student of behavior used this method, the problem would have been formulated directly in terms of the method, as follows: What is the influence of visual word-stimuli upon the patellar tendon reflex under such and such conditions? The fundamental error in the psychologist's procedure is that the problems formulated and the conclusions drawn can have no real bearing upon the methods employed and the results secured, since the psychologist takes as his general problem the reconstruction of his subject's environment and not the study of his behavior. When problems are formulated in terms of available methods, the scientist is much less prone to spend his energies in the fruitless effort to solve problems which at the present moment lie far beyond the best available technique. The student of behavior is not altogether guiltless here, for occasionally he also formulates problems which

---

[18]Burtt, H. E. and Tuttle, W. W. The patellar tendon reflex and affective tone. Amer. Jour. Psychol., 1925, 36, 553-561.

are quite unrelated to the methods employed in their solution. The difference between such a mistake on the part of a behaviorist and by a similar mistake made by a psychologist lies in the fact that, by the definition of the subject matter and goal of his science, the psychologist is forever committed to this error, while in the case of the behaviorist only a momentary lapse from rigid scientific method has occurred.

In the description and criticism of the psychologist's methods, we have by implication given many of the characteristics of the methods used by the anthroponomist. It is only fitting and proper, however, that we should describe certain characteristics of these methods more in detail. As in psychology, so in anthroponomy, chief reliance is placed upon the social method as a method of gathering data. The anthroponomist will at times work upon himself as subject, but he appreciates the great difficulty of controlling and checking many factors which influence behavior where the subject and the experimenter are one, and *he absolutely refuses to use this individualistic method as the basis for interpreting the results of his scientific labors.* The methods of the anthroponomist always involve the presentation of stimuli and the consequent arousal of behavior in the subject. Sometimes one stimulus is emphasized in the experimental situation so that this stimulus finally may be said to control the behavior. Sometimes the subject is merely placed in a general environmental situation and his behavior observed. So far as is practical, the specific stimuli which determine the behavior are recorded and the experimenter notes what seem to him to be the important aspects of the response. Where the conclusion is drawn that the red stimulus, in a red-green discrimination experiment, *e. g.,* controls the behavior, there is no implication that the red stimulus is effective *by itself.* Many other stimuli are cooperating, particularly stimuli from the stomach of the hungry subject and stimuli from the muscles and skin. The conclusion, in reality, is that, under these experimental conditions where the stimuli from the skin, muscles, viscera, ears, etc., are kept *constant,* the *deciding* factor in controlling the response is the wave-length difference between the two visual stimuli. To be sure there are configurations of stimuli at work and the organism does act as a whole, but under the conditions of the experiment described, the most significant conclusion to be drawn refers to the stimulus which plays the deciding role. Wherever it can be shown that the subject's behavior is controlled by a particular grouping of stimuli, that conclusion should be drawn. Any other use of the Gestalt concept seems unnecessary.

This brief discussion of the stimulus-response nature of behavioristic experiments leads me to state three further points: (1) The psychologist conducts exactly similar experiments, but he is so engrossed in his effort to reconstruct the subject's environment and so hypnotized by the significance of language behavior that he slurs over the essential character of his observed facts in his desire to attain the goal which he has set himself. If Burtt and Tuttle, for example, had realized that, in dealing with their so-called affective processes, they were dealing with a bit of behavior, the first step that would have been taken would have been to assure themselves that this particular bit of (visceral?) behavior was present. Having shown its presence as a result of the word stimuli, they could then have studied the facilitory and inhibitory relations between this behavior and the knee-jerk. (2) Some psychologists have said that the behaviorist, when he uses the stimulus-response concept, ignores the contribution which the organism makes to the nature of the behavior. This seems to me to be a remarkably uncalled-for accusation. Has not the behaviorist always appealed to the results of heredity and previous training as factors which cooperate with present stimuli in determining behavior? Was there ever a behaviorist who explained maze behavior without calling upon the retained effects of previous training for a part of his explanation, or a behaviorist who ignored childhood peculiarities in accounting for adult behavior? (3) The third point concerns the psychologist's criticism of the behaviorist's use of the stimulus-response category. By what right, so the criticism goes, does the anthroponomist say, "I used a red light as the stimulus," or "I trained the subject using a cube and a sphere as stimuli." Since the behaviorist accepts the theories of physics and chemistry as adequate for the explanation of nature, it is said that all stimuli should be stated by him in terms of these sciences. This criticism ignores the fact that the behaviorist, like the physicist, accepts a common-sense view of the environment as the *milieu* for his experimentation. This we have been at great pains to point out earlier in the present lecture. The anthroponomist has no more hesitancy in saying that he gave water to his chicks in order to see whether they would drink than a chemist has in saying that he has completed the analysis of water into H_2O. The chemist does not find it necessary to drop the word water and substitute for it some electron-proton substitute. Wherever the situation demands that the wave lengths of light, the vibration frequencies of sound, and the chemical constituents of odorous substances be stated, the behaviorist meets the demand, but not otherwise. As anthroponomy advances to ever more and more rigorous experimentation, it is to be expected that such specifications of the stimuli and of the organic conditions will occur more and more frequently. Until that time, let us proceed in a matter of fact way, suiting our specifications to the practical needs of the moment.

It would be a hopeless task to canvas in one lecture all of the points at issue between psychology and anthroponomy. We shall, therefore, limit ourselves in the remainder of our discussion to a brief statement concerning the third problem formulated above, "What are the results of the science?" With reference to anthroponomy it only need be said that the results secured bear directly upon the nature of the human individual as he is found working in the fields, bathing in the surf, or pursuing his intricate way in the great cities of Earth. The anthroponomist himself specializes more upon language behavior, learned responses, and the facts of inter-stimulation and response than any other scientist, and in addition he cooperates with others in the study of various additional aspects of man in so far as these affect organic behavior. All of these results are possible without omitting from the resulting picture of human nature any observable and verifiable datum. The anthroponomist even goes further and offers various hypotheses concerning the nature of the inner and outer environments as these are reported by his subjects. Nowhere is it necessary to introduce the concept of consciousness, or experience, conceived as another mode of existence, or as another aspect of the physical world.

The psychologist thinks that he secures two types of results, one he assumes concerns consciousness, or experience, and the other we all agree is behavior. The behavioristic results of the Wundtians have been deplorably slight in amount when one considers that most of their experiments have involved stimulus-response situations in a subject other than the experimenter. The adherents of biological functionalism have been more fortunate in their results in spite of their theory that mind is an instrument of adjustment in the struggle for existence. This outcome of their work has been possible because their systematic point of view has encouraged the direct study of man. It is only to be regretted that they have mixed up experience and behavior so thoroughly that the conclusions which they have drawn from their experimental work must in many cases be rejected, and in many cases the work must be done over under the guidance of another systematic point of view. No combination of "experience" and behavior is necessary or possible in the accurate portrayal of human nature. If we consider the results secured by the most consistent and logical students of (so-called) consciousness, the followers of the Wundtian tradition, we see that these results consist of a vast array of least discriminable aspects of experience, blueness, tonality, contact, pain, sweet, noisiness, intensity, clearness, duration, and others.

When we turn to the new school of Gestalt psychologists, we find that experimental results are stated in terms of unique configurations and not in terms of the abstract and highly artificial products of the Wundtian school. This is an advantage to the extent that new aspects of the environment are discovered, an advantage, i. e., if we think that the way to understand man is through a study of the environment. As yet the Gestalt movement has not worked far enough into the problems of systematic psychology to reveal just how it will treat these problems of general theory. The movement so far has been limited largely to the field of "perception" and to an elaboration of the concept of the organism as a whole. Sooner or later, however, it must face the many other problems of classical psychology, as these appear in such questions as: the natures and inter-relations of "perception," "imagination," "affection," "attention," and "thinking." I can see no evidence as yet which would lead me to believe that Gestalt psychology as a science of "experience" will escape many of the cul-de-sacs into which the psychology of discriminable aspects of experience has fallen. After all, a Gestalt is merely another unique but more complex aspect of the environment. And it will be just as difficult for the adherents of that point of view to classify and synthesize unique Gestalten as for their opponents to synthesize unique elements or unique least discriminable aspects of the universe.

It is sometimes said by Gestalt psychologists that the chief result to be obtained by their method of approach to psychology is an insight into the neural processes of man and that the study of Gestalten is merely a means to this end. Köhler in particular has emphasized this, and he has in addition sought in a brilliant way to apply the principles of physics to the problems of neural processes. There is much, therefore, in Köhler's psychology which is in harmony with Loeb's tradition in biology and with Weiss's theories in anthroponomy. And yet, in spite of this, I cannot react optimistically toward such a program for two reasons: (1) Ever since the days of Wundt's physiological psychology, the students of psychology have sought neural correlates for complex as well as for simple experiences with little or no success. On what grounds, therefore, are we to expect better success from the attempt when made by the Gestalt psychologists? To be sure they will propose theoretical neural functions different from the ones proposed by the Wundtians. So much is certain, because the Gestalt psychologists are seeking neural correlates for Gestalten and not for the least discriminable aspects of experience. (2) My second reason for pessimism with reference to the attempt to dissect neural functions by means of environmental studies is the same as my reason for rejecting a science which studies human nature by means of analyses of the environment. Why all this indirectness? If one wishes to study neural functions, why not study them directly? Why not begin where the physiologist has left off and carry on from that point? The work of Franz, Lashley, and Coghill will throw more light on neural functions than fifty years of speculation by the Gestalt psychologists added to the fifty past years of Wundtian speculation, because Franz, Lashley, and Coghill are attacking their problems directly and in the light of the present status of the sciences dealing with that problem. *If the Gestalt psychologists are able to formulate an hypothesis which will be valuable in the understanding of neural function, it will be a result of the stimulus-response data which they will inevitably accumulate in their studies and not a result of the experiential hypothesis with which they, like the Wundtians, burden their use of the social method of investigation.*

We have at last reached the end of the task assigned to us. So far as time has permitted, we have compared psychology and anthroponomy with reference to subject matter, methods, and results. The outcome, as I would have you see it, is that anthroponomy stands out as a common-sense, direct attack upon the problem of human nature, omitting no observable and verifiable datum from the picture. Psychology, on the other hand, is an indirect method of reaching the goal, an indirect method moreover which is inseparably bound up with the ancient philosophical concepts of mind and consciousness as aspects of the universe which differ from the physical. With this my work is done. It remains for you and those who follow to support the point of view which in your judgment offers the better possibility of reaching that intriguing goal, the understanding of human nature.

"Our past is clean forgot,
Our present is and is not,
Our future's a sealed seedplot,
And what betwixt them are we?—
We who say as we go,—
   'Strange to think by the way,
Whatever there is to know,
   That shall we know one day.'"

PART II

Dynamic Psychology

Robert S. Woodworth

CHAPTER V

DYNAMIC PSYCHOLOGY*

By Robert S. Woodworth

The combination of words, "Dynamic Psychology," has not at present, and never has had, any great vogue. In comparison with the "rational psychology" and "empirical psychology" of a century or two ago, with the "structural" and "functional" psychology of twenty years ago, or with the "introspective" and "behavioristic" psychology, the "Gestalt" psychology or the "psychoanalysis" of the present time, "dynamic psychology" has an unfamiliar sound, and may well arouse the query, "What new iconoclasm is emerging into view?" In reality, however, dynamic psychology is neither new nor revolutionary. It is an attempt to lay stress on certain problems which psychology has always regarded as belonging to it; or, in a more ambitious sense, is an attempt to characterize psychology as essentially a study in dynamics.

Of the few authors who have employed the phrase, some mean by "dynamic psychology" a part of the subject, while others mean to imply that psychology, when properly conceived, *is* dynamic psychology. F. L. Wells has used the phrase as a convenient caption to cover studies of emotions, wishes, trends, conflicts and inhibitions. J. H. McCurdy has done the same. T. V. Moore limits the scope of his extensive and valuable treatment of "Dynamic Psychology" to the affective and conative sides of mental life.

On the other hand, C. L. Herrick, some twenty-five years ago, urged that psychology might well make use of dynamic concepts throughout its field of study. I myself, not many years since, while seeking to envisage psychology as a unitary enterprise, having a common aim in spite of great divergencies in the definitions proposed and the methods advocated, was led back to the now archaic phrase of the older psychologists, the "workings of the mind." That was what they said they proposed to study, and essentially the same, so it appears to me, is the aim of modern psychologists of all schools. We may dodge the futile questionings that attend the use of the word, "mind," and substitute "organism" or "individual."

*Powell Lecture in Psychological Theory at Clark University, December 12, 1925.

Then, to dodge physiology as well, we may simply explain that by organism we mean the organism *as a whole,* and perhaps we have reached as adequate a definition of our science as we can hope to attain for some time. At any rate, the phrase, "dynamic psychology" carries this notion of "workings," and may serve as a reminder of the common aim of all psychologists.

It is agreed on all sides that psychology studies processes. What the behaviorist observes, and what the introspectionist observes, both come down to *process,* sequence of events. Structure we observe only in the figurative sense in which a complex process may be said to have structure. We are concerned with antecedents and consequents, cause and effect, stimulus and response, the combination of factors and similar dynamic relations.

Psychological dynamics is not limited to the study of feeling, emotion, conation and muscular and glandular action. We study also sensations as dependent upon their stimuli, we analyze out the various factors in the perception of depth or distance, we examine the process of learning, and formulate laws of association or recall. The whole subject is permeated with dynamics.

Perception is a chapter in psychology that is especially in need of dynamic concepts. A plurality of stimuli, as in a chord or clang or in McDougall's dot figure, gives rise to a unitary percept, such as recognition of the chord, hearing the timbre of an instrument, seeing a definite figure in a scatter of dots. Here is a real problem. How is the unitary percept related to the plurality of tones or dots? The associationists attempted a solution by introducing the concept of "simultaneous association." Originally, association meant successive association, one idea calling up another, an antecedent event arousing a consequent. Simultaneous association means nothing more than that the elements are together. The dots are together in the field of view, the tones of the chord are heard together. Being together, they are said to be associated, and that is all there is to it. The explanation breaks down in face of the dot figure, since the assemblage of dots, when looked at steadily, takes on different groupings, one after another. The same is true of many other "ambiguous" figures. It is even true of the clang or chord, which may be heard in different ways, now centered about one of the constituent notes, now about another. There is more than a mere togetherness of the dots or notes; there are groupings, and the same elements appear now in one grouping, now in another. The qualitative differences between the groupings are not accounted for by simultaneous associations. In fact, "association" does no more than call attention to the problem. Stimultaneous association is an undynamic concept, and part of the aim of dynamic psychology is to clear the decks of such concepts.

Little, if anything, is gained by substituting the concept of synthesis, or of apperception, for that of association, Just a general synthetic activity of the subject, putting dots or tones together, really leaves the matter just as simultaneous association left it, and does not account in the least for the different perceptions that occur in face of the same assemblage of stimuli. What is needed is something specific, differing from moment to moment as the perception differs.

The really dynamic concept to fit the case lies ready to hand, and is no other than the concept of stimulus and response. The dot figure, or other ambiguous figure, is a stimulus to which more than one response is possible. The plurality of stimuli, acting together, arouse the unitary response of seeing a particular figure. Previous experience, and present internal conditions, are factors in determining which of the possible responses shall be touched off at any moment. Here, as often in reflex action, multiple stimuli converge upon a unitary response.[1]

This interpretation of perception evidently has much in common with that of the Gestalt school. The figure or chord percept is conceived as a unit, almost as an element, and at least not as a sum or synthesis of elements. The dot figure percept is not composed of the dots as elements, but can properly be called a unit in its own right. It can be prepared for as a unit, as when the subject looks for a certain figure in an assemblage of dots; and, once present, it can function as a unit in suggesting something similar to itself or otherwise associated with itself.

Mention should also be made of the important "complex theory" of Selz.[2] ("Complex" is here used in an entirely different sense from that of the psychoanalysts). What function as units in thinking and association are often not such "elements" as tones, colors, dots, or even words, but figures,

---

[1] I have argued in the same vein in the Psychological Review.
[2] Otto Selz, Über die Gesetze des geordneten Denkverlaufs. Stuttgart, 1913.

chords, phrases and other similar "complexes." Selz proposes his complex theory as a substitute for the "constellation" theory. The difference, and the line of evidence which he adduces in favor of the complex theory, can be illustrated in the case of multiplication.

When one is set to find products, the stimulus, "3 and 9," immediately arouses the response, "27," with no intrusion of the response "12," which, as the sum of the given numbers, is even more strongly associated with them than 27 is. The constellation theory explains that the actual response is the resultant of two tendencies, the associative tendency, which leads towards the sum, product, or any response habitually associated with the stimulus, and the determining tendency to find products. The explanation fails, since 12, which is firmly associated with the stimulus, "3 and 9," is also a product. The search for products would be satisfied with 12, since 12 is the familiar product of 2 and 6, or 3 and 4; and the general associative tendencies would probably favor 12 over 27. Evidently 27 derives its advantage from the fact that it is, not simply a product, but the product of the given numbers. What the stimulus calls up, therefore, is, not simply numbers, but a "complex" such as "3 times 9 are 27." Such elementary parts of the multiplication table, though complex in a sense, are learned as units and function as units in the work of multiplication. The set to multiply puts into readiness, not numbers which happen to be products, but these elements of the multiplication table.

That figures, chords, and other such "complexes" are units, unitary responses, and function as units in perception and recall, is essential to the dynamic theory of perception which I am trying to present. So far, this theory is in agreement with the Gestalt conceptions. But something more is essential to the dynamic theory. This something more may be made clear by reference to Dewey's critique of the doctrine of sensory elements.

Dewey's criticism[3] follows the general line taken by James[4] in his rejection of the analysis of sensations. James urged that when, by dint of previous training and by careful focusing of attention, an overtone is heard out of a clang, the clang

[3] John Dewey, Human Nature and Conduct. New York, 1922. p. 31.
[4] William James, Principles of Psychology, New York, 1890. I, pp. 502-504.

experience was not thereby analyzed, but a new experience was being obtained. The auditory stimulus remained the same, but a new response was made to this stimulus. One may admit that the stimulus has been analyzed, but not the sensation. Dewey adds this further consideration: the hearing out of the overtone, far from being a primitive type of reaction to the stimulus, is one that is only possible to a specially trained observer. How absurd, then, to take this highly sophisticated form of observation as furnishing the primitive elements of auditory experience! As experience, apart from the physical stimulus, the clang is more primitive than the overtones that are said to constitute the clang.

Certainly this reasoning is cogent and pertinent. Yet one question remains: In the sequence of events that starts with the physical production of the fundamental and overtones, and ends in the perception of the clang, or of certain overtones in the clang, is there not an intra-organic stage equivalent to an indifferent assemblage of partial tones, a stage consequent upon the stimulation of the ear, and antecedent to perception? Let us follow the sequence of events. The several sets of waves, of differing vibration rates, are first compounded into a complex wave motion of the air, and it is in this form that the auditory stimulus reaches the ear. The ear seems not to respond to the wave form as such, but to break it up into its constituent simple waves. The ear is said to be an analytic organ, and the evidence for this analytic power of the ear is the fact that, after suitable training, the observer can hear the separate overtones out of the tonal mass. Probably the organ of Corti, and certainly some part of the auditory mechanism, possesses this analytic power, and furnishes as its stage in the sequence of events, an assemblage of tones, the fundamental and overtones. Without this stage to work from, to respond to, perception of the overtones would be impossible. It is an "indifferent" stage, in that it can lead either to the experience of the clang or to the hearing out of overtones.

Much the same can be said with regard to the dot figure. The retinal image is an indifferent assemblage of dots, not grouped in one way rather than another. Presumably, the retina, and also the first receptive visual centers, respond pretty faithfully to the retinal image, and do not introduce the configuration which we find in the percept.

It is at least a fair hypothesis that the first conscious stage in the process has this character of an indifferent assemblage, and that the figured percept is sequent in time to the indifferent stage. If we call this indifferent, unfigured stage the stage of *sensation,* then the seeing of the separate dots, or the hearing out of the overtones, is a genuine analysis of the sensory stage. It is not an analysis of the percept, but it is an analysis of the antecedent sensation.

If the objection is raised that introspection affords no support for this preliminary indifferent stage—that the configuration is there as soon as the stimulus is seen or heard at all—I would reply that there is some evidence, though none of it is well worked out as yet. The evidence is of several kinds.

(1) In looking at the dot figure, or at any ambiguous figure, though shifts occur from one configuration to another, the background or mass of the visual whole seems to remain constant. The dots or lines remain the same all through the shifts or grouping. This is as it would be if the configuration were superposed upon an indifferent sensation mass.

(2) When the stimulus is unfamiliar and not very clearcut, there is sometimes an interval of sensation before configuration appears. This is as it should be. Unpracticed perceptual reactions should be relatively slow and halting, whereas much-practiced perceptions of familiar assemblages of stimuli would probably occur with a latency of not over a tenth of a twentieth of a second, an interval too short for introspective observation.

(3) In object blindness, word deafness, and similar losses of function due to localized cerebral lesions, sensation remains, while configuration, at least of the normal type, is wanting. This is as it should be if configuration represented the activity of a different brain mechanism from that of the first receptive areas which, we may suppose, are active in sensation.

(4) In recall, configuration often comes back clearly, while the sensory mass is vague and lacking in body. This is as it should be if configuration were a response separate from sensation, ordinarily aroused by the sensory stage, but capable of other attachments so as to be arousable in other ways and apart from sensation.

The evidence ought to be sufficient to lend some respectability to the hypothesis of a sensation-perception sequence. In fact the evidence is as good as could be expected in the absence of intensive work on the problem. The promptness with which the perceptual stage would probably supervene upon the sensory, and the prolongation of the sensory stage (with continued stimulus) so as to overlap and blend with the percept, must necessarily make it difficult to demonstrate two separate stages in the process.

This hasty consideration of a problem in perception may serve to indicate the broad scope of dynamic psychology, as covering topics quite apart from emotion and movement, and as operating with a variety of dynamic concepts, and not solely with impulse and similar principles.

It will probably be clear without discussion that a dynamic psychology need not take sides in the controversy between introspectionists and behaviorists. It can utilize data obtained by either introspective or objective observation; sometimes the one and sometimes the other will serve to indicate the stages in a process going on within the organism. From its disinclination to adhere definitely to either the behaviorist or the introspective wing of psychology, dynamic psychology is exposed to the accusation of being merely eclectic, of seeking to avoid extremes and preferring the "middle of the road." Such an accusation is not wholly fair, since dynamic psychology has its own problem and can rightfully seek light wherever trustworthy information is to be had.

Behaviorism, as a set of taboos—touch not, taste not, handle not the unclean thing, i.e., the sensation, the image, or anything with an odor of introspection about it—tends to clog the works and hamper progress. On its positive side, however, behaviorism is distinctly a study in dynamics, and it is doing much to force psychology to the use of dynamic concepts, and to cause those that have no dynamic value to become obsolescent.

Phenomenological psychology appears to stand at the opposite pole from behaviorism, yet it too, by its efforts to get away from every-day modes of description and to describe sequences of events with a minimum of extraneous matter, may serve the purpose of dynamic psychology, so far as its descriptions are verified. What we need is a description of processes as they actually occur. The descriptions and concepts that satisfy us in daily life are apt to confuse and distort the sequence of events. We need, specially, to be on our guard against valuation and teleology. When we say that a process occurs because it is useful to the organism, we have lost our sense of direction, and are putting the cart before the horse. To be sure, the outcome of an act may be the cause of further processes, but not of the process leading up to the act itself.

But to say that dynamic psychology does not operate with concepts of value, as tools in its own work, is not to say that it must have nothing to do with the facts of preference, success and failure, likes and dislikes, loves and hates, purposes and fears, as they actually occur in life. All such events in the process of living are to be included; only, we need a straight, undistorted account of them.

From what has already been said, the attitude of dynamic psychology to the purposivist and the mechanistic tendencies in psychology may be sufficiently clear; yet the matter deserves somewhat closer attention.

Purpose is a real fact in human life, and, if not purpose, at least striving towards a goal is a real fact of animal life as well. Quite apart from the philosophy of purpose and striving and their place in the world process as a whole—which is not a psychological question—purpose is one of the phenomena which psychology must include in its story. A dynamic psychology must study purpose in relation to its antecedents and consequences, its causes and effects.

Some authors, as especially McDougall,[5] appear to teach that any thoroughgoing causal interpretation of human behavior and experience implies shutting one's eyes to the facts of purpose and striving. There is certainly some confusion here. There can be no contradiction between the purposiveness of a sequence of actions and its being a causal sequence. A purpose is certainly a cause; if it had no effects, it would be without significance. Moreover, for anyone to harbor a purpose, he must believe in the causal nature of the stream of events in which he means to work. His purpose seeks to control the course of events, by adopting means that can be relied on to produce the desired outcome. Without some experience of dependable causes to be utilized as means, a purpose could scarcely take rise.

Shall we say, then that a purpose, though a cause, is itself uncaused, that it has no genesis, no motivation, no stimulus? I know of no facts tending to such a conclusion. On the contrary, so far as it is possible for us to influence other people and control their behavior, it is by way of controlling their desires and purposes. We can control their hands and

[5]Outline of Psychology. N. Y., 1923.

feet and vocal organs, for the most part, only by controlling their desires. We make appeals to them, we appeal to their self-interest, their loyalty, their interest in this, their dislike of that, and by such means we excite in them purposes that eventuate in action. Animal behavior is similarly controlled by the use of suitable incentives.

If man has certain native propensities, if these are awakened by certain stimuli, if they are the basis of sentiments and purposes, then, undoubtedly, every purpose has its cause in a double sense: it has its genesis in the life history of the individual, and, at any time, it has its exciting stimulus. The whole study of purpose would be futile, if purpose were not the effect of definite causes, as well as the cause of definite effects.

Purpose is not belittled by recognizing it as the effect of antecedent causes. Every cause is itself the effect of antecedent causes, and its own effectiveness as a cause is not thus diminished. Your purpose of giving somebody a happy surprise on Christmas Day is no less a purpose, and no less effective, because it originated in your love for that person (which itself is the effect of causes lying back in your life history), and in your memory of joyful surprises on former Christmas Days. Your purpose would be futile if it had no effects, it would be incredible if it had no causes. It is a link in a causal chain, but it is just as fine a purpose for all that.

Therefore, I say, there must be some confusion of ideas when the fact of purpose is brought up as if it made a dynamic, cause-and-effect psychology impossible or even wicked. Rather, this and similar facts are grist for the dynamic mill, and, when well ground, should produce the most valuable sort of knowledge for the understanding and control of human conduct.

With purposivism, as a philosophy of all nature, or of all animate nature, dynamic psychology has nothing to do. In order to concentrate upon its own job, psychology needs to keep away from philosophy, or, at least, to maintain a clear distinction between what is psychology and what is the philosophy that happens to appeal most strongly to the particular psychologist. I contend that the injection of purposivism, or of animism, into a psychological discussion is irrelevant and distracting. Vitalism, indeed, can be treated as a scientific question, but it is not a question for psychology. It is a question for cellular physiology, since the crucial considerations refer to the life processes of the cells, not to the behavior of the individual as a whole.

Psychology is not called upon to give its adherence either to vitalism or to a mechanistic conception of life. If a scientific decision between these two views is possible, it will be reached by physiology, not by psychology. Psychology is not mechanistic, any more than it is vitalistic; nor even is a dynamic psychology mechanistic, though it deals with causes and effects. Dynamic psychology follows the course of events in the life of the organism as a whole. The self-same course of events can be followed by physiology, with its more refined or at least more microscopic technique. A chimpanzee, let us say, joints together two sticks of bamboo and uses the jointed pole for reaching a banana. This is a psychological description; much more and finer detail might be added and the description still remain at the psychological level. Now the physiologist may undertake to describe this same series of events, in terms of the action of the different muscles, of separate muscle fibers, nerve fibers, synapses in localized nerve centers, and so on. He would be describing the same real process—not a "parallel" process—but his description would employ different concepts and would be, in general, very different from the psychologist's description. It would be much more minute than the psychologist's description, but not necessarily any truer. It would not include the relationships observed by the psychologist, and would not be so useful for purposes of prediction and control, if we wished to know what the chimpanzee would *do* in a given situation. Still other observers, as the physical chemist, might describe the same real process, analyzing it in still minuter detail, and working, we may say, at a still lower or deeper level of description. Now the physical chemist or the physiologist may approach a mechanistic description of the chimpanzee's actions, but the psychologist does not come within shooting distance of such a description. It lies out of his level altogether.

Both introspective and objective psychology, we may remark in passing, are working at the same general "level," intermediate between the level of the sociologist above and that of the physiologist below. Both are working at the level at which the actions of the individual as a whole come into view. Thus introspectionists and behaviorists logically belong within the confines of the one science of psychology. Though they may have their family jars, they are not likely to consent to a divorce. I would liken dynamic psychology to the child that holds this family together, were that not rather out of keeping with my insistence that dynamic psychology is essentially much older than either behaviorism or introspectionism, which have arisen recently, as a matter of fact, in the strife for more adequate methods in psychology. Dynamic psychology can use the data of both. I would go so far as to say that it is the dynamic point of view that gives significance to either introspective or behavior data.

Dynamic psychology is not physiology; it is not, necessarily, physiological psychology. The latter works the two levels together, or correlates psychological with physiological findings—a most valuable task. But it is one thing to recognize the value of such correlation, and quite another thing to teach that the only worth-while goal of psychology is a physiological description. Psychology is primarily responsible for its own level, and its own particular goal is such a generalized description of the individual's activities, in causal sequence, as will make possible prediction and control within this field and level. Contact with the social and physiological levels, above and below, is extremely valuable for psychology, especially in a dynamic sense.

If the aim of genetic psychology, in a general way, is to trace the course of events, and to seek for uniform sequences that may have the value of causal laws, this general problem can be seen to break up into a number of more special problems, according as the course of events is followed over a long or over shorter periods of time. Genetic psychology, the life history of the individual, his curve of growth and senescence, are concerned with the sequence of events over long periods of time. The process of learning, the practice curve, the curve of forgetting, the curve of fatigue and the diurnal course of efficiency, follow the sequence of events over comparatively short, but still considerable periods of time. Studies of reflexes, emotional responses, reaction times, and the dependance of perception upon sensory stimuli follow sequences that run their course in a few seconds at most, and illustrate the most detailed type of analysis which psychology has found it feasible to undertake. Because the more minute the analysis, the more searching and fundamental it appears—though this is in part an illusion—the concepts of stimulus and response, applicable to this minutest analysis of process, have come to have a dominant position in the array of dynamic concepts employed by psychology.

Though the concepts of stimulus and response have long been employed, they have of late been more emphasized than formerly, and are beginning to awaken some rather trenchant criticism. Possibly no better use can be made of the present occasion than to attempt a slight contribution to this discussion, and to the clarification of these fundamental concepts.

To some critics, these concepts have seemed too obvious to have much significance. We are challenged to make any general statements concerning stimulus and response that are not too trite and self-evident to merit any attention. Can anything at all surprising, and yet true, be said of stimulus and response?

Well, for a first attempt, let us notice that "stimulus" is not to be identified with "cause." The stimulus is decidedly not the adequate cause of the response. The response may reveal much more energy than was present in the stimulus. The same stimulus may, on different occasions, give rise to quite a variety of different responses. In these and other ways, the relation of stimulus and response is not the relation of cause and effect.

The stimulus may be said to be part of the response, the other partial causes being the structures of the organism, its stores of energy, and in general its condition at the time when the stimulus affects it. The stimulus is related to the response as the blow of the trigger is related to the motion of the bullet from the muzzle of the gun. The stimulus excites the response, but the energy and form of the response are determined by the organization of the individual.

So much, however, is an old story. Let us proceed to something less obvious and more open to debate. The organization of the individual is often conceived as built up of units which may be named reflex arcs, or reaction arcs. Such a unit is conceived as extending all the way from the receptor through the center to the effector. In terms of activity or behavior, letting S stand for stimulus and R for response, we say, according to this conception of reaction-arcs, that behavior is composed of S-R units. S is not to be considered apart from R, nor R apart from S, for S-R is a functional unit. These S-R units are harnessed both abreast and tandem, and thus integrated into complex modes of behavior. Native equipment consists of a stock of such units, and learning consists in the integration of these units into acts.

Though this conception has, and long has had, considerable vogue among psychologists, there are objections to it, which, in my opinion, are fatal. Evidence at hand appears to show that:

(1) No S-R unit is a unit in the full sense. There may be a few exceptions, such as the patellar reflex, where the R can be aroused only by one S. Other reflexes, however, are elicited by any one of a number of different stimuli. In the case of the pupillary reflex, the narrowing of the pupil is elicited either by increased illumination of the retina or by focusing of the eye upon a near object. Dilatation of the pupil is elicited by diminishing the light entering the eye, by turning the eyes from a near to a distant object, and by a variety of other stimuli, such as a sudden loud noise, a bitter taste in the mouth, a sudden touch on the skin, a sudden pain. Much the same is true of other reflexes. In Sherrington's terminology,[6] each reflex, such as the flexion reflex or the scratch reflex, has a "receptive field" of greater or less extent, by stimulating any part of which the reflex can be obtained. Instead, then, of thinking of S-R as a unit, we have to think of R alone as the real unit. This unit covers the activity of the peripheral motor organ and of the nerve center which directly controls it. Each R is accessible to several S's, more accessible to some than to others. Behavior is composed of R units, rather than of S-R units. Native behavior consists of an assortment of such R units, which can be elicited by a variety of stimuli, though not by any stimulus at random.

(2) Even when a given S-R combination is functioning fairly regularly as a unit, the fact of conditioned response shows that this S-R unit can be broken up, and a substitute S attached to the R. This fact, which would be impossible if S-R were a genuine unit, is perfectly in line with the conception of R as a unit, requiring some S to arouse it, but attached more or less loosely, more or less closely, to several S's, and capable of becoming more closely attached to an S with which it was only loosely attached at the outset. Integration of behavior units would be very difficult, if not impossible, to conceive, if S-R were a genuine unit, fixed and indissoluble, for then all new connections between the units would have to be

---

[6]Integrative Action of the Nervous System, New York, 1906.

established at the periphery (where it is very doubtful if new connections can be formed), while a modifiable center would be of no service whatever.

To reach a true picture of behavior, then, we should ideally start not with S but with R. Having made an inventory of the R's at the disposal of the organism, we should next inquire regarding the various S's by which each R could be aroused. We should note combinations of R's arousable as integrated totals by the same S, and also combinations of S's effective in arousing an R which perhaps is not readily aroused by any single S.

Responses are integrated when two or more of them become attached to the same stimulus, so as to be aroused in combination by this stimulus. Stimuli may perhaps be said to be integrated when two or more of them become attached to the same response. Stimulus-response "units" do not, as such, become integrated, since every integration involves the break-up of pre-existing "units" of this sort.

Finally, note should be taken of Thurstone's recent onslaught upon the "stimulus-response fallacy in psychology." Paraphrasing his argument, in the light also of earlier discussions by Dewey[7] and by Sherrington,[8] we may say, and with good reason, that very seldom does a stimulus find the organism in a completely resting, neutral and unpreoccupied state. Ordinarily, a stimulus breaks in upon some activity in progress, some "incomplete reaction," to use Thurstone's expression. This activity has a trend towards some goal, immediate or remote. We have, then, not first stimulus, then activity of the organism; but first an activity going on, next an intercurrent stimulus, and then the activity modified in response to the stimulus. The response to the intercurrent stimulus is determined as much by the pre-existing activity as by the particular stimulus of the moment. If the incomplete activity is very intense, as in the case of two dogs fighting, such a stimulus as the master calling or even jumping in with a stick to separate the dogs may have scarcely any effect. At other times, a very faint stimulus, anticipated and prepared for, has a pronounced effect.

The relations of stimulus and pre-existing incomplete activity are well illustrated in the process of reading. The reader

[7] The Reflex Arc Concept in Psychology, Psychol. Rev., 1896, 3:357.
[8] Integrative Action of the Nervous System.

is in the midst of a story, and eagerly reaching forward to learn what is coming next. The successive stimuli from the printed page are seized with lightning rapidity and utilized for just one purpose, from among the many responses which these stimuli are capable of arousing. The actual response is determined, we say, by the context as well as by the word seen at any instant. More precisely, the actual response to each successive word and phrase is determined by the activity set in motion by what has already been read, and tending forward in a definite direction. The successive word stimuli do not deflect this motion from its course, but are so responded to as to further the motion already in progress.

What has been said of reading could be said as well of hunger or sex activity or of fighting or flight from danger. Here the organism may be said to be in the throes of a need which is the controlling factor in the activity. Whether the concept of "need" is a useful dynamic concept is perhaps open to doubt; it smacks considerably of the sort of teleology that we do well to leave aside. In the actual process, what we call "need" is a prepotent activity, *i.e.,* an activity not readily deflected, moving forward without responding to stimuli disconnected with itself. What we see is an activity going forward in a definite direction and rendering the organism unresponsive to certain stimuli, while unusually responsive to others.

These considerations apply in the study of sensation and perception as well as in the study of motor activity. In the laboratory, when we wish to analyze behavior by isolating certain responses and tracing out their antecedents and consequents, we try to do away, as far as possible, with pre-existing incomplete activities, and get the subject into a neutral, or at least a receptive state. Then we apply known stimuli and note the responses. Instead, however, of thus simplifying and standardizing the pre-existing state of the organism to the maximum, we may choose to apply a given stimulus when a known activity is in progress. What we then get are "false reactions," "illusions," and the like, knowledge of which is equally valuable with the knowledge obtained under simplified conditions. But, evidently, a knowledge of responses, and their relations to stimuli, under the simplest conditions of pre-existing activity, furnishes a base line that is essential in any accurate survey of the whole field of activity; and thus it is that what we may call the "stimulus-response psychology," the most de-

tailed form of dynamic psychology, is of genuine and fundamental importance, in spite of the criticisms, revisions and
elaborations of its concepts contained in recent discussions,
and briefly presented in this lecture. The fact that such discussions occur is evidence of the significance of the concepts of
stimulus and response, and at the same time an indication that
"dynamic psychology" is a fair characterization of much, at
least, of the psychological enterprise of the present time.

PART III
Gestalt

KURT KOFFKA

CHAPTER VI

MENTAL DEVELOPMENT*

By Kurt Koffka

That mind develops, individually during any person's life, racially in the history of mankind, and phylogenetically in the evolutionary series of the animal kingdom, is today a truism. What we are interested in is *how* this development takes place. To give concrete substance to our discussion of this problem we shall make a survey of the different stages of mind by considering what mind is able to do. In this attempt we find no great difficulty in grouping our material. Restricting ourselves to the sphere of the vertebrates, we can roughly distinguish three types of behavior—using this word without any theoretical bias—and can exemplify these types by a number of instances:

Type I. (a). Sneezing and coughing; the reaction of the pupils of the eye to light; eye-movements of fixation.

(b). The suckling of the new-born infant; the pecking of a chick just broken from the egg; the building of nests; lastly the entire life of ants or bees.

Type II. The behavior of animals in certain kinds of experiments of the puzzle-box or maze-type, and in the tricks we see performed in vaudeville shows.

Type III. The behavior of chimpanzees as observed in the experiments of Dr. Köhler; or to select another instance out of an indefinite number, your behavior in attending this lecture or mine in preparing and delivering it. Our classification, whatever its theoretical bearing may be, is not entirely arbitrary; for psychology has named each of these three types. We call the first reflexive and instinctive activities, the second trained or drilled performances, and the third intelligent achievements. For brevity's sake I shall sometimes refer to them simply as reflexes and instincts, training, and intelligence.

These three types evidently represent different stages of mind and we may expand each of them so as to include all possible stages in our scheme. Then the problem of mental development reduces itself to the problem of the connection

---

*Powell Lecture in Psychological Theory at Clark University, April 29, 1925.

between these three behavior types: which is the original type of behavior and how have the others grown out of it? We can, for our purposes, discriminate two main theories of mental development, one being unitarian, and deriving all behavior from one fundamental type, that of the reflex (Ia), while the other is pluralistic and maintains an essential difference between the three types; the higher ones being, in the course of evolution, added to the lower ones.

Let us examine the first of these theories. It starts with the assumption that our behavior type Ia, the reflex, is the original type and it uses a very popular description and explanation of the reflex. Reflexes as very simple and comparatively regular responses to definite stimuli are explained by the hypothesis that they are the function of a very simple apparatus, the reflex arc, consisting of afferent and efferent neurones and the connection or bond between them, which in this way connects the situation and the response of the organism. Thus this conception of the bond is the starting point of this view of mental development. But it is more: It is the supreme principle by which this theory achieves an admirable simplicity. For according to this view every action of an organism is explicable in terms of such connections,—in other words, every action carried out by an organism is determined solely by the bonds or connections involved. The original connections, and consequently, the original reaction-tendencies go far beyond the realm of mere reflex action, embracing the entire so-called instinctive activity.

Now instinctive and even most of reflexive activity appears to be highly adjustive; the animal does what is good for it in its environment. But from the point of view of this theory this adaptiveness is not a property of these actions themselves, but is instead, a mere impression which they give to the onlooker. The actions are not determined in any way by the intrinsic nature of the situation, but altogether by these pre-existing bond-devices. The situation enters only as the agency which turns the key, presses the button, makes the machine go. But, like a real machine, the animal can only act according to the pre-established system of bonds, whether such an action be adequate to the circumstances or not.

The connection between situation and response is therefore purely contingent and consequently we do not know why a certain situation affects a certain pathway, we can only state that it does do so. We ought then to be able to change the response to a constant situation by merely changing the bonds involved in such a pathway.

What this really implies will become evident when we take up a few of our initial instances. The theory means that a chick newly escaped from the egg pecks at a grain, seizes and swallows it, not because this is the sensible response to this particular situation, but because its neurones are connected with each other in such ways as to secure these reactions in this sequence. If we were able to change these connections the animal would, for instance, first make the swallowing and then the pecking movement. Or, another example, taken from Watson's experiments on babies: If in a dark room we introduce a bright spot, the baby turns its eyes towards this spot and fixates it. It does so, merely because of its innate connections without regard to the situation, and again by shifting those connections we ought to be able to change this response in such a manner that, for instance, the baby would be made to look towards the left when the bright spot appears on the right. This experiment happens to have been performed, though, naturally, not with babies but with monkeys. Marina dissected the inner and outer muscles of the eyes of monkeys and connected them crossways. An impulse sent to contract the external muscle of the right eye ought now to result in a movement towards the left and *vice versa*. Consequently, in our experiment the monkey should react just as we have predicted; it should look to the left when a bright spot appears at the right. Speaking more generally all the monkey's eye-movements in the horizontal should have been the reverse of normal. In reality, however, nothing of the kind took place. As soon as the wounds healed the animal moved his eyes just as normally as it did before the operation. That means that in spite of the changes made in the devices, the movements continued to be performed so as to produce the same sort of achievement.

Thus the conception of a merely contingent connection between situation and response breaks down even at the reflex level. And we are left with the problem: how can a certain result, rather than a reformed system of devices, determine organic movements? Without the slightest leaning towards vitalism we shall have to face this problem. But before we do so, let us turn to the explanation of our second type of behavior, training, which according to this theory is the only way in which learning takes place.

It is the pride of this theory that it has been able to explain acquired behavior in the same terms which it employs for original behavior. This extension of the explanation is not so difficult as it may appear at first sight. The only assumption required is that in animals which are able to learn, the original bonds are not absolutely fixed but may be modified according to specific laws. What this means is best explained by an example taken from Thorndike's experiments. He puts a hungry cat into a cage, the door of which is shut but can be opened by turning a lever, and before the cage he places some enticing food. The first time in the cage the cat will make all sorts of movements which have nothing to do with the lever, but in the course of its aimless movements it may accidentally strike this lever, and by this action achieve its escape and the possession of the coveted food. In a later experiment, say the tenth or twentieth, the cat will turn the lever without any other movements, as soon as it has been placed in the cage. It therefore appears that the cat acquired a new reaction towards the old situation. But speaking strictly from the point of view of this theory, the effect of learning is rather of a negative than of a positive kind. For, according to this view, any one of the innumerable reactions which the animal made in the first experiment, was connected to this particular situation by bonds of neurones. We can not assume as a rule that a situation has only one set of bonds connecting it with one single response; instead we must believe that every single situation possesses a great number of different connections of varying strength and directness leading to very different reactions. The process of learning consists, then, merely in strengthening certain sets of bonds and weakening all the others. The chief laws by which this result is to be achieved are those of frequency, recency, and of effect. While the two first are readily understood, the law of effect requires a few words in explanation. It embraces the fact that it is the appropriate, the successful act that survives, and expresses this fact by saying that such connections as have led to *satisfaction* gain an advantage over such as have not done so.

Like original behavior, acquired behavior, then, is determined by devices, taking place over neurone-bonds which have undergone some change but which, this change once completed, are determinants of action just as exclusive as were the originally effective bonds. Consequently the relation between situation and response remains contingent, and all learning proceeds by chance. Again we ought to be able to change the reactions by shifting the connections, but if we do so, we get the negative result previously reported because the acquired activity continues unaltered. Of course the law of effect was meant to modify this point and to account for progress in mental development. But as it stands it fails to achieve this task, since in reality it is not a law of *effect,* but a law of *satisfaction* which is a very different matter, because the satisfaction is not the satisfaction of success, but something which follows success without having any meaningful connection with it. Thus, according to Thorndike's own teaching, when in the previously described experiment the cat has learned to turn the lever it does so, not because it understands what the turning of the lever means, but because this particular movement, belonging among the original responses to the situation of being confined,—in which situation the existence of the lever is absolutely immaterial,—has in many cases led to satisfaction by giving the animal freedom and food. For this reason the movement is stamped in, and this particular set of bonds between the initial situation and the particular movement is therefore strengthened to the detriment of other connections which at start were just as ready as this one. Just as the existence of the lever was immaterial for the production of the movement to turn it, so now this movement is immaterial to the pleasure derived from the tasting of the food. Chance made the movement with the lever and chance, in the arbitrarily contrived situation of the puzzle box, connects the striking of the lever with freedom and food. Thus this law of satisfaction is not a law of effect, for which reason it has been a sore point in the theory, even from the beginning. Satisfaction comes after the critical event, after the movement which it is assumed to stamp in; therefore it must have a retroactive force. It is not only difficult to explain how such a backward force can be exerted, but once retroaction is granted we have to state how far back this force will reach. Why should it extend precisely to the really relevant movement when the animal does not know that this movement is relevant?

More recent observations have shown that it is the effect and not the subsequent satisfaction which is the determining factor in learning. In Köhler's experiments one of the apes, after solving a particularly difficult problem in order to secure some bananas, did not interrupt this newly invented procedure to taste his booty, but continued to fish with his new tool to get all sorts of useless things after all the bananas had been collected.   Also in Kuo's experiment improvement of the achievement went on although the imperfect performance led to exactly the same ulterior satisfaction as did the improved act.   But if the effect and not the added satisfaction is relevant, we shall again have to discard the idea that the connection between situation and response is merely contingent.

And yet this concept of the merely contingent relation has dominated our whole psychology of experience for it has even a wider application than we have so far pointed out.   Bonds are not only formed between receptors and effectors, but also between ideas in the famous "associations."   Again an association connecting a perception with an idea, the sight of lightning with the expectation of thunder, would be purely contingent connection, based merely on the frequency of the concomitance of the events.   No other connection being recognized, this means that originally there can be no order in our perceptions—all order must come from experience as the chance repetition of contiguous events.   From this point of view all our rational concepts would seem to be illusory, because they imply more than contingent connections.   But even if that were so, there remains one fact unexplained: for how does this illusion arise?   Even if it be an illusion, it is at least a datum, an undeniable fact.

Just as the puzzle-box (and maze) experiments give experimental support to the first part of our theory, so the second rests upon very elaborate experiments on the learning of nonsense-syllables.   Both these types of investigation, however, involve highly artificial conditions.   In both cases the object of experimentation, the animal or the human observer, is confronted with a situation which is completely meaningless.   There is, for instance, nothing in the syllable *pum* that indicates that the syllable *dat* is to follow it.   In other words: no nonsense-syllable calls for its successor in the series.   And the same argument applies to the puzzle-box; it is so constructed as to surpass all possible understanding on the side of the animal, and therefore, though it may call for the expenditure of effort for freedom, it can call for no *specific* action to achieve this end.   This again is in contradiction to the theory from which we started and which maintains that by inherited devices each situation is connected with quite a number of specific reactions.

We have used the phrase: a situation calls for a reaction. What does this mean? When before the eyes of an animal we put food inside an open box the animal will enter the box and fetch out the food. This situation does, so we may say, call for a certain reaction. But is this not simply an instinctive reaction? If we grant this, what have we gained? If we have given up our understanding of instinct as a ready made set of neurone-bond devices, how does this name help us in understanding these factors? But does our term, "the situation calls for," do any more? With this question in mind let us glance at certain experiments in which the animal solved problems under natural conditions in a situation that revealed openly all the parts necessary to the required achievement. Tomorrow Professor Köhler will report at length upon his experiments to which I have just referred. Therefore I shall only mention here some very general features of his results. His chimpanzees solved their problems *not* by trial and error; the correct solution was not slowly and painfully selected out of a number of inexpedient movements, the correct activity began abruptly from a stage of deliberation, continued in an unbroken curve and took place always with regard to the relevant part of the situation. It was not a product of chance, neither were these actions instinctive. What then remains?

Shall we have recourse to the pluralistic theory mentioned in the beginning and assume that a new factor, the intellect, must be the cause? To do so would, on the one hand, be equal to a renunciation of a theory of development; on the other hand, it would not even be an explanation of the facts. To ascribe an action of our first type to instinct is no more an explanation than to attribute an action of the third type to intellect.

There remains but one other possibility: the situation forces the animal to act in a certain way, although the animal possesses no pre-established special devices for the act. How is this possible? I shall develop the answer to this fundamental question by the help of a concrete and well-known instance which has become precipitated into a proverb, *viz.,* the burnt child shuns the fire. Fortunately Dr. Watson has taken this change of behavior out of the sphere of mere armchair psychology by providing us with experimental evidence on the subject. His experiments, which he performed with an infant beginning the 150th day of his life, showed that at first the burnt child did not shun the fire at all, but would grasp for

it again and again although it came so near the flame that it
flexed its fingers and withdrew the hand. The change seems
to have come very suddenly. On the 220th day the child, instead of grasping for the flame, slapped at the candle and
afterwards reached for it but a single time. How can we
understand this transformation in the response? To state that
the stimulus, candle, is originally connected with several responses, among them being those of grasping and of slapping,
and that the first of these became weakened by dissatisfaction, is quite inadequate. The suddenness of the change and
the new reaction which superseded the old one are left entirely without an explanation. In other words: why did this
fortunate infant, instead of simply shunning the fire, slap at
it?

If we use common-sense psychology we would say: the infant slaps the candle, because he has learned to dislike it, just
as he grasped for it at first because it looked so attractive to
him. This common-sense explanation is essentially different
from the behavioristic explanation in one point: it connects
the action not with the stimulus but with the perception of the
stimulus, and the change of reaction with a change in the perception. An attractive object calls for one kind of behavior,
a repulsive object for another. Thus we meet again our initial
problem: a situation calls for something. And now we see
that the situation does call for, if at all, not as a stimulus,
but as a perceived, phenomenal situation. We see further that
the relation between stimulus and phenomenal situation is not
univocal: because the same stimulus may evoke different perceptions. Since this fact is abundantly confirmed by scientific
experimental psychology it would seem as though we could
afford to accept our common-sense explanation. Couched in
scientific terms, it would run like this: Our direct responses
to stimuli are receptor processes which in many cases will be
on the mental, perceptive level: such a direct response is, however, only the beginning of the total response: the perception
issues in action according to its constitution, the action is a
natural continuation of the perceptive process and is determined by it and not by pre-established connection-bonds.
Change of response to a constant stimulus does not take place
by alternation in the function of ready-made devices, but is a
result of a change in the perceptive process produced by the
stimulus. Lastly: a stimulus upsets an equilibrium on the receptive side of the system; this upset equilibrium results in

a movement which tends to bring the system to a new equilibrium and consequently the reaction must vary with the way in which the equilibrium was disturbed, that is with the receptor process, with the phenomenal situation.

From this follow several important inferences: (1) responses of our first type, reflexes and instincts, can not be explained ultimately by the reflex arc. The organism has at birth a constitution such that some stimuli will upset the equilibrium in one direction, others in other directions: some situations will be attractive, others repulsive. To confine ourselves for the moment to this difference, from attractive situations will result positive, approach reactions; from repulsive situations, negative, avoidance responses. (2) Learning consists in many cases primarily in a change of the perceptive process. It can, therefore, no longer be considered as an association, the mere tying together of two contingently contiguous ideas, or the selection of pre-established pathways by trial and error. This means that the perceptive process has its own constitution, shape, patterns; we must ask not only, and not even primarily, where, in which neurones or brain cells, does perception occur; but chiefly: how does it occur and what is it like? When learning takes place, when such a process changes, we must ask: what sort of a change is this? Learning, then, is not merely a matter of memory, because before a process can be remembered, it must have occurred, and therefore in all learning we have to distinguish between two problems: (a) how is a process remembered and how is it forgotten? This problem of memory is the one problem to which the theories previously discussed have reduced all learning, by explaining it in terms of association or selection. (b) How is the process, which is to be remembered achieved for the first time? This problem of achievement is really the more important of the two. It brings us back to our question: How can the situation force the animal to do something which it has never done before? This is really the problem of achievement.

(3) We also find an answer to a question raised in our first discussion of the reflexes, viz., how a certain result rather than a system of devices can determine organic movements and how it can call for a certain achievement. We see now that there is no mysticism, no vitalism involved in this. If we consider every response as the result of a disturbed equilibrium we can predict that such a response will be in the di-

rection of a new equilibrium, since every process in nature must comply with this law. Our task is to establish the fact of the equilibria of an organic system, and the causes by which as well as the direction in which this equilibrium may be upset.

The problem of mental development now takes on an entirely new aspect. Instead of considering such development as a change in connections or associations we have to view it as a transformation of processes. Our next task will therefore be to describe the nature of the original processes and of their various forms of transformation. This will finally lead us back to the causal problem: how the situation can enforce these changes.

Our first two questions will be approached *pari passu*. The discussion of the change that takes place will also reveal the original properties that undergo change. Let us return then to our burnt child example. The transformation that took place in this case may be called one of *meaning*: the attractive candle became repulsive. By calling this change a change of meaning we designate the fact that the perception of the candle points beyond itself in one of two directions. Originally the flame was attractive, that is, it appeared to the child as an object *towards* which something had to be done; afterwards it became repulsive, that is, it appeared as an object *against* which action should be taken. In both cases the perception had the character of incompleteness, and a change has taken place in the specific nature of this gap. In other words: experience, in this case, does not create meaning, but *transforms* meaning; which implies that meaning itself is not a product of experience — mental development does not lead from the meaningless to the meaningful, but from one kind of meaning to another kind of meaning. Mind without a meaning we should never expect to encounter.

It would transcend the limits of this lecture, were I to attempt to confirm this result by showing how, on the one hand, it is borne out by the facts of child psychology, and how, on the other hand, a purely empiristic explanation of meaning leads to a vicious circle. But in as much as my whole argument seems to rely on this one experiment of Watson's, I may recall a much older observation made by Lloyd Morgan which is in all essentials similar to the instance from which we started. If we substitute for the child a chick and for the candle a cinnabar caterpillar which is conspicuous by its im-

pressive black and yellow rings and apparently distasteful to
the chick, we shall find a close analogy in the two instances of
behavior. The chick at first pecks at the caterpillar as it will
at any other object of appropriate size, after which it drops
its victim with signs of disgust. Since very often this transformation takes place after the first experience and without
the need of repetition, the next time this chick catches sight
of such a caterpillar it will run away with signs of fright
sounding the danger note. Lest my opponents should try to
take the edge off my argument, and reproach me with anthropomorphism by contending that I have no earthly right to
ascribe either desire or disgust and fright to a chick, I will
discuss the same fact with another set of concepts. Let us
dismiss the *mind* of the chick altogether. What we must retain, however, are the receptor-processes which are aroused in
his system by the action of the caterpillar on his sense organs
and which, according to the explanation we have established,
are the direct causes of the movements that constitute the
overt behavior of the animal. We should then have to say
that at first a receptor-process in the visual organ of the chick
is of such a nature that it issues in approach, whereas after
the first pecking it issues in flight. In both cases the receptor-
process was incomplete, as it continued into motor processes,
and but the *kind* of incompleteness differed in the two cases.
It seems therefore a natural and legitimate generalization if
we apply our concept of meaning to these receptor-processes,
quite apart from mind; meaning has then a very objective
signification. And yet our explanation in the new terms is essentially the same as what it was in the old terms, where learning consists in a transformation of meaning. I need only to
indicate that just as the concept of meaning can be transferred
from mental to neural behavior, so can the other concepts we
have employed such as desire, disgust, fright, and ever so many
others. This again means that the taunt of anthropomorphism
has not hurt us. Furthermore it may be noted that both our
examples are usually reckoned among achievements of training.

Returning now to the burnt child, this example has made us
acquainted with the process of change of meaning. We have
not yet exhausted this example for now we can raise the
question of how this transformation came about. Why had so
many repetitions of the experiment no effect and why did the
result appear so suddenly when it did come? Again our an-

swer is given in terms of a description of the event. What happens all along in the child's mind?—or, if you prefer to ignore the existence of the mind, use instead the concepts we have just introduced in the case. of the chick. At first the infant sees the attractive flame and reacts correspondingly; then the child feels pain and withdraws the hand. According to the theory of association and the law of dissatisfaction—which is the reverse of the law of satisfaction—this occurrence ought to be sufficient to establish in a very short time in the child's mind or in its organism an association between the sight of the flame and the withdrawing of the hand. But to all appearances it does not do so. As long as the occurrences in the child's mind are not changed, no transformation of the response will take place, because the flame remains desirable. Only when the pain comes, not merely after reaching for the flame, but from the flame itself, can a transformation take place. Now the flame itself thwarts the wish of the child, it ceases to be an attractive and becomes a repulsive object. This transformation of meaning is therefore the consequence of another process of change. Flame and pain were at first two different things: one plus one. Afterwards they grow together and become a unit. The two have ceased to be two and have become one.

Here we find another process of transformation which we may well call unification. Another example of simple unification is furnished by an experiment performed by Bühler, with a method developed in animal psychology, upon his own child. A piece of rusk was placed slightly out of the infant's reach, with a string attached to it which came within reaching distance. Before the end of the 10th month, the child was not able to secure the rusk by means of the string. While vainly reaching for the rusk it would push the string aside. String and rusk were two different objects calling for different reactions. Later on, when the child pulls the string and secures the rusk, string and rusk are no longer one plus one, but now form a unity in which the string is a subservient part. This achievement has been ascribed not to training but to intelligence. Change of meaning gave us the clue that meaning was an original property of the receptor processes. Can we take a similar clue from the process of unification? Or is unity of a manifold always the product of experience?

Comparative and experimental psychology have provided us with abundant material for the proof that unitariness is likewise an original property of perception. Instead of spreading out this material I shall approach the question from another angle by demonstrating a third kind of transformation: Just as two may become one, so may one become two. Dr. Köhler's ape experiments contain many pregnant examples of this. But as he will report upon them himself, I shall indicate an entirely different field of mental activity in which this kind of transformation, which we, appropriately, call analysis, has taken place. I refer to the field of magic and its relic superstition. To destroy the original unity between a presage and the happy or unhappy event that followed it: to dissect this originally coherent unit, whose coherence was like that of the tones of a melody, meant a progress in cognition. How difficult it may be to take two for two and not for parts of one, is shown by the many forms of superstition that still lead a vigorous life all about us. That analysis is a difficult process, even more so than unification, was also a result of Köhler's experiments. This is another indication that the unity of the manifold as such is not a product of experience, since the effect of experience is that of breaking up such units.

It should be stated that our unit is not the mental element of the association psychology, because being the unit of a manifold, it deserves to be called a whole. Inside of such wholes there occurs a new type of change which may be called articulation. Again Köhler's experiments contain splendid specimens of such processes. To appeal to your own experience: Just recall the change that takes place in your idea of a new city or a part of the country during the first weeks of your stay there. The originally more or less chaotic field gets more and more organized, certain main directions develop, a few chief points determining the rest are singled out, and accordingly your behavior in the new surrounding changes. Can we infer that articulateness is original or is it altogether a product of experience? Again our answer must be that some kinds and degrees of articulation must be inherent in the original responses, for without this there would be complete chaos, in which none of the other properties could exist. Mere chaos can neither be meaningful or unitary. To cut a long story short, we find at the beginning, in our most elementary reactions, even at the level of the reflexes and instincts and again in training and in intelligent performances, unitary, articulate, meaningful wholes; to which we apply the name of Gestalt, configuration, structure. Development starts, not with chaos or with a multitude of mental elements without order or meaning, but with structures, however primitive their character may be.   Development proceeds by transformation of such structures.   Gradually, by a number of smaller or larger leaps and bounds, we achieve different orders, different articulations, different meanings.   I have just tried to sketch a few of the main processes which occur in this development in very general outline.   The picture has to be completed.   We must apply our general principles to concrete cases, we must study the different achievements in this genetic sequence, and must learn to understand how one achievement facilitates or even makes possible another achievement.   This task, though its actual execution is just in the beginning, falls outside the scope of this lecture.   One problem, however, I must take up: What is the cause of these transformations?   Our answer, naturally, can only be very general.   Wherever change occurs the phenomenal situation aroused by the real situation is incomplete, unstable.   It tends to become stabilized.   But whether it can become so depends upon the kind of situation and upon the individual organism.   We call an organism that succeeds in filling the gap clever, and one that does not stupid, but it is obvious that these terms are always relative to the situations; for there are many situations in which all of us are utterly stupid.

The last reason then for all these changes lies in the original processes themselves.   All processes not stationary exert pressure upon the system to become stable; if the system can yield to this pressure, then the result is achieved.

We can express these facts in still another way: Wertheimer was the first to state a law, which has served as a good guide in our experimental research and which has been given theoretical support by Köhler.   This law, the law of precision, maintains that any configuration will become as perfect as the prevailing conditions admit.   Vague as it seems in this formulation, it has a definite meaning in several concrete instances and will become more and more defined the further psychology progresses.   In the closing words of this lecture I shall indicate an application of this law and thereby supplement in a casual way the picture I have drawn of mental development.

So far I have been almost exclusively concerned with what may be called intellectual achievements.   But what of the moral side of mind; what of a man's character and personality?   Must these escape our scheme of development?   I think not. The behavior of an organism shapes configuration also in time. Not only the simultaneous but the successive is also structured. The larger these wholes and the greater their unity, articulation and meaning, the more perfect is their gestalt, the more personality will they express.

Is the theory so sketchily drawn before your eyes unitarian or pluralistic? It is pluralistic in as much as it embraces an indefinite number of different structures and many forms of configurative changes; but it is not pluralistic in the sense of assuming a number of separate faculties like those of reflexes or instincts, training and intelligence. It is unitarian, not in reducing every process to the mechanism of neural bonds or associations, but in its attempt to give ultimately an explanation of development by means of the universal law of Gestalt.

Wolfgang Köhler

CHAPTER VII

INTELLIGENCE IN APES*

By Wolfgang Köhler

The following pages contain the description of some types of anthropoid behavior and a few remarks intended to make us better realize what problems are given in those cases. That animal psychology has to be a science of behavior and that the introduction of animal consciousness as an acting factor in problems and explanations would only lead into confusion is my opinion as it is the axiom of behaviorism in this country. If, notwithstanding that, I frequently use terms which may suggest the heresy of assuming consciousness, the reason for it and my innocence will become apparent with time. I can *not* agree with Watson in his method of condemning all difficult-looking problems in the nervous system as pure mysticism and after effects of the introspection time. That gives a simple science with only a few concepts; but a good deal of the world of behavior and its problems does not occur in this science. I therefore make a difference between a dogmatic behaviorism which narrows its own world of realities, problems and theoretical possibilities as if knowing beforehand what kind of things can occur in an exact world,—and another behaviorism which wants to see as many forms of behavior, problems and theoretical possibilities as possible, deeply convinced that even his amplest view of the world will probably come far short of the wealth of phenomena themselves. I prefer the second.

If we observe the faces of anthropoid apes, of monkeys and of dogs, quite naively, we get the impression that those faces show very different degrees of "understanding" or "insight." Observation of the animals in action and experimentation on them prove that our expectation was justified, at least with regard to the high place we would tend to give to the apes.

Let us take as an example Hunter's method of delayed reaction[1] which I shall describe in a simplified form for our purposes. If one of the higher vertebrates sees in front of himself three open doors and in one of them food, he will, if he is hungry and the circumstances allow it, move in the direction

*Powell Lecture in Psychological Theory at Clark University, April 30, 1925.
[1]Behavior Monographs II, 1, 1913.

11

of this food and eat it. If in different cases different doors are used as "doors with food" the reaction will, of course, change its direction correspondingly. To choose the right door becomes more difficult, however, if the animal remains enclosed in a box at the time the food is presented to him in one of the doors, so that he can see the food through this obstacle but is released only after the food has disappeared in the box behind the door. Animals below the monkeys find great difficulties with this task. Even if the interval of delay between exposure of the food and reaction is of some seconds or a minute only, the after effect of the past perception (in human language: "It was *that* door!") seems to become confused, and in some cases one cannot be quite sure whether an after effect of this kind does exist at all or whether positive results are produced by quite a crude and low form of behavior.[2]

In experimenting with chimpanzees, I used a somewhat different method. The ape was sitting behind the bars of his cage. On the other side of these bars I made a hole in the ground, put some fruit in it, and covered the hole and the surroundings with sand. The ape, who with great interest had observed what I did, could not reach the place of the food because it was too far away for his arm; but when I was careless enough to come too near his cage he immediately seized my arm and tried to push it in the direction of the hidden food, as he would do whenever he could not find a method of approach towards his food himself. Of course this was already a delayed reaction. But as I wanted a larger delay I did not do him the favor, and the ape began soon to play in his room apparently not giving any attention to the place of the food. After three quarters of an hour a stick was thrown into his cage from the side farthest from the fruit. The ape accustomed to the use of sticks as instruments, instantly took it, went to the bars nearest the place of the food, began to scratch away the sand exactly in the right spot, and pulled the fruit toward him. Repetitions of the experiment with other positions of the food had the same result.

Since the reaction was always surprisingly correct I made the interval of delay much greater. I let the apes see how

---

[2] With animals of a highly developed olfactory sense the utmost care is needed in order to avoid olfactory cues at the time of reaction. However, in the case of anthropoid apes this danger is not very serious, since their olfactory senses is, as one may easily prove, more or less at a level with our own.

I buried the food somewhere in the earth of the very large playground and brought them, immediately afterwards, into their sleeping room so that they went on the playground not before the following day when more than seventeen hours had elapsed, more than half of them spent sleeping. One of the apes, when leaving the sleeping room, did not hesitate a moment but went straight to the place of the food and found it there after some searching.[3]

In another experiment a stick was hidden in the wooden framework of the roof, where the apes could not see it from the ground. Again they observed with great interest our unusual action. But we at once brought them into their dormitory. The next morning, when one of them came back into the same room, he discovered some bananas on the ground outside the cage and too far away for his arm. As apes, accustomed to the use of sticks, do under these circumstances, he looked around in exactly the way of a man seeking something, but could not find such a tool. After some seconds, however, his eyes went up to the place where the stick was hidden the evening before. He could not see it, but he climbed at once in the shortest possible way up to that part of the ceiling where the stick was hidden, came down with it, and scratched the food towards him. I repeated the experiment with all the chimpanzees who had seen how we put the stick in its place in the roof. They all independently solved the problem in the same manner.

"Memory" works in two different ways at least. Many animals and men learn to react to a given situation in a specified manner, i.e., they develop habits. There are great differences in the speed of learning, in the number of different situations for which a reaction may be learned, and in the complexity of reactions which are learned. But even the earthworm shows "memory" of this general type by acquiring a very simple habit of moving in a definite spatial form. In the second type of memory something more seems to be required: An important part of a situation is not actually pres-

---

[3]One might say that the place of the food attracted the ape not because he knew there was food but because, in consequence of my digging, this place looked unusual and was only therefore attractive to the ape. It did not look unusual to my eyes as I had covered the whole region with dry sand. However, to meet this criticism better I made several holes in the ground after the apes were enclosed in the house and filled them afterwards in the same manner as the right hole. But the ape went to the right one.

ent in perception, but it was seen somewhere at another time, and its existence may be taken account of in the response, if that knowledge is still active or becomes active in the given situation. Where we have memory of this kind it makes the life and behavior of an animal look incomparably larger and freer than all habit formation can do. But there is not much evidence of it in most animals, and I do not know if even monkeys would show such a surprising behavior as I found in the chimpanzees.[4]

But perhaps these experiments do not examine intelligence in the strict meaning of the word. Therefore I describe another type of behavior which may have more to do with intelligence proper. You must know one of the usual forms of experimentation with animals. The subject is confronted with two or more objects and learns to choose one of them, depending upon its position in space or its color or some other discriminating quality. This effect is produced by rewarding the animal each time it chooses the right object and perhaps punishing it whenever it chooses the wrong one. Learning of this kind is usually a slow process without any indication of higher processes being involved. The curve of learning which shows how the number of wrong choices decreases with time has an irregular but gradually descending form. One might expect an ape to solve simple tasks of this type in shorter time. But that is not always the case. Often the period of learning in anthropoids is at least as long as with lower animals. However, the *form* of learning is sometimes quite different from what is found in the case of lower vertebrates.

When Yerkes made experiments of the general type described[5] with an orang-utan, this ape did not make any real

---

[4] "Delayed reaction" in animals lower than apes has seemed to some degree explainable by the fact that the animal. when the original stimulus (for instance, the food) is shown, quite naturally turns in the corresponding direction, and that it often remains in this bodily orientation by a kind of simple inertia after the stimulus is withdrawn, whereupon very probably it will go on in this right direction after release, if no other incentive makes it turn to the left or to the right. Of course, the chimpanzees did not remain in the right orientation, neither in three quarters of an hour nor in seventeen hours. Their delayed reaction cannot be explained so simply. To be sure, many cases of delayed reaction in lower animals cannot either.

[5] It does not matter for our present discussion that the experiments were dealing with "multiple choice" instead of the simpler sensory discrimination.

progress at all for a long time, whereas some animals much lower in rank solved the same problem without great difficulty. But finally, when the experimenter had almost lost hope of making the orang solve his task, the ape after one right choice suddenly mastered the problem completely, *i.e.*, never again made a mistake.   He had solved the problem in one lucky moment, his curve of learning showing an altogether abrupt descent.[6]   Some of my experiences on the learning process in chimpanzees are very similar to this observation of Yerkes. Sometimes the same surprising fact is found in children, and one can hardly avoid the impression that this ape behaves like a man under similar circumstances who, after a while, in a certain individual experiment, would grasp the principle of the problem and say to himself, "Oh, that's the point! Always the dark object!"; of course with the consequence that he, too, would never make a mistake again.

We do not well describe experiments of this type by saying, as we usually do, that an animal in such a situation learns to connect certain stimuli with certain reactions and that this connection is "stamped in."   This formulation of the process gives too much importance to the memory or association side of the problem, and it neglects another side of it which may be even more important and more difficult.

Although so much has been said against "anthropomorphism" in animal psychology, we have here a persisting case of this error, committed not by dilettants but by very eminent men of science.   The experimenter is interested in a problem of sensory discrimination and builds an appropriate apparatus which shall present "the stimuli" to the animal in question. When he looks upon the situation which he has created himself, this situation is completely organized for him, "the stimuli" being the outstanding features of it, and all the rest forming an unimportant background.   Consequently he formulates the animal's task as one of connecting "these stimuli" with certain reactions, reward and punishment enforcing this connection.   But he is not aware of the fact that now he has credited the animal with the same organized situation which exists for himself, the experimenter, in consequence of his scientific aim and problem.   Certainly the experimenter sees the stimuli as dominating the situation whenever he looks upon it.   But why should the same organization exist in the sensory situation of the innocent animal?   Experience shows that an

---

[6]Behavior Monographs III, 1. 1916.

objective situation may appear in very different organizations. Formation of groups and forms in the field is the natural outcome of many constellations of stimuli. Some part of the field may also have an accent, or be dominating, spontaneously. However, under the influence of interests, of previous experiences, etc., this original organization tends to change into new ones. We have not yet studied these processes in the case of animals, but one thing appears evident from the first moment: It is altogether improbable that an animal, when confronted with a new situation of discrimination experiments, should at the outset have the same organization of the field which exists in the experimenter's thought and perception.

Perhaps in this respect the animal's perception of the field is much more different from that of the experimenter than a young student's first perception of brain tissue in the microscope is different from that of the trained neurologist. This student cannot react immediately, and in a definite way, to the differences in the structure of tissues which dominate in the professor's microscopic field, because the student does not yet *see* the field in this organization. Even so, the student at least knows that in this situation his actual experiences of temperature, touch, muscular sense, noises, smells, and the optical world outside the microscopic field shall be without any importance. Nothing of this eliminating knowledge is given to the animal, who is put in an apparatus and there shall learn "to connect the stimuli with the reactions," but who really is subjected to a *world* of sensory data in the surroundings and in himself. Whatever the first organization of these data may be it cannot possibly correspond to the very special organization which the experimenter sees. Therefore the question arises as one of the greatest importance: What role does the actual manner in which the situation appears to the animal play in his reactions and in the learning process? And further, is learning going on independently of this factor and of possible changes in the organization of the field? Or is reorganization, which would make "the stimuli" outstanding features in the field, perhaps an important part of the problem? In this case, does the animal need so many trials as it really receives for the building up of a connection of stimuli and reaction, or does he need those trials for the right organization of the field, so that eventually there *is* the right thing to undergo the right connection? Finally, does the stress of reward and punishment exert any influence in the direction of such a reorganization? If not, how else is the reorganization produced?

As yet we cannot answer these questions, so far as the lower vertebrates are concerned.   But the observations of Yerkes and my own make it rather probable that in anthropoid apes at least the same thing may occur under favorable conditions that is so common in man: After some experience in a new situation he has to deal with, a sudden change into a reorganization appropriate to the task, with the accents on the right places.   We may even suspect that afterwards not very much time is needed for a connection between the now outstanding stimuli and the reaction, if ever there was a real separation of the two tasks.   Animals often learn so surprisingly fast under the natural conditions of their life, when an object *they are already attending to* shows "good" or "bad" properties.

If there is something in these remarks, we may be compelled to make a revision of our theories of learning. But certainly not without new experience! Because, though we already know something about organization and reorganization of sensory fields in man, we know hardly anything about it in animals; and therefore I propose to experiment about it. We have methods for it. Even so, however, we may at least venture one simple hypothesis; namely, that in animals, as in man, the manner of presentation of the stimuli in a field will have a strong influence on the forthcoming organization. A practical consequence of this hypothesis is that we should be able to help the animals very much in their learning by presenting the stimuli in such a form and in such surroundings and general conditions that they tend to become the dominating factors of the situation spontaneously. (It is not the place here to explain how that may be done.)

But the situation consists of more than the sensory field only. There is reward and punishment in it; and in the animal, as their consequence, there is presumably something like physiological stress as the working motor of the reorganization and learning. We speak of them as of separate things, but it is reward, punishment and stress *in the reaction to the field* which seems to bring about reorganization and learning. It might be, therefore, that a more intimate connection of stimuli and reward or punishment will shorten the period of learning considerably. The electric shock, for instance, applied to the legs, is not intimately connected with the task of getting a red spot as "the negative stimulus." There is only a very loose connection between them in space and time. If that spot *itself* would make a sudden movement against the animal and so frighten it whenever it goes the wrong way, we should certainly have a situation much nearer the animal's learning in common life and a more efficient one because the negative stimulus is directly made outstanding thereby and at the same time immediately imbues itself with "negativity."

With chimpanzees I went further. Clever apes can even be "taught." By all possible means you may draw their attention to the color of two boxes (or their difference) and you may show at the same time that inside the box of one color there is nothing; whereas behind the walls of the other color there is a banana. Whenever I proceeded so, forgetting the rule that an experimenter shall not play any direct role in experiments with animals, a striking increase of right choices used to be the immediate effect. And why not forget that rule, provided our principal intention in the actual experiment is not the study of the most clumsy form of learning but to make the chimpanzee master his problem as fast as possible? We teach our children this way, and only a bad teacher would not be able to verify afterwards if the result of learning is independent of himself. Nothing easier than to find out in a chimpanzee if afterwards the result is genuine or depends upon a wrong cue (the experimenter).[7]

Since it seems to me of some importance for our science that animal psychologists acknowledge these new problems in the general field of learning, I wish to defend myself against one reproach. Do not these problems exist only if we introduce the consciousness of animals? So many of the expressions used in the description of experiments and in the exposition of the problems seem to involve the assumption of consciousness. If that is so, the orthodox behaviorist will jump back and solemnly declare that he has nothing whatever to do with those rather mystical organizations and reorganizations of the field or the situation and that as a man of natural science he will go on formulating his problems in terms of stimuli and reactions.

My answer is that none of my expressions was meant to imply consciousness. Nobody can describe the behavior of

---

[7] In a new method which we found working well with apes, we eventually eliminated from the study of the sensory field all learning by chance reactions. (Psychol. Forschung I, 390. 1922.)

higher animals in its rich and concrete reality without using
terms which are ambiguous in so far as they mean behavior but
may at the same time imply consciousness. I always use them
in the first meaning. Let us take an example: "The ape observed with great interest what I did." Can an ape "observe,"
can an ape have "interest" without having consciousness? Can
I state that his "observation" was directed upon my actions
without assuming consciousness in the ape? I do not know
whether in those cases the ape has consciousness or not. And
I can go on without knowing it, because "to observe a thing"
is a term which in everyday life, too, has a perfectly objective
meaning, a certain visible and very characteristic behavior towards something being called so. I deny absolutely that we
always or even often mean consciousness or think about consciousness of the people when we see the chemist, the policeman, etc., "observe" a chemical reaction, a suspicious car, etc.
It is the same thing with "interest." A man or a chimpanzee
looks "interested." A visible and again a highly characteristic
attitude is meant in most of the cases where we use this word.

But why not use terms which are free from all ambiguities
and can only suggest objective attitudes and forms of behavior? Because we have no terms of this kind. Or, if
there are some, they are not manifold and nuanced enough to
suggest to readers all the many attitudes and forms of behavior which are seen in the higher animals or man. To describe the contraction of all the muscles which are employed
when the chemist, the policeman, or a chimpanzee look "interested" would be beyond my forces. And, by the way, nobody would understand me, unless I added the remark: "You
know, I mean those movements which, as a whole, produce
the interested attitude," and there we would be again!— On
the other hand, if once for all the meaning of those terms is
restricted to behavior, where is the danger in using them?
And if we should decide never to use them, one consequence
would be unavoidable: Our description of behavior would
become extremely poor, not more than a meager rest of the
concrete world of behavior would be accepted in our science;
and our theoretical concepts would very soon be exactly as
poor and meager as our material.

However, this defense holds for the description of behavior
only. The behaviorist would at once point out that in explaining the alleged problem of organization I have mentioned
the animal's perception of the field and laid much stress on

the organization in which the field appears to the animal. But I must answer again that for my use of these words it has no importance whether or not the animal has consciousness. Only two assumptions are contained in these formulations. The *first* is that in the higher animals some parts of the central nervous system are the place of sensory processes, corresponding to the stimulation from without, just as certain fields of the brain in man are shown by an overwhelming evidence from pathology to be the stage of sensory processes. And I use the words "perception of the situation" when I mean the totality of these processes.   One would be condemned to clumsy and boresome forms of speech if convenient terms of this kind were forbidden by the puritans of behaviorism.—The *second* assumption, which introduces the physiological side of "Gestalt" psychology (as applied to the sensory field), is a working hypothesis about a general property of those sensory processes.   Even the behaviorist who formulates his problems in terms of stimuli and reactions must assume that something happens between the former and the latter in the central nervous system.   He tends to deny that any *specific* problems are to be solved in this region, between sense organs and reacting organs.   But this also is an hypothesis and a rather vague one, to be sure.   One problem at least must be accepted as such.   We have conductors between the sense organ, the eye, for instance, and the reacting organs; and these conductors lead from one to the other as a kind of dense network.   Either I assume that from one point of the retina one conductor goes absolutely isolated to one reacting organ, a second conductor from another point of the eye again isolated goes to the same or to another reacting organ, and so on.   In this case there is really not much to ask about the intermediate region.   Or, I realize that the network is not very apt to be a sum of totally isolated conductors.   And in this case I must admit that the simplest rules of physics are to be applied to the network, the processes in one conductor becoming functionally dependent on the processes in all the others, and vice versa.   "Conduction" between the sense organ and the reacting organs means now a problem of specific process distribution, in its most general aspects similar to problems of process distribution in physics.   And the effect on the reacting organs, and therefore on behavior, will directly depend on this process distribution.   It is this dynamic distribution to which I am alluding when I speak about organization of the sensory processes. And I cannot see that so conceived this term means anything mysterious; though the main thing about it is to discover the concrete properties of the distribution of which we know but little. Of course this organization depends upon the stimulation, but certainly not in the manner it would depend upon it if all conductors were isolated from each other. And to say that a study of behavior must be the investigation of reactions as dependent upon "the stimuli" turns out now to be a somewhat confused program, very apt to hide this fundamental problem altogether: How do the sensory processes depend on a given set of stimuli? How, therefore, the organization of the field, and how the reactions? We shall speak about it later on.

One may consider as a third assumption (though it is a necessary one) that the distribution or organization of sensory processes shall not depend upon the constellation of stimuli only but on the total interior situation in the animal, too, so that influences like hunger, fear, rage, fatigue and organization in earlier experience can produce changes in a given distribution. But in this respect the behaviorist, if once he admits the problem of organization at all, would certainly have the same opinion.[8]

More than one psychologist would say that an animal who (like Yerkes' orang) suddenly "grasps" the principle of a situation in learning experiments thereby shows a genuine type of intelligent behavior. But we can apply another test of perhaps more significance. An example frequently to be observed in the classroom will show you what I mean.

I try to explain to my students a somewhat difficult demonstration of a mathematical theory, putting all my sentences together with the utmost care in the right sequence and with all possible clearness. I shall probably not have much success in my first performance. Something remains dull in the faces of my audience. So I repeat what I have said, and perhaps in the course of the third repetition one face here, another there, will suddenly undergo a marked change toward "brightness." Soon afterwards I may call the owner of one of those changed faces to the blackboard, and he will be able to give

---

[8] I shall not deny that the emphasis I lay upon this problem is largely determined by observations on man, even by observation of what I see. But why not? Most of the best work done in animal psychology was suggested by experiences in man. So the experiments in color discrimination, on the Purkinje phenomenon, on contrast, on the effect of distribution in learning, etc.

the demonstration himself,—we might say, to imitate what I performed before. Something has happened between the sentences of the demonstration in this clever student's mind, something important enough to become immediately visible in the change of his outer aspect and to make a new performance possible.

If we try to apply this experience to experimentation with apes we can't, of course, make use of speech, in giving the model, and instead of mathematics, too, we have to choose another kind of problem. What is the effect on an ape if he sees another ape or a human being perform a certain action which, if imitated by the ape, would be of the greatest advantage for him? Here perhaps the objection may be raised that an ape imitating what he sees done by others does not at all show intelligence. Are not monkeys and apes endowed with a special instinct to imitate almost all acts which they see performed in their neighborhood? If, then, they do it under experimental conditions, too, what can we conclude?

But in this case the widespread opinion is an absolutely wrong one, and the idea or the belief that monkeys and apes are constantly imitating the behavior of others seems to have the following origin. Monkeys and apes make a strong impression on us by some striking similarity between their behavior and the behavior of man. Don't they use their hands in the same manner as human beings? Don't their faces show similar "expressions" to those of man in many states of emotion? All this is easily explained, if the primates find a special pleasure in copying, or are mechanically compelled to copy the attitudes and the behavior of man. However, monkeys and apes who are caught somewhere in the woods of Central Africa or Asia show the same similarity with man's behavior from the first moment, before any experiences with the behavior of human beings could begin to have such an influence. The similarity with man is a natural one and does not prove at all the working of a strong "instinct of imitation."

In fact, there is not such an instinct. Imitation is almost as difficult for apes and as rare in them as it is in lower vertebrates. One does observe imitation of different forms or types in apes, but not so very often, and only after certain conditions are fulfilled. One first type of imitation which I saw with surprise in chimpanzees is very well known from observation in children. When the workman has been in our house and the children have, of course, observed with greatest interest what he was doing, we may see, on the same or the following day, how the children with the help of some objects, a book, a stone, or a wooden board, are copying what seemed to them essential in the performance of the man, in sawing, nailing or boring. Let me call this behavior of children a "serious play." It *is* a play, but it is serious at the same time, as many plays of our children are,—the child feeling himself important in assuming the role of the artisan. If somebody laughs about the play, the pleasure in it is usually spoiled.

I would call the following behavior of a chimpanzee imitation of the "serious play" type. On the playground a man has painted a wooden pole in white color. After the work is done he goes away leaving behind a pot of white paint and a beautiful brush. I observe the only chimpanzee who is present, hiding my face behind my hands, as if I were not paying attention to him. The ape for a while gives much attention to me before approaching the brush and the paint because he has learned that misuse of our things may have serious consequences. But very soon, encouraged by my attitude, he takes the brush, puts it into the pot of color and paints a big stone which happens to be in the place, beautifully white. The whole time the ape behaved completely seriously. So did others when imitating the washing of laundry or the use of a borer.

Our modern civilization has made us judge all things with special regard to their practical value—I think, too much so. My chimpanzee's painting is just a play without such a value. Therefore we ask if the ape will also imitate when the model is an act of practical importance for him, *i.e.,* will he do it in a form which is "more than play." There are cases of this kind.

One day a chimpanzee was not fed in the morning, his food being fastened on the ceiling of the room. A box was put on the ground some yards apart, but the chimpanzee did not use it. Indeed he never had used a box as an instrument before. In vain he tried to reach his food by jumping or by climbing up on the walls and along the ceiling. Eventually he became so fatigued that he went several times to the box to sit and relax a little, while his eyes looked sadly up to the food. After many hours in which no indication of the solution of the simple problem became visible I took the box, put it under the food, climbed up and touched the food with my hands, then stepped down again and threw the box some yards away. In less than a minute the chimpanzee began to eat because, now, he took the box and used it as I had done, only that he did take the fruit with him.

Another example: when food was fastened in the ceiling near to the house of the animals, they would open the next door, turn it in the direction of the fruit, and climb up as in the case of the box. One day I made this trick more difficult by fastening the door on the wall by means of a hook and a ring, in order to see what a chimpanzee would do under these new conditions. The ape whom I chose for the experiment tried to open the door, but failed completely since he did not give any attention to the hook and the ring. Chimpanzees do not easily see that such a small object (hook and ring) can be of importance for the movements of a large one (the door). Finally, the animal gave up, but he watched me attentively when I approached the door, lifted the hook and turned the door a little. At this moment he gave a cry of surprise, very similar in chimpanzees to the corresponding emotional expression in man, and I hardly had re-established the connection of hook and ring when the ape was already at my side, opened the hook, turned the door towards the food and solved the problem.

These cases may easily produce an illusion as though imitation were really an easy matter and not an achievement of some significance. But we have only to repeat one of these experiments with a less intelligent ape in order to see that certain conditions must be fulfilled before imitation becomes possible. One of the chimpanzees at Teneriffe was almost stupid; at least when compared with the other apes. He had been present a great many times when other chimpanzees had used the box as a tool for reaching objects in high places. So, eventually, I expected this animal to be able to do the same thing when left alone in such a situation, i.e., with a banana somewhere in the ceiling, a box some yards apart on the ground. The ape went to the box; but instead of moving it in the direction of the food, he either climbed up on the box and jumped from there vertically in the air, though the food was elsewhere, or he tried to jump from the ground and to reach the banana. The others showed him the simple performance a number of times, but he could not imitate them and only copied parts of their behavior which, without the right connection in the whole act, did not help him at all. He climbed up on the box, ran from there under the banana, and jumped again from the ground. Decidedly the right connection of box and food in this situation was not yet apparent to our chimpanzee. Sometimes he moved the box a little from its place, but as often as not away from the food. Only after many more demonstrations of the simple act did he finally learn to do it in a manner which I cannot describe briefly. One sees there is a serious task in learning by imitation even for a less intelligent *ape*. An *intelligent* chimpanzee, observing another in this little performance will, for instance, soon become aware that moving the box means from the first moment moving it to a place underneath the food, the movement will be grasped as one with this essential orientation, whereas a stupid animal sees first the movement of the box, not relating it instantly to the place of the food. He will observe single phases of the whole performance, but he will not perceive them as parts related to the essential structure of the situation, in which alone they are parts of the solution. Of course this right organization is not simply given in the sequence of retinal images which the action of the imitatee produces.—It is with imitation as with teaching. When teaching children we can only give some favorable conditions or "marks" for the new things which the child has "to learn," and the child has always to furnish something from his side which we may call "understanding" and which sometimes seems to arise suddenly, corresponding to the marks given by us. Nobody can simply pour it into the child.

If apes in some cases are able to "see" the necessary connection between the parts of a performance which they observe and the essentials of the situation, the question naturally arises whether or not the same apes sometimes *invent* similar performances as solutions in a new situation. An ape who sees a box obliquely underneath some fruits hanging down from the ceiling will soon try to reach these fruits from the top of the box. Since the box is not quite correctly situated and therefore the ape perhaps cannot reach the food immediately, does he "understand the situation" and move the box a little until it is more or less exactly below the food. I have described elsewhere how chimpanzees really solve simple problems of this type without the help of teaching or the model performance of another. As this description is now translated into the English language there is no need of repeating it at this time.

But let me mention one side of the ape's behavior in many

of these experiments. An ape who has often used a stick as
an instrument, when he found his food on the ground beyond
the bars of his cage, finds it there again beyond the reach of
his arms. But no stick is in his room, only a little tree is there,
a stem dividing into two or three branches. For a long time
the ape does not find a solution. He knows about sticks and
their use, and now there is a tree. But he does not see parts
of the tree as possible sticks. Later on he suddenly finds the
solution, goes to the tree, breaks off one of the branches, and
uses it as a stick. But it appears to me important that for
quite a while the tree does not seem to have any connection
with the problem. Human beings, accustomed to analyzing
and reorganizing the structure of their surroundings with relation to a problem, would see the branches as possible sticks
from the first moment. In order to understand the ape's behavior from the human standpoint, we must take a somewhat
more difficult structure than the simple tree with its branches.
Let us suppose that for some reason or other you want a
wooden frame of the following form: ⌐   In your room
there is not such a thing. Some other wooden frames namely:

W◇ ◯
◯ R 8
◻ ⌣

do not look in the first moment as if they would be of any
use in your situation, even if you apply the saw, which may
be the only instrument available. To be sure, after I made
the preceding remarks about the ape you begin to analyse
these forms because you must suspect now that there I have
"hidden" the frame you want. And so you find it very soon
in the R But wouldn't you give up, perhaps, in the case that
such a suspicion were not aroused beforehand, those forms
looking like casual parts of your surroundings? For the mental level of the chimpanzee, the tree seems to be, with regard
to the stick (the branch), what the group of forms and especially the R. is for us with regard to that frame: The part
which we might use is not an optical reality *as a part* in the
whole which is given originally. It may become such a reality
by a transformation. Reorganization of the surroundings
under the stress of a given situation would then again be an
essential side of the task and at the same time its main difficulty.

I know that several psychologists will not easily believe that my description of intelligent behavior in apes is correct. An almost negativistic attitude has developed in animal psychology, so that we all are afraid of being criticized on account of anthropomorphic tendencies if our description of animal behavior is not denying but showing some higher forms of processes. Therefore I have made moving pictures of some experiments of this type. They are much more convincing than all words and arguments which I might add in order to corroborate my statements; but we have no technique to give this strongest argument to the readers of a scientific journal.

CHAPTER VIII

AN ASPECT OF GESTALT PSYCHOLOGY*

By Wolfgang Köhler

What we call "Gestalt psychology" means a new point of view and a new procedure in various respects, and in several parts of psychology, so that it is far beyond my power to give a complete and adequate idea of it in one lecture. If I try to speak in general terms about it, my statements will needs sound vague and you cannot see how they are to be applied in concrete cases. And if I try to show how, in a more special field of our science, the problems and the procedure of Gestalt psychology develop, many sides and consequences of the new concepts cannot possibly become visible, and you shall probably take as a central position of Gestalt psychology what really is only one of its applications. Since, in my judgement, the second danger is less important than the possibility that very general statements would not give you any concrete idea at all, I prefer the risk which is the natural consequence of exemplification in a special kind of problem; and I shall try to show you how Gestalt psychology treats some sides of our sensory experience, more especially, how the new ideas deal with the visual field in a state of rest.

One of the fundamental methods of natural sciences is *analysis*. The psychologist, therefore, confronted with a complex field of vision, for example, feels naturally inclined to analyze this field into smaller and simpler entities whose properties he may study with more ease and with more hope of clear results than an immediate consideration of the whole field would yield. Generally he does not ask himself what this procedure purports and if, perhaps, the term analysis has more than one connotation. He simply analyzes down to very small parts of the sensory field—let us call them the "sensations"—which do not contain differences, which show a minimum of area, and so seem to constitute the simplest parts of the field. Only gradually do we now become aware of the fact that at this very starting point of investigation at least two ambiguities must be carefully avoided.

Let us take an instance from the physical world: If we want to study the air which is surrounding us in this room,

*Powell Lecture in Psychological Theory at Clark University, May 1, 1925.

we also shall feel inclined to analyze it. We may do that in different ways. Either our attention picks out a "differential" of this volume of air, *i. e.,* an extremely small volume which may be regarded as homogeneous in density, temperature, etc.; or we concentrate our attention on one molecule, say O_2. In the first case, everybody knows he is not treating a *real* element of the air, he knows the differential is not defined by some objective physical properties, as if its interior were kept together somehow, no such keeping together occuring beyond the limits of the differential between *different* differentials; he knows, therefore, that the limits of the differential are existing in thought only. On the other hand, when taking the molecule as the final product of our analysis, we mean exactly an element of the other character: It is well defined physically as a real unit; mutual inner forces which keep the interior of it together are not, in comparable degree, uniting parts of one molecule with those of another. In order to get differentials our thought imagines arbitrarily separating surfaces in the medium; where a molecule is, begins and ends is a question which nature has made out; the molecule is an *objective* unit.

Does a sensation belong to the first or the second type? If we do not like to answer this question for the sensation as a supposed part of "consciousness", I will ask the same question for the physiological processes underlying the sensory field. It would hardly be indifferent for the sensation or the sensory field whether the process corresponding to the sensation must be treated as a differential or as a molecule of the total field. We should probably make different theories of sensory experience corresponding to our choice of one or the other of these fundamental possibilities. In the psychological literature, however, this alternative is hardly mentioned. So far sensation is a vague concept, and the conquences of our use of this concept will correspond to this state of affairs.

The second ambiguity of our concept, certainly related to the first, may again be made clear by an example from physics. I can connect two rooms by a number of tubes or pipes; and I can, in one room, press water into each of them separately, so that in the other room jets of water come separately out of each pipe and fall in separate receptacles. In this case we have real elements before us, isolated streams of water, which are so totally independent of each other that from the standpoint of physics no problem is left referring to the whole of

streaming water.   On the other hand, I can connect two points
of a network of wires with the two poles of a battery of gal-
vanic elements.   Immediately the electric current through this
network is established, forming the so-called stationary distribution in the net, in the wires connecting it with the battery,
and in the battery itself.   Nobody can prevent me from concentrating my attention upon one small part of this conducting
system and upon one small part of the physical process going
on constantly in it.   I may do that in my attempt at making
the theory of the process.   But the next step I have to make,
if the theory shall agree with the facts at all, must consist in
my admitting that the small part of the process I have in view
is *as* it is, not for its own sake and independently, but only
in so far as in the other parts of the system the corresponding
processes are going on.   The stationary distribution of electric current in a given system is a dynamic equilibrium of the
whole system, not to be reduced into independent branches of
current.[1]   What occurs in one wire of this system, therefore,
cannot be compared functionally with the stream of water in
one of the pipes of our other example.   In this pipe I shall find
the streaming absolutely unchanged, whatever may happen and
be changed in the other pipes; the streaming in one of them is
a function of the local conducting properties in this pipe only.
In the case of electric currents in a conducting network, any
change in any place will immediately alter what happens in
"the small part" of it which we were considering.   If, therefore, I like to analyze, in the case of the pipes, I may do it.
No harm will be done, provided my analysis finds the real
elements (independent stream in one pipe).   But if my analysis picks out a part of that stationary current distribution, I
must confess in the next moment that here analysis cannot
mean the same thing, since I find a local state of affairs which
cannot be understood as long as I do not consider the whole
process.   It cannot be understood because it does not exist
without the dynamic influences throughout the whole system
(and vice versa).

Is a sensation, or is a physiological process corresponding
to it, like one of those streams of water in separate pipes, *i.e.*,
functionally independent?   Or is it like that "small local
process" in the network conducting the electric current, *i.e.*,

---

[1] It is instructive to know that in the early days of the investigation of currents this situation was exactly as embarrassing for
physicists as the problems of Gestalt are now for us.

does it exist in its actual state only as dependent upon the dynamic equilibrium distribution in a larger area? Evidently this alternative is at least as decisive for our theory of sensory experience as the former; but though dynamic equilibrium is a word mentioned in some of our more modern textbooks, we do not see as yet that the fundamental differences between the two assumptions were recognized and the concrete consequences worked out. For a long time we have all of us practically applied the standpoint of the pipes when treating the sensory field. When, now, we are told that the contrary seems to be more probable for several reasons and that we should not go on with the pipes, we easily become angry and say that we never did formulate such a radical principle as that of the pipes. In this we are probably right, because we never had a clear idea of the functional alternative, no idea that there was something important to decide one way or the other, and rather unconsciously *worked* in that line only. But I think somebody *should* have stated that radical principle, because it is of so much higher scientific value to make a clean, clear mistake, which is the best antecedent of progress, than to remain in that phase of vagueness where not even mistakes can be made—and afterwards be displaced by something better.

One remark may be needed here to show that the two alternatives are not simply identical. The molecule as representative of an objective unit and the independent stream in one pipe seems to be so similar; yet we must not exaggerate the parallel between them, because though a molecule in the air is a physical unit held together by forces which do not connect in a comparable degree parts of one molecule with those of another, still what happens with the molecule may be determined by its being the "part" of a larger whole (and vice versa). If it has a charge (*i. e.* is an ion), for example, it will move in the electric field and influence other charges by its own field so that perhaps finally its movements will become one dependent little part of just such a whole process as we described above. Therefore a molecule or any other physically defined unit may either be an altogether independent unit like the stream in one separated pipe or it may, still retaining its property of more specific unitedness, have a life which can only be rightly understood if we consider a larger system in which we find it.

Is a sensation of the molecule type? Let us try to answer with complete naiveté as if there were no psychology already existent.

I look up to the homogeneous blue sky of today, and find it continuous. Not the slightest indication of its being composed of real units, nothing of limits or of any discontinuities. One may answer that my simple observation is not the method to decide this point, but I cannot agree with this argument since we need, first of all, concepts for the description and the understanding of our immediate experience; and the sensation loses considerably of its importance as a fundamental concept, if, taking it as something of the molecule type, we find nothing to substantiate this idea in direct observation. The continuity of that region of the sky or any homogeneous field is a positive property of it. And we see that our fundamental theoretical concept in this form does nothing to make this property understood. On the contrary, a special hypothesis would be needed in order to explain how in spite of the existence of sensation molecules the homogeneous field becomes a continuum. Therefore the only thing produced by this useless assumption is a complication of theory. And I lay the more stress on this fact as we shall see very soon that there do occur parts in sensory fields which are real objective units, though they certainly are not "sensations." The concept of sensation tends to hide for us the importance of these other realities and has done so for a considerable time, very much to the drawback of psychological progress.

Since the concept of a *differential* does not mean anything like a real unit but only signifies the small uniform part of a medium, field, or process which our thinking regards more especially in a certain moment of our theoretical consideration, sensation as a differential can evidently not be verified in experience. It has nothing to do with experience directly. Perhaps it does not help us very much in our thinking, but at least so long as we remain aware of its completely arbitrary nature it will not conduct us into errors.

Having found that we may keep sensations in our system as differentials, if we want to, we have to ask whether these differentials we are considering in a quiet field of vision are to be regarded as independent or as dependent differentials in an equilibrium distribution of larger area. Feeling that this is the very kernel of our problem we should give our answer slowly, gradually approaching the decision by a series of observations. Before starting we remember that our procedure shall be as naive as possible, so that it does not matter if our observations follow a line where psychologists do not usually

search for anything fundamental.   It does not matter either
if, for a while, we seem to lose sight of our problem and seem
to go in a new direction.

One of Wertheimer's papers[2] describes observations of the
following type:

(1)   You look on a series of spots (Fig. 1) whose dis-

FIG. 1

tances are alternately of a certain larger and smaller width.
If I say that these spots appear spontaneously in groups of two
(which "belong together") so that the smaller of the two distances is always in the interior of one group, and that beyond
the larger distance a new group begins, etc., you probably will
not find the statement or the phenomenon very impressive.

I therefore introduce a change substituting straight parallel
lines for the spots (Fig 2), at the same time increasing the

FIG. 2

difference of the two distances a little.   The phenomenon of
group formation is now a little more striking.   How "real"
it is you can feel when trying to form other groups in the series;
namely, so that any two lines with the larger distance between
them form one group and the shorter distance is the space
between two consecutive groups.   You see that this requires
a special effort.   To form *one* of the new groups may be rather
easy; but to make the change for all of them *i. e.,* for the
whole series simultaneously, is more than I, for instance, can
achieve.   Most people never will get this other grouping as
clear, stable and optically real as the former one; and in the
first moment of relaxation or fatigue, you instantly see again
the spontaneously existing groups as before.   It is as if some
forces were holding the pairs of nearer lines together.

Is distance in itself the decisive factor?   Two spots or

[2]Psychologische Forschung 4, pp. 301 fol. 1923.

two parallel lines may be regarded as a rather poor boundary enclosing space between them. In our figures they do so better when nearer together, so that we might perhaps formulate our principle in the sentence that the members of a series better enclosing space between them tend to form groups. This new principle seems to work because it covers the fact that the parallel straight lines form more striking and stable groups than the spots. Evidently they enclose space between them better than do the spots. And again, we can change our last figure by adding some short horizontal lines so that the larger space between the more distant parallels begins to be better enclosed (Fig. 3), and the result is that it becomes easy to see

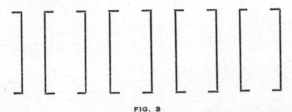

FIG. 3

the pairs of more distant lines with their annexes as groups, even before the open distance between those annexes is made smaller than the distances of the parallels nearer to each other. But let us be cautious. Perhaps we have two different principles, that of distance and that of "enclosing".

(2) In the next figure all members of the series follow each other at equal distances, but there is a regular change in the properties of those members (Fig. 4). It does not matter

○ ○ ● ● ● ○ ○ ● ● ● ○ ○ ● ● ●

FIG. 4

whether the difference is of this type or a difference between yellow and black, for instance. Even in a case like this (Fig. 5) you observe the same phenomenon, namely that the members

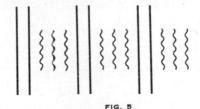

FIG. 5

of the same "quality" (whatever it may be) form groups and
that a new group begins where we have a change in the quality
of members. Again you convince yourself of the reality of
this observation by trying to see the series in another grouping
than that. Probably you will not be able to see the series as
solidly organized throughout when trying to enforce any of
the other mathematically possible formations of groups.

(3) The description of our observations is not yet complete.
If we look back upon the series of parallels, we see that the
formation of groups is not an affair of those parallels only.
The whole area *in* a group, half enclosed between the parallels
nearer to each other, white like the surrounding paper, still
looks different from it and also different from the area between two consecutive groups. In a group there is a certain
aspect of "solidity," or we might even say: "there *is* something";
whereas between the groups and around the whole series we
have "emptiness" or "there is nothing." This difference
described and discussed very carefully by Rubin,[3] who calls it
the difference between the characters of "figure" and "ground,"
becomes the more remarkable since the whole group, including
its half enclosed white area, appears to "stand out" in space
from the surrounding ground. At the same time we may remark that the parallels, which, as it were, solidify the enclosed
area and lift it a little from the ground, "belong to this area"
in one more meaning: You see that they are the edges of this
enclosed area, but are not in the same manner edges of the indifferent ground outside the group.[4]

There is more to describe in the aspect of even such a simple
field of vision. But, lest you might feel that I intend to lead
you into unimportant details, I hasten to carry our observations
on into a new direction.

(4) The groups formed in the series of parallels included
pairs of them. We add third parallels in the midst of each
group and find, as one may have expected beforehand, that
these three lines so close together still form groups and that
the grouping is even much more striking now than before
(Fig. 6). We may add two more parallels in each group between the three already drawn. Not much of white is left

[3]Visuell wahrgenommene Figuren I. Kobenhaven, Christiania,
Berlin, London: Gyldendal, 1921.
[4]Similar laws are found to apply to the formation of units in
temporal series (Wertheimer, Psychol. Forsch. 4; Koffka, The
Psychol. Bull. 19, 1922).

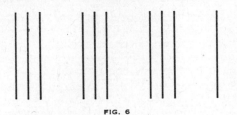

FIG. 6

now in the group and the stability of group formation is still increased (Fig. 7). Some steps more and the areas of our

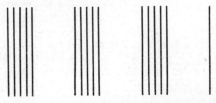

FIG. 7

groups are uniform black rectangles. There would be three of them; everybody looking upon the page would see these "three dark forms." And our gradual procedure has taught us that to see the black content of each of those areas, as "one thing" united in itself, outstanding as one from the ground, is only a very extreme case of the formation of group units which we were observing first. It is not a geometrical truism—it has nothing to do with pure geometry—that continuous uniformly colored areas or spots in differently colored homogeneous surroundings appear as wholes, units; it is a primitive experience in vision. And we have seen that it is an extreme example of the fact that, with neighbours of equal properties given, group units are formed. This principle was seen working with increased effect the denser we filled the area of the group. It cannot stop working when the group becomes a continuum. (I hardly have to mention that our uniformly colored wholes might have thousands of different forms, usual ones like the rectangle, to which we are accustomed, or quite unusual ones like some spot of ink on the paper or a little cloud in the sky.)

You see why I started showing the group formation in the case of separate members: It is easier to acknowledge the problem there *as* a problem. To be sure, the unit of our black rectangles is much more stable than that of our first spots and parallels; but we are so used to uniformly colored areas

surrounded by other color "being one" that the problem here
is not grasped so easily. Most of the observations of Gestalt
psychology are of this kind: They touch facts of such a general occurence in every moment of our life that, therefore, we
have difficulties in seeing anything remarkable in them. This,
too, is the reason why they are scarcely mentioned in psychology.

Again the progress of our observations obliges us to look
back. We formed series of spots or straight lines and observed their grouping. Now we have learned that these members of our series themselves contain the same problem or
phenomenon, in so far as they already are extended and uniformly colored units. The consequence is that we find formation
of units in different "order" or "rank", e. g., straight lines
(lowest order) and groups of them (higher order). If a unit
exists it may still become part of a larger unit or group of
higher rank. Whether it remains exactly the same thing when
undergoing this absorption is a question which shall occupy
us later on.

(5) With the "being one," the continuous unit has retained another property of the discontinuous group: It still
has the "figure" character as something solid, outstanding from
the empty ground. Imagine now that we substitute for the
rectangle, printed in black, a black rectangular paper, covering
the same area and carefully pressed against the page. Evidently nothing of importance is changed; this paper is "one"
and has the character of something solid on account of similar
reasons that the printed rectangle had before. Imagine further
that this paper begins to grow in the direction at right angles
to its surface and the surface of the page. It becomes thicker
and is soon a black block or "thing" in space. Again nothing
functionally important is changed. But we see that the application of our observations has become much larger. Wherever "a thing" is visible as "one" and as something solid the
same principles are concerned which we first became acquainted with in the formation of groups. There are still other influences working in our appreciation of things as units and as
solid, but we have no reason to think that those principles of
primitive group formation we were considering (and others I
could not mention here) lose their force when we have to do
with things in three dimensions instead of spots or rectangles.[5]

_____

[5] "Things" again may become members of groups of a higher order.
Instead of spots we might have a series of men and still observe
the formation of groups. In architecture one knows enough about
that (compare the grouping of pillars, windows, statues, etc.).

I am thoroughly aware of the fact that here we are confronted with a subject for thorough discussion. Why should such solid units *in vision* so generally correspond to real things in the *practical* meaning of the word? And every day experience seems to show that this correspondence exists. What would be our life if it were not so! There are two answers to give. The first is that a great many objects or things in the practical meaning have objective properties which make them likely to be seen as *optic* units too. There is the world of objects which man has created himself for his practical purposes. Without much thinking he makes and has made them so that in color and other properties they are apt to appear as units. Of course, nobody gives his piano a painting which would make parts of it easily combine into optic units with different parts of the surroundings, making the piano disappear. *Natural* objects often follow the same principle, because what has one common origin in nature or belongs together in nature as one thing will rather likely show some common surface properties in color and otherwise, whereas the surroundings have different surface properties as being of a different origin and different physical nature. So the mountain separates from the sky, a cloud again from the sky, the blackbird (even at rest) from the lawn, the stone from the sand, and the cliff from the sea.—The second answer is that, wherever our primitive optic principles are not favorable to the formation of units in correspondence to real things, it becomes more and more difficult to recognize, to find or to see these real things, until at last we do not see them at all. Who has never in his life stared upon an odd form at some distance which he could not explain to himself and which, after a slight change of standpoint (therefore change in arrangement of stimuli *i. e.* conditions for grouping) suddenly broke up into one well-known thing and perhaps parts of other well-known things? The moment before the primary optical unit formation had created an absolutely unknown optical thing, because the arrangement and the properties of stimuli happened to be so. Paint the pencil, the books, the ash tray, the eraser, the paper knife, the rule, and the desk each in some colors distributing them in irregular spots so as to have no relation to the total form of the object— you will see that your accomplishments in life are a little slowed down because you are constantly seeking. Without painting: Observe under what circumstances you do not find your pencil for ten seconds, though it is openly before you on your desk.

In most cases you will observe that the position of the pencil, relative to other objects, and some similarity of its surface properties to those of the objects at its side, had united it with them optically and so made it disappear as a relatively independent optic unit. The art of making puzzle pictures is an application of these facts—the parts of a man, for instance, are absorbed by the surroundings—and the last war, with all its art of camouflage, has shown how far the optical destruction of real objects can go, even if nothing disturbs the projection of those objects on the retina.

Most things are certainly *known* objects for the adult. This means, for instance, that when seeing a pipe we see it as something with a specific function in smoking, and of course this "meaning" of that optical unit on our desk is brought into it by experience. It does not follow at all that the optic unit of it *as such* is a product of experience. As yet we have only seen that the *existing* unit may become imbued with some functional meaning by experience. On the other hand, I shall not deny that experience has an influence upon our seeing those units. But here we must avoid a circle. I saw a certain object often in earlier life and under conditions of surroundings favorable for its being seen as a unit. The effect is that I find myself more likely to see it again as "one thing" even under conditions where the purely optical constellation is less favorable for it and optical absorption of it or its parts into other units would probably occur without the influence of previous experience. So this influence of previous life, instead of showing how experience *makes* units out of something else, *presupposes* the existence of the unit as such in previous seeing. It is an experience *about those units* which afterwards becomes effective. The more one avoids the rather common but dangerous phrase, that this or that thing "must of course be explained by experience," the more one tries, in our case, for instance, to consider concretely how experience might produce units (and out of what?), the less plausible becomes this rather superficial statement. Recently we have made experiments on this question which are not yet published, and we are surprised to see how easily even that effect of experience which I have admitted is overcome by showing a well-known form in a constellation in which the primary tendencies of unit formation are working against our seeing that form. One example (not at all a very strong one) may demonstrate this fact (Fig. 8). The first aspect of this constellation of straight

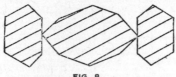

FIG. 8

lines is usually: A drawing consisting of three parts, two irregular hexagons including a lengthy other form between them. There is a strong tendency to see closed surface-forms as against figures consisting of lines only. Therefore, the K, whose constituents are openly given in the contour does not come into existence, one of its parts helping to form the first closed surface to the left and the rest limiting one end of the lengthy surface. When demonstrating cases of this kind I often hear the argument: You forget that we have not seen the well-known K *in such a connection* before. But that is exactly what I say: The influence of experience is not strong enough to overcome spontaneously even such a simple arrangement which tends to be organized into other and less familiar forms. If nothing in the surroundings were changed, we would of course instantly see the letter as we saw it at other times; but in this case no experience would be needed for explanation. (In this example one can see the K very easily, after being helped to. In other cases it becomes altogether impossible really to see a well-known form in a given constellation, even when one is absolutely certain about its constituents being geometrically and physically present.)

An observation showing that no experience is needed for a first formation of units in the visual field is given in cases where blind born persons gain their sight by operation. Psychology used to be interested in these cases because of the problem of third dimension and of the correlation between space in touch and in vision. Whatever the outcome for these problems, one point is quite obvious in the description of first vision under these circumstances, though very characteristically the investigators do not mention the problem as a problem: It may be an open question whether the patient recognizes a square as a square which before he knew only by touch. But certainly he understands the investigator very well when asked what the form there is, showing thereby that he has there something outstanding as one in his field of vision at once.

We began our observations intending to decide whether or

not the sensation is an *independent* differential. Our first result, however, has led us back to another concept, namely that
of an objective unit.   In order to show what I meant with this
term, I mentioned the molecule in the atmosphere as a unit
which is not arbitarily conceived in thought, but objectively
given by the strong intercourse of interior forces, which hold
the molecule together, in contrast to the comparatively low dynamic interrelation between the molecule and its surroundings.
I chose the very small molecule as a model because the question
was if we had to regard sensations, supposedly small things,
as similarly small objective units; and we found no indication
of their existence as such.   But the concept of an objective
unit in the defined meaning is not necessarily restricted to small
things.   A crystal, for instance, in the saturated solution in
which it forms is an objective unit, in such a similar meaning
as a molecule that some physicists have really called it an enormous molecule.   Are there objective units in a field of vision?
Yes, there are and we have been considering them now for
some time.   It is not arbitrary and abstract thinking that makes
those groups or spots or rectangles or things in my visual field.
I find them there as optical realities not less real than their color,
black, or white or red, etc.   As long as my visual field remains
the same (is not changed by internal or external influences)
there is little doubt about what belongs in one of those units
and what not.   And if we have found that in the visual field
there are units of different rank, a group, for instance, containing several spots, the larger unit containing smaller ones
of still stronger unitedness, exactly the same occurs in physics
where the molecule as one larger objective unit (defined by a
comparative break of interconnection at its limits) contains
smaller objective units, the atoms, whose interior is again enormously stronger united than the molecule is.   There is no
contradiction and no vagueness in objective units containing
smaller units. And as it remains an objective fact in the physical material, where the boundaries of its units and perhaps
of sub-units are, so in the visual field no arbitrary analyzing
thought should interfere with observation: Experience is
spoiled if we begin to introduce artificial sub-divisions where
real units and boundaries of one or the other rank are open
and clear before us.   This is the principal reason why I think
that a concept like sensation is almost a danger. It tends to
absorb our attention, obscuring the fact that there are observable units and sub-units in the field. Because in the moment

we give up our naiveté in description and theory and think of the field in terms of unreal elements, these unreal little things appear to our thought side by side, indifferently filling space, some of one, some of another color or brightness, etc., and the observable units with their observable boundaries do not occur in this pseudo-description. I do not exaggerate. Look on the development of the psychology of vision: All the more important observations relating to the real units, etc., began to be made in the last thirty years only, though the facts were before us thousands of years, wherever psychologists or other people looked into the world. Artificial theory made us a little blind for them.[6]

It will be worth while to mention here one more ambiguity of the term analysis in psychology. I may either consider in theory one little part of the visual field, *i. e.* when thinking about such a field—about this we were speaking hitherto; or I may, looking on an actually given field, proceed by *actual analysis in vision*. In the second case, when finding, for instance, the letter K in Fig. 8, I really have changed the visual field, the units and the boundaries in it. There is a letter now which did not exist before in the field and the units which were given before are seriously changed. To really see the letter and the closed areas of that figure at the same time and undisturbed is more than I can achieve. Probably it is as impossible as to have the two really separate atoms of O and the molecule O_2 at the same time. Of course it is highly interesting to produce such a change in the field; what happens or does not happen in such an actual operation may even give very valuable hints on the nature of the units we are operating upon. But in no case must one expect to find the whole truth about a given unit by transforming the field and creating new units in it. I would not find out all about a molecule O_2 when describing two atoms O which I have really separated; and also, the separate atoms O, which I describe, did not exist as really the same thing in the molcule. This is a point we shall treat later on more thoroughly.[7] For the moment it is more important to mention that from the standpoint of Gestalt psychology there is after all *one* analysis which is perfectly genuine, allowed and productive in all cases: The simple de-

[6]G. Humphrey, The Journal of Educational Psychology **15**, 1924.

[7]The fact in itself that the change of subjective attitude toward the field can to a certain degree alter its properties, units, etc., must be regarded as being a very interesting problem. As yet it has not been studied thoroughly enough. (Köhler, Psychol. Forsch. **6**, 1925, pp. 396 fol.).

scription of the field in terms of real units and sub-units as their real parts, in terms of their boundaries, sub-boundaries, etc.

The question we wished to answer was whether or not the local state of affairs in a sensory field is an independent process, so that the whole field may be regarded as a mosaic of them. On our way we found something about extended units in the field, and the same facts we were considering there give an answer to our present question too. How can local processes which are independent of and indifferent to each other be at the same time organized into larger units of well observable extent in some areas? How, again, can relative break of continuity at the well observable limits of those areas be understood, since these limits are not limits everywhere between little pieces of a mosaic, but only appear where one group or unit ends? The hypothesis of independent little parts is unable to give an explanation. All the concepts we found necessary above for the description of the field have no relation whatever to the conception of independent local elements. And more concretely: Where our groups or units are formed can certainly not be deduced by considering the conditions in one point, then independently in the next, etc. Only a consideration which takes account of how the local conditions for the whole field *relate to each other* begins to approach an understanding of those facts. Not the local white along a white line drawn on a black field makes this line a real optical unit in the field; there is no specific unit and no line before the surroundings have a *different* color or brightness. This difference of stimulation around as against equality of stimulation within the line must in the given arrangement be the fact which produces a specific unit. And in the same manner for units of higher order: Not the independent or absolute conditions in one of our parallels, then the conditions in the next one, make them form one group, but that these lines are *equal, different from the ground,* and so *near* to each other—three prerequisites which again show the decisive role of *relations* of local conditions. And let us be careful not to forget the ground. Because, if a certain group is formed, say two parallels, being half a centimeter from each other, I only have to draw two more parallels on the outside of this group and much nearer to the first parallels than these are to each other, and the first group is destroyed, two other groups being formed by the parallels which are now

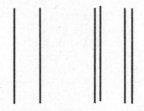

FIG. 9

nearest to each other (Fig. 9). Only so long as we had uniform white in the neighborhood of our first group did this group exist. I change conditions in this neighborhood and what was the interior of a unit, now becomes a gap between two others. One consequence more follows immediately: The characters of "figure" and "ground" are so absolutely dependent upon the formation of units in the field that, since these units cannot be deduced from an aggregate of independent local states, the appearance of an area as "figure" or "ground" cannot either. And still another fact as argument: We draw two parallels and produce a group; we draw another congruent pair but considerably more distant from the first than the distance between the first lines is, and go on increasing the length of our series. The result is that *all* the groups in the series become more solid than each of them would be when given alone. Even over distances of such an amount the conditions in one place have an influence on what happens in another, and vice versa.

The fact that not the local properties of given stimuli but the relations of those properties to each other (the total constellation of stimuli, to use a better word) are decisive for the formation of units, suggests at once the idea that dynamic intercourse in the field decides about what becomes a unit, what is excluded from it, what is "figure," and what falls back as mere "ground." Indeed, at the present time not many psychologists will deny that, acknowledging those real units, etc., in the visual field, we have at once to draw the adequate consequences for that part of the brain whose processes are corresponding to our field of vision. The units, sub-units, boundaries, the difference of "figure" and "ground" must exist there as physiological realities.[8] There must be a unit of pro-

[8]Wertheimer, Experimentelle Studien über das Sehen von Bewegung. Zeitschr. f. Psychol. **61,** 1912. (Also: Wertheimer, Drei Abhandlungen zur Gestalttheorie. Verlag der Philos. Akad., Erlangen 1925.) Köhler, Die physischen Gestalten in Ruhe und im stationären Zustand, pp. 173 fol. Verlag der philos. Akad., Erlangen, **1920.**

cess containing three comparatively separate sub-units when
we look on Fig. 8; and at least partially this unit of physiological process must be disturbed and give place to a new one
not existing the moment before when we begin to see the K.
Remarking now that relative distance and relation of qualitative properties are the main factors determining the formation of units, we remember that exactly such factors ought to
be decisive for it if it were the effect of dynamic intercourse
in the physiological process throughout the field. Most physical and chemical interaction we know of depends upon the
relation of properties and on mutual distance between the
material in space. Now, differences of stimulation produce
points, lines, areas, of different chemical reaction and in certain spatial relations to each other on the retina. If there is
transverse connection between the longitudinal conductors of
the optic nerve somewhere in the optic sector of the nervous
system, mutually dynamic intercourse ought to depend upon
the relations of qualitative properties and space which are at
a certain time existing in the total optic process, streaming up
to or into the brain. No wonder, if we find phenomena of
distribution, etc., showing direct dependence upon those relations.

But physiological conclusions of this kind will appear better
founded if first we consider another side of our descriptive
problems. Intimately related to the existence of real units
and boundaries in the field of vision we find the fact that there
are *"forms"* in this field. It was practically impossible to exclude them from the foregoing discussion, because wherever
we see those units they have forms,[9] this being the reason
why in the German terminology those units are called "Gestalten." Again, the reality of forms in visual space is a fact
which cannot be understood from the standpoint that the visual
field consists of independent local elements. If there were elements of this kind forming a dense and perhaps continuous
mosaic as the "stuff" of the visual field, then we should have
no real forms in this field. Mathematically, of course, some
aggregates of them might be considered together, but that
would not correspond to the reality in which at a given time
some concrete forms *are simply there* in vision, not less than

---

[9] I do not think that the term "configuration" is quite adequate
as a translation of the German word "Gestalt." The word configuration seems to mean elements put together in a certain manner, and
this is a functional idea which we must carefully avoid.

colors and brightnesses. And first of all, mathematically, *all* imaginable patterns might be considered in such a field of independent elements, whereas in vision always quite *individual* forms are before us under given conditions.[10] If, now, we examine these conditions upon which the real forms depend, we naturally find again the qualitative and spatial relations of stimulation. Naturally, because the now well-known *units* appear in the individual forms we are seeing, and we had to realize previously that those units are somehow a function of those relations. I remember from my own slow development in this respect how difficult it is to make a sharp distinction between any aggregate of stimuli, *i.e.*, geometrically existent patterns of them, and optic forms as realities. On this page there are certainly some black points which, considered together, would be a large group of this real form,—(Fig. 10).

FIG. 10

Do we therefore *see* such a form as visual reality? Certainly not. But let those stimuli be *red* and perhaps brought nearer together and all people who are not color blind or half blind for forms by brain lesion would instantly see this group as a form. Also, to use our old example: We first did not see the form of the letter K, but another with three separate units, and only when these units gave way at least partially there appeared at once the definite form of K. And do not think that these were some exceptional cases painfully sought, for the purpose of my argumentation: There is no field of vision you have in everyday life in which you might not find thousands of geometrical patterns of all varieties; but you do not see such forms because other *existing* units with other forms have, as it were, spent and distributed the field amongst them.

All this is not only true for forms in a plane or in the paper; it is as much the truth for the things or objects in our surroundings. And so I wish to warn you against the misunderstanding that these problems of real units and their

[10]Köhler, Komplextheorie and Gestalttheorie. Psychol. Forsch. **6**, pp. 386 fol. 1925.

forms might perhaps have some importance for æsthetics or for other considerations of a supposedly higher level only whereas they were foreign to the practical stuff of everyday life. There is no object, no man you have to deal with, whose optical reality is not a concrete demonstration of the same scientific situation. If, in thousands of years, people have never become fully aware of it, it is not astounding that we still have difficulties in realizing how full of problems one glance into the world is.

"Perhaps you are right," somebody might say here, "in so far as your units and their forms have psychological reality and importance. It also seems probable that for units and their forms the constellation of stimuli is at least as important as the absolute stimuli themselves. But why not assume that some psychic factor, which we might look for, collects the local elements into units and gives them forms at the same time? Your tendency is to deny the existence of independent sensory differentials and to consider those units and their forms as the outcome of dynamic intercourse in the total stream of the optic process itself. But you would not go so far as to assert that the real nature of a local process is determined by the relations of stimulation in a large area. Is not, after all, the color or brightness which is somewhere in the field the fundamental reality in it? And this color at least does depend upon its local stimulus. White is white, black is black on the surface of this paper, whatever may be the units and forms in which they occur. They *are* independent local processes."

There are two points to answer. That color is a more important or more fundamental side of our visual field than the objects in which they appear or the forms of those objects would not be easy to prove. Our vital reactions are determined by the objects, one single property of which the colors are. And if a color be ever so extended, but at the same time be the mere ground on which an object appears, what determines our naive reactions from thinking down to eye movements will be the *object* in 99 out of 100 cases, though its color might be a poor gray. And the second point: Colors *are* dependent on the constellation of stimuli throughout the field. The black on this page is at once transformed into a bright white, the white around it into a black, a gray spot may become a red one, a red one white, without the slightest change in local stimulation, if only you change the total constellation or quality of stimulation around the spot sufficiently. Everybody knows that we have only to reduce the light reflected from the white on this page to a small amount and to keep the black letters reflecting exactly the amount of light they are reflecting now in order to get white letters on a black ground. No need to dwell upon the other cases. Because of simple physical reasons really strong changes of this kind in the surroundings of one smaller area which itself remains unaltered are rather rare, and so we do not easily become aware of these phenomena. Neither are we much struck by the more frequent fact that a change of stimulation, for instance, produced by change of illumination in a part of the field, leaves the white of an object there much more constant than the radically different local stimulations can account for. Since the relation of stimuli is not changed when only the illumination becomes stronger or lower for our object and its surroundings at the same time, the nuance, the white of this area, does not change very much either.

I know, you say: "But that is contrast!" Whatever the name of it, we have to do with the facts behind the name and the type of functional interrelation involved. The facts are that local color also shows its dependence on a *set* of stimuli, whenever we change the average properties of stimulation in the surroundings a little more than is usually the case. If we make the experiment with this printed page, for instance, the result shows clearly enough that the black of our letters is really black only under conditions of much higher brightness surrounding it.

And there is one fact about the contrast which makes it altogether impossible to eliminate it from our discussion as something old, well-known, and not connected with this problem. Quite a series of observations has recently shown that the tendency to treat the visual field as a mosaic of elements was particularly dangerous in the work on contrast. All of these new observations agree in one essential point, namely that the existence and the "amount" of contrast is in the highest degree dependent upon the units or forms which appear in the field. We find contrast of various degrees, but we find also the opposite of contrast under different conditions of unit formation. Even without any change in the constellation of stimuli, if by change of subjective attitude we produce a real change in the units of the field, the effects which are ascribed to contrast may suddenly appear in striking degree or altogether disappear as the case and the units may be. Apart from the contrast, and more generally, several investigators were able to show that it is easy thoroughly to alter local colors by making their area enter one group or another in the formation of real units.[11]

Instead of small units of the type of molecules we have found larger units and forms in the visual field which come into existence and disappear, depending mainly on the actual conditions of stimulation. The manner in which stimulation determined those units showed that the physiological foundation of their existence must be dynamic intercourse in the optic stream, the units being *dependent* real parts in this stream, and every local process, if we want to consider it more especially, being a *dependent* differential. It follows that such a differential and its properties as we are considering in abstract theory, cannot be rightly understood without going back to the total sensory constellation in which they only are what they are.

We draw a physiological consequence: If the local process in an extensive system is by dynamic intercourse in this system a dependent differential, it will change, and so will the process in the whole system, until equilibrium is reached in a stationary distribution without further change. We were treating visual fields in the state of rest. They must be the psychological correlate to a stationary equilibrium distribution in the corresponding processes of the brain. There are enough cases in physics where a process originating in a system under a certain set of conditions develops its stationary distribution in extremely short time. The time in which the equilibrium of an optic process is developed must also be rather small. Because, if we give a set of stimuli suddenly, say by projection, the phase of "something happening," which we observe, has an extremely rapid appearance, and in a moment we see the field, its units and their forms at rest.

To avoid misunderstandings I may add that, in a state of stationary equilibrium, the field is by no means "dead." The mutual stresses in the phase of field formation (which of course are themselves interdependent) do not disappear when the stationary distribution is accomplished. They only have now (together with the processes) those intensities and direc-

[11]Koffka, Zeitschr, f. Psychol. **73**, 1915. Koffka, Psychol. Forsch. **4**, 1923. Fuchs, Zeitschr, f. Psychol. **91**, 1923; **92**, 1923. Benary, Psychol. Forsch. **5**, 1924. Köhler, Psychol. Forsch. **6**, 1925, pp. 411 fol.

tions everywhere in which they balance each other. The total process in stationary distribution is still a *store of energy,* distributed in the field.

Physiological theory has to solve two different problems with regard to the described properties of the field of vision. These properties, as they really are, involving dependence of the local state on *relative* properties of stimulation in a wider range, including, further, the formation of units, their forms, etc., have appeared almost marvelous, so that they often were considered as the outcome of supernatural mental forces. The first task, then, must be to show that, in the general functional aspect, properties of this kind are far from unusual in physics. So the more general difficulty is removed, by demonstrating a corresponding type of processes in exact science, particularly if we can show that, under the circumstances given in the optic sector of the nervous system, processes of that general type are very likely to occur. If that is done, the second task will consist in finding that *individual* kind of physical (or, if you prefer, physiological) process which may be assumed to be the physiological reality underlying a field of vision. This second task is by far the more difficult, given our lack of physiological knowledge. We have hardly begun to seek our way towards a solution of it, and so I return here to the first problem.

The main difference between the functional ideas which are usually applied to the central nervous system and the functional concepts of Gestalt psychology may perhaps be formulated as follows: A process starts somewhere independently and its way is determined by a well-conducting path pre-existing by inheritance or formation in earlier life. The process, then, arrives somewhere, as a stone which I throw hits the window, and produces those effects which it must produce under the conditions given at this place of arrival. That is the prevailing functional idea of today. The conducting path determines the consequences of the process, since, with another connection, absolutely different results would be produced in quite another place, and the process between two places is independent of the mutual relation of properties in these places, existing the moment before the process begins. So something "blind" is one of the principal characteristics of this functional concept, one place being influenced suddenly from without; it has "no vote" in the matter. If evolution or association has not built up the right conducting path, anything may happen in the central nervous system.—Of course there are conductors in the theoretical ideas of Gestalt psychology, too; but they play a very different role here, being—in a sensory field, for instance—a rather indifferent quasi-homogeneous network, which in itself does not prescribe what the outcome of nervous dynamics shall be, or where a process shall go. This is regarded as mainly determined by the relation of actual physiological properties in the different places, and so is the distribution of conduction in the whole network. Our good will to find the "mechanism" or the "machinery" for special nervous processes has made us almost eliminate what is a dominating factor of a great part of physics: There differences of temperature, of pressure, of concentration, of potential, *i.e.*, of relations of properties, throughout the system in its actual state, determine what part exerts what influence on what other part in the next moment. No special constraining and isolating conductors are responsible for the result—the medium in itself would conduct everywhere in every direction—and the really occurrent distribution of process is itself depending upon those physical facts, as they are at a given time. Processes of this kind are not "blind" in the manner described above, since it is a mutual affair between places and their properties whether a process originates between them and what kind of a process it shall be. Neither must we expect nature to produce a horrible confusion without special constraining arrangements for the "right" conduction; because the outcome of this "freer," though absolutely necessary, dynamic interaction is everywhere in physics a very regular and orderly spontaneous distribution of process with very striking features, reminding one of biological phenomena. Since all places are dynamically interrelated with all others, even the interaction between two of them in a given moment is found dependent upon the actual state of the whole system; and so we understand why the total process can and must obey one law for it as a whole: It approaches the equilibrium distribution, which is not an affair for its single parts but for the whole range of the system. For a long time we have believed in the predominant and almost exclusive importance of rigid arrangements in the nervous system which were supposed not to take part in the process or to be influenced by the actual situation, but only to enforce the right ways of nervous stream "from without." The above observations seem to suggest that we have overdone this principle. They tend to show that finally we must try also to apply the principles of direct and freer dynamics,[12] as they are working in physics. To be sure, the usual older concept is not actually in contradiction with physics, but it corresponds to one possibility in physics only, omitting those types of physical systems altogether which are by far the richest in functional properties and consequences and behave a little like systems in biology.[13]

At least one glimpse on the more special way in which this general idea may be applied to the optic sector of the nervous system: In consequence of unequal stimulation in different areas of the retina, different areas of a cross section of the optic sector contain unequal chemical reactions and so contain unequal chemical material in crystalloid and colloid form. If these unequal areas are in functional contact, they certainly are not in equilibrium. There is "energy able to work" in the system wherever areas of unequal properties have common borders. Here in the contours must be the main source of energy for dynamical intercourse. It would be so in physics or physical chemistry under corresponding circumstances.[14]

Our assumption gives a physiological correlate for form as an optic reality. From the standpoint of independent elementary processes such a correlate could not be found. Their indifferent mosaic would contain no real forms or, if you prefer, all imaginable but not real forms in each case, namely for a mind who would pick them out of the mosaic. Evidently only a kind of process which cannot be split up into independent local elements would be acceptable as a correlate of real form. Now, the stationary equilibrium of the process which we assume to underly the field of vision is a distribution of stress and process in space,[15] which only maintains itself as this whole. Therefore we make it our working hypothesis that in

---

[12]The word "free" is used here in a meaning which does not contradict strict necessity at all, exactly as a physicist speaks about different "degrees of freedom" in a system: A system has more or less freedom in physics, the lower or greater the number of special arrangements is which constrains the free dynamic intercourse of its parts. In the usual hypothesis about the nervous system, we give its processes as little freedom as possible.

[13]Köhler, Gestaltprobleme und Anfänge einer Gestalttheorie. Jahresbericht über die gesamte Physiologie, 1922. Berlin, Springer, 1924.

[14]Köhler, Die physischen Gestalten etc., pp. 1 fol., p. 185, pp. 195 fol.

[15]The concept of space requires a special consideration here since in the brain it cannot simply be measured in cm, cm^2 and cm^3. (Köhler, Die physischen Gestalten, p. 232 fol.)

all cases this distribution is the physiological correlate to the space properties of vision and especially to form. Since our conception of a physiological unit is necessarily in so far relative, as any sharp decrease in the intimacy of dynamic intercourse at the boundaries of an area shows its interior to be a real unit, we can without contradiction treat the whole optical process as one for a given time, and still assert the formation of specific (*more* intimately connected) units with their forms in it, depending on the spatial constellation of stimuli.

We consider the case of such a real form and unit a little nearer. We said that the form of a unit is determined by the properties of stimulation *in relation to each other*. It is well known that many years ago Mach and von Ehrenfels drew the attention of psychologists to a property of forms (and more generally Gestalten) which is only a consequence of that fact. If we change the absolute properties of stimulation, the form of a unit remains the same for a wide range of the change, provided the total constellation of spatial and other *relations* of stimulation is not changed. On a homogeneous background the objective circle is seen as the same form though we change the fixation point considerably. A change of color does not matter if only the interior and the background remain homogeneous and remain different from each other. We may reduce the diameter or increase it; that does not matter either, so long as this change does not pass certain limits. Of these possibilities of "transposing a form" the first ones do not require a special consideration in our physiological theory because one sees at once that our physiological assumptions lead to the same results. But about "transposing in size" some words may be needed, and I give the example of a very simple equilibrium distribution in physics in order to show that there the same thing occurs and must occur.

A number n of condensers is only connected by very thin wires, and the direct mutual influence by the electrostatic field is practically excluded by very large distances between them. If we give this system a total charge of amount e, this charge will distribute itself spontaneously on the surface of the condensers. Then, calling the electrostatic capacities of the condensers $C_1, C_2 .. C_p .. C_n$ in the equilibrium distribution, the charge e_p of one of them will be:

$$e_p = \frac{e.\ C_p}{C_1 + C_2 + \cdots + C_p + \cdot + C_n}$$

This charge remains in the condenser p as long as the other charges remain in the other condensers and vice versa. The simple formula shows that correspondingly this charge e_p is a function not only of the local conditions (C_p), but also of the conditions everywhere else in the system (C_1 etc. appearing in the denominator) as is the case with all equilibrium distributions—and with units in the field of vision. Hence a change of conditions in one point of the system affects the distribution throughout. But there is *one* type of changing conditions which does not make the distribution react at all. Multiply or divide all capacities by the same factor—which may be done in reality by increasing or diminishing their linear dimensions in equal proportion—and the local charges or the whole distribution do not change at all. e_p is depending on $\dfrac{C_1}{C_p}$ etc., only. I might as well have written:

$$e_p = e.\ \frac{1}{\dfrac{C_1}{C_p} + \dfrac{C_2}{C_p} + \cdots + \dfrac{C_n}{C_p}}$$

The *relations* of relevant properties (capacities) have not been altered, and so the distribution has remained invariable under the transposing of spatial properties. Invariability under transposing is therefore not at all a thing peculiar to sensory experiences. (For simplicity's sake I chose an example where the spontaneous distribution is one of rest. But we find quite similar facts in cases of spatial *processes* as depending on spatial conditions.)[16]

---

[16]Our example may be used also as an illustration of a "freer" system. No previous isolating arrangement of conductors determines what charge is conducted to what condenser. At any branching point the current might take all open ways in all degrees of intensity. Still, in a given system, we have one equilibrium distribution only, because the current everywhere is fully determined by the mutual relations of actual properties (potential) throughout the system; so it streams and changes until all stresses are in balance for the whole.

The application of the general principle to the optic sector of the nervous system will then consist in our assuming that stimulation and relations of stimulation produce the energy for a process in the optic sector.   The distribution of this process will depend primarily on the retinal constellation of areas of different stimulation, on the general properties of the conducting net and on influences which are exerted upon the optic sector from other parts of the nervous system and the organism as a whole. You see from my last words that perhaps we are not allowed to treat the optic process as one problem of Gestalt and not to include a still larger system.

Eventually I should like to show, at least in some cases, how, with this standpoint in sensory psychology given, the consequences necessarily reach much further.

We have seen that the existence of a geometrical pattern of stimuli on the retina does not at all determine whether I see certain forms or not, because if we change the surrounding pattern or even our attitude only, the outcome may consist of quite different units and forms.   Therefore *"recognizing,"* which in the majority of cases is not a recognizing of color or brightness but of the form of a unit, of an object, for instance, will one time occur, another time not, depending upon the principles we were discussing, i.e., upon the reality of units and forms.   Rubin has shown that in very impressive experiments.

It is the same thing with *"meaning"* and with *"reproduction."* Certain stimuli and groups of stimuli will not reproduce anything at all before the right unit or form, which acquired in experience a meaning or a reproductive force, becomes a physiological and psychological reality.   How should anybody pronounce the name of the letter K when looking on Fig. 8, before he sees this form as an optical reality?   But, in other cases, one can show in an even more convincing way how decisive this existence or non-existence and the properties of real optical forms in the field are.   I made experiments of this type:

The subjects are shown pairs of figures like, *e.g.,* Fig. 11, for a short time.   After awhile reproduction experiments are made showing the subjects in one-half of the cases a *real* part of the original, for instance the straight line to the left in our example; in the other half much *more* of the geometrical pattern is shown, but so that "the part" shown does not correspond

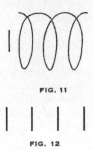

FIG. 11

| | | | |

FIG. 12

to an optical reality in the original, for instance Fig. 12. We are used to thinking that reproduction becomes easier the larger the fraction of the original is which we give. We might predict from our principles, and we find it proved by experimentation, that this purely quantitative factor does not mean very much and may easily be overcome by something more important. Which half of the cases yields more and more correct reproductions? The first one where *"less"* of the original is exposed! And why? Because there I show something that did exist very nearly so in the original, whereas in the second case I show something that certainly did not occur in the original as a psychological and physiological reality and therefore did not acquire a reproductive force. The subject *did not see* the three straight lines more to the right in the group of four, and the first to the left, now forming one member of the group of four, has lost much of its relative independence and thereby has changed its character so far that it does not reproduce now as it reproduces when given alone. [Some experiments made by Shepard and Fogelsonger in this country seem to become explainable from the same principle.][17] This example will perhaps prove better than much description or discussion of "Gestalten" how essentially the understanding of mental life and of the corresponding physiological processes depends upon our discriminating between really existing forms and elements arbitrarily analysed in thought.

We further have evidence for believing that the coordination of certain simple motor reactions to a visual field depends on our principles directly. If, in the stereoscope, one vertical line is exposed to one eye and a second to the other so that with a given degree of convergence of the two eyes the lines appear nearly parallel and at a rather short distance from each other,

[17]Psychol. Review **20**, 1913.—For the explanation Psychol. Forsch. **6**, pp. 379, fol. 1925.

we find them uniting into one line almost at once. It is well known that in this case our eyes turn without our intention into that degree of convergence which brings the two lines upon two corresponding verticals of the two retinae, the two physiological *processes* becoming probably more intimately united under these circumstances than with any other degree of convergence. But we have seen already that parallel lines near to each other [seen in a monocular field of vision, or both of them with both eyes] form a group or belong together as if under mutual attraction. Doesn't it look as if, under the conditions given in our stereoscopic observation, these forces were accomplishing the same thing more thoroughly by really uniting the parallels? An examination of the situation from the standpoint of physics seems to show that such a thing might really occur. We saw that in the equilibrium distribution of process the field is still full of stresses which are for the moment in balance, but represent a store of energy. So in vision there seems to be stress tending to bring the two parallels together. In physics, if such a field is functionally connected with movable parts, amongst whose movements some definite form of motion would release the still existing stresses of the field, this movement will immediately occur, produced by the energy of those stresses. These only *"waited,"* as it were, for an opportunity to let their energy work, for instance influencing movable parts in the direction of a better equilibrium. The better equilibrium in physics lies always in the direction of those stresses which tend to produce some change, but which in our physiological case *cannot do it directly in the field*. If possible, then, they will do it by a detour influencing the muscles of the eyes as moveable parts in the direction of release of their energy. There is nothing supernatural in such an orderly physical process, no process with or without detour can ever produce changes which are not directed toward a more stable equilibrium of the whole system. We have only to adopt this view for the case of the optical part of the brain and its nervous connection with the muscles of the eyeballs in order to have a new explanation of fixation movements which is founded on principles of Gestalt theory and physics.[18] Of course the hypothesis needs a careful working out for the concrete conditions given in the nervous system and in the muscles of the eyes. But the more we work in this direction the more facts seem to show that we are on the right way.

---

[18]Köhler, Jahresbericht über die gesamte Physiologie 1922, pp. 536 fol.

About one other and far more important extension of Gestalt psychology only some brief remarks are possible here. We dealt with forms or groups of very different degrees of solidity. There are cases in which all attempts of destroying, in actual analysis, a given form in favor of a certain other form are in vain. But distribute the furniture of a room in an irregular manner through this room: you will have rather solid and stable units, the single objects, but no equally stable and firm *groups* will be formed spontaneously with those objects as members. Still equality or similarity and dissimilarity of color and other properties, relative distances, etc., are tending to form groups; but you observe that one group formation is easily displaced by another, depending on slight changes of conditions, probably in yourself. It is evident that, under such circumstances, the influence of changes in the subjective attitude towards the field will be much higher than in the case of the solid units or stable groups. Even forces of no peculiar intensity will now be strong enough to produce new groups in a field which—with the exception of the objects in it—does not resist very much because its interior tendencies of group formation are too weak. [If we wish to remain consistent in our form of theory, subjective attitude and change of it must also be represented in the physiological field as physical states or stresses and changes of them, which influence the formation of physiological groups.]

The members of these groups, the objects, are however more than purely optical entities under most conditions of life. They commonly appear as imbued with "meanings," "functional properties," and so on, by experience. And these secondary properties, when actually present, must be almost inherent now in the optic physiological process units of objects, because in extreme examples we have the strong impression of actually *seeing* the acquired properties in the objects, even if there is no possibility of their having a purely optical origin. I cannot tell you briefly how Gestalt psychology would treat this fact. For the moment we may state only that in practical life, of course, seen objects have more properties than we have had to treat as yet. Do not forget however that one necessary prerequisite (for seen objects being imbued with their functional properties) is always their real optical existence as forms in the field. If you apply "camouflage" to them, or if the optical units do not actually exist for some other reason, the functional properties do not appear either.

Supposing now a field to be given, in which objects have no strong optical tendency towards formation of stable groups, our subjective attitude will often tend to group them with regard to acquired functional properties; not necessarily so that objects of equal functional value are grouped together, rather more frequently so that objects which *belong* together in one actual practical task of performance stand out together in the field. Here, however, we must be careful to avoid a mistake. The subjective attitude may easily be taken as something foreign, acting from without like an independent power on the content of the field, for instance, forming groups in it. In real life quite a different thing usually happens. The chimpanzee behind the bars of his cage seeing a banana beyond them too far away for his arm is, when healthy and not overfed, immediately in a well defined subjective attitude; the banana there "arouses his appetite," that is, the relation between his inner conditions alluded to and the aspect of the fruit makes the banana outstanding in the field, makes the "functional value" of it very alive and produces the corresponding stress towards the fruit, both things being sides of one and the same fact. *There is no arbitrary subjective attitude;* the appearance of this object and the animal's attitude towards it are changed correspondingly and, at the same time, determined by the relation between the animal's inner condition and one real part of the field. If we consider, not the visual field separately, but the larger whole in which it really occurs, namely the total situation including the inner conditions of the animal, we find the subjective attitude as well as the functional value produced *in mutual dependence.* The subjective attitude, then, does not come more "from heaven" than changes which it produces in the visual field; and we become aware of this fact when we do not restrict our consideration arbitrarily, that is again, if we do not make an artificial analysis.—After a short while we see the chimpanzee looking around for a stick. Evidently this attitude is not less determined in the total situation than was the direct tendency toward the food. But again this new attitude has remarkable consequences upon the objects of the field. A man can easily observe in himself in a similar situation and one can see in the behavior of the ape, that many objects which are not real sticks but something similar to them, appear very soon "as sticks" in the functional meaning of the word, if no real stick is found.[19] The tree with its branches

[19]Köhler, The Mentality of Apes, p. 37, 1925.

however may for a long time remain "one thing," too much a unit optically to let the functional value of a stick enter the branches, since these are not seen as optically real parts—at least by the chimpanzee. If finally this unit is destroyed under the pressure of the subjective attitude of "seeking a stick," we certainly have a case of a unit changed by the subjective attitude; but once more this attitude itself is changed at the same time and in a corresponding manner: as soon as the attitude of seeking makes the branch a real part of the field, that attitude itself undergoes the change from "seeking" to "breaking off." After all we seldom have the subjective stress alone, it is a stress *between man* (or animal) *and the field* or some part of it, determined by the relative conditions of both sides in this *total situation*. Therefore, in principle, no change will occur on one side without a corresponding change on the other.

I draw some conclusions: Reorganization of the field by subjective stress, if the field is not too stable, seems to be an important side of intelligent behavior. We suspected this before when describing the behavior of apes. But the subjective stress is as much a function of the field as the field is of the stress, both being dependent sides in the total situation. And, of course, only if the subjective attitude is so concretely related to the actual field, can the corresponding stress have effects on the field which lead to the "solution of the problem" given in this field. In the total situation, including inner and outer conditions, the inner and outer sides of what happens seem to be in a similar functional interdependence as prevails for instance between the dependent areas of the visual field. If that is true, the dynamic intercourse between field and subjective stress must follow the same rule, that is, develop in the direction of equilibrium, which as yet I have only applied to the field, the eye movements, etc.

With these remarks I return to my starting point: Though here I have mainly tried to explain the procedure of Gestalt psychology in its treatment of the visual field, this is by no means the only application which the functional concepts developed above admit. They can be as well applied to the full reality of mental life and we are beginning to do it. But since we need firm ground under our feet we prefer to *introduce* our standpoint by showing how it works in vision, because there we have the best methods for concrete, experimental decisions.

PART IV
Purposive Groups

MORTON PRINCE

CHAPTER IX

THREE FUNDAMENTAL ERRORS OF THE BEHAVIORISTS AND THE RECONCILIATION OF THE PURPOSIVE AND MECHANISTIC CONCEPTS†

By Morton Prince

I

Of course all students of Behaviorism cannot be shipped in the same boat for they would soon begin to quarrel like all other psychologists. There are several types differing from one another in their points of view and doctrines. Woodworth recognizes four different types.* Therefore I do not suppose it is possible to define Behaviorism or Behaviorists in terms to which all who claim to be good and true believers would agree. So it would not be fair to impute to one type an error that may only be true of another type. Nevertheless I think it is reasonably accurate to say that Behaviorism is an attempt to explain human (and of course animal) needs, motives, desires, impulses, emotions, thought—in short conscious activity—and the resulting (as commonly supposed) bodily activity in terms, not of consciousness, but of the neural and glandular processes correlated with the former and of the bodily motor behavior which they admittedly induce. Accordingly it is not necessary to take account of consciousness at all, but only of the objective processes which are correlated with consciousness, and which enter into the chain of causal events eventuating in bodily behavior. Whether or not consciousness has anything to do with determining our actions, behavior conduct, bodily reactions can be adequately explained by the mechanisms of the nervous system considered as reflex processes organized into systems (patterns) and the resulting motor activities of the individual. Some behaviorists go so far as to hold that consciousness has nothing whatsoever to do with our bodily reactions and conduct.

Thus, in his recently published book a leading and esteemed Behaviorist, after opening his exposition with the definition of Psychology as "The Science which studies behavior and consciousness," lays down the principle that consciousness has nothing to do with determining behavior. It needs to be

†Powell Lecture in Psychological Theory at Clark University, December 15, 1924.
*Psychological Review, July, 1924.

studied, of course, like any other biological event; "no scientist," he says, "can afford to ignore the circumstances *attendant* on the events (of behavior) he is observing. Introspection on conscious states is both interesting in itself and necessary for a complete account." But, he maintains, for all that, consciousness does not explain behavior. It is only an epiphenomenon and apparently any given behavior would occur just as well without it as with it. *"Consciousness,"* he goes on, *"is in no way a cause of the bodily reactions through which the needs are fulfilled. Explanation is not derived from desire, feeling, will, or purpose, however compelling these may seem to our immediate awareness, but from the sequence of stimulation—neural transmission—and reaction. Consciousness often accompanies this chain of events; but it never forms a link in the chain itself."*

Desire, feeling, will and even *purpose* are thus recognized as events, but they are useless events for all the good they do in determining our actions. Our actions may accomplish our will and fulfil our purpose but we are very foolish in believing that our willing or purpose had anything to do with them. So, also, Huxley taught just fifty years ago when he explained to us that consciousness was related to the mechanism of the body as the steam whistle to that of the locomotive engine.

"The consciousness of brutes," said Huxley, "would appear to be related to the mechanism of their body simply as a collateral product of its working, and to be as completely without the power of modifying that working as the steam whistle, which accompanies the work of a locomotive engine, is without influence upon its machinery." Their volition, if they have any, is an emotion indicative of physical changes, not a cause of such changes.

Again, "It seems to me that in men as in brutes there is no proof that any state of consciousness is the cause of change in the motion of matter of the organism." If these positions are well based, it follows that our mental conditions are simply the symbols in consciousness of the changes which take place automatically in the organism: and that, to take an extreme illustration, the feeling we call volition is not the cause of a voluntary act, but the symbol of that state of the brain which is the immediate cause of that act.**

Hughlings-Jackson† and Charles Mercier‡ taught the same doctrine; so the Behaviorists are harking back to the past.

*Italics mine.
**Fortnightly Review, November, 1874.
†"Evolution and Dissolution of the Nervous System" and other papers.
‡"The Nervous System and the Mind."

This is a very convenient principle—up to a certain point, when, as I hope to be able to show, it lands us in a veritable and impenetrable jungle where we can no longer follow the course of the behavioristic reactions. For the "steam whistlers" very conveniently get rid of the parlous problems of both introspection and inferences from objective events in others, the only methods by which consciousness can be studied; but it may be doubted whether it is true, as our author maintains, that "a material advance has been made in psychology since the adoption of the mechanistic and behavioristic viewpoint" by not "including consciousness or 'mental' entities in the sequence of cause and effect." It is certain that the behaviorist who adopts this principle cannot give in his own mechanistic terms, excepting in the simpler reflex actions, a complete and true explanation of behavior that is "accompanied" by conscious events. His explanation stops short just when it begins to be interesting.

If he could give such a satisfying explanation, we should have presented to us a book in which behaviorism was *explained* from beginning stimulus to the ending motor activity without a reference to such whistling events as emotion, or images, or imagination, or temperament, or intelligence, or will, or purpose. This would be Part I. Then for what he calls a "complete" but not causal account in Part II we should have a superfluous description of the epiphenomena—the tootings of the whistle, the conscious processes.

Such a book has never been written and, it is safe to say, never will be; though "there are a few psychologists who maintain that, since consciousness cannot explain events, it has no place in the science which studies behavior," and Watson has bravely written a partial "Psychology" trying to do without mind.* So far from this being a "serious mistake" from the point of view of steam-whistlers, as one leading behaviorist thinks, it seems to me to be the only logical attitude that can be taken if the "principle" be adopted; but then it is not psychology.

---

*Watson warns his readers that they "will find no discussion of consciousness and no reference to such terms as sensation, perception, attention, will, image and like. These terms are in good repute, but," he says, "I have found I can get along without them both in carrying out investigation and in presenting psychology as a system to my students. I frankly do not know what they mean nor do I believe that any one else can use them consistently."—Psychology from the Standpoint of a Behaviorist; p. 8.

I have purposely refrained from mentioning (perhaps I ought to say, my physiological processes have, through stimulus and response, adapted my pen to the present situation so as not to mention) the name of the clever author I have quoted, because I am not criticizing any one in particular and I hope he will so understand it. He happens to be for my purpose a happy and brilliant exemplar of the principle and has had the courage and clarity of thought to state explicitly and without reserve the doctrine he and other behaviorists adopt, just as Huxley did fifty years ago—to say exactly what he means and to mean exactly what he says, a most admirable quality of mind.

Now, to come at once to the point: one of the fundamental errors of the behaviorists (of one type) is the denial of consciousness as cause of bodily reactions. As I wrote a long, long time ago;* *"How* consciousness causes bodily change is one question and *that* it does so is another. We may not be able to say *"how* it does it, but *that* it does it is beyond dispute."* The *how* and the *that* are two different questions. I believe we can answer both. But even if I am mistaken in thinking we can answer the first, I still believe it is futile to deny that mental processes cause bodily processes. I may be permitted to quote what I wrote in 1891 as it expresses my view today:

"Now I do not wish to speak except with the highest deference for those who hold opposing views. I know how easy it is for the mind to deceive itself in matters of this kind; how difficult it is to free one's self from the ideas which by long habit are connoted by language, and which consequently prevent our viewing a thing from a new aspect. But I do wish to emphasize the fact that any doctrine which ultimately leads to denial of volition as a cause of action is, as Mercier would say, 'nonsense', and doomed to failure. If one is moved to sympathy at the misery of a beggar, and following one's sympathy one gives a dollar to that beggar, the giver is satisfied that his feelings of sympathy—his states of consciousness—directly controlled his muscular acts and moved his fingers to take a dollar bill out of his pocket and give it away. This is a fact of direct experience, and is worth a whole volue of scientific erudition.

If, under the influence of anger, I strike a man, there is little use in my trying to shift the responsibility from my temper to the shoulders of my grey matter, and in my telling the world that my outburst of temper was only a sort of 'steam-whistle'; that it told me what my right hand was going to do, but had no more to do with the hitting than has the judge on the bench who is going to try my case.

Popular language correctly expresses the facts in such cases, and any scientific doctrine which attempts to explain the relation of

*The Nature of Mind and Human Automatism, p. 25, J. B. Lippincott Company, 1885. (Out of print.)

mind and body, and does not recognize this truth, will never be accepted by common-sense people. The contention of those who hold the doctrine which will be developed later, is that the 'steam-whistle' advocates have been logically driven to their conclusion; but the reason for this is that though their logic is faultless, their premises are wrong, the conditions of the problem not being thoroughly understood. Well-known truths regarding the nature of so-called 'matter' have, in practice, been neglected, or their full bearing on the question been overlooked. That there is a solution of this question, which on the one hand does not disregard these truths, and on the other hand recognizes volition as a cause of muscular action, we believe. This solution thus far for the most part has been neglected; but the reason for this is plainly because it has not been understood, and not because any serious objection has been urged against its final conclusion.*

I should like to hear a Behaviorist (of this type) arguing his case before the Judge and making the plea that he was only an automaton and that his "criminal intent" had nothing to do with his criminal act; that it was his neurones, or his ductless glands, or his conditioned reflexes that did the crime. I would love to hear the Judge say; "Yes, quite so; five years in jail. Next case," and then humming to himself (paraphrasing from Shylock): "Until thou canst rail the seal from off my bond, thou doest but offend thy lungs, young man, to speak so foolishly."

I wonder why the counsel for Loeb and Leopold did not put a Behaviorist on the stand as an expert in psychology! Why, the whole of criminal law and criminal responsibility is based on "criminal intent"— the doctrine that consciousness is the cause of bodily actions. It is the seal of "criminal responsibility." Just imagine the Fifteen Judges of England in the famous McNaughton case, instead of laying down the time-honored (if not medically honored) test of responsibility ever since incorporated in common law: "Did he know the nature and quality of his act, or if he did not know it, did he know that what he was doing was wrong?" Suppose, instead, they had laid down the test: "Were the conditioned reflexes of his neurones or ductless glands adjusted to the ethical codes of society? What a delightful opera bouffe Gilbert and Sullivan would have made of it, rivalling Pinafore!

The Behaviorists may be certain of this: any psychology that does not recognize that consciousness is a cause of our actions, will be treated as nonsense and will never be accepted or seriously considered by common-sense people.

---

*Morton Prince: Hughlings-Jackson on the Connection between The Mind and The Brain. Brain, 1891, vol. XIV, p. 250.

II

A second fundamental error of Behaviorists is to suppose, leaving the question of consciousness aside, that behavior can be today completely explained in terms of the correlated neural and other bodily processes alone. I am ready to agree it would be a great desideratum if it could be done. But it cannot be done for the simple reason that we have not even the rudimentary knowledge that will allow us to follow the reactions to any stimulus beyond the afferent receptors, through those cerebral pathways that are correlated with mental experiences. Possibly in the years to come we may be able to do this but it will be in the dim, dim future. Just imagine trying to follow the "adequate stimulus" through and pick out the systems of neurones—neurograms, I have thought it useful to call them—involved in any complicated mental process and determining behavior. And yet without doing so it would be impossible to explain the behavior. Take, for example, the comparatively simple case of going to market to purchase your dinner. You look over the different viands offered you, reject a beefsteak, and after considering different meats, select a fine brace of ducks. What neurograms or ductless glands determined your behavior culminating in your final choice? Your hunger stimulus and habit reactions may get you to the market. But even then, what particular neurograms were involved? But pass over that. Why did you reject the beefsteak? Was it a visual or olfactory, or gustatory stimulus? And if so, why did it result in rejection? What neural and other systems came into play? Did the stimulus awaken neural systems correlated with thoughts of excessive price and economical concepts, or conditioned gustatory reflexes of aversion, or some other? And if so, which? You can't even make a sporting guess. But psychological analysis (not psycho-analysis) would reveal—what? Why, an unpleasant episode of childhood (long forgotten) by which beef-steak became linked, not with an unpleasant gastric experience of nausea and vomiting after eating a beef-steak, but with a *person* whose conduct towards you had shocked your susceptibilities. No objective laboratory technique could have possibly revealed this episode, though the "word-reaction" method might have allowed you to suspect the involvement of the person and to postulate a conditioned reflex, or pattern reaction. But what reflex and what system of bodily processes was involved? Well, pass again over the rejection of the beef-steak.

What stimulus and neuronic systems determined your final behavior in choosing the ducks for your dinner?

They looked tempting to be sure. Do you think it was only by reason of an awakened gustatory conditioned reflex? I do not suggest awakened pleasant gustatory images, that would be a too subjective explanation. Here again psychological analysis would reveal episodes of the past, episodes of duck shooting, outings on Chesapeake Bay when you bagged many a duck, sat for hours in a blind with intense excitement, lived in a shooting camp with convivial friends, before the days of prohibition, lived on ducks that you had shot yourself, etc., etc. All this experience was linked up with duck and made your eyes open wide when you saw (optical stimulus) the fine brace in the butcher's stall and determined your behavior to buy.

It was the "setting" of these past experiences which was the efficient determining factor. Some, perhaps, would call this setting a "pattern." "Pattern" or "setting," you may introduce it into a mechanism of conditioned reflexes, if you like; but how could you have discovered these reflexes and pattern, or setting without psychological (introspective) analysis, and even now can you point out the particular pattern and reflex paths? Can you describe concretely and specifically the factors otherwise than in psychological terms?

Take an actual case from my note book; a woman flies off into an extraordinary violent fit of anger ending in hysterics and other symptoms eventually landing her in my consulting room as a patient. The stimulus was the apparently innocent refusal of her husband to protest against the firing of firecrackers under her window on a Fourth of July. Will you tell me what neurological and glandular pattern determined that behavior? I can tell you the cause in psychological terms for it was a setting of experiences dating back many years, but without introspective analysis you will search in vain. Even after being found, by introspective methods, you cannot put your finger on the particular physiological mechanisms (neurograms and glands) which, as conditioned reflexes or habits, did the job.

The best you can do in all such cases is to find by *introspective* methods the experiences of which the residua became systematized (with glandular systems) into a "pattern" or "setting" as dispositions (innate and acquired) and then say, *ex hypothesi,* these residua functioning in mechanistic fashion after the manner of conditioned reflexes (or some other manner) determined the behavior, while the psychological elements were only "symbols in consciousness."

If all this is true of such simple behavior as that of the instances I have used, how much more hopeless it would be to discover the bodily processes (neural, glandular, and others) involved in such behavior as working out a plan for a League of Nations, or the mathematics of the Einstein theory of relativity, or of the orbits of atomic electrons.

III

The third error of the behaviorists is in confining themselves to only one method of observation and experimentation —the objective method. For the successful solution of the problems of science, when any given method has been carried as far as it can and fails to be adequate to resolve the further intricacies of the problem, new problems that have been brought to view by the very successes of the method, then new methods have to be discovered that will be adequate for pursuing the research along new lines to meet the new problems.

Of course in physical science all methods are limited to objective ones because the physical sciences deal only with phenomena and cannot touch the ultimates as we can with conscious processes. The physicist finally, therefore, comes up against a stone wall and can go no further, as when he reaches the problem of the ultimate nature of energy, or of the electron. As Bertrand Russell points out, electricity "is not a thing, like St. Paul's Cathedral; it is a way in which things behave. When we have told how things behave when they are electrified, and under what circumstances they are electrified we have told all there is to tell . . . Electricity is not like red paint, a substance that can be put on to the electron and taken off again; but is merely a convenient name for certain physical laws." But, I may add, the physicist goes further than this. He says that the electron is electricity itself, but stops there, though, as a matter of speculation he may add it is the way something else behaves, *e. g.*, the ether.

From one point of view this is a limitation of physical science, but even within his fields the physicist adopts new and many methods as called for. So it is with the problems of the medical and biological sciences. What would we think of the medical clinician should he say, "Oh! I am a stethescope doctor. I only use the stethescope to diagnose diseases of the body,"—though he runs up against a stone wall, when the problem of bacterial infection of the blood becomes the vital one? Or of another who should say, "I am a blood doctor. I only examine blood,"—though the problem shifts to the kidneys? Or of another who boasts, "I am a urinary doctor. I only examine the urine,"—though the problem shifts to the brain? Or of another, a psycho-analyst—"I only use free-associations,"—though free associations lead him away into philosophy and psychology?

Plainly, different problems require different and often many methods, according to the nature of the problem.

So when the Behaviorists inquire into the problems of psychology it may be pertinently asked, is the objective method adequate to resolve completely the problems involving consciousness. When he follows the "adequate stimulus" beyond the sensory receptors, does he not run up against a stone wall, or, at least, lose his path in a jungle.

Let us take one of the least complex problems, or at least one that offers preeminently objective phenomena for research —the behavior resulting from, or determined by, emotion. The occurrence, in conjunction with emotion, of bodily processes (open, as they are, to physiological investigation and having given rise to the James-Lange theory) eventuating in certain types of behavior, has led to the formulation of the concept of so-called "heredity pattern-reaction," or mechanism, as an explanation of emotional, or emotional-instinctive behavior. But is this a complete explanation? Will the discovery of any particular visceral, glandular or other bodily process in connection with particular behavior, explain the *why* of the behavior which subjectively appears to be not mechanistic but "purposive"; why in one situation the individual withdraws from a given stimulus, in another examines it intently, in another approaches it with an embrace, according as he experiences a sentiment of aversion, curiosity, or affection?

Why are these pattern reactions so specifically different? And why does the behavior seem to the individual to be purposive, if it is not? There would seem to be here something over and above the visceral (etc.) process and which is of the order of consciousness. This something (the emotion and cognition) seems at least to be a part of the reaction and to enter into the causal change of events, from stimulus to behavior, for given the emotion we can predict the ensuing behavior. If this be so, the behaviorist must at this point renounce his objective method and resort to some other that will allow him to deal with consciousness.

The only answer the behaviorist can give is that the emotion (and cognition) is an epiphenomenon, the tooting of the steam-whistle that tells by its toots what particular visceral processes are involved in the causal pattern reaction, and that if our physiological knowledge were sufficiently intimate he could predict equally well the behavior; or, as an alternative, that the conscious process and the bodily process are only different aspects of the same thing. As to the first alternative, of consciousness as an epiphenomenon I have already said enough. If the latter alternative be adopted the conscious experience is just as much a causal factor as the physical process and calls for a different method of research.

Thus, if these points are well taken, the Behaviorist, whether he be a steam whistler or some other kind of parallelist, or an interactionist, or a panpsychist, or some other kind of monist, is compelled by the force of circumstances, by the hard facts of nature, willy or nilly, to shift to some other method after he has carried his objective method as far as he can. And the only method open to him that we know of now is the introspective method of which there are many kinds.

The attempt to interpret all behaviour in physiological terms has led to most extraordinary statements on the part of some Behaviorists.

Watson in his "Psychology from the Standpoint of a Behaviorist," would teach that "emotion is an heredity pattern-reaction involving profound changes of the bodily mechanism as a whole, but particularly of the visceral and glandular systems" (p. 195); and that "thought is the action of language mechanisms" (p. 316); is "highly integrated bodily activity and nothing more" (p. 325); and that "when we study implicit bodily processes we are studying *thought*". By this Watson does not mean to identify thought with the cor-related cortical activity of the brain—not at all; but with all the bodily processes that are involved, implicitly and explicitly, in the production of spoken, written and sign language—the muscular activity of the vocal apparatus, diaphragm, hands, fingers, eye-movements, etc. (p. 324).

Now my dear Mr. Watson—if you will do me the honor to allow me to address you personally—I have the greatest respect for you and for your work. You have, at least, made the psychological world "stop, look and listen." You have made an impression on the thought of the day and have made your brother psychologists think and reconsider their basic under-

standings, and in doing this have been a big influence in direct-
ing thought and awakening interest in your points of view. If
any one thinks this easy, let him try it himself. I have tried
it in a modest field and cannot see that I have had any marked
success; so for this reason I take off my hat to you. But, Dr.
Watson, don't you see that when you define "emotion as an
heredity 'pattern-reaction'" of bodily mechanisms, you are
talking just nonsense? You are putting together words that
severally have meaning into a sentence that has no meaning.
It is obvious that you are compelled to make some such definition in order to consistently adhere to your scheme of a psychology described in terms of bodily reactions and mechanisms
without consciousness. But emotion is not a pattern reaction
of visceral and glandular systems or any other anatomical
organs. Emotion is a mental experience, an event of consciousness. You may hold, if you like, that emotion is *conditioned* by pattern reactions of the visceral and glandular
systems; or that it is a mental experience correlated with,
or even, perhaps, the awareness of such reactions; but to say
that it *is* such physiological reactions is nonsense. Emotion
is emotion and nothing else, and certainly nothing like visceral
and glandular activity.

Likewise *thought* is nothing like muscular activity. Images,
for example, are elements of thought. Just imagine my
asserting that my images of this hall and this audience—my
visual pictures of your upturned faces, of the "fair women
and brave men" I see before me, are muscular contractions.
A queer sort of mental blindness, queer thinking, and not very
flattering, you would say. But there is one sense in which you
might be justified in employing this definition without writing
nonsense, although I can not make out from the context
that you have this meaning in mind. You could identify
emotion and thought with the particular physiological processes
of the body you mentioned, in the same sense that the physicist
identifies sound with waves of the atmosphere, and light with
electro-magnetic waves. But it is apt to be overlooked
that when the physicist says that sound and light are such
waves, he does not mean that literally. It is only a convenient
form of expression. All he means is, that which the organism
apprehends as sound is motion or waves of the atmosphere;
and that which the organism apprehends as light is motion or
electro-magnetic waves or ether waves. Sound and light are
the reactions of the organism to these waves: the waves excite

the conscious reaction in us. If there were no beings with ears there would be no sound and the universe would be deathly still; if there were no beings with eyes there would be no light in the universe: it would be pitch dark as it probably is for some insects and other living things. There would be waves in the atmosphere and waves in the ether but they would not be apprehended as sound or light, respectively, just as there are atmospheric waves going on all the time, above and below a certain "pitch" which we cannot hear; and there are electro-magnetic waves beyond each end of the spectrum, infra red and ultra violet, which we cannot see. But the universe is full of them all the same. There are living things for which the world is absolutely silent and others for which the world is absolutely dark. Some living things undoubtedly apprehend ether waves not as light but in some other mode; and atmospheric waves not as sound but by some other sense. So what the physicist means is that sound and light are modes of consciousness by which the organism apprehends different kinds of motion in the universe. He is not so foolish as to confuse motion with sound.

Now in this sense you can *logically* hold, if you like, that emotion is a conscious mode of apprehending by the organism the "heredity-pattern reactions of the visceral and glandular systems," or with James and Lange that the stream of sensory impressions from these systems become fused into an emotion, but this is not identifying the emotion with the visceral reactions any more than is the wave theory of light an identification of visual perception with ether or electro-magnetic waves. Nor, does it help out the behavioristic concept. Unless emotion can be shown to be an epiphenomenon—a steam whistle—it remains to be shown that it does not enter into the causal chain of events inducing behavior; or lacking that, it remains for you to find, if you can, its correlated brain processes and show that *they* do not enter into this chain.

Likewise you may logically maintain that thought is a mode of apprehending the kinetic sensations streaming brainwards from the activity of the muscular systems involved in language; but psycho-physiologically considered, it takes a pretty bold behaviorist to maintain, for instance, that a visual image, or an auditory image, or a tactile image, all of which are elements of thought, is a mode of apprehending kinesthetic sensations, or to identify such images with the muscular activity itself. The only alternative would seem to be to take a novel monistic view and correlate thought with muscular activity after the same fashion that psychology commonly correlates it with brain processes. Here we have parallelism, or panpsychism with a vengeance. Brain processes seem to be chucked overboard, bag and baggage, to lighten the ship of behaviorism, or as useless stowaways. And as to images and wishes and motives and criminal and moral intents which we thought we had some reason for thinking had something to do with our behavior, they too are only delusions and if we want to know what our thoughts, wishes and motives really are, why, just study our muscular systems that subserve language!

IV

The Identification of Conscious and Neural Processes

Let us return now to the first error of the Behaviorists. If I am right in holding, as I believe I am, that consciousness is "a cause of the bodily reactions through which the needs of the organism are fulfilled," the error of those who deny it lies in the false major premise that mental processes and brain processes are parallel events in the same organism and in the minor premise that parallel processes cannot act upon one another. Grant these premises and the conclusion is absolutely sound that consciousness cannot be a cause of bodily processes. But one or the other premise or both must be false because the facts of experience contradict the conclusion. The theory, therefore, is unsound.

I recall that my aged professor of philosophy at Harvard, when I was a student there, many years ago, had a question which he used to put with great gusto, and a snort, to each class. When the time came he called me up. "Prince: Supposing that fact and theory don't agree; what then?" he snorted. I knew the answer he wanted, but, student-like, wishing to tease the old man, I replied, "So much the worse for the theory, Sir." "No, no, no; Premble, Premble, Premble." Premble arose and with the tact of a good boy answered, "So much the worse for the fact, Sir." "Quite right, quite right," snorted again the old professor. It seems to me that this is practically the standpoint of the Behaviorists (of one type) and constitutes a fourth error.

It is obvious that the real question at issue is the old mind body problem. This problem, as I have long held and have argued in opposition to the usually held view* and will try presently to show, is, in my view, one of *identification*—the identification of consciousness with the *reality* of brain processes, with the brain processes from within. Before arguing once more this contention, it will be well to set before ourselves exactly what the theory undertakes to identify. For this purpose we should think of the ultimate nature of matter from the point of view of the physicist and as revealed by modern researches. This modern conception of matter simplifies and clarifies the physical data involved in the problem, if not the problem itself. While formerly the atom was held to be the unanalyzable unit of matter, we are now taught that the atom is a microcosmic solar system of electrons and protons, units of negative and positive electricity, the former revolving in orbits with tremendous rapidity around a complex nucleus of electricity— a unit of positive electricity in the case of hydrogen, a complex unit of negative and positive electricity in the case of other elements—a sort of infinitely minute cosmos. All the physical and chemical properties of so-called "matter" are nothing but the activities of electricity. In other words and in sum and substance, matter, as we know it through our senses has disappeared, having been resolved into negative and positive electricity, or more specifically units of the same in motion, acting and reacting upon one another and associated with, or being in themselves, units of energy.

This is a marvellous conception and a marvellous reconstruction of our knowledge. The properties of matter, such as mass, hardness, crystallization, atomic weight, chemical affinity and reactions, are resolved into the activity and manifestations of units of electricity; while that which we apprehend directly as heat and light and indirectly as ultra violet rays, X-rays, radio rays, and other rays, are modes of electro-magnetic motion, shot out by the energy of such electrical units.

When we look out upon the world of objects about us we must recast our mode of viewing them and of thinking. We must learn to think in terms of those mysterious concepts, electricity and energy, if we would try to resolve the deeper, ultimate problems of life and mind, as well as those of the physical world. When we look out upon the rocks and houses

*Op. cit. (above): also; Professor Strong on the Relation between the Mind and the Body, The Psychological Review, November, 1903; The Identification of Mind and Matter: Philosophical Review, July, 1904.

and trees and plants and animals, we must try to view them in terms of billions upon billions of negative and positive electrons —electrical units—in tremendous activity and motion, sometimes sending out units of energy into the world of space and always acting upon our senses in such fashion that we apprehend them all, not as they are but as material objects. The only known constituent of the ponderable matter of the universe is electricity.

It is as if we were looking at one of those drop curtains at a theatre which an exhibitor, by an arrangement of lights, makes disappear by its becoming transparent, and allows us to see through upon a scene behind. At first we see before us houses and trees and people painted in realistic form upon the curtain. Then all these things fade away; they and the curtain become so transparent that their places have been taken by little bullet-like objects, atoms of the elements, most of which are arranged in tiny, irregular shaped groups called molecules. Nowhere do these little objects coalesce into a continuous mass but everywhere they are separated from one another by relatively enormous spaces. If we could examine them closely, we would find that these atoms and molecules have the same properties as have their masses. Atoms of gold look and are just like a mass of gold; a molecule of glass just like a mass of glass.

Now, as we look, the illumination is again modified, so that we can see still deeper. The atoms and molecules have disappeared and their places are taken by innumerable, infinitely small "particles" which are in constant motion, flying around and about, sometimes with almost infinite velocity. Many revolve in orbits about others, like the planets in the solar system, but here the orbits and the systems are restricted within the confines of what we a moment before saw was the atom. Others fly out of these confines in streams into adjoining space and send out waves of energy to even distant spaces (radio-activity). Some rush towards others, as if attracted by something; others rush away from the same "particles," as if repelled. Often there are head-on collisions and then we see waves of motion of enormous rapidity, like "rays," shooting out into space. Some of these waves stimulate our senses and are apprehended as light and heat; and some do not and can therefore be recorded only by mechanical devices. These are X-rays, radium-rays, etc.

Now, let us stop here and listen to our exhibitor who is a

physicist. He explains that all the "particles" in their motions produce certain phenomena and obey certain laws and he calls these phenomena phenomena of electricity, and these laws, laws of electricity; and so the particles are termed electricity, or, more specifically units of electricity in motion. And then, again our physicist tells us he is compelled to postulate some kind of motive power that drives the electrical units into motion and sends out the waves of electro-magnetic motion into space. Realizing his own subjective feeling of exerting "force" when he pushes some resisting object into motion, he thinks of it anthropomorphically, perhaps correctly, as force or energy; and accordingly postulates the motive power of the electrical units as an entity and calls it energy.

Now, at this point our exhibitor, the physicist, again changes his lights, but reverses the order of appearances. The world of electrons fades away and the world of atoms and molecules, the complex configurations of the electrons, reappears as larger spots where the electrons were. Then in turn these fade away and the world of material objects—rocks, water, trees, animals —reappear as configurations, where were the complex groups of atoms and molecules. So our exhibitor has allowed us to see deep within the world of objects and to recognize that this world is only the mode by which we apprehend through our senses, the actual physical world of electricity and energy.

V

But what about the brain processes of the physiologist, the brain processes which we apprehend as such in the same way as we apprehend the rest of our material world through our senses and which we conceive, as atomic or molecular activity, physical or chemical, to be correlated with consciousness? These, too, disappear under the analysis of the physicist. Let us not forget that we must likewise learn to think of these activities as those of enormously complex groups (called atoms and molecules) of units of electricity, and groups of groups, motivated by and associated with units of energy and, perhaps, radiating energy. As a recent writer on the atom from within has expressed it: "Whether we are interested in speculative questions like those (of life and death), in less speculative but yet unsolved questions like the mechanism for the transmission of stimuli by nerves, or in the purely practical matter of the efficient organization and operation of the multiplicity of machines which condition our daily lives, we must seek explanations in terms of energy and electricity.

"Widely different branches of science are now known to be dealing with the same fundamentals of electricity and energy. For the first time in centuries there exists the material which a genius could synthesize into a universal science, in which physics and chemistry, biology and geology, will lose their identities in a common set of principles."*

While waiting for such a genius perhaps I may be permitted, to try my hand, in a humble way at synthesizing mind and matter into a common principle.

It is, then, of such mysterious entities that we must think in trying to find a solution of the correlation of mind and brain. I say "mysterious" for what is this intangible entity electricity? And what is the entity energy? These are the two fundamental entities of the new science and if we would follow its teachings, we must learn to think of all scientific problems in terms of these concepts. What is their ultimate nature? What is an electron from *within?* What is energy from *within?* The answer of the physicist is that that is beyond his province, that he only deals with phenomena, and the laws of their relations, and therefore cannot deal with the ultimate nature, the reality of anything.

In a sense the terms electricity and energy are only word pictures. They are subjective *concepts* which we are obliged to postulate to explain the phenomena, to give the phenomena meaning. Thus, though energy is conceived and postulated as the motive power of the physical universe, the only way it is evidenced to our senses is as motion, or as changes in the form of motion of the electrical units (electrons and protons) and as "wave" motions in circumambient space (light, heat, etc.). What it is itself is unknown and by the objective methods of science it is *unknowable.* Nevertheless "to every moving particle, whether electron, proton, atom, molecule, or more evident mass, we ascribe a portion of this unknown."**

---

*Milk: Within the Atom, p. 9.
**These principles have been clearly summed up by John Mills as follows:
"When we cause a body to alter its state of motion, either by changing its speed or its direction, we are conscious of exerting what we are pleased to call a force. When we observe the gravitational tractation of body and earth we speak of a force of gravitation as acting on the body. Bodies upon which the earth under similar conditions exerts equal forces we call equal in weight. Unfortunately weight is but a particular kind of force and force itself is an entirely subjective concept without any objective reality. Whatever may

Likewise, while the existence of "particles" has been demonstrated by physicists and these have been termed particles of electricity, or units of electricity, electricity itself is a concept, the ultimate nature of which is unknown and by the objective methods of science is *unknowable*. Science can only determine its laws of behavior.

Even positive and negative electricity, (electrons and protons) may be only different manifestations of something else manifesting itself in these two different phenomena. Consequently, Bertrand Russell finds it necessary to utter a word of warning:

"It may be found, however," he says, "as a result of further research, that the æther is after all what is really fundamental, and that electrons and hydrogen nuclei (protons) are merely states of strain, in the æther, or something of the sort. If so, the two 'elements' with which modern physics operates may be reduced to one, and the atomic character of matter may turn out to be not the ultimate truth. This suggestion is purely speculative; . . . . Our imagination is so incurably concrete and pictorial that we have to express scientific laws, as soon as we depart from the language of mathematics, in language which asserts much more than we **mean** to assert. We speak of the electron as if it were a little hard lump of matter, but no physicist really means to assert that it is. We speak of it as if it had a certain size, but that also is more than we really mean. It may be something more analogous to a noise, which is spread throughout a certain region, but with diminishing intensity as we travel away from the source of the noise. So it is possible that an electron is a certain kind of disturbance in the æther, most intense at one spot, and diminishing very rapidly in intensity as we move away from the spot. If a disturbance of this sort could be discovered which would move and change as the electron does, and have the same amount of energy as the electron has, and have periodic changes of the same frequency as those of the electron, physics could regard it as what an electron really is without contradicting anything that present-day physics means to answer. And of course it is equally possible that a hydrogen nucleus (proton) may come

---

be the character of the alteration in the relative motions of the bodies of a system the alteration is but the manifestation of a change in the disposition and availability of that uncomprehended motive power of our universe which we call energy.

"Energy and the electrical elements are the postulates of the new science, the entities in terms of which all explanations of scientific phenomena must be made.

"To our senses, whether aided by apparatus or not, this motive power, or energy is evidenced only by changes in the state of motion of the electrical elements. To every moving particle, whether electron, proton, atom, molecule, or more evident mass, we ascribe a portion of this unknown. The amount which we assign to any particle depends upon the speed with which it is moving and upon its electrical composition." (Within the Atom, p. 39.)

to be explained in a similar way. All this is however, merely a speculative possibility; there is not as yet any evidence making it either probable or improbable. The only thing that is probable is that there will be such evidence, one way or another, before many years have passed."*

As a matter of pure speculation I would add we may even go further and resolve units of electricity into units of energy or manifestations of the same. For a mass is a collocation of units of electricity, but mass as a consequence of the theory of relativity is energy itself.

When we think, then, of brain processes, we must learn to think of processes, physical or chemical, in terms of their final analysis by the physicist; that is, processes of which the component factors are mysterious units of negative and positive electricity, or mysterious units of energy, or both.

We are compelled, then, to say that a brain process that we are trying to correlate, or identify with consciousness is a phenomenon of electricity and energy. Beyond this we have not the faintest idea of what concretely a brain process is. We must not overlook that fact. Accordingly, *the problem of identifying consciousness with brain processes becomes the problem of identifying it with processes which are revealed to us through our senses as electrical units in activity and wave-motions of energy.* But we must not forget, what the physicist sometimes does forget, that these are not ultimates. *They are only phenomenal manifestations of an unknown something.* The nature of this something the physicist cannot even guess at. He can only postulate concepts—the immaterial entities electricity and energy to account for certain phenomena. But these entities are not only unknown but unknowable by the objective methods of science. The postulated something may be spiritual (whatever that may be), or of the order of the *psychical,* or something else that is *not* matter, but is *immaterial.* Whatever it is it is not material in the sense of the material phenomenal world as known to physics and to account for which it is inferred. It is *immaterial.*

VI

We may now consider the problem itself. The theory for which I am arguing is this: that ultimate unknown something which reveals itself objectively to our senses, which we apprehend through our senses as phenomena of electricity and as phenomena of energy, the *unknown immaterial reality* of elec-

*The A B C of Atoms, pp. 141-143.

trical units and units of energy is the same *in kind,* is of the same nature as that which is known as conscious experience. Or, simplifying the statement as a generalization, that same immaterial reality which, as a concept, is postulated in the objective world (the brain process) as phenomenal units of energy becomes, under certain conditions of configuration and activity of its units, consciousness; just as under other conditions of this kind it manifests itself to our senses as atoms and molecules of electrical units with corresponding physical and chemical properties and as electro-magnetic motion. In other words, consciousness is the *reality* of a particular portion of energy— the energy of the universe-in-itself, the unknowable of physics, the brain processes (of the physiologist) "from within." Thus the psychical becomes identified with that which is postulated by the physicist as the unknowable energy of the universe, by the physiologist as the brain process.

Now, see how by this theory the real problem interestingly shifts. It is no longer the old problem of parallelism, or interactionism. Instead it becomes the question: How is it to be explained that consciousness—a feeling, an image, a color, a pain, can appear under such a different form as units of electricity, electro-magnetic motions? Surely our experiences of the two are totally unlike.

The answer would seem to be simple and obvious: Electricity and energy are the mode in which the reality of the brain process—consciousness—is apprehended, actually (or ideally immaterial) through the senses by another organism, the reaction of this organism to the reality; in fact it is the only mode by which, if apprehended by a second organism, it could be apprehended. For if apprehended through the senses it must be in terms of those senses; if through the visual sense, it must be apprehended as visual perception—form and motion; if through the auditory sense, as sound; if through the tactile sense, as tactile perception; and so with the other senses.

According to the theory, then, mind and matter become synthesized in a common principle; for consciousness is identified, not with electricity (and energy) as objectively apprehended, but with the *reality* of these concepts, the unknowable of physics; or if you prefer, the brain process of the physiologist *from-within.* If the theory is sound, how clear it becomes that there are not two processes in the same organism, parallel with one another, but only one process, the conscious process. The brain process of the physiologist, and electricity of the physicist, are the modes in which the conscious process is ideally apprehended by a second organism.

A moment's thought is sufficient to see how the theory clarifies the parlous problem of parallelism, which has been the thorn in the flesh of psychological science, and relegates the epiphenomenalism of the steam whistle to that limbo where such absurdities belong. Interactionism, too, disappears as a problem, for, there being *only* one process, there ceases to be the question of how one kind of process, the mental, can act upon another of a different kind.

VII

We are now at last, you will be glad to hear, in a position to take up the main point of our thesis which we set out to elucidate—namely, the reconciliation of the purposive and mechanistic concepts. Unfortunately it was necessary to lay this preliminary foundation. It ought to be self-evident how this reconciliation follows as a logical necessity.

Brain processes, that is to say, neural processes, are reflex processes. That we can all agree to. It is the only way in which a neural process can be activated, can function and determine behavior. Reflex processes are by nature mechanistic. There is no doubt about that. But neural reflex processes are *ex hypothesi,* the mode in which conscious processes are apprehended through the senses by the methods of the physiologist. If that be the case, and if consciousness is the *reality* of neural reflex processes, then conscious striving and impulse, *that which we call will and purpose, if apprehended objectively through the senses would necessarily be apprehended by these methods as reflex and mechanistic processes.** It is the only form in which will and purpose could be manifested when so objectively apprehended.

So, when we think in terms of mind, we must think in terms of will and purpose; when in terms of physiology, in terms of mechanism and reflexes. In *principle* it is immaterial which terms we use. But we must not deny the former, will and purpose, as having equal validity with mechanisms and reflexes, nor forget that consciousness is the real thing, while mechanistic processes are only symbols of the real.

---

*This interpretation was worked out in my Nature of Mind and Human Automatism (1885), pp. 93-98.

Thus going a step further, Pan-psychism and Pan-material-
ism are interchangeable terms;** and so purposive and
mechanistic psychology may be reconciled.

Practically, however, as we know almost nothing about
brain-processes, nothing of their nature, and cannot possibly
even guess the concrete brain process that is correlated with
(identifiable with) any particular mental process; and as we
cannot, therefore, follow a stimulus through its intricate and
complex reflex course of complex brain processes until it
emerges in motor and other pathways as behavior—in view of
all this ignorance we are perforce compelled to explain the
causal antecedents of behavior in terms of mind, of will and
purpose, and not of reflexes.

It would, indeed, be a happy thing, if we could explain
behavior in objective terms (brain processes), in view of the
uncertainties and fallacies of the data derived by introspection, open as they are to all sorts of interpretations, for we
should then be able to use more exact quantitative methods
of objective science. But it cannot be done. So, if we want a
complete and causal explanation of behavior, we can only
use mental terms and get over the difficulties of introspection
as best we can. Will and purpose are facts of experience and
as such facts determinants of behavior. They give us a complete and adequate explanation thereof, one upon which the social organizations and sociology are founded, and upon which
the explanations of behavior made use of by social psychology
must be based, if it is to be recognized as entitled to a place
amongst the sciences. Nevertheless, if we can reconcile two
apparently conflicting points of view, as I have endeavored in
this exposition to do, it will redound to the advantage of psychology, and perhaps it is not too much to say, of our conception of the universe.

**Morton Prince: The Identification of Mind and Matter.

CHAPTER X

AWARENESS, CONSCIOUSNESS, CO-CONSCIOUS-NESS AND ANIMAL INTELLIGENCE FROM THE POINT OF VIEW OF THE DATA OF ABNORMAL PSYCHOLOGY†

A Biological Theory of Consciousness*

By Morton Prince

I

My task is not an easy one, for psychologists are not at all times a happy family. They have not as yet learned to live harmoniously together on the basis of a common understanding of what they mean by such concepts as those which are presented in the title of this lecture, nor of the facts of experience for which they are supposed to stand. They should not consider it out of place, if they were reminded of the old proverb about "a house divided against itself." But what is lacking in a common understanding is made up for by the positiveness of statement and the cock-sureness of opinion of each member of the family, leading sometimes to acrimonious discussions in matters of pure theory and making one think of the sects of the Donatists and Orthodox Christians of olden times who belabored one another with cudgels because they could not agree in matters of dogma and doctrine. I fear that psychologists, being human beings first and searchers after truth afterwards, are like all mortals, too often concerned with maintaining their own points to which they have committed themselves rather than discovering the truth. Perhaps after all we cannot expect the latter until "this mortal shall have put on immortality."

So now to our task, but with as open a mind as we can muster and, if possible with sustained clear thinking.

At the very outset we are confronted with a technical difficulty, namely, ambiguity of terms. Both consciousness and awareness have several meanings in that each term is used in several different senses and interchangeably as well as exclusively. Thus, for example, consciousness is used to denote the being conscious, or aware *of* something—of objects (en-

†Powell Lecture in Psychological Theory at Clark University, December 15, 1924.

*An abstract of this lecture was read at the International Congress of Psychology held at Oxford, July 26—August 1, 1923. (See Proceedings and British Journal of Psychology.)

vironment), or thought, sensations, perceptions, feelings, or of self *by* some thing, or some one, or self, or "I," as when I say I have a consciousness of such or such a thing; or, I have a consciousness of self; or of my internal feelings.

But it is also used to denote simply thought, sensation, perception, feelings, images, etc., *i. e.,* a process, each by and of itself regardless of whether it is *per se* awareness of something by something: as when we speak of consciousness as contrasted with the physical world, or of thought, sensation, feeling, as elements of consciousness, or of the content of consciousness.

Awareness is also used with the same two meanings, although that of awareness *of* something *by* something is by far the more common. Indeed some assert that awareness without a subject is a contradiction in terms. It connotes a subject who is aware. Consciousness, on the other hand, has no such necessary connotation in some folk's minds, though the contrary is asserted by others.

Nevertheless, consciousness and awareness are often, if not commonly, used as synonyms, it being insisted by those who so use them that they have identical meanings. Cognition also is used as a synonym for awareness and consciousness and with similar double meanings.

All this is bad enough, leading, as it does, to inevitable confusion owing to the fallacies resulting from using the same terms in different senses. But it is worse than this. There is no common understanding of the psychological facts for which the terms stand in whichever sense the terms are used. Thus, for instance, it is held by some orthodox psychologists that, as a fact, there is and can be no consciousness that does not include in its content both some thing, some subject, some person, some experiencer, some self that is conscious and a consciousness of some thing. An elementary state of consciousness, or, more correctly, a conscious process that does not include these other elements does not, they say, in fact, occur. This concept, of course, postulates consciousness as equivalent to and identical with awareness.

The question plainly is one of fact which can only be determined by investigation. It is one of the most important problems of psychology and cannot be resolved by theoretical reasoning and logical deductions from the meanings of words. Its importance lies in the fact that it opens up, as I will presently explain, the whole question of the actual occurrence and nature, indeed the possibility of subconscious processes, that is, of consciousness of which we are not aware, and therefore, of the structure, mechanisms and functioning of the mind. And more than this, upon the answer to this question hangs the possibility of forming a biological conception of consciousness.

But first let me touch upon the more specific and narrower question as to whether the postulated *experiencer* involved in this notion of consciousness as awareness can be based on a demonstrated specific awareness of a self.*

Psychologists are divided into three camps—the self-psychologists, the selfless-psychologists and the middle grounders. The first group maintain that the content of every conscious process includes a self—an awareness of self, a self-consciousness. Hence that all consciousness is a consciousness or awareness of something by a *self*.

The second group, the selfless ones, claim to be unable to find any self, or consciousness of self by introspection; deny its reality and hold that mental processes function without any such reality. The "I" and the "You" are merely compulsory expressions required by the necessities of language.

The middle-grounders admit the self in that we are aware of self in, for instance, feeling and willing, but not in perceiving and imagining which may go on without any self or self-consciousness. I must class myself *in principle* with these last —the middle grounders.

Of course there are also the indifferent non-combatants who take no heed of the self at all—a sort of plague-on-both-your-houses attitude—and go on talking about awareness, and content, and objects of awareness as if the question of *by* what, or *by* whom could be ignored. The implications of their language, however, are that something is aware though what is not defined. But this vagueness is also true, and specifically so, of the self-psychologists. These do not attempt to analyze the self, to define its structure, to say what it is, even whether it is animistic or psychological; whether it is "an anima or an animus sitting," as you may remember Tristram Shandy's father used to say, "like a tadpole all day long both summer and winter," dabbling its feet in the fluid of the pineal gland. It has no analyzable psychological structure. For it is said to be an "ultimate datum"; to be "indefinable," "*sui generis* and

---

*Compare Mary Whiton Calkins' admirable critical discussion of the problem: "The Self in Scientific Psychology"; Amer. Jour. of Psychology, October, 1915.

therefore incapable of definition"; it "is a kind of thing which one can merely indicate but which one can as little demonstrate to the I-blind as one can demonstrate color to the color-blind"*—a veritable tadpole theory.

Surely we must allow, in view of all this confusion, that the Behaviorists have some excuse for joining in the cry, "A plague on both your houses"! and saying, "we will have none of consciousness; away with it. We are going to disregard it entirely and explain behavior in terms of physiological processes alone," though they ought to add, "if we can."

This question as to whether there can or cannot be consciousness that has no awareness by. "some one who is conscious of some thing"—some person, some subject, some self, that thinks and experiences and is aware, this question is, as I have already intimated, of fundamental importance to psychology. For, obviously, if consciousness (experience), when considered identical with awareness, always includes an I, and if "we cannot talk of experiencing, without an I which experiences," as Dunlap, Mary Calkins, Oesterreich and others of that camp insist, then a sub-consciousness—that is to say, a coconsciousness (as I prefer to term it) or coawareness, or an "unconscious," term it what you will, is a paradox and an absurdity. It is mere nonsense. Consciousness is conceived of as limited to and only what may be called our personal consciousness. And this many insist upon on this very ground, entirely ignoring the findings of abnormal psychology including therein artificially dissociated and activated mental processes. One must admit that logically they are right, if the premises be granted; but their premises, so abnormal psychology teaches, and as it seems to me, are unsound; and abnormal psychology relies on precisely the same methods and the same kind of data and the same logic as does traditional normal psychology. I don't want to be one of those pestiferous friends who are always telling unwelcome, if wholesome, truths, but our mutual friend and collaborator Abnormal Psychology insists on telling us a lot of disagreeable truths to which, as the easiest way out, the "normal Psychologist," taking a tip from Nelson with his blind eye at the battle of Copenhagen, finds it exceedingly convenient to turn a deaf ear and to pretend he does not hear them. And among those truths, or at least claimed truths, are

---

*Oesterreich; quoted by Miss Calkins. It is fair to say, though, that the I is not considered as something having an existence beyond and beside experience: "Experiences exist in the self."

a lot of sensations and feelings and thoughts of which a given subject is not aware and which are therefore called *co*conscious. They are not in the content of his awareness.   There is no use saying that they are *not* types, or orders of consciousness, for they are.   They are certainly non-physical and they are both psychical and psychological.   Nelson saved his skin by winning the battle, but I can't help thinking these psychologists of the normal are yet to win and save their skins.

The data of abnormal psychology and of dynamic psychology include a large number of percepts and "ideas" and sensations, dissociated from the personal consciousness, from awareness by the self, and from anything that thinks or perceives.   They are processes, of course, and these processes are not synthesized with that other complex or process which is called a self, an "I" or a personality.   Until these facts, as I believe them to be, are recognized and frankly utilized as data, I can't help thinking we shall never be able to understand consciousness as processes, nor biologically, and therefore animal intelligence and instinct.

II

CONSCIOUSNESS REGARDED AS COGNITION

In venturing these criticisms on the negligent attitude of the self-psychologists of course I have only in mind that concept of consciousness which identifies it with awareness by a self, a subject, an experiencer, who (logically we can only say "who") is inherent in every conscious process.

But there is another conception of awareness which is germane to the problem in hand and this we must take a few moments to consider.   I am sorry and must ask you to bear with me a while longer before taking up our main theme.   It is a much more subtle notion in that it means the identification of consciousness with a particular kind of awareness.   You will see that it is a much more defensible notion in that it can be reconciled with the data furnished by subconscious processes as derived from experimental and abnormal psychology.   This must now be examined.

According to this subtle notion, awareness is identical with cognition-of-something, but neither the one nor the other need involve a *self* that is aware; the very simplest conscious process is *in itself* and *by itself* cognition of something.   Therefore, no self or experiencer would seem to be required, unless it be the "organism."   But to call it the organism, as I will presently insist, is the introduction of an objective and biological term in the psychological equation.

I am not sure that this conception of awareness has been explicitly stated in these terms, but it is, at least, so implied in certain expositions of consciousness as set forth by well known writers.

Thus it is maintained, for instance, by William McDougall, for whose work I have great admiration and with whom I am fundamentally in accord,—it is maintained by him, with Mary Calkins' approval, that every sensation, every perception even of the simplest and most rudimentary kind in the simplest and most rudimentary organism conceivable, is *cognition* and therefore awareness of "something there."

"The simplest mind," he forcibly argues, "we can legitimately conceive is, then, one which would respond to a sense-impression, not merely by 'having a sensation' but by an act of **knowing**; this act we could only describe as becoming aware of **something there**, an **object in space**, no matter how completely undefined the nature of the object as thought of and the nature of its spatial relations. Such a mind, of simplest possible structure, must be conceived as consisting of one cognitive disposition linked with a single conative disposition. Such a mind would respond to every sense-impression that affected it at all (no matter what its nature) with simple **awareness** of **something there** and a vague undirected impulse of appetition, of striving towards the object."*

This, if I understand him correctly, amounts to saying that every sensation is, itself, *per se*, cognition and awareness, but not by a self.

Here cognition and awareness are robbed of one of their attributes and are given another and particular meaning. If this be true of the simplest mind in the simplest organism, then it must, also, be true of the simplest dissociated and coconscious sensation, or image, of the human mind, and of this, as I shall presently point out, there is some experimental evidence that may be adduced in support.

This is the only meaning that I can conceive can be given

---

*Outline of Psychology, p. 260. Bold face mine.

It is difficult to reconcile this view, if I do not misunderstand him, with his argument for the substitution of the term **experience** for consciousness. Just as "All experiencing or thinking" he says, "is the experiencing or thinking of [by] **some one**, some person, some organism," and "whenever we refer to a fact of experience we imply **some one** thinking of **some thing**," so consciousness "stands for the fact of being conscious of something" and "implies some one who is conscious of something."

These two conceptions of consciousness, one requiring a subject that is aware (conscious) of something, the other only awareness of something, the response of a simple cognitive disposition without an apparent subject, can hardly be reconciled.

to cognition and awareness under this theory. Only on the adoption of such a meaning can consciousness and purposive behavior be attributed, as McDougall "provisionally at least" does, to such microbes as the protozoa (on the basis of Jenning's observations and conclusions). Likewise a dissociated "prick" of a pin may be felt, and, according to the evidence, in fact *is* felt coconsciously by an anesthetic hysteric as a subconscious perception of "something there" and even as a pin there, but not by a self. And so with many coconscious, dissociated sensations, images and perceptions. It is difficult to reconcile this conception of consciousness with that for which McDougall has argued when adopting the term "experience" in place of consciousness; namely that "consciousness implies *some one* who is conscious of something."

Undoubtedly he would further explain to us that the awareness of the "simplest mind," of a protozoan, and of a dissociated bit of consciousness for "something there" is by the "organism," for he sometimes substitutes this term for the subject "who" (or I). But to say that the "who" is the organism is a poorly masked camouflage for it is substituting biological objective terms for psychological terms, and introducing the ambiguous middle. If we are going to have a subject, it is a high potentate, the psychological "who" to whom we want to be introduced and not a conglomeration of such common folk as the liver and gall bladder and muscles, or any material "who."

After such a ruthless elimination of the self, the question of awareness would seem to become a purely academic, if not a philosophical one, and to be practically of no importance.

It does seem queer, not to say paradoxical, that such a dissociated isolated conscious process as a simple sensation, or a complex of sensations (perception) of which the personal consciousness is not aware, can be a cognition of something in the environment without there being anything that cognizes—a cognition that is not a cognition by something. How can we speak of a cognition that is not a cognition by something? If it is insisted that the cognition must be by a self or subject, then we may ask how many selves or subjects are there in a given personality. We may have any number of independent dissociated conscious processes, independent so far as awareness of each other is concerned. Does each one of them imply a self? If so it would seem that there must be any number of selves.

A way out of the difficulty may be found in the following considerations. Probably no sensation after the first experience (if not before) ever occurs as an isolated experience. It is always integrated with other sensory events—kinesthetic and pressure sensations, visual and tactile images, sensory localizing impressions, etc.,—whether because of inherited integrations or acquired experiences. The whole of these are integrated into a complex which, as a setting, gives the sensation meaning. A prick from a pin, we will say, is integrated even with revived visual images of a pin, as well as with numerous other sensory impressions. It is this whole structural complex which functions when (the other senses being neglected) the skin is pricked. It is comprehensible that such a complex may well be in itself a specific cognition of something there—of a pin, an apperception of the stimulus.* It *is* the pin for consciousness.

At any rate, if all that is meant by "awareness" is that kind of, or so much consciousness or cognition as is presumed to be present in the protozoa and to determine its reactions, as so cautious and conservative an investigator as Jennings thinks justified; or the kind that may be possessed by William James' theoretical polyp (quoted by McDougall with approval) which thinks, "Hello! thingumbob again"; or so much consciousness as may be present in higher animals, like the crawfish of Thorndike's and Yerkes' experiments, presumably without any self, or self-awareness, one can accept for all practical purposes the concept of consciousness that identifies it with cognition without a subject (save the material organism).

Indeed, I think that the data from Abnormal Psychology I am going to marshal and the thesis I am presenting better supports the position of the purposive behaviorists against the mechanists, the tropists, the conditioned reflexers, and others, than that other insistence of McDougall that consciousness stands for and "implies some one who is conscious of some thing."

The practical questions are: Are dissociated mental processes of which the self is not aware, themselves conscious processes? If so, are they devoid of a self, a subject, and self-awareness? And if the answer is affirmative, what can such simple conscious processes by themselves as dissociated coconscious sensa-

---

*I am not sure whether such a structural complex is not analogous to, or identical with the Gestalt concept.

tions, images, perceptions, etc., devoid of self and all self-awareness do? How far are they capable of choice and can they adapt the organism to the situations of life and thus determine so-called purposive behavior—in short, exhibit intelligence of various sorts? And how far are they paralleled by such primitive types of consciousness as presumably occur in the animal world? If such processes are self-less and yet can determine purposive behavior and if they can be so paralleled by the primitive types of the animal mind, we shall be able to give a psychological interpretation of animal behavior and form a biological conception of consciousness.

With the narrower question of the reality of a specific self in what I may call our every day "personal consciousness," let it be borne in mind, I am not concerned.

In order to avoid the confusion from the double meaning of terms, I shall at once precisely define the meaning in which I shall use the terms "consciousness," "awareness" and "cognition."

I am going to use "awareness" in the first of its two common meanings and "consciousness" in the second of its meanings as defined at the beginning: that is to say—

By awareness I mean an awareness or cognition *of* something *by* something, (an "I," self, subject, experiencer, or something that is aware).

By consciousness I simply mean thought, sensation, perception, image, feeling, sentience, or anoetic consciousness without any implication of its being itself awareness, *i.e.*, cognition of something *by* something. Whether there is or is not such consciousness is a question of fact to be determined by investigation. The evidence for the veridity of this concept I propose to present.

Awareness thus becomes a type or order of consciousness and the two are not used as synonymous terms.

By cognition I mean *knowing* or awareness of something there without necessarily there being a subject that knows, though of course there may be such. It is a modified and particular type of awareness. This subjectless cognition I hope to be able to justify.

III

THE EMPIRICAL DATA

I propose now to examine the content and activities of the simplest conscious processes with a view to determining (a) whether they include anything that can be regarded as awareness *by* something—a subject, an experiencer, a self; (b) the character of the behavior, if any, which they determine, *i. e.,* whether purposive or not; (c) the degree of intelligence exhibited by such simple processes; and (d) how far they may be regarded as analogues of the lower orders of the animal mind.

Such simple conscious processes suitable for study are found in the dissociated and more or less segregated processes occurring in certain abnormal conditions, such as hysteria and dissociated personalities; in artificially produced conditions, such as suggested post-hypnotic acts; and in normal states, like intense concentration of the attention and absentmindedness; and in that no-man's land of dreams, automatic writing, etc.

The very simple dissociated coconscious processes found in these and other allied conditions and the behavior which they determine enable us to study consciousness reduced to its simplest terms—sentience, sensations, perceptions—segregated from the complex self and from the highly complex order of conceptual thinking with which, as experienced probably only in man, sensations and perceptions are normally inextricably commingled and integrated.

It is a fair assumption that such simple dissociated processes are analogues to primitive orders of mind and the simplest of them approximates McDougall's theoretical "simplest mind we can conceive . . . one single cognitive disposition linked with a single conative disposition." Of course such a mind is an abstraction for every mind is more complex than this; and so is every dissociated process, and many may be very complex. Indeed dissociated processes may be of every degree of complexity from the simplest to the highest, approximating a wholly integrated mind.

But many are exceedingly simple compared with the completely integrated human mind, probably as simple as many types of primitive minds belonging to the lower forms of animal life. A study, then, of simple dissociated processes ought to throw light on the problem of awareness, and give an insight into the kind of behavior which can be determined by the simpler minds which, as we infer, are manifested in the lower orders of animals.

Of course no dissociated process is completely isolated any more than is any conscious process of normal everyday thinking. The one as much as the other is organized in a "setting" of dispositions deposited by past experiences in which it has its root and which conditions the reactions of the process to given stimuli or a situation. Nevertheless, the same must be true of primitive animal minds.

The phenomena I shall make use of are the inferred coconscious (subconscious) processes revealed in:

1: Hysterical anesthesia.
2: The fringe and ultra-marginal zone of consciousness during
    a) normal attention:
    b) certain types of absent-minded acts and impulsions:
    c) suggested post-hypnotic acts:
    d) phobic attacks.
3: Certain types of extremely dissociated personalities.
4: Coconscious images in various conditions.
5: Coconscious solutions of mathematical problems.
6: Coconscious somatic and coenesthetic sensations and anoetic consciousness.
7: Tics and hysterical and suggested contractures.

The method employed in all but the last of these conditions is chiefly introspection in states of repersonalization, *i. e.,* hypnosis, abstraction, so-called dissociated personalities etc., but in some observations, where it could be employed, introspection by the presumed coconscious process itself was employed and described by subconscious writing.

The fundamental principles underlying the method are:

(1) That by introspection in these states memories of conscious processes previously segregated and excluded from the awareness of the personal self can be brought within the awareness of the newly repersonalized subject; and also that communication can be established with these subconscious processes by means of automatic writing; or that they can be made to manifest themselves by other sorts of behavior of one kind or another.

(2) The assumption that these segregated bits of conscious processes roughly correspond to the simpler types of consciousness and, therefore, to the theoretically simplest mind, and that the behavior they determine to that which such a mind determines.

It will be well at this point to make clear what is meant by coconsciousness, or more correctly coconscious processes, and for this purpose give some examples of the data upon which this concept is based and which I also desire to make use of for a biological conception of consciousness.

1. I cannot do better than begin with the old and classical phenomena of *hysterical anesthesia*. These have long been known to students of abnormal psychology. I prefer to begin with them, because they are as important as they are old and have not been as yet adequately analyzed; and because psychologists, who undertake to interest themselves in the problems of awareness and consciousness, rarely give any signs that they have heard of them and much less take cognizance of them as data, nor seem to realize that they may be possible factors in the problems.

Hysterical anesthesia is a loss of sensation by the personal consciousness due to dissociation from functional causes. It may involve only some of the senses, or all of the senses, and only part of the body, or the whole of the body.

Now, given an hysteric of a certain type with absolute anesthesia of the skin, no tactile stimulus is felt, much less perceived, *no matter how intensely the attention is concentrated* on the stimulated area. The lack of awareness of the tactile stimulus is not due, therefore, to lack of focusing the attention; *i. e.,* to the unfelt sensation—a prick of a pin, or the touch of a hand, or the burning of a hot iron, or whatever it may have been— having been in the fringe of awareness. There was simply and plainly absence of awareness.

Now put that hysteric into another state of mind, or personality, that is to say hypnosis, and he recalls, first, that there did actually occur the sensation of a "prick" or "touch"; and, second, that when it occurred he was unaware of it. He further insists that it was a veritable sensation-in-being. More than this he recalls and insists that there was a coconscious perception of which he was at the previous moment unaware, and in evidence thereof, when put to the crucial test, he describes accurately what the experimenter did—that he pricked the hand five times, drew a figure on the skin, put a pair of scissors, a knife, a key in the hand, bent the third and fifth fingers, and so on. These he now claims to remember were true coconscious perceptions of which the hysteric was unaware in spite of concentration of attention.

Again modify the experiment. Instead of hypnotizing the hysteric try tapping the so-called unconscious dispositions by automatic writing at the moment of the tactile stimulus. The writing now describes accurately the tests and insists there are at the very moment coconscious sensations and perceptions experienced synchronously with the tactile stimulus by that which writes, while at the same instant the subject testifies he is not aware of the stimulus. More specifically, that which writes feels and perceives while the subject is unaware.

Now, unless we refuse to accept the psychological interpretation and insist, as Münsterberg used to hold, that the tactile stimulus is only recorded as a neurological disposition to be later awakened as a conscious memory,* we have here a very simple coconscious process—a sensation, or a perception—which is also a "cognition" of the environment; for the consciousness is not simply a sensation of pain, in the case of a pin-prick, but a realization that it is the prick of a *pin,* and in the more complicated tests a recognition of objects such as scissors, key, etc., as has been already mentioned.

Is the coconscious cognition, revealed in such observations, that by a co-self, a co-subject, or co-experiencer, for such it would have to be in view of the unquestionable fact that the hysteric-subject is unaware of the co-experiences? This is a subtle problem. To so interpret the data would require the postulation of a plurality of coexisting selves, or a reconsideration of our conception of the nature and structure of a self. It will be better to postpone giving an answer to the question until all the data are in hand. Assuming, however, provisionally that the answer is negative, that such simple coconscious processes do not justify the postulation of a plurality of I's or selves, the significance of the phenomena in question for the problem of awareness and consciousness is that *consciousness is not synonymous, coextensive or identical with self-awareness, or awareness by a self, or by a subject, or an experiencer or anything.* If the residua left by the simplest coconscious experience of the kind here cited is to be regarded as "one cognitive disposition linked with a single conative disposition" (Mc-Dougall), there remains the question, what kind of behavior can such dispositions determine? To answer this question we will examine dissociated coconscious processes occurring under other conditions.

---

*The physiological interpretation lands us in a whole peck of difficulties. It does not get rid of the coconscious interpretation **in principle** because it would have to admit that the written memory was a hallucinatory memory and, if so, as hallucinations are not neural but a conscious process, the theory postulates a coconsciousness, a co-hallucination. Further it would have to explain the writing itself as due to neurological processes. There are also a large variety of other subconscious phenomena which it would have to explain.

2. In *absentminded acts* there is commonly dim sub-awareness by the subject of the act, but there is a type in which no such awareness of it, or of the conscious process which determines it, can be detected. But this process can afterwards, in hypnosis, be recalled to memory as having been a coconscious one, often rich in visual imagery. It may be quite complex and determine complicated purposive behavior, such as we all know absentminded acts may be, sometimes to our mortification. It exhibits cognition but not by the personal self as the experiencer. In this case consciousness or apperception itself, apparently, *is* cognition, unless some other self can be found.

3. Of the various conditions in which dissociated coconscious processes are found, the one in which they are, perhaps, most beautifully studied by experimental methods is that of artificially *suggested post-hypnotic acts*. These, as you all probably know, are acts performed by a favorable subject in a waking state as a result of a suggestion given while he was hypnotized. The subject, for example, is told in hypnosis that after waking, at a given signal, he will arise from his chair, walk across the room, take down a certain book from the bookcase, carry it to some part of the room and place it in a given place, and so on. If the subject is a good one the act will be performed as suggested in a sort of absentminded way without even, it may be, his being aware of what he is doing. Indeed such acts are in principle absentminded acts.

Now, in experiments of this kind I have found that there is a conscious process of which the subject is unaware which determines the act. In the example I have cited there is at each step in the act a coconscious visual image of and preceding the next step to be performed. Thus there develops the image of the subject walking across the room—whereupon he arises and absentmindedly walks across the room; an image of the bookcase—he arrives at the bookcase; an image of a hand reaching for the designated book—he reaches for and takes down the book, and so on.

These coconscious images of which the subject is not aware are found in a good many conditions besides absentminded and suggested post-hypnotic acts. They occur in frankly repressed thoughts, in the subconscious perseveration of dreams after waking (*e.g.*, automatic kleptomania), in artificially induced hallucinations, in automatic writing, in concentrated attention as when we are in a "brown study," and various other conditions. In some conditions they come and go repeatedly, or may remain more or less stabile, or they may behave like cinema pictures and symbolically represent elaborate thoughts or ideas. Sometimes they erupt into the personal consciousness and then the individual becomes aware of them as hallucinations or visions. Indeed this is the psychological mechanism of the visions of saints and sinners; but saints and sinners are aside from the subject in hand.

What I want to call attention to now is that further investigation has shown, as I believe, that, first, these images are elements in a conscious process of which the personal consciousness is unaware—a coconsciousness—and which may be very simple in composition, or of greater or less complexity; and, secondly, this process may determine intelligent purposive behavior of various types varying from kleptomanic attacks to subconscious writing; and, thirdly, it has all the characteristics of intelligence and cognition. Whether or not this co·consciousness is awareness in the sense I have used this term, *i. e.*, by something, a subject, a self, is a question we shall presently consider.

4. When we come to study *coconscious perceptions* in normal every-day life, we have a mass of observations showing perceptions of the environment and of the body of which the personal consciousness is not aware—auditory, visual, tactile, kinesthetic, coenesthetic, etc. These are of sounds in the street, voices, visual images of the environment, sensations of warmth, cold, and discomfort, of positions of the body, tension, and coenesthesis, generally, streaming in from the body, none of which enters the content of the personal consciousness at all. They are all comparable in principle to the perceptual phenomena I have already described of hysterical anesthesia.

As to behavior, the coconscious bodily sensations may cause shifting of the position of the subject, or general restlessness, and sometimes discontinuance and change of occupation, or location without the subject realizing the reason therefor.

In these three classes of phenomena, then,—absentminded acts, suggested post-hypnotic acts and coconscious perceptions of normal every-day life—we have dissociated bits of consciousness, *i. e.*, conscious processes consisting of little more than simple perceptions dissociated from the personal self, but which nevertheless are manifestly cognition and determine behavior, not of a reflex order, but intelligent and adaptive to a purpose or end. If they can be shown to have no specific self of their own, they give an insight into the nature of a self-less consciousness like that which we imagine the lower animals possess, and the sort of behavior it can determine.

The phenomena I have cited are sufficient, I think, for my purpose without detaining you with a further recital of actual examples of the performances of coconscious processes in other normal and abnormal conditions I have referred to, such as automatic writing, mathematical calculations, subconscious perseveration of dreams after waking, phobias, tics, and other states.

IV

AWARENESS BY COCONSCIOUS PROCESSES

Now, if the veridity of dissociated coconscious processes of the kind I have cited be accepted, the important question remains, is the *co*consciousness self-less, and has it self-awareness, and does it involve an awareness by a self or subject, or experiencer, or something? Is, for example, the simplest dissociated and coconscious sensation or even perception of a pin-prick an awareness of something there by a coconscious self, even though the personal self feels nothing? In short, can it be said to have any real awareness, or is it *per se* self-less cognition? The last question is a very subtle one.

Theoretically if there is a coconscious self—an experiencer—this self would have to be a second self differentiated from the personal self, for the latter is ignorant of the coconscious process, and there would have to be as many selves as there were differentiated dissociated experiences—and of these there may be any number.* It looks to me as if we were going to get into hot water, or at any rate into very troublous waters, if we are going to attribute every dissociated conscious process, no matter how simple, of which the subject is unaware, every coconscious perception, every bit of automatic writing, every motor-automatism, to an "I." Kipling's ape, Bimi, you will remember, got into terribly hot water because he had "too much ego in his cosmos," but our cosmos would be a whole universe of egos.

But the problem is too important as well as difficult to be turned aside by a jest. Whether or not there is a self which is differentiated from the subject-self and may be called a co-

---

*Of course I am excluding coconscious personalities, like "Sally" (case of Miss Beauchamp), which represents very complexly organized coconscious systems with a veritable second self. They throw light on the structure of the self which, in my judgment, contrary to that of the self-psychologists, is analyzable and definable.

experiencer who co-experiences the simplest dissociated co-sensation or co-image (assuming the fact of co-experience to be accepted as veridical as those who are familiar with the phenomena do accept it) of which the subject is unaware is a subtle question and one not easy to answer. It is a matter of interpretation dependent upon the evaluation of the evidence. An affirmative interpretation would require the postulation of a plurality of coexisting selves, and probably a recasting of our conception of the nature and structure of a self and a more exact knowledge than we now possess.

A plurality of coexisting selves is theoretically possible, particularly as we know that in the complex conditions of so-called multiple personality, dual (or more) selves occur, but if we are to ascribe a self to every dissociated conscious process, it looks as if the animistic psychologists are going to have a hard time of it. Perhaps we ought to have more exact knowledge of what a self is before reaching a conclusion on theoretical grounds, particularly on any theory of cognition.

But we have considerable positive testimony though it must, of course, be evaluated as relating to the question at issue.

The empirical evidence entirely denies self-awareness to such coconscious experiences. The introspective testimony of my dissociated subjects, who in that condition recalled vividly and precisely these subconscious experiences, has been unanimous that these experiences were without selfconsciousness, that in their content there was nothing that the personal pronoun "I" could be applied to. The subject could not say, and there was nothing that could say, "I saw this," "I felt that"; the perceptions, feelings, etc., were not synthesized into a self or personality. The conscious events were just sensations, perceptions, images and "thoughts" and nothing more—no agent, nothing that could be called a *psychological* "experiencer." This evidence contradicts Wm. McDougall's view alleging to be a "fact that there is only one agent in *all** forms of mental activity, you or I, he, she, or it, an agent that can properly be denoted only by a proper name or pronoun, or generally as the 'subject'." Here was a type of mental activity in which no such agent could be discovered.

If it be said that the organism was the agent, the experiencer that experienced, then it may be replied that this is using both the noun and the verb in a different sense—in an objective and biological sense and not in a psychological one, and we are

---

*Italics mine.

guilty of the logical crime of the ambiguous middle term.   To
say that the "organism experiences" has no meaning for psychology, and it is a very different thing from saying that "I" or
"you" experience—the one is only biological and objective, the
other is psychological.

Now, please don't close your minds and go away with the
opposing thought that such phenomena as I have cited are rare
and therefore may be disregarded.   Whether they are rare or
not (and they are not), like "flowers that bloom in the spring,
tra, la, la, has nothing to do with the case."   They may be as
rare as Dinosaurian eggs, or a tadpole sitting on top of the
Washington Monument, but if a single dissociated selfless conscious process can be established that is devoid of awareness
and yet can determine intelligent purposive behavior, a fundamental principle is thereby also established that becomes the
basis for a biological concept of consciousness and the understanding of animal behavior.

The deeper significance of these findings is, first, that consciousness is not always to be limited to and therefore synonymous and identified with the awareness of the every-day personal self.   Otherwise, a subconscious, or coconscious, or unconscious process would be a paradox.

Second, a self is not essential, as some maintain, for consciousness, nor, paradoxical as it may seem, for cognition, nor,
as Ach implies and agrees, as a result of his experiments on
normal subjects, does all personal experience involve consciousness of self.   So the conclusion that conscious processes may
function without there being any self-awareness or awareness
by a self does not wholly rest on the findings of abnormal
psychology.   It also is in keeping with the studies of Michotte
and Prüm on themselves and four other normal subjects.
These experimenters, who found direct introspective evidence
of a self and self-activity, distinguished this experience from
other sensational and affective experiences *without* self-consciousness.

Third, another point of significance, especially for a biological
conception of consciousness, is that a dissociated selfless consciousness of a primitive type, can determine intelligent purposive adaptive behavior of a kind that parallels the behavior
of the lower animals.

V

ANIMAL INTELLIGENCE AND BEHAVIOR

In the course of our discussion of coconscious phenomena I

have already called attention to the intelligent purposive behavior which even the simplest coconscious process, without
any self or self-awareness, can determine. This behavior, as
we have seen, varies in complexity all the way from maintaining
the posture of the body for a given purpose, or the adaptation of
the posture and the relation of the subject to the immediate
situation of the environment (if the evidence is accepted) to
more complex purposive acts such as those called absentminded behavior, the complicated actions following suggestion in hypnosis, defense behavior (in phobic attacks and conflicts with the volition of the "conscious self") and impulsive
actions such as kleptomanic behavior, to say nothing of solving
mathematical and other problems and of constructive imagination exhibited by a dissociated consciousness without self-
awareness.

Such behavior is commonly called automatic although it can
be shown, as I believe, to be determined by conscious processes
of which the self is not aware. This would seem to give some
insight into what very possibly may be the central conscious
factor in instinctive and other types of animal behavior. We
are so accustomed from our intellectual experiences, to think of
awareness by a self as essential for purposive and intelligent
behavior, that it has been difficult to conceive of consciousness
being involved in instinct and learning by experience in the
lower animals. Hence the behaviorists, who are now having
wild joy-rides in America, have sought a way out by conditioned reflexes. But the findings I have just cited, as well
as a large variety of other findings in the field of the coconscious, discovered by abnormal psychology, show another way
out; *viz*: that consciousness without any self, or "awareness"
can determine behavior of an intelligent purposive kind. Such
a dissociated consciousness may be regarded as a relatively
primitive consciousness and it may well be the type of mental
activity in animals.

At any rate the resulting behavior which it motivates, as I
will presently point out, is comparable to that of the lower order
of animals; and therefore a study of the different orders of
dissociated consciousness and the resulting behavior would
reasonably seem to give an insight into the central conscious
factor in animal behavior including cognition and the affective
element in instinct. Indeed I think we may say that the behavior of animals, from the lowest through intermediate levels
to nearly the highest (where self consciousness may be devel-

oped) can be paralleled by similar sorts of behavior carried out
by dissociated conscious processes in man, whether they be of a
normal, abnormal or artificially induced character. By such
automatic conscious mechanisms, the "trial and error" behavior
studied by animal psychologists may be better interpreted than
by the mechanistic principles of conditioned reflexes, tropisms
or other physico-chemical reactions. To this I will presently
return.

From this point of view we may say that examples of all the
different types of animal behavior and of the inferred animal
consciousness, according to the stage of evolutionary development reached, can be found recapitulated *under various conditions* in man.

The discovery, if I may be permitted to use so strong a term, of
dissociated imagery and perceptions, which, through the processes of which they are elements, determine intelligent behavior, without any awareness *of* processes, or pertaining *to* the
processes (as in suggested post-hypnotic behavior and in various other types), offers an interpretation of the mechanism of
animal behavior which has been so baffling. In animal behavior I include the "trial and error" phenomena which have
been the study of animal psychologists. Loath to interpret this
as "intelligence" of the anthropomorphic sort, in which reasoning and volition and an implied self are fundamental factors,
mechanists, like Loeb, and behaviorists, like Watson, have
sought to find an adequate explanation in tropisms or in pure
conditioned reflex responses without intervention of consciousness—an explanation which seems to be satisfactory to the
mechanistic behaviorists but to nobody else. On the other
hand it is difficult to accept the actuality of reasoning and its
implications in so lowly an animal as the crawfish which learns,
through "trial and error" to avoid obstacles and reach its goal
by a selected path. I have in mind the experiments of Yerkes
and Thorndike. But if it is true that in human beings conscious processes involving perception and images, dissociated
from the psychological self and without anything that is aware
of anything, can exhibit memory and determine complicated
intelligent purposive behavior which fulfils an aim and reaches
a goal, it would seem that we have here the analogue of a fairly,
and relatively, primitive consciousness and that a similar though
simpler sort of consciousness may well exist in lower animals
that have organs of sensation, and may determine the behavior

in "trial and error" experiments.   Such an hypothesis is not only tenable but is of wide reaching significance.

To be a little more explicit, if the data of abnormal psychology be accepted, the hypothesis derives considerable support in that the behavior of the lower animals, let us say the crawfish, is determined by a consciousness of a primitive type (without awareness) that is also found in man; namely, that has as components an assortment of sensory images of past experiences (or memory) of a simple sort and less specialized than in man, sensations of present experiences, feelings, and impulses, derived or not from innate mechanisms (instincts)—the whole organized by experience into a complex without awareness, though it may be "cognition," but capable of determining purposive adaptive behavior. *Just such complexes in dissociated conditions have been revealed in man.*

The crawfish, for instance, has eyes and a gustatory and a tactile apparatus. If it has eyes we are compelled to infer that it has visual sensations, however vague or unsystematized; and if it has visual sensations, it would seem to be a necessity that those sensations would be revived as "images" according to psychological laws by associative experience—or, in other terms, memory; and so likewise with gustatory, coenesthetic, and tactile sensations and images, thus a complex of memorial images and the processes to which they belong would be organized by experience, and it is the complex as a whole that would function To take particular instances, the "trial and error" behavior of Thorndike's crawfish would be explained by the organization of kinesthetic and visual images of past trials with gustatory memories of the food finally obtained and feelings of appetite satisfied—the whole complex providing the impulses to behavior and guiding the movements of the animal in a purposive fashion. The same mechanism would adequately satisfy the accomplishments of McDougall's white rat and Airedale terrier* to both of which he rightly, as I think, attributes intelligent purposive behavior. Both animals learned by "trial and error" to accomplish what in man would be called "intelligent" acts. Analogous behavior we have in man manifested by the phenomena I have already described. To eliminate all consciousness as a causal factor is to make consciousness a pure epiphenomenon and to revert to the "steam whistle" theory of Huxley.

---

*Outline of Psychology, pp. 190 and 196.

No less an accurate observer and cautious authority than Jennings, whom McDougall pertinately cites, finds it impossible to explain the behavior of protozoa by the hypothesis of reflex response to stimuli and regards such behavior as requiring the intervention of some sort of consciousness analogous to that which we have to postulate in higher animals.

"We have asked" he says, "merely whether there exists in the lower organisms objective phenomena of a character similar to what we find in the behavior of man. To this question we have been compelled to give an affirmative answer. So far as objective evidence goes, there is no difference in kind, but a complete continuity between the behavior of lower and of higher organisms."

As to the presence of consciousness in micro-organisms he concludes:

"Paramoecium . . . makes such an impression that one involuntarily recognized it as a still subject, acting in ways analogous to our own. Still stronger, perhaps, is this impression when observing an Amœba obtaining food . . . The writer is thoroughly convinced, after long study of the behavior of this organism, that if Amœba were a large animal, so as to come within the every-day experience of human beings, its behavior would at once call forth the attribution to it of states of pleasure and pain, of hunger, desire, and the like, on precisely the same basis as we attribute these things to a dog . . . We attribute consciousness to the dog, because this is useful; it enables us practically to appreciate, foresee, and control its actions much more readily than we could otherwise do . . . I believe it beyond question that we should find similar attribution to it [Amœba] of certain states of consciousness a practical assistance in foreseeing and controlling its behavior. Amœba is a beast of prey, and gives the impression of being controlled by the same elemental impulses as higher beasts of prey".

In attributing consciousness to such low forms as the protozoa of course we do not think in anthropomorphic concepts, in terms of human consciousness. We must rather try to conceive, if we can, of psychical processes as contrasted with chemical and physical processes, but sufficiently specific and differentiated as sensibility to determine purposive adaptive behavior. By "sensibility" is to be understood, a primitive consciousness, or primordial consciousness without the attribute of thought or feeling though it is sentience. But we may attribute to it the capacity of registration, conservation, and reproduction of experience. According to the view of some, all living matter has these functions; which means of course, memory, which in turn, in the last analysis, means the capacity to adjust through experience to situations of the environment. By the theory then, if not demonstrated fact, of sensibility, the behavior which Jennings found in the protozoa might well be explained without attributing the more highly specialized anthropomorphic consciousness to these low forms of animal life. And we may be justified in correlating the introspective findings of vague coenesthetic consciousness, that I have cited, with the primitive and even anoetic consciousness of animals and interpret them as sentience. After all, this is only taking that other step that reaches monism; is it not?—the identification of consciousness, or "mind stuff," with the ultimate reality of chemical and physical processes, the theory which I reached and elaborated in my first lecture.

There is to be found, then, functioning in the *human organism* all the different types of psychical and psychological processes which occur throughout the scale of the whole animal hierarchy at the various stages of evolution reached, from the dim sentience of the protozoa to that higher intellectual activity which culminates in thought and self awareness; and, as a working hypothesis, it may be held that in man every evolutionary stage of consciousness is recapitulated and represented, beginning with what is probably mere sensibility of the simple cell, through the highly specialized sensations and perceptions, without awareness, to the more conscious processes of thought, and self awareness. Through such considerations we are led to that biological conception of consciousness which I have endeavored to unfold.

CHAPTER XI

THE PROBLEM OF PERSONALITY*
How Many Selves Have We?

By Morton Prince

The theory of personality is fundamental to the problems of Social Psychology and of Abnormal Psychology. It may be said that at least an elementary understanding of the psychology of the component traits of personality, if not of their dynamic mechanisms, is essential for poets, dramatists and other writers of fiction; and, above all, for biographers, if they would understand the apparently paradoxical and often contradictory traits manifested by their characters. For such an understanding involves an understanding of what is called human nature. I have therefore thought the problem appropriate for this lecture.

The frequently advanced theories of personality are, to my way of viewing the problem, inadequate or incomplete in that they do not take into consideration and give an explanation of all the facts involved. Among such facts left out—and there are many—are those of the normal everyday alterations of character, those of the asocial personality, those involving the problem of character versus intelligence and those commonly called abnormal alterations, or phases of personality, but which are manifestly due not to abnormal but to the normal functioning of mental processes under altered conditions.

Furthermore, the theories most in vogue are predicated either on the one hand on the debatable premise of "instincts" having very specific functions and determining very specific purposive behavior—concepts unacceptable to some; or, on the other hand, on the still more debatable premises of the naïve modern Behaviorist who defines personality in terms of bodily reactions to the environment, without taking note of the psychological mechanisms involved, and thus would reduce every trait of personality to conditioned reflexes, relegating the mind

*Powell Lecture in Psychological Theory at Clark University, December 17, 1924.

An abstract of this lecture was presented at the meeting of the British Association for the Advancement of Science, Psychological Section: Toronto, Canada, August 6-13, 1924.

to the superfluous position of the steam whistle on the locomotive, as Huxley did half a century ago.[1]

TRAITS OF PERSONALITY AS ENDURING DISPOSITIONS ORGANIZED IN SYSTEMS (NEUROGRAMS)

Common, as well as psychological observation, teaches that
every individual exhibits a greater or less number of native
and acquired intellectual endowments, certain acquired mental
traits, certain acquired habits of mind and body, certain moods
and certain innate affective conative tendencies, which determine his reactions to the situations of life and particular circumstances of the environment.

For example: Intellectual endowments would comprehend native
capacity for and acquired knowledge of, mathematics, music, language
and special fields of learning, capacity for constructive imagination,
logical judgments, etc. Amongst acquired mental traits may be
classed sentiments, ideals, and beliefs; amongst habits, modes of
thought, opinions, prejudices, etc., and amongst innate affective
tendencies are to be found all those impulses and driving forces
which are recognized as derived from or correlated with the emotions,
feelings and appetites, and are generally called instincts or instinctive
tendencies.

Most of these components, those that are acquired by life's
experiences are peculiar to and vary in each individual, but
the innate instinctive tendencies are common to all individuals.
The sum of the different components as a whole constitute
personality; and according as the components vary in character
and quality and the modes in which they are assembled, or
integrated with one another, will characters differ.

For convenience of description we may extend the meaning
of the term "traits" to include *all* the different components
and so I shall do. Now the individual traits of personality
are to greater or less degree fixed and enduring—those that
are innate permanently so: others acquired by experience, like
habits and sentiments, fixed and enduring until modified by
new experience; and then as new formations this quality is
still continued.

It is obvious that this quality of fixed persistence implies
some kind of enduring dispositions and these we are com-

---

[1]Attempts have been made to classify personalities (or more correctly, characters) into types, such as the introverted, extraverted,
noetic, cyclothymic, autistic, etc. (Jung, Conklin, Rosanoff and
others.) But such classifications do not touch the real problem.
They are merely descriptive of end results. They do not explain
anything. What we want is an explanation of the Why and How.

pelled to formulate in physiological terms, in terms of correlated neural dispositions organized to a greater or less degree into potentially functioning whole or systems. An organized system of neural dispositions I have thought useful to denote by the term "neurogram"[1] a neural record of mental and other experiences.

It is impossible to conceive of a mental experience, or process like a thought, or a sentiment, or a feeling, enduring, as such, after it has passed out of the awareness of the moment. We cannot think of it as stowed away somewhere, as you stow away a penknife in your pocket, or a book upon your bookshelf. The very fact of it being a process indicates that it ceases to exist as such. We are compelled to conceive of it only as conserved by means of a correlated brain disposition potentially capable of being stimulated to activity and therewith reviving the original mental experience or process. The nature of the correlation depends upon what theory of the mind-body problem we adopt—parallelism or monism. But in any case, if we bear these concepts in mind, we may avoid pedanticism and speak, interchangeably and indifferently, of physiological dispositions or mental dispositions, as the functioning of the former—ex hypothesi—necessarily carries with it corresponding mental processes. But let us remember mental disposition is a figure of speech.

The innate and acquired mental "traits" of personality, then, are conditioned by physiological dispositions. But just as physiological dispositions are (or may be) organized into systems, so of necessity the processes of the correlated mental experiences are correspondingly organized. As the one is, so must the other be. Accordingly mental "traits" (as I have defined them and aside from pure native endowments) comprehend, besides the innate instinctive tendencies, systems of potential or actual activities organized by experience within themselves and with the innate, instinctive conative activities and conserved as physiological dispositions.

DEFINITION OF PERSONALITY

We may, then, define Personality as the *sum total* of all the biological *innate* dispositions and tendencies of the individual and all the *acquired* dispositions and systems of dispositions; or, more specifically, as that psycho-physiological collocation of traits (meaning *all* the native and acquired intellectual endowments, all the habits, sentiments and other mental systems, *plus* the inherited emotional instincts, appetites and other tendencies) by which the mind manifests, or may manifest itself, i. e., actually or potentially, and of which certain variable components determine the reactions of the individual to the circumstances and situations of life.

---

[1] The Unconscious, p. 109.

I say "actually or potentially", because there are two facts that should be noted: First, there are many "traits" which though enduring components of the personality may be only rarely manifested. Potentially, however, they are there and may determine, given the situation and the circumstances, the reactions of the individual. This is particularly seen in the emotional tendencies, such as anger, fear, mirth, play, etc. That is to say, a person may be of such a placid temperament that he may almost never be known to manifest anger, which may seem to be absent from his personality, yet potentially the innate disposition is there and given some adequate circumstance the anger reaction will be called forth. And so with fear and other emotional tendencies.

Similarly with acquired sentiment. There may be organized within the structure of the personality sentiments which are rarely in activity; there may be even antagonistic sentiments involving the same object and incompatible with each other—love and hatred of, or aversion to one and the same person or thing, each having been created at different times under different conditions of the organism or by different experiences. Within habitual situations and conditions only one of such antagonistic pairs habitually functions but the other opposing sentiment, nevertheless, endures as a potential disposition capable of functioning. For let the situation and other conditions be sufficiently altered and it will be switched into activity. And so it is with the other components of personality.

I would impress upon you and I beg you to hold constantly in mind, lest I be misunderstood, that *for the moment I am concerned only with the structure of the mind and not with the dynamic forces contained in its traits*—the conscious and the subconscious strivings and urges, the "drives" and conflicts— nor with environmental situations as stimuli. These two factors largely determine what variables or traits shall in any given situation be manifested as character. But the structure of the mind conditions these dynamic forces and the reaction to the environment. I shall later, in due time, consider these other dynamic factors.

All Neurograms and Traits Not Assembled Into a Functioning Whole

Now a fact to be noted and which must be taken into consideration by any theory of personality, is that, of the various and many organized dispositions, or neurograms, comprehended potentially in the whole personality and when functioning providing the traits, all are not assembled under all conditions and at all times into a functioning whole. The individual reacts at one moment with one set of traits and at another with another, perhaps of an opposite character. Indeed he may possess, as I have said, traits that are antagonistic to one another, such as sentiments of hatred and love, or interest and disinterest, for the same object; or he may manifest both charitableness and uncharitableness; intelligence and stupidity; etc. Obviously such opposing traits cannot be manifested at one and the same moment. But let the conditions of the organism be altered, such as occurs in fatigue, or illness, or intoxication, or states of dissociation, or moods; or let the conditions of the environment be altered and one or the other of these opposing traits comes into functional activity. The dispositions underlying its opposite then may be said to be dissociated from the functioning systems of the personality, or be suppressed, or switched off. In other words, that which is the functioning part of the personality undergoes alterations from time to time, one set of traits being predominant at one time and another at another. There occurs a dissociation, or switching out, of some dispositions and re-synthesis, or switching in, of others.

CHARACTER A PHASE OF PERSONALITY AND NOT A FIXED STABLE THING

The terms "personality" and character are often loosely used interchangeably as synonyms. I am afraid I have done so myself. But it would be better to use "personality" in the comprehensive sense for the *sum total* of all the enduring traits and their underlying organized dispositions, potential and active, innate and acquired, possessed by the organism, and reserve "character" for those traits and dispositions which are predominant or characterize the personality at different moments, determining at such moments the reactions of the organism. From this point of view *personality* would change only as traits were modified by, or new traits were acquired by experience. The *character* would change not only in accordance with new experiences, but in accordance with changes in the internal conditions of the organism (strivings, conflicts, moods, intoxications, etc.) and with changes in the environmental situations. These character-changes are different *phases* of personality in that they represent selected groups of the total of the variables of personality. It is a matter of dissociation and re-synthesis of variables— that is, of organized systems of dispositions and corresponding reactions.

The practical point is, the character of the personality is not a fixed stable thing, but may be altered from time to time. It is a variant of the personality. Some individuals are not the same in character in the morning and evening; nor under adversity and prosperity; nor in sorrow and happiness; nor in sickness and health; nor in the different relations of life—those of business and the home and society, etc.; nor, as is proverbial, in wine and sobriety—as Mr. Volstead and Mr. Bryan, who would take all the joy out of life, would have us remember. Personality has many phases, or variants.

So the functioning part of the personality is subject to alterations from time to time, manifested in changes of character and corresponding reactions. The resulting phases are normally observed and in popular parlance are commonly spoken of as "sides" to the personality, or character. They are particularly obtrusive under abnormal conditions, internal and external, and are then called abnormal alterations of personality—such as intoxications, trance, fugues, hypnosis, deliria, sleep, multiple personality, etc. But such abnormal states are only complex systems formed by dissociation and synthesis out of the variables—various components of the whole personality. So they, too, are all phases of personality.

Multiple Alternating Phases in Every Day Life

Yet nearly all writers of fiction and even biographers have failed to recognize—what in these modern days the most advanced criminologists and penologists have recognized— that man is a many sided creature and woman, if I may venture to say it, particularly so. No one is wholly good or wholly bad; or wholly hard or wholly sentimental; or wholly self-centered or wholly altruistic; or wholly self-assertive and self-reliant or wholly shy and self-depreciative; and I may even say wholly intelligent or wholly stupid. William James classified human beings as the "tough-minded and the tender-minded"; but no one is wholly tough or wholly tender. So every one has different sides, as we say, to his personality, each side manifesting its particular traits and conduct, which are the expressions of its particular interests and sentiments and ideals; its instinctive emotions, and feelings; its impulses, and desires, and moods. And according as which side is uppermost will a person appear to his neighbors and to the world as a person of this kind of character or that kind.

An acquaintance of mine, for example, is a practical business man, a steel manufacturer. In the management of his business he displays the characteristics of a capable executive and money maker. His character, expressing his interests and ideals and impulses at such times, is only that of a business man bent on industrial and financial success.

But from time to time he shuts himself up in his room, bars out the world and his friends and even the enticements of every social pleasure, and alone with his violin as a companion loses himself in the land of dreams—of music and emotion and sentiment until the wee sma' hours of the morning. At these times the business self disappears, and a dream self of emotion and sentiment, oblivious to all else, takes its place.

So also will a person appear as a shrewd, hard, selfish, ruthless egotist in his dealings with business competitors, when one side is uppermost; and to the public, when it is the other side, as a compassionate, generous, philanthropic altruist, interested in bettering the welfare of his fellow beings by the use of his millions.

Or, again, in this country a type of political boss used to be not uncommon (and is still not as extinct as the dodo). When one side was uppermost, he would appear ambitious, unscrupulous, uncharitable to his opponents, and a grafter on the public treasury; and then, under different conditions and in a different environment, which called out the other side of his nature, he would exhibit in private life to his family and friends, a character of high ideals, honest in private dealings, exemplary in morals, kindly and charitable, beloved by all who knew him.

Or again, may I take the personality of Abraham Lincoln which has been such a puzzle to his biographers, and is now puzzling a distinguished biographer, so he tells me, who is writing a new life. There were at least two sides to Lincoln's personality. There was the uncouth, coarse-minded hilarious Lincoln, constantly repeating the unprintable jests and language of the youths of the rough pioneer life that was the lot of the early settlers and of the sordid vulgar civilization of the primeval forest. And there was the sad Lincoln, the idealist whose thought was not only the manifestation of a sublime character, but embracing the loftiest concepts of human nature, was expressed in language that recalls in purity and beauty the most inspiring ethical and poetic imagination. No wonder his biographer, unversed in psychology, is puzzled.

In the realm of fiction the dramatist is forced by the conventional canons of his art, if not by lack of wisdom, and for the purposes of dramatic effect, to depict but one side of the personalities of his characters.   Consequently there is probably not a character of the drama, excepting possibly Dr. Jekyll and Mr. Hyde, of which the whole personality has been portrayed. Iago, devil that he was, probably at home with his children, if he had a home and children, might have been the picture of an angel father.   Melancholy Jacques, if he had had a couple of cocktails before dinner, might have forgotten his pessimism and shown, *in vino veritas,* another side of his personality and entertained his company as a hilarious jester.   Even Hamlet, though a good subject for a psychopathic hospital, if he had returned to his University at Wittenberg would have probably forgotten for one night, at least, all about his philosophies of life and his lamented father and exhibited himself in that other joyous, rollicking mood or character for which he very likely was known in the congenial surroundings of his boisterous student days.

The world still awaits the great dramatist who will draw, if it be possible, a complete picture of a human personality, true to nature and under the confining canons of art.

It would be hazardous in me to draw examples from amongst the fair daughters of Eve, lest I might find it expedient to take the first train out of this good city after this lecture.   But I venture the opinion that human nature is all the same in whichever sex it is incarnated.   From such insight as has been vouchsafed me from the revelations within the confessional box of the physician's consulting room, I suspect that man and woman are pretty much of a muchness.   The multiform sides of a woman's nature differ from man's only in form and their conventional expressions.

The contrasting sides, however, of the gentler sex are much less conspicuous to the world than man's and are more easily overlooked.   In woman, as every woman knows—but few men—one or more sides of the character are by the necessity of social customs camouflaged.   From childhood she is taught by the conventions of society, by the social tabu, to restrain and repress, often even from herself, many impulses and cravings which are born within her, as well as many thoughts and sentiments which she has acquired by experience, by contact with the world and therefore by riper knowledge.   The repression under the social codes of these, the natural expressions of a part of her personality has belied her nature which has been confined for centuries in a cage hung with opaque curtains, like unto the spiritualist's dark cabinets.   But within her social cabinet, all sorts of urges of human nature have been seething.

In these days we have the great movement for emancipation of the sex. Woman at last, after centuries of repression, is coming into her own and is being allowed to give free expression to her personality. We have already seen remarkable manifestations of her abilities, her aspirations and her desires and her capacity to compete with man, and, I fear, expressions of her personality, hitherto unsuspected by naïve man, in other unconventional directions. What may happen with complete emancipation of the sex I am not rash enough to prophesy.

But to go back: in each of the examples, real and imaginary, above cited—and I might draw in different individuals from life, dozens of contrasting and contradictory pictures—it would appear that in the different relations of life the personality presents contradictory traits and conduct, and, in popular language, we might say different "selves" alternating with one another from moment to moment. But these "selves" are plainly only different sides or phases of the same personality.

In which of these sides, or which of these characters is the personality the "Real Self?" Is either side the real self? Or is one more than the other? Would the individual himself know which he or she is? Certainly no one is more real than the other.[1]

When a person uninterruptedly exhibits one fixed, strongly marked phase of his personality during a considerable period of time it would seem as if a cleavage, so to speak, had occurred, the cleft for the time being separating certain groups of traits from the others without any bridge between them. And, as a matter of fact, this cleavage sometimes literally occurs, as I will presently demonstrate to you.

Again, the contrasting phases of personality may be distinguished by differences of mood, each mood being marked by its own strong feeling tone or emotion, or by exaltation or depression, with corresponding sentiments, habits, thoughts, ideals and resulting conduct.

---

[1]Strictly and precisely speaking such phases of personality cannot be described as "selves." The problem of the self is a narrower and special problem involving other and special factors. Yet it is true that a differentiated phase of personality may include a self different in its psychological structure from the self of another phase; and this structure may be distinguished by a characteristically different idea of self, self consciousness, self regarding sentiment, etc. As we shall presently see there may be two (or more) veritable alternating selves constructed out of the components of one personality.

That this differentiation of the personality into distinct
phases or groups of traits, or sides of the character, express
it as you will, is not a mere figure of speech, but an actual
fact of the structure of the mind may be demonstrated experimentally, and is often observed in everyday life when, as
the result of emotional shocks and the internal forces of the
mind, the personality is broken up into its component parts
and one side split off from the other sides. I might cite many
experiments and observations of my own, but to eliminate
personal bias allow me to mention an interesting experiment
by another observer. This experimenter, while engaged in
some hypnotic experiments on a young man of twenty-two
who was "essentially normal and responsible, of robust character and of decided intellectual ability," found to his surprise
that this young man fell, *entirely independently of suggestion*
and as if by accident, into at least four distinct phases or moods
each of which may be well characterized as a self.

The first phase, the ordinary or quiet mood was very similar
to his normal self when awake. He was of a nature quiet,
speculative and restrained, well bred and courteous in demeanor
and of a religious and idealistic temperament. If a suggestion
was made not consonant with this character it was rejected at
once and any amount of insistence would be in vain.

In the second phase, called the "gay mood," into which, on
its first appearance, he suddenly *without warning* and to the
surprise of the experimenter, changed out of the first phase,
the subject became extremely hilarious and absurd, jested in
an easy way, displayed a tendency to practical jokes on the
experimenter, kicked his clothes about the room and was generally obstreperous and fantastic, both in speech and behavior.
Then, of a sudden, without warning or suggestion of any kind,
he reverted to his former quiet, gentle, restrained self. On
other occasions in this gay mood, which frequently occurred,
he showed himself to be a "gay Lothario," for he displayed
an astounding lack of the ordinary conventions or proprieties,
professed a contempt for either religion or morality, and a
disregard for any responsibility in his actions, becoming in
his own language, a child of nature, non-moral though not
vicious. Any suggestion not consonant with this mood was,
as in the first phase instantly rejected.

The third phase was a "malicious" mood. In this he became a sort of "Jack-the-Ripper." He exhibited a strong wish

to inflict pain and frequently asked permission to stab the experimenter in order to have the gratification of seeing blood flow. Indeed he was detected surreptitiously extracting a penknife from his pocket with a view to satisfying this inclination. He confessed to a wish to vivisect, or, failing that, to strangle. (These traits may sound to you preposterous, but permit me to say they are all well known and recognized by criminologists as frequently the basis of the horrible crimes that from time to time shock the public. They are the manifestations of sexual perversions and are known as Sadism. Jack-the-Ripper, whose frightful abominations—killing and mutilating his victims—shocked the world many years ago, was plainly a Sadist.)

The fourth phase into which the young man fell in the same way was a "depressed" mood, the very opposite of the gay phase. Now he exhibited himself as a melancholic—a melancholy Jacques—utterly and beyond bounds miserable and ready for no reason that was apparent to burst into tears.

Each of these moods, or so-called selves, carried its own different set of emotions, tastes and mental attitudes. As I have said, suggestions not consonant with the particular mood he was in were rejected. And the whole manner of the man in each exhibited an absolute contrast of expression, conduct and mode of speech, just as we all do in our different moods (not like those of this young man, I hope), according as we give expression to the gay traits of our personality when, as the unwitting beneficiaries of a piratical little fleet of British steamers and the twelve mile limit, we still celebrate; or the vicious traits in a fit of anger, such as were deliberately taught to the Tommies, the Poilus and the Doughboys when they went over the top; or the sorrowful traits at the loss of a dear one; or the sedate, melancholic traits—as when we listen to a lecture on the Problem of Personality.

Now an interesting point is that there was no break in the continuity of memory for these different moods or selves any more than for our own. He remembered them all completely, and how he felt and thought and acted. Their appearance was beyond his control; thus again resembling our own changes of mood, and they were independent of suggestion. He graphically described them as if he were a magic lantern with many colored slides passing in sequence before his eyes and through which he looked; and as the world would be colored by those slides, so he felt and thought about it.

I see no reason to hesitate to accept these findings because
I have independently, and often, observed the same phenomena,
though of course the psychological composition of the moods
or phases was different. As instances let me cite only three
cases which I have intensely studied.

A young woman whom I had frequently hynotized, but only
for the purpose of therapeutic suggestion, one day spontaneously changed from a reserved, depressed, respectful self-
abased, saintly character, dominated by religious ideals and
longings, to a gay, sprightly, childlike, saucy young girl, car-
ing not a rap for religion or saints. Then later another phase,
strongly contrasting with the previous two came into being.
This phase represented a mature, practical woman of the
world, a Realist, neither saintly nor childlike, but manifesting
traits of ambition, self-assertion, and self-reliance, with an
exceedingly bad temper and resentful of control, determined
to dominate her environment.

In the second case, leaving a subject hypnotized in the room,
when I returned I found that a very serious-minded, depressed,
self-reproachful lady, about forty years of age, overburdened
with cares and anxieties and responsibilities, and a nervous in-
valid, something of a Mrs. Gummidge-sort-of-person, had suddenly changed to a mood in which she felt herself a care-free,
gay, young girl, full of the joy and happiness of life, enjoying
the full vigor of physical and mental health. These changes
also occurred when awake. In this mood she would do, from
a social point of view, all sorts of reckless but harmless things
which she strongly reprobated in her customary mood. Then
after this gay youthful mood passed off, *there being no dis-
continuity of memory*, this lady would be much distressed at
her previous behavior and could not understand why she had
felt and thought and acted as she did.

The third case is that of a young woman with no very striking
psychological characteristics except those of depression, a
marked feeling of inferiority and dependence, vascillating in
purpose, and an absolutely asexual temperament. But in another phase she became a person of an entirely different character, self-assertive, and self-reliant to an obtrusive degree, ambitious, voluptuous, conceited about her supposed musical and
dramatic talents; she regarded herself as the reincarnated soul
of a Spanish courtesan and singer of the XIII Century, a
sort of "Carmen" of the operatic stage.

These phases or moods into which these three subjects of

mine respectively passed must be regarded not only as different phases of the same personality, so different were they in feelings, and attitudes of mind, and sentiments, and conduct, but as different selves.

For the variant phases also included in the integrations distinct psychological selves which respectively were specifically differentiated from the more habitual selves and characterized by very specifically different ideas of self, self-regarding sentiments and self-consciousness. Each phase in each case distinctly repudiated any unity of self-consciousness with the self of the other phase or phases of the personality and insisted on being consciously an independent self. Into this detail however, I cannot enter here.

At any rate, psychological analysis of the minds of these three persons and a study of their life histories, revealed beyond any manner of doubt that the secondary phases, or moods, were compounds of traits, i. e., of systems of innate and acquired dispositions, which were components of the whole personality of each, but which had been repressed and suppressed by conflict because incompatible with the paths of life chosen by each. Now when the lid had been taken off, these components came to life and were split off from the rest of the personality, which in turn was suppressed, thus forming a new phase. (The mode in which this happens I will come to later.)

Now on the basis of such cases—and many of them have been studied and analyzed—it is safe to say that if the young man I have just cited who showed the three moods, the "gay" mood of Don Juan, the "malicious" mood of a Jack-the-Ripper, the "depressed" mood of a melancholy Jacques, besides his own natural goody-goody mood—if he had been analyzed in a similar way, it would have been found that deep down in his nature there were longings to be a gay Lothario, without qualms of conscience; that there were also certain urges, impulses and desires of the sexual instinct to express themselves in sadism, i. e., cruelty and the shedding of blood; and it is also dollars to doughnuts that there were good reasons for the depression, in that life seemed to hold out little to him in the way of fulfilling his aspirations, and perhaps self reproaches for fancied failure to live up to his ideals. These traits and tendencies were all integral parts of his nature—his personality, but to his credit had been controlled, repressed into the subconscious, if you like, and probably concealed even from himself. But now, through the dissociation that occurred from the hypnotic procedure, the lid had been taken off, and they sprung to life as different selves of his personality. No wonder he seemed to himself, as he said, to be looking through the colored slides of a magic lantern and saw the world as it was colored—by the multiplicity of his different selves.

These surmises may seem surprising and unbelievable to the uninitiated; but when you begin to dig down into the roots of personality of any one, you never know what you will find. If Shakespeare had dug down deep into the hidden recesses of the minds of Hamlet, and Iago, and Jacques, he would have been astonished at what he found.

So nobody knows what will be found in any of us until you begin to dig.

In actual everyday life, in healthy minded people, it is not difficult to find examples of the same principle, even in men who have achieved positions of eminence in the world. There was William Sharp, the novelist, who, when one side of his character was uppermost, was the vigorous, practical man of business, the bread-and-butter winner, a masculine character as known to the world. And then there was the other side, a feminine side; a mystic that saw visions, lived within his imagination and intense emotions and sentiments, but unknown to the world, and wrote his novels under the feminine name of Fione Macleod, a secret kept until his death. Fione he considered his Real Self, so much so that as William Sharp he wrote letters to himself as Fione, and Fione wrote to William Sharp. And yet William Sharp was a level headed man. Which was the real self? The masculine William or the feminine Fione? Or was one more than the other?

I could, if it were proper, cite similar examples from persons I have known.

When the contrasting sides of personality are of a moral character, contrasting the good and the bad in human nature, the resulting effect is more striking and dramatic—sometimes shocking.

Robert Louis Stevenson, as every one knows, after pondering much on the duality of man's nature and the alternations of good and evil, for a long time cast about for a story to embody this central idea. Finally he wrote the wonderful story of double personality "The Strange Case of Dr. Jekyll and Mr. Hyde." It was meant to be only an allegory to present the two sidedness of human nature, good and evil. Real cases of double personality were then not known in actual life, so Stevenson, in his imaginative creation, constructed better than he knew and anticipated the discoveries of psychological research.

I have recalled to you Stevenson's imaginary creation because, allowing for literary exaggeration, in all fundamentals and many details it is so true a picture of what is actually observed in cases of double personality that it can be used almost as well as an actual case from life.[1]

What sort of structure, then, has personality that such strongly contrasting phenomena as I have described can issue out of it?

THEORY OF PERSONALITY

By what theory can it be explained how it comes about that an individual can exhibit so many and such extreme and even seemingly paradoxical phases, or alterations of his character, and such contrasting, contradictory traits and behavior?

Let me clear the ground and premise by saying that the dual nature of man, so often moral in the contrasting traits, the fact that impressed Stevenson's imagination and upon which he pondered, is easily explained psychologically. It would take me too far afield to go adequately into the explanation tonight. I will content myself with simply outlining the general principles of purposive behavior for which we are chiefly indebted to William McDougall as the leading present day protagonist. Our motives are for the most part primarily derived from our inherited primitive instincts or instinctive dispositions with which every child is born or which soon develop within him—the instincts of pugnacity, and greed, and curiosity, and sex, and fear, and sympathy, and self-abasement, and self-assertion, and the tender parental instinct of love, etc.

These instinctive dispositions are innate, born in us and inherited. Many are biological in that they are common to all the higher animals and serve for the preservation and reproduction of the species. If the fox did not possess the instinct of fear, by which he is driven to flight from danger, he would stand still in the presence of his enemy and all the foxes would soon be gobbled up and the species would die out.

If the lion was not born with the instinct of pugnacity or anger, he would not have the driving force to fight and kill his enemies and the animals he devours. If he did not have the instinct of curiosity he would not be impelled to investigate every strange object that might be a dangerous enemy. And so on.

---

[1]It is of psychological interest and instructive to those occupied with the problem of the mechanism of dreams that Stevenson dreamed this story and for his first draft simply wrote down the next morning at white heat the scenes as he dreamed them. Of course he afterwards rewrote and elaborated. The dream, it can be assumed, was only the constructive working out in allegorical form of previous thoughts which very likely had their origin in personal mental conflicts. This feat does not stand alone in literature. Poe's "Ulalume" and Coleridge's "Kubla Khan" and "Ancient Mariner" are said to have been composed as dreams.

. Each instinct, too, has a special aim, the fulfillment of which alone satisfies it: to escape from danger in the case of fear; to overcome opposition in the case of anger, and so on.

All these primitive instincts, each one being characterized by an emotion—of fear, anger, or wonder, or greed, or hunger, or love— every child inherits. During early infancy its motives are entirely derived from them and every act that is not simply a reflex one is determined by them. It has little more than emotions and feelings, and every so called purposive act is instinctive. We may say every child, during this period, is little more than a savage, governed only by instinctive motives. As he develops he is soon taught to bring these under control and to use them only in accordance with the social codes and those of ethics and manners.

At first the infant is a thief; he stretches out his hand, impelled by the instinct of greed, to seize and appropriate whatever he sees, your watch or your diamond pin. Then Mamma says—"No, no, naughty, naughty" and he soon learns control.

He is a would be murderer, for whenever thwarted he falls into a fit of anger and would kill his mother or nurse. Again he is taught control.

He is a coward, for he has a panic of instinctive fear at the slightest noise, and again he is taught control, and so on.

Then as the child develops he begins to acquire experiences of the world, of the persons and objects about him. He begins to have ideas and thoughts of this world, for he is taught the ideals and sentiments which the codes of morals, and ethics, adopted by society, demand; and by this education the primitive instincts are linked to these ideas and objects. Thus the instinct of love becomes attached to his mother, and to ideas of the good; the instincts of fear and aversion are associated with the bad and evil thoughts, so that these are repelled. Thus *on the one hand*, our ideals, though they probably have a driving force of their own, are reinforced by the driving force of the instinctive emotions and, *on the other hand*, the instinctive tendencies are brought under control or repressed.

So, starting in infancy, the whole of our social education, from the time of the nursery to adult age, is devoted, *on the one hand*, to the cultivation of the use of instincts in the service of right social conduct; to instilling ideas in the mind and linking them with these instincts and their emotions; to the development in this way of those sentiments, ideas and moral principles, and codes of ethics and manners and habits which society sets up as standards of good conduct; and, *on the other hand*, to the repression and modification and regulation and control of those instinctive tendencies, which, given free play, induce asocial conduct, like cruelty, and avarice, and greed, and dishonesty, and libertinage; but which when modified and controlled can be brought to the service of society as, for instance, when anger is aroused in the cause of righteousness, and the sex instinct in the cause of idealistic love and the perpetuation of the race. If this control were not so accomplished, we might all run amuck down the streets, impelled by our primitive instincts, as happens in times of political revolutions, such as in the Russian Bolshevik revolution, and in the days of Terror in the great French Revolution when the primitive instincts broke loose and men reverted to barbarism.

It is easy to see, also, I think, how in this way our experiences, our ideas and instincts are organized into complexes, as we technically say, or systems, each pertaining to special subjects or objects, or to the satisfaction of special aims, or aspirations and longings. And these systems when fully developed become what we may call sides or *character traits* of the personality.

Now it too often happens that in certain individuals, and always to a certain extent in everybody, the social education has been inadequate and failed. Then the barbaric, primitive instincts are not completely repressed and controlled and harnessed. On the contrary, under the social influence of the environment they form asocial sentiments and ideals; or they still retain their independent activity, free from control, and when aroused, seek their aims and accomplish the fulfillment of their desires. They then motivate asocial conduct and become an evil side of the personality.

It may be that in such an individual we have an alternation of character traits. This happens when, under ordinary conditions and in one environment, the good instincts and the moral ideas and principles dominate and that side of the character is uppermost. The evil side is quiescent, or camouflaged and out of sight. Then we have one self, the moral self. But change the conditions and the environment and above all introduce a conflict between repressed desires and the moral self, and the evil side of such a person, with its primitive instincts and desires, is aroused, the good is repressed and sinks out of sight, and we have that upon which Stevenson had so long meditated and finally presented in his allegory of Dr. Jekyll and Mr. Hyde—"The duality of the man's nature and the *alternation* of Good and Evil."

No sound theory of personality can disregard, as is usually done, the data derived from the study of cases of multiple personality. For the multiple nature of man, or to state it in a different form, the different selves, of which our minds and personalities are compounds, may be most clearly recognized, as I have already intimated in the frankly abnormal cases of this kind observed in actual life. They are not uncommon and many have been studied. They are of interest, not because of the dramatic phenomena they exhibit, but because of the light they thus throw on the structure and mechanisms of the human mind, on the composite nature of man, and on the many little selves of which the mind is composed. In these cases the mind is analyzed much more clearly than any psychologist can do it. For by the internal conflicting forces of the mind itself, as I will later explain, and not by any artificial procedure like hypnotism, or suggested dissociation, the mind is split up. A cleavage takes place between its different mental complexes, or systems, or what I have called sides of the personality, resulting in the formation of different corresponding selves, each self living an independent life and alternating and sometimes coexisting with the other self or selves. But all are parts of the whole personality.

In illustration simply of these principles the three cases of altered personality I have cited may be taken as examples. When they were submitted to intensive and prolonged analytic study it was revealed beyond a reasonable doubt that, to take one of them as an example, the youthful phase of the second case was in part a resuscitation of the traits of girlhood which had been outgrown in the course of life's mature experiences. These traits consisted of youthful sentiments of love, aversion, etc., for objects, persons, activities, etc., such as are characteristic of irresponsible youth.

Amongst the sentiments were many which were the direct opposite of and antagonistic to those of the mature personality. Such, for example, as liking for objects, persons and activities for which the latter had intense aversion and even hatred; while again some sentiments, such as those of maternal parenthood, were completely switched out and lost; and similarly with habits of thought and behavior.

The traits of this phase, also, included habits of thought and behavior which could be identified with those of that early period of life to which they genetically dated back and belonged. These sentiments and habits were in large measure motivated by the instinctive impulses of play and longings for pleasure, joy and happiness. These different component instinctive tendencies could be easily differentiated and recognized. All these traits were organized into functioning systems. On the other hand, many habits of the matured character were dissociated. The codes of social conduct and habits which governed the social behavior were those which belonged to youth, while the social codes which were intensely held and lived up to by the mature woman were completely dropped out of the altered character.

Besides this regression to the traits of youth, this altered personality, or, more correctly character, exhibited a clearly differentiated and larger system, the genesis and growth of which could be distinctly traced. Beginning with a rebellious aversion to a certain condition of life, by successive accretions from the subsequent experiences of life, and the incubation and maturation of repressed desires, this primitive aversion became developed into a large complex of systematized habits of thought, sentiments, longings and impulses which finally became constellated with the youthful traits into a functioning whole, in rebellion against the previous mature sentiments, codes of ethics and behavior and social obligations of the personality.

There was thus a constant succession of conflicts between mental systems—the old and the new—ending in disruption of personality and the evolution of a new character possessing traits of sentiments, habits of thought and behavior, and instinctive tendencies antagonistic to those of the original character. There was even evolved a new self, with a different idea of self and self-regarding sentiment—so different that this new formed self could not consciously identify itself with the previous self. There were two selves with one body.

The conflicts were not motivated by subconscious wishes of a hypothetical "libido," but were between antagonistic systems motivated by various emotional instinctive tendencies.[1]

Studies of other cases of multiple phases of personality have yielded findings precisely similar in principle.

Then, again, there are many phenomena in the field of abnormal psychology, other than those of dissociated personality, that enable us to detect the organization of the structure of the personality in complexes and systems of complexes of innate and acquired dispositions. But the limits of time forbid the citation of these.

The alterations of character manifested in multiple phases of personality (of which I have cited examples) and conditioned by the structural organization of the mind in units of innate and acquired dispositions, and complexes and systems of such units do not, as we have seen, stand apart from the normal. Though such alterations are called abnormal, they are determined by the normal activities of the units functioning normally, but under conditions that do not permit harmonious adjustment with one another and adaptation of the individual to the environment. The prototypes of such alterations are to be found in normal individuals under normal conditions in everyday life. Thus the alterations of character manifested normally in moods, in fatigue, under stress and strain of emotion and excitement, the so-called "brain-storms," etc., are precisely the same in principle, are conditioned likewise by the structure of personality, and are the manifestations of a temporary variant—the formation of a new phase of a personality out of its numerous components. The process is that of

---

[1]For a complete analysis of this case see: "The Psychogenesis of Multiple Personality," *Jour. of Abnormal Psychology*, Oct. 1919; also my "The Unconscious" 2nd Ed. Lectures XVIII-XX. For a similar analysis of the Beauchamp case see "Miss Beauchamp: theory of the Psychogenesis of Multiple Personality," *Jour. of Abnormal Psychology*, Vol. XV, 1919-20.

dissociation and synthesis, brought about by the internal forces of the dispositions of the mind.

So it becomes evident that fundamental to all these problems is the conception of the structure of the mind and human personality. In the light of the findings of experimental and abnormal psychology we must abandon the older notion of the mind being a unity, at least in the sense that all active processes are unified in consciousness and that those processes of which we are conscious include all mental processes. Rather we must regard the mind as a complex of units, or, rather, of unitary systems of experiences and instinctive dispositions. Such systems become organized by the experiences of life and derive their most intensive driving force from the urge of the emotional dispositions organized within them. Sentiments of love and fear and aversion and curiosity and many others, derived from the linking of these dispositions and experience, are contained in the structural systems and each has its own urge to find expression. The complex integration of all these systems into one composite whole is the mind's structure.[1] One might say that the mind is a composite of a lot of little minds, each concerned, however with its own business and its own interest and aim. Normally each little mind or unitary system enters the field of consciousness in orderly fashion, when called upon, according to the circumstances of the moment and the environment: and behaves in a way that adapts the individual to his environment; though with due regard for the interests and aims of the other little minds with which, after the fashion of compound reflexes, it is structurally integrated. But sometimes, under stress and strain, there is conflict between the unitary systems, one or more of these little minds are repressed by an autocratic Kaiserlich system so that it cannot enter consciousness, and then, impelled by its own uncontrollable urge, it may turn like the proverbial worm; or, to change the simile, take the bit in its teeth, and, taking on independent or so-called automatic activity, kick up a devil of a row in its subconscious prison cell, and do all sorts of horrid things. Then we have what we call symptoms due to conflict. Or, again, we may induce by technical methods of experimentation, some of these units to function subconsciously and independently. Ordinarily and normally, however, the units of the mind behave harmoniously

---

[1] For a more extensive discussion of this theory see: "The Structure and Dynamic Elements of Human Personality," *Jour. of Abnormal Psychology*, Vol. XV, 1919-20; also, my "The Unconscious," 2nd Ed., Lecture XVII.

as dynamic elements of one large system. Some emerge into consciousness, some remain submerged in the subconscious storehouse of the mind to be called upon when wanted as systematized memories; while many, still remaining subconscious, become stimulated into active processes and act upon and modify the processes of conscious thought and behavior. But all, the conscious and the subconscious, are one mind. Let us never forget that.

The Disrupting Force of Conflicts

What is it, then, you may again ask me, that makes the difference between these cases that you call multiple personality and those which you describe as manifesting multiform, alternating and conflicting traits?

Why is it that, if we all have multiform natures, or more correctly speaking, two or more sides to our nature and if we are made up of a lot of little minds, why don't we all split up into separate personalities, each with its own self, bobbing in and bobbing out, alternating with one another like Dr. Jekyll and Mr. Hyde, if we have an evil side; or, if not, as I hope, only incompatible desires, into different contrasted selves—serious minded or pleasure loving; worldly or saintly; gay or melancholic; practical or idealistic, like some of the cases I have told you about?

The answer involves a principle of the mind that has occupied all poets, dramatists, novelists and students of human nature since literature began, and of recent years has been accepted and made use of by all psychologists who have studied the troubles of the human mind.

It is the principle of mental conflicts—the conflicts of antagonistic and irreconcilable desires and urges and impulses which have distracted and always will distract and torment poor human beings, and which have been the basis of some of the greatest tragedies of literature and actual life.

A person, let us say, is torn by two conflicting desires which means impulses, one belonging to one side of his nature and one to the other; one to be good and one to be bad—one, to take a recent case of mine called "Mary Jane," to follow the puritanical path of dull, monotonous, prosaic, joyless virtue and morality, and one to kick over the traces and give rein to the joyful impulses of pleasure, of the primitive instinctive urges of a gay but forbidden life.

Or, let us say, without introducing the moral question of good or evil, there is by the circumstances of life, as in the case of a Mrs. O. I have studied, a condemnation of the individual to a dull, monotonous, banal life of duty and joyless work, and at the same time longings for a higher life, to give expression to the aspiration of the personality in art, or literature, or on the stage.

Or, if I may take a third example, a young life devoted, like that of Miss Beauchamp, to religious and moral perfection, seeking to develop the personality, literally and meticulously by the precepts of the highest moral and religious ideals of the teachings of Christ, renouncing, *on the one hand,* the natural, harmless joys and pleasures and excitements of youth, and, *on the other,* the natural realistic interests and ambitions of the grown up man or woman, while at the same time there is incomplete adjustment to all those renunciations. In spite of the religious and moral aspirations, there still persist unacknowledged both the youthful desires and impulses, and the worldly ambitions and impulses making up two other sides of the personality. Obviously these various desires and impulses are in conflict and irreconcilable.

These examples I have drawn from actual instances that I have known and studied. In each instance a rebellion has been started. Beginning with a rebellious group of wishes and ideas, this rebellion grows, like a rebellion in the social or political organization, drawing within itself more and more dissatisfied elements of thought and new wishes and new ideas of self, and fancies of a new life that might be, which would fulfil the aspirations of a new self. Thus a side to the personality is formed and the beginnings of another personality, another self come into existence.

In each of these cases we have a conflict of irreconcilable desires. Both or all cannot be satisfied. The individual cannot adjust himself to the life he has chosen, or which has been forced by circumstances upon him, because of the unsatisfied desires; desires which are unacceptable because of moral or other scruples.

The inevitable results, if the individual is of an unstable, over-conscientious, neurotic disposition. The dynamic force of the conflict, that is of the unacceptable desires and impulses that cannot be satisfied, represses or dissociates the other side and ruptures completely, or almost completely, the mind. There is a complete cleavage between the sides of the character, between the rebellious side, or the rebellious self, and that side, or self, which is rebelled against. If the rebel wins the king is dethroned, the government is put out of business; or, as we say in psychological language, the original self is dissociated and repressed, for the time being annihilated. Then the new rebellious self sits on the throne with a new government in power. So complete is the rupture and so powerful the repression that even memory may be repressed and lost for all the experiences of life antedating the rupture; that is to say, the new rebellious self can recall nothing of his previous self, or vice versa, or both.

The new one differs of course from the old one. His conduct corresponds with the thoughts and feelings and sentiments and desires which constituted the rebellion and he proceeds to satisfy them; and so we say we have a second personality. This means that the traits—the ideals, the sentiments, the impulses, etc., of the other side of his personality are dissociated or repressed.

This goes on for a time—it may be a few hours or days or months—then something happens; something stimulates, that is, awakens the desires and sentiments and feelings of the old original side of the personality, the original self. There is again a conflict and if the old self wins, the new one is repressed in turn, and the old one appears and sits on the throne again. In political parlance the reactionaries have thrown the revolutionaries out of the window. And so it goes, one self alternating with another self and we have what we call a double personality.

The answer, then, to the question you put to me, "Why do we not all split up into multiple personalities?" is plain: because we have no mental conflicts between our opposing desires and impulses *which we cannot satisfactorily adjust or control*. Of course we all have conflicts, but the desires and impulses and tendencies which are unacceptable to the other side of our natures are not so intense that we cannot adjust them to our satisfaction, or control them; they are not so intense as to become a seething rebellion against the situations and conditions of life; or against our accepted ideals and sentiments; or against those codes of ethics and morals which have been instilled in us in childhood—which is to say our consciences.

Or, it may be, that *we have no consciences* that may be shocked by such desires and impulses. The codes of ethics and morals have failed to be instilled so deeply as to be "categorical imperative" principles. Hence none of these desires are unacceptable. In fact they are accepted and there is a joy in satisfying them. The conscience is not shocked any more than was Dr. Jekyll's, who intentionally changed himself by a drug. There is no conflict and the personality is not disrupted. Indeed we have a way, even when, deep down in our hearts we know they mean forbidden fruit, of justifying them to ourselves. By a process of sophistical reasoning we justify self-indulgence, whether it be of play, or activities and modes of life which are incompatible with duties and responsibilities assumed.

If, then, I have spoken truly, I think we can say that, although we have only one mind, out of its various elements there can be formed more than one character, and that we are entitled to call those different phases of the personality that alternate with one another different selves, whether they are actual independent, dissociated personalities, or only extreme and changing moods, or strongly contrasting groups of traits. The name that we give is, after all, a verbal question. The practical facts are the important matter. So to illustrate once more:

If there had been an irreconcilable conflict, and if it had been strong enough and could not be otherwise compromised, any of the characters I have described at the beginning might have been dissociated into two or more independent personalities. The first, the music-loving business-man might have split into a money-making steel manufacturer robbed of his musical talent and into an idealistic unpractical dreaming musician. The second into a hard, selfish miser and into an idealistic philanthropist. The third into a criminal boss politician and into a lovable moralist, and so on. But—there were no conflicts, no consciences to be shocked, etc.; and so they only manifested moods, or alternating traits.

May we not, therefore, say, in answer to our question, we have as many selves as we have moods, or contrasting traits, or sides to our personalities?

RECAPITULATION

I may summarize the theory I am presenting in the following brief recapitulation.

The personality is not a unity in the sense of being a functioning whole. It comprises many different components of which various ones and a varying number from time to time engage in activity as mental and physiological processes and manifest themselves as traits of character. These are the variables. Personality, accordingly, is not a stable thing but exhibits many alterations under changing conditions.

Of the variables, all are not assembled under all conditions and at all times into a functioning whole. The individual reacts at one moment with one set of traits and at another with another, perhaps of an opposite character. Indeed he may possess, as I have already pointed out at the beginning, traits that are antagonistic to one another, such as sentiments of hatred and love, or interest and disinterest, for the *same* object; or he may manifest both charitableness and uncharitableness; intelligence and stupidity; etc. Obviously such opposing traits cannot be manifested at one and the same moment. But let the conditions of the organism be altered, such as occurs in fatigue, or illness, or intoxication, or states of dissociation, or "moods"; or let the conditions of the environment be altered and one or the other of these opposing traits comes into functional activity. The dispositions underlying its opposite then may be said to be dissociated from the functioning systems of the personality, or be suppressed, or switched off. In other words, that which is the functioning part of the personality undergoes alterations from time to time, one set of traits being predominant at one time and another at another. There occurs a dissociation or switching out of some dispositions and re-synthesis or switching in of others.

The different variables, manifested as "traits," are systems of dispositions, innate and acquired, integrated into lesser and larger functioning systems.

The innate dispositions are those which condition and determine the reflexes, the native tendencies and appetites and the instincts, in which last I include the emotions. These are inherited psycho-physiological arrangements.

I have purposely avoided getting entangled in the battle of the instincts.

But everyone agrees that the dispositions which condition and upon which the native tendencies and emotions depend and which determine some sort of behavior, whatever that may be, are inherited. And everyone agrees that these dispositions become integrated by experience with the acquired dispositions deposited by the experiences of life. And nearly everyone will agree with McDougall and Shand that the conative force of these dispositions when excited to activity, provides impulses which give driving force to the acquired dispositions with which they become integrated. And if this be so, it will be agreed that these impulses tend to carry, or to co-operate in carrying, the activated acquired dispositions, i. e., our ideas, sentiments, wishes, etc., to fruition, whether or not (Woodworth) they are the sole driving force, or purposive in character.

You may call such inherited psycho-physiological arrangements "instincts" or instinctive tendencies, or "patterns" or what you please; that is a matter of concepts and terms. What matters is that there are inherited psycho-physiological arrangements which behave as units, determine impulsive behavior of some sort, become integrated with the deposited acquired experiences of life and organized with them, co-operate, at least, through their impulsive force in determining behavior. And if this be so, these innate units are components of the structure of personality—*primary units* they may be called.

As to these acquired dispositions, such phenomena of dissociated personality as I have cursorily cited—and the intrinsic forces of the mind dissect its structure far more accurately than can the psychologist—such phenomena reveal that the enduring experiences of life are organized and conserved in complex systems in which are integrated the innate dispositions;—acquired systems they are, which on the psychical side are experienced and re-experienced as *sentiments* and *cognitions* and *beliefs* and *perceptions* of objects and situations and memories and images, with their *meanings;* and as *tendencies* and *desires,* etc. (How they are acquired is a genetic question.)

The physiological basis of these are neural dispositions, or neurograms, which when activated are consciously experienced as systems of mental processes. Each system, in a way, functions as a psychic whole.

These acquired systems may be termed *secondary units* and and all and each are necessarily, so long as they endure, components of the structure of the personality. These units, again, become further integrated with one another and more or less firmly knit into *larger* systems and *constellations* of systems to form what is popularly called the personality. In the course of life, from the cradle to the grave, under the genetic influence of so-called "culture," a vast number of lesser and larger systems are organized and conserved. All of them, however, do not persist as active traits, or components of traits. Many fall into "innocuous desuetude" and lie fallow, having become unsuitable for the adjustment and adaptation of the organism to the changed environment and situations of life. Others may be inhibited or be repressed by conflict with antagonistic systems and in that case may take on further growth by sub-conscious incubation and maturation. In any case, however, so long as they are conserved, they are potentially capable of activity and, in fact, often do become activated under alteration of the conditions within and without the organism. This switching out and switching in, suppression and repression and resuscitation of enduring systems result in the ephemeral normal alterations of character of everyday life; but, when the product of irreconcilable mental conflict of sufficient intensity they result in those abnormal alterations manifested as multiple phases of personality.

Such, in brief, but without attempt at demonstration, is the theory of personality which I would offer for your consideration as best explaining all the phenomena manifested in both normal and abnormal conditions.

We have little more than passed the threshold of the entrance into that wonderful structure, the human mind. Great discoveries await us. That is the promise which the future holds out. But I believe that promise is based on the condition that we shall make use of those methods upon which science has depended for its discoveries in every field of knowledge—experimentation and provisional hypotheses confirmed by exact methodical observations.

William McDougall

CHAPTER XII

MEN OR ROBOTS?*

By WILLIAM McDOUGALL

I

In the two lectures which I have the honor to give on the Powell foundation I am responding to an invitation to defend Purposive Psychology, or, in other words, to defend the proposition that man's acting and thinking are purposive. I seem to be in a position analogous to that of an anatomist called upon to defend the proposition that man is a biped, or that of a physiologist required to prove that man breathes air. That is to say I am expected to support by argument a fact familiar to all men through first-hand experience, a fact so familiar and well established that it has become embodied in the very structure of all languages and is recognized and acted upon by all men in all the practical conduct of daily life.

This is a strange and embarrassing position for any man of science. To demonstrate the obvious, to bring forward elaborate arguments in support of well recognized facts, must always seem an ungrateful and somewhat absured procedure. Yet just such procedure is a duty thrust upon me by the strange course of development of psychology, the science of human nature.

It is necessary to clarify the situation and to define the task before me by referring briefly to this course of development. At a time which now seems remote, but which, regarded in historical perspective, is comparatively recent, it was the prevailing tendency to class together all expressions of striving towards a goal, all purposive activities, and to attribute them to a single faculty, 'the Will.' This faculty was supposed to coöperate upon occasion with various other faculties, such as Memory and Reason. And it appeared that these other faculties frequently seemed to work independently of the Will. That fact seemed to justify the setting apart of the Will as a distinct faculty. Then came the revolt against faculty

*Powell Lecture in Psychological Theory at Clark University, December 10, 1925.

19

psychology; and in the main, under the influence of Locke and Hume, the psychology of Ideas prevailed. The followers of this 'new way of ideas' claimed that all the processes of the mind, and all human behavior, might be adequately described and explained in terms of Ideas, or impressions and Ideas. It was claimed that we need to make only three fundamental assumptions about the nature of mind, or the mental nature of man: first, that he is capable of receiving impressions, i.e., sense-impressions; secondly, that he naturally retains these impressions in the form of Ideas; thirdly, that these Ideas, retained in the storehouse of the mind, are linked together according to certain simple rules, the so-called 'laws of association,' and are apt to reappear in consciousness, one after another, in a manner determined wholly by these associative links and by intercurrent new sense-impressions.

Throughout the eighteenth and nineteenth centuries, many psychologists and philosophers were intoxicated by the seeming success of these principles. It seemed to them that the new principles, so charmingly simple, enabled them to dispense entirely with the faculties, and especially with the faculty of the Will. All instances of purposive activity, they said, could be adequately described and accounted for by recognizing a peculiar kind of Idea, called an Idea of an end or goal. Ideas of this kind, however, were not essentially different from other Ideas. They were supposed to work or function in just the same way as Ideas of other kinds; that is to say, the Ideas of goals were implanted by sense-impressions and, like all other Ideas, faithfully obeyed the Laws of Association and associative reproduction.

Confidence in the all-sufficiency of psychology of this kind was greatly increased by the discovery that, as knowledge of the structure and functions of the nervous system increased, all descriptions in terms of Ideas could be plausibly translated into terms of brain-processes; the Ideas were assumed to be locked each in its separate brain-cell or group of cells; and the links of association were conceived as material links between such brain-cells. Then at last it seemed that a real explanation of mental life became possible, an explanation in terms of the physics and chemistry of the brain. Recent studies of the "conditioned responses" have given a new confidence to those who regard the principle of association as capable of explaining every manifestation of skill and knowledge. For these observations seem to them to give more precision and a more definitely mechanistic meaning to the principle of association.

This is the line of thinking which, beginning with Hartley, has culminated in the mechanistic behaviorism of Dr. Watson and his followers. Those who accept it say that we do not need to trouble about Ideas; but only need concern ourselves with physical impressions and physical responses. For they imagine that they can adequately imagine all the brain-processes that intervene between sense-stimulus and motor response, without seeking any aid from introspection. It is the alarming popularity in this country of this new way without Ideas that lays upon those of us who cannot accept it the embarrassing obligation to appear as champions of the simple obvious and commonplace truth that man is a purposive being, that, from the cradle to the grave, his life is one long round of purposive strivings, of efforts to attain, to make real, those things which he imaginatively conceives to be good or desirable. The spread of that other way of thinking among psychologists has gone so far that those few of us who do not accept it are regarded as cranky persons wedded to mediaeval metaphysics, queer survivors from the dark ages who, by reason of some twist in the brain, are incapable of joining in the triumphant march of modern science.

The author of a recent amusing play has imagined the construction of machines in the shape of human beings, machines so ingeniously put together that they can be set to perform much of the routine labor now performed by men. And he has called such machines *Robots*. He has supposed a Robot to be so delicately responsive to stimuli, that you could dictate a letter to it, and the Robot would proceed to write it out on the typewriter. Now there is, in principle, nothing absurd or impossible in this supposition. The mechanists in psychology ask us to assume that men are such Robots, carried to a higher degree of responsiveness than that depicted by the author of the play. And the view that men are merely such improved Robots is now being dogmatically taught to thousands of young students in the psychological departments of the universities of this country. The question before us is then—Is the assumption that men are Robots a good or useful one? Is it at the present time a profitable working hypothesis?

My own view is that it is not a good working hypothesis

in the present state of knowledge. I propose to try to show you good grounds for that view. Let me first say that I have no desire to defend the psychology of Ideas. In my estimation the word 'idea' is one that has long outlived its usefulness in science, however convenient it may be for popular usage. No doubt, the word served a useful purpose in the hands of Locke and Hume (and its German equivalent 'Vorstellung' played a similar part in the hands of Herbart and others) in enabling them to lead psychology away from the errors of the older faculty psychology. But what an Idea may be no one has been able to say: no one has been able to use the word in a way that is not essentially misleading. For the word 'idea' implies a thing or entity; and all the theory of association of Ideas, as well as the psychology of Herbart, was permeated and distorted by the influence of this implication, that our mental life, that all thinking, consists in the successive appearance of these entities, Ideas, before the footlights called 'consciousness,' and in their disappearance into a mysterious unknown region called the unconscious.

Very early in my career as a psychologist, I planned to write a psychology without Ideas, a feat now accomplished in my 'Outline of Psychology.'*

For every form of the idea-psychology, not only suffers from the misleading implication that Ideas are entities that somehow exist in their own right, but also suffers from another grave defect, namely, it leaves us without any intelligible theory of action, it cannot relate the Ideas with the bodily activities in which our mental life expresses itself. It inevitably leaves the Ideas up in the air; it cannot find any way of planting their feet among the solid facts of cerebral currents and muscular contractions. It is true that the theory of ideomotor action was an attempt to remedy this defect; but, as is

---

*I believe and have long believed that the next important advance of logic will consist in the banishment of Ideas and their equivalent, Concepts, from that discipline.

In this respect, as in several others, I am happy to find myself in agreement with leaders of the *Gestalt* school. Prof. Wertheimer has recently written: "Wenn man sich recht überlegt, was im lebendigen Denken ein Begriff ist, was das wirkliche Kapieren eines Schlusses ist, wenn man sich überlegt, was das Entscheidende bei eimem mathematischen Beweisgang ist, bei dem Ineinderhängen, dann sieht man, dass mit den Kategorien der traditionellen Logik hier nichts gemacht ist." (Ueber Gestalttheorie, Symposion, 1925.)

now pretty generally recognized, that theory failed hopelessly, if only for the reason that it flew in the face of obvious facts.

It is of interest to note that Dr. Watson and I have been led by our perception of the same fact, the unsatisfactoriness of the idea-psychology, to two very different positions. Both of us became acutely conscious of the fact that the idea-psychology was unable to render any acceptable interpretation or explanation of human conduct, that it propounded no intelligible theory of action. Both of us were impressed by the fact that the psychology of the nineteenth century neglected unduly the facts of behavior, and that, in calling itself the science of consciousness, it was turning its back upon the more important problems of human nature, the problems of conduct. As long ago as 1905 I began my attempt to remedy that state of affairs by proposing to define psychology as the positive science of conduct, using the word 'positive' to distinguish it from ethics, the normative science of conduct. I hoped in this way to draw more attention to the neglected problems of behavior. And in 1908 I went further with this program by publishing my Social Psychology. In that book the problems of conduct were given first place; the purposive or goal-seeking nature of all human activity was emphasized; and the hormic theory of action was developed in some detail. Watson took up the same cue some years later, and, being primarily interested in animal psychology, in which field there is no possibility of any direct observation of conscious activity, and in which the student is inevitably confined to the observation of bodily behavior, he proposed to effect the needed reform, not by redressing the balance in psychology between the introspective and the objective methods of study, but by the simple expedient of upsetting the balance completely. He proposed to throw overboard as useless the introspective methods of study and all that we had learnt in that way; and, having absorbed the dogma that all events are mechanically explicable and that all human and animal action is merely mechanical reflex action more or less compounded, a dogma which owing largely to the influence of Herbert Spencer was then fashionable, he proposed to ignore completely all those features of behavior which imply its purposive nature and which can only be stated or described in terms which imply the direction of action towards ends, the seeking of goals, the striving to bring about a change. Thus, by repudiating one half of the methods of psychology and resolutely shutting his eyes to three quarters of its problems, he laid down the program of Behaviorism and rallied to its standard all those who have a natural distaste for difficult problems and a preference for short, easy, and fictitious solutions.

Let us notice that the psychologists of this group, who call themselves 'Behaviorists,' are not propounding any new doctrine of a positive kind. The view that all events are mechanically explicable is as old as Democritus; the view that animals are purely machines is at least as old as Descartes; the view that all human conduct is explicable on the theory of the compounding of reflexes was developed in great detail, and with an assurance as complete as Dr. Watson's, by Herbert Spencer more than sixty years ago. The only novel feature is the proposal to ignore completely a very large range of facts of the utmost interest and importance, facts of two orders: first, the fact that each of us consciously perceives the world about him, consciously desires to modify it in ways which he consciously conceives, consciously strives and plans to effect such changes; secondly, the fact that almost all human and animal behavior, considered strictly objectively, seems, with various degrees of clearness, to express such perception, such desiring, such conscious planning and striving, such conscious concern with the future. All that is positive in the methods and principles of Behaviorism has been actively practised and taught by many biologists for many years, by such men as Albrecht Bethe, Jacques Loeb, Bechterew, Pavlov, Uexküll, and others. All that is novel in the behaviorist program is the resolute pretense that the facts of human consciousness are of no interest to the student of human nature, present no problems worthy of consideration and may profitably be ignored.

Let us notice next that the school of avowed behaviorists has very quickly split into two rival parties. The one party, that led by Dr. Watson, which we may conveniently call the party of strict behaviorists, or the S.B. party, adheres to the original program; it is characterized by its refusal to recognize both the facts of conscious activity and the fact that behavior can not be adequately described, and still less intelligibly interpreted, without using language which recognizes the goal-seeking nature of all behavior.

The other and smaller group is best represented by Prof. E. C. Tolman. The behaviorists of this group refuse to recognize, or to be interested in, only one of the two great classes of facts ignored by the S. B. party, namely, the facts of conscious activity. They recognize fully the facts of the second order ignored by the S. B. group, the objectively observable fact that behavior is obviously a goal-seeking process. They mark their separation from what I have called strict behavorism by contemptuous reference to it as behaviorism of the Watsonian variety, and by devising for it the elegant and expressive designation "muscle-twitchism."[1] This group of behaviorists may be conveniently distinguished as teaching purposive behaviorism or P.B.

The situation is further complicated by a third group of psychologists who, while showing much sympathy with the S.B. party, belong neither to it nor to the P.B. party. They are well represented by Prof. F. A. Allport.[2] They are separated from the S. B. by the fact that they neither deny nor totally ignore the facts of conscious activity. They give the impression that they would much like to do this, but have not the courage of their desires. They see that to deny the whole realm of introspectively observable facts is too flagrantly absurd and that to ignore them may be a little dangerous. But they are allied with the S.B. party by their neglect to make use of the introspectively observable facts and by their acceptance of its "muscle-twitchism." For them every instance of human conduct or animal behavior is merely a mechanical reflex response to a sensory stimulus; and they resolutely shut their eyes to all the objective (as well as the subjective) evidences that behavior is a goal-seeking process. Thus, in spite of their recognition of the fact that human beings are consciously active, the psychologists of this group are in practice and procedure very near to the strict behaviorists; they may well be called the exponents of 'Near Behaviorism' or N.B.

Purposive psychology may best be vindicated by showing the inadequacies of these three types of behaviorism, Strict Behaviorism, Near Behaviorism and Purposive Behaviorism.[3]

---

[1]Prof. Tolman speaks of "behaviorism of the proper sort" as being "not a mere Muscle Twitchism of the Watsonian variety." "Behaviorism and Purpose." Journal of Philosophy, Vol. XXII, 1925.

[2]In his "Social Psychology."

[3]I say nothing about the type of psychology which confines itself to the study of the introspectively observable facts, and ignores the problems of behavior. Psychology of this type, however interesting and important may be its contributions to our knowledge of human nature, can never be more than one part or specialized

Strict Behaviorism

Strict Behaviorism denies to itself all acquaintances with a vast range of most interesting facts and problems. It abolishes, by the simple process of refusing to look at them, all the old and fascinating problems of the relations between the mental and the physical, including all the vast field of psycho-physics, all that part of psychology which is concerned more particularly to study and to formulate exactly the relations between sensory stimuli and sensory experience. For the S.B. all the monumental work in this line of Thomas Young, Johannes Müller, Weber, Helmholtz, Hering, and a multitude of others is a closed book. S.B. equally debars itself from taking any notice of dreams, crystal visions, hallucinations, delusions, pains and subjective symptoms of every kind, all the multitudinous departures from normal modes of experience which are only revealed by introspective reports; and thus shuts itself off from all possibility of learning anything from the psycho-analytic movement, which, whatever its errors, has proved to be a movement of the first importance.

The hardy S.B. replies "What of that? If I refuse to be interested in all these topics, you can't force me to be interested." And he dismisses all the schools of psycho-analysis with a few contemptuous words. He contends that only the bodily movements which constitute outward behavior are of any practical importance; and he believes that two very simple conceptions suffice for the explanation of every instance of behavior, namely the reflex and the conditioned reflex. He pretends that, armed with these alone, he can penetrate every secret of the human heart and mind. Why then should he countenance any laborious study of the disordered feeling and thinking of the neurotic and the madman; why seek to elicit, why ponder

---

branch of the science of human nature, one that restricts itself to very special methods and problems. Though some of its exponents are inclined to claim for it that it is the whole of psychology, they represent a viewpoint which is fast passing away. I will make only one comment in the form of a citation from a recent article of Dr. Max Wertheimer; "es gibt psychologische Theorien und recht viele psychologische Lehrbücher sogar, die, trotzdem sie dauernd nur von Bewusstseins-elemente sprechen, materialistischer, dürrer sinnloser, geistloser sind als ein lebendiger Baum, der vom Bewusstsein auch vielleicht nichts in sich hat. Nicht darauf kann es ankommen, woraus materialiter die Stückchen des Geschehens bestehen, sondern auf den Sinn des Ganzen, die Art des Ganzen, muss es ankommen." Ueber Gestalttheorie, Symposion, 1925.

over, interminable reports of his phantasies, his dreams, his internal struggles, his torments, his terrors, his impulsions, delusions and obsessions? All such experiences, so long as the patient does not allow them to gain expression in bodily action, are barred by the S.B. Wait till the internal tumult expresses itself in a homicidal act; then the behaviorist will step in and explain the whole affair with the magic words "badly conditioned reflex."

The S.B. and the N.B. are misled by their dogma into such monstrous error, not only in their dealings with human beings in the practical exigencies of social life, but also in their experimental procedures. Thus Dr. Watson, obsessed by his doctrine, experiments with new-born infants, and, failing to find in them any clearly marked tendencies and capacities beyond a few very simple ones which can plausibly be described as reflexes, triumphantly jumps to the conclusion that, as regards all innate mental endowment, all men of all races are exactly alike. He utters the final word upon the question of racial differences (one of the most difficult and important questions confronting us and one which can only be settled by the prolonged research of many workers, research which is only just begun) by saying: "I defy anyone to take these infants at birth, study their behavior, and mark off differences in behavior that will characterize white from black and white or black from yellow."[1] In the light of his profound observations on new-born infants he denies not only the existence of all the instincts of the human species, but also all hereditary mental traits, capacities, talents or characteristics of every kind, other than the few reflexes he finds in those new-born infants. "Our conclusion then, is that we have no real evidence of the inheritance of traits—Let us then, forever lay the ghost of inheritance of aptitudes, of 'mental' characteristics, of special abilities."[2]

Animal behavior is the chosen ground of the behaviorist; it was through studies in that field that he was misled into his perverse unfortunate endeavor. There, if anywhere, (or in

---

[1]Pedagogical Seminary Vol. XXXII, p. 296.

[2]Dr. Watson's defiance is magnificent, as magnificent as the similar defiance of the late Mr. Bryan in face of the evidence for human evolution. It is disconcerting and portentous that a man whose reasoning processes are habitually of the kind illustrated above should be widely acclaimed in this country as a leader in a great field of science. The fact gives furiously to think.

relation to the new-born babe, his other favorite object) his descriptions and interpretations should appear plausible and adequate. But, even there, he cannot describe, much less interpret, the facts in any useful and profitable manner without departing from his principles.[1] His simplest experiments postulate the animal's purposive or goal-seeking tendencies. He puts a hungry animal in a cage or a maze and places food just beyond his reach; or puts the food in a box, knowing or assuming that the animal will try, will strive, to get at it. And all the successive actions of the animal are intelligible only in terms of this assumption. It is true that it is possible to describe the successive movements of the animal in purely objective terms, just as it is possible to make a Kinematographic record of them. But such a description, no matter how minute and exact, leaves the actions quite unintelligible so long as all references to the goal and the striving towards it are really excluded. The behaviorist pretends that each movement displayed is a reflex reaction to some sense-stimulus; and it is perhaps true that sense-stimuli play a part in determining the particular form of each movement. But all the successive movements have a meaning, a significance, for us, and are intelligible to us as behavior, only when we regard them as incidents of one process of striving, a process that has conative unity. No matter how carefully the behaviorist may exclude from his descriptions and interpretations all implication of this aspect of the movements, he does not exclude it from his thinking; he implicitly makes the assumption which explicitly he professes to repudiate.

It is worth while noting that even the movements of the parts of a machine cannot be profitably or intelligibly described and interpreted in purely objective terms, i.e., without reference to the purpose of the man who designed and made the machine. Take any machine, even the simplest: We may describe in the greatest detail, its structure and the sequences of movements of its parts, without either understanding the machine or leading the hearer of our description to understand it. We cannot understand the machine and its movements without knowing what the machine is designed to do, what its function is, what it is there for, in short, what purpose it is designed to serve, in what goal-seeking process it

---

[1] I recognize that interpretation or explanation is only description in more generalized terms: but the distinction is useful and valid.

forms a link. The machine, in a sense, embodies a human purpose; it is designed, constructed, and put in action *in order to* facilitate the accomplishment of some purpose, some plan, to satisfy some desire, to make easier and more certain the attainment of some goal. It is for that reason, and that reason only, that we naturally and properly speak of the machine as being in order or out of order. No purely physical inorganic structure in the construction of which human design has played no part, can properly be said to be in order or out of order; unless we regard it as embodying the purpose of, and as designed by, some non-human intelligence, some non-human mental being. The solar system in many respects resembles a machine; but, unless we regard it as designed and constructed in order to render the earth habitable for men, or for some other purpose, there can be no meaning in describing it as in order or out of order. If, through collision with a star or a comet, the course of the planets were changed in some radical fashion, there would be no sense in saying that the system was out of order. And so with a machine, say a typewriter or a linotype machine: if pressure on a key does not bring down the right letter, we say the machine is out of order; but the statement has meaning only in virtue of its implicit reference to the purpose which the machine is designed to serve.

If, then, we cannot understand or intelligibly describe the movements of the machine without reference, implicit or explicit, to the purpose it serves; how much less can we intelligibly describe the movements of men or of animals without such reference, whether in particular or in general terms.[1]

---

[1]One of the sources of confusion in this matter is the two-fold sense in which the words 'purposive' and 'teleological' are used, the intrinsic and the extrinsic meanings. There is the intrinsic sense in which human conduct is purposive, teleological, or goal-seeking; and there is the extrinsic sense in which the movements of the parts of a machine are purposive, teleological, or goal-seeking. The most mechanically minded man does not scruple to ask—What is the purpose of this lever, or of that cog or switch, in a machine? And in the same way he does not scruple to ask—What is the purpose of this bone or that muscle in an animal's body? But he uses this language without reflecting upon the significance or implication of his words. If the question of his meaning is forced upon him, he is likely to reply that his words are merely a convenient, but incorrect, form of speech; that of course he does not mean that the starting lever foresees and intends the starting of the machine, or that the bone or muscle of the animal foresees or intends the movements in which it plays a part. And he is confident that in

Yet just this is the program, the goal, the purpose of the S.B.
and the N.B. Their purpose is to achieve general descriptions
of behavior in language which shall exclude all reference to
purpose; the goal they seek is description of behavior without
reference to its goal-seeking nature; they strive toward a
description which shall exclude all reference to, all implication
of, striving. Thus they cannot move a step, cannot even lay
down their program, without stultifying themselves.

The supreme and final test of any scientific principle or
hypothesis is the pragmatic test. How does it serve as a guide
to observation and experiment? This test, when applied to
the principle or hypothesis of the S.B., at once reveals its inadequacy, its falsity, its misleading nature.   ·

As a matter of fact, the S.B. does not in practice abide by
his principles. When he sets out to make experimental observation of a man or animal, he does not ignore the purposive
nature of behavior; he puts his subject under such conditions
as he believes will induce it to strive towards some goal. He
puts the animal in a maze or a cage from which, he believes,
it will strive to escape; or he offers it some incentive to

---

both cases all the movements are mechanically explicable: and
that therefore the word 'purpose' in all cases of both classes implies a fallacy. In the older discussions of teleology, the words "purposive" and "teleological" were chiefly used in the sense in which
we apply them to a machine. It was asked—Is the solar system,
are volcanic eruptions, lightning, and the flow of rivers purposive?
The question meant—Are these things or processes designed, constructed, or set in action, as our machines are, in order to serve
some purpose? And the answer of science was—No, they are not.
The same question was asked of the structures and processes of
the animal body. And for a long time science accepted the positive answer; regarded the animal body as a machine cunningly
designed to realize the purpose of its Designer and Creator. Then
came the Darwinian theory: and science saw that it was no longer
necessary to regard the structure of each animal species as the
product of a designing Creator, and said—The structures and movements of the animal body are not teleological or purposive. When
the teleological interpretation of bodily movements in the extrinsic
sense of the words was thus rejected, the other kind of teleological
interpretation, the intrinsic meaning, fell also into disrepute, owing
largely to the failure to distinguish between the two meanings of
the words, between intrinsic and extrinsic teleology. It should be
noted that intrinsic and extrinsic teleology do not imply one another. They do not stand or fall together. Rather they may be
regarded as alternatives. The more fully we accept intrinsic purposiveness in organisms, the less do we need to postulate extrinsic,
purpose and conversely.

strive, food, or a mate, or a rival, or a terrifying object. He has some general notion of its striving tendencies; and his experimental procedure is guided by that knowledge, while he pretends to proceed without reference to such tendencies.

Much experimental work, both on men and animals, has been far less productive than it might have been, if the striving aspect of behavior, the purposive nature of all our activities, had been recognized frankly and explicitly, instead of implicitly and furtively. For in very many experiments the question of supplying adequate incentives to striving is all-important. I might illustrate this fact at great length from the records of experiments made by many psychologists. It must suffice to point out that in quite recent years the importance of the incentive to striving has begun to receive practical recognition in both human and animal experimental psychology, with much profit to the procedures adopted and to the results attained.[1] The common conclusion arrived at, being that which common sense has accepted for long ages, is that

---

[1] A few references must suffice: W. Köhler, The Mentality of Apes, p. 65.

Simmons, The Relative Effectiveness of Certain Incentives in Animal Learning, Comp. Psychol. Monog. 1924.

E. B. Hurlock, The Effect of Incentives upon the constancy of the I.Q. Pedagog. Seminary, Sept. 1925.

H. F. Whiting and H. B. English, Fatigue Tests and Incentives, Journ. Exp. Psychology, Feb. 1925.

W. F. Book and L. Norvell, The Will to Learn, an Experimental Study of Incentives, The Pedagog. Seminary, Dec. 1922.

I may add that in my own prolonged experiments with rats, realizing the primary importance of incentives that will evoke strong striving towards a goal, I have adopted the plan of putting the animals into a tank of water in which is a single island or platform. The rat placed in water at once swims vigorously to and fro, exploring the boundaries and all available channels of the tank. And careful observation of the behavior on repetition of the situation will convince any impartial observer that, after the rat has found the platform a few times, the platform becomes for him a goal which he actively seeks. I venture to claim that a due regard to the importance of incentives has in this case led me to a method of great value in animal experiment, one which, by standardizing the incentive and evoking constantly a maximal energy of striving toward a goal, greatly shortens the duration of each experiment and renders the successive performances of the same animal, and of different animals, much truer indices of the animal's capacity to learn than the performances under the commonly used method of rewarding the animal with food and making food the incentive of its behavior.

the more effective the incentive, i.e. the stronger the urge, or impulse, or striving, evoked, the more rapidly and efficiently does the animal or the human being overcome difficulties and attain its goal.

The demonstration of the inadequacy, the relative futility, of all attempts to ignore the purposive, the goal-seeking, nature of all behavior may best be taken from the mouth of the purposive behaviorist. Two of my colleagues stand out as leaders of this group, namely Profs. R. B. Perry and E. C. Tolman. The latter has recently published a series of articles concerned with this topic, basing his conclusions on the careful observation and analysis of animal behavior under experimental conditions.[1]

In the first of these articles, Prof. Tolman sets out by rejecting decisively the proposal to abolish instincts and the endeavor to interpret instinctive behavior as merely the result of setting in action a chain of reflexes. After referring to countless instances of animal behavior which exhibit extreme variability of action, variations not attributable to variations of the sense-stimuli, Tolman writes: "Indeed these and countless like observations have given the pure reflex *pattern* theory its *final coup de grace.*" He rejects equally decisively the view that what we call instincts can be identified with habits. "Instinct behavior *is* fundamentally different from habit-behavior. For, although undoubtedly inheritance plays its part in both and environment plays its part in both, still variations in heredity are primarily responsible for the differences to be observed in the one and variations in environment for the differences to be found in the other." He shows that most of those authors who profess to avoid all reference to goal-seeking do not in reality do so, but rather introduce it surreptiously. He rightly insists that the instincts or, as he alternatively calls them, the "innate determining adjustments," are to be "recognized by the teleological patterns of the final goals which they achieve. The subordinate movements and objects involved may be all acquired, but the general pattern of the goal is innate and constant."

In the third article, Tolman rightly insists on the goal-seeking character of animal behavior, and writes: "It appears that

---

[1]"The Nature of Instinct" in the Psychological Bulletin, April 1923; "Behaviorism and Purpose," in the Journal of Philosophy, Jan. 1925; "Purpose and Cognition: the Determiners of Animal Learning" in Psychological Review, July, 1925.

goal-seeking must be defined not only as a tendency to *persist* in more or less random fashion until food is reached but also as a tendency to *select* within limits the *shorter* (and probably also the easier and pleasanter) of two or more alternative ways." And he shows that such goal-seeking is initiated, not merely by sense-stimuli, but by the animal's appreciation of the situation in which it finds itself, what Tolman prefers to call its "initial cognitive hunches"; and that in turn the goal-seeking is guided and terminated, not merely by some new sense-stimulus, but by the animal's appreciation of the nature of the new situation brought about by its activity. All this is based upon minute and exact experimental observation and analysis of animal behavior; and it leads Tolman to the conclusion that we cannot hope to make progress in the study of animal behavior unless we frankly apply to animal learning "some sort of purposive (goal-seeking) and cognitive (object-adjustment) categories"; and that "practically, it seems that the current tendency to talk and think primarily in terms of such inadequate and premature physiological concepts as are now on hand is in part responsible for some of the barrenness of our present animal research."

These conclusions of Prof. Tolman's are perfectly in line with the work and conclusions of Professors Köhler and Koffka, two leaders of the *Gestalt* school. Both, basing themselves upon intimate studies of animal behavior, have shown by the most careful and elaborate reasoning how hollow and misleading is the pretense of the S.B. to be able to describe and interpret the actions of animals either as series of reflex responses to sense-stimuli or as habit responses; they have shown that those observers of animal behavior who pretend to demonstrate the absence of all intelligence and purpose in animals merely prove their own domination by a perverse purpose, namely the purpose to demonstrate the adequacy of mechanical categories. They show conclusively that you cannot describe intelligibly and adequately the behavior of animals without using language which implies that the animals do not merely respond to stimuli, but that they seek goals and appreciate the several factors of a complex situation in their relations to one another and to the goals they seek. For example, Köhler describes the following behavior of a chimpanzee. "Sultan grabs *at* objects [food] behind the bars and *cannot reach* them with his arm; he thereupon walks about *searchingly*, finally *turns to a* shoe-scraper, made of iron bars in a wooden frame, and *manipulates it until* he has pulled out one of the iron bars; with this he *runs immediately to* his *real objective,* at a distance of about ten metres and *draws it toward him."* I have italicized the words of this description which imply the purpose and refer to the goal of the animal in accordance with common sense and good sense. The consistent S.B. would have to describe this simple bit of behavior very differently, as a series of disconnected movements, movements each of which is a response to some sense-impression of the moment and is unconnected with the other movements of the sequence by any reference to, or implication of, the connection of them all in one sequence as steps in a single goal-seeking process, a single continued striving towards the objective, sustained by the animal's desire for food. Of course such a description is possible, but not only would it be long-winded and clumsy, but also it would be inadequate and positively misleading. Köhler goes on to say: "In this case it is pretty clear that the whole proceeding, part by part, contains *several* constituents which are meaningless when isolated. (1) Instead of keeping to his objective, Sultan goes away from it; this is quite senseless when taken by itself. (2) He breaks up one of the station's iron shoe-scrapers, and this, taken by itself, has nothing whatever to do with his objective.—(1) The animal by no means strides away from the objective in the free careless way which we are used to, in him and the others at times when they are seeking nothing, but goes away like some one who has a task before him. And here again, I wish to warn against anyone speaking of 'anthropomorphism' of 'reading into' the animals etc., where there is not the least ground for such reproaches. I merely ask whether it does not look different from somebody strolling about idly. Of course it looks different. Whether we can exactly analyze our total impression in both cases, has nothing whatever to do with the case. Now all I wish to state is that the two general impressions that are contrasted here *occur in chimpanzees, exactly as in man;* and it is these 'impressions' which are not at all 'something that has been read into' the chimpanzees, but which belongs to the elementary phenomenology of his behavior, that are meant when we say, for instance, 'Sultan trotted about gaily' or 'he went over the ground looking for something.' If *this* is an anthrophomorphism, so then is this sentence: 'Chimpanzees have the same tooth formula as man.' So as to leave no doubt whatever as to the meaning of the expression, 'Walking about searchingly,' I should like to add that nothing is said therein as to the 'consciousness' of the animal, but only as to its 'behavior.' (2) While playing with the shoe-scraper Sultan's activity is concentrated exclusively on *loosening one of its bars;* but even when described more precisely thus, this action remains *irrelevant with reference to the real purpose as long as it is considered in isolation."* Prof. Köhler thus brings out clearly the fact that the train of action described has a conative unity, is a sequence of actions, all of which are steps in one continued process of seeking a goal, of striving to attain the objective, and that any description which ignores this fact, any consistent description by the strict behaviorist, must be useless; and worse than useless, because positively misleading.

The particular instance described above is only one of a multitude of similar instances in which the animals obviously take steps in order to attain their goals; instances such as piling up boxes *in order,* by climbing upon the pile, to be able to reach bananas hung high on the ceiling; or joining two pieces of bamboo *in order* to make a stick long enough to reach a banana lying outside the cage.

Again, in criticizing the S.B. theory that all learning or improvement of action is merely a process of habit-formation, by the chance succession of movements and the mechanical association of such movements as are most frequently repeated to form a habit, Köhler writes: "the facts we are speaking of, by the way, seem to represent almost a reversal of what the theory we have discussed regards as the effect of repetitions. According to it, procedure developed by accident becomes smoother through practice, and more like a genuine solution. This may be true, where the theory applies; the chimpanzee's *genuine* solutions, at any rate, do not become more valuable in themselves through constant repetition, even if they appear more quickly. For one who has actually watched the experiments, discussions like the above have something comic about them. For instance, when one has seen for oneself, how in the first experiment of her life, it did not dawn on Tschego for hours to push the obstructing box out of the way, how she merely stretched out her arm uselessly, or else sat down quietly, but then, fearing the loss of her food, suddenly seized the obstacle, and pushed it to one side, thus solving the task in a second—when one has watched that, then to 'secure these facts against misinterpretation' [the misinterpretation of the S.B.]

seems almost pedantic."[1] And in general Köhler says of the S.B. interpretation of the learning process—"No single experiment fulfils this requirement, as practically none is performed twice over in the same way,—indeed the movements by which any single one is performed vary very much—*the only limit is the sense of the proceeding.* For this reason no observer, even with the best of efforts, can say: 'the animal contracts such or such a muscle, carries out this or that impulse' *this would be to accentuate an unessential side-issue, which may change from one case to another;* which muscles carry out which action is entirely immaterial."

Further, criticizing a common illegitimate extension of the S. B. theory, which we owe originally to Thorndike, and which asserts that success stamps in (in the brain) the accidental associations of movements that have led to success, Köhler writes: "the animals produce complete methods of solution quite suddenly, and *as complete wholes which may, in a certain sense, be absolutely appropriate to the situation, and yet cannot be carried out. They can never have had any success with them,* and, therefore such methods were certainly never practiced formerly.—After all this, as far as I can see, even an adherent of that theory must recognize that the reports of experiments here given do not support his explanation. The more he tries to advance more valuable data than the general scheme of his theory, and really thing out and show how he would explain and interpret all the experiments in detail, the more will he realize that he is attempting something impossible."[2]

Köhler does not hesitate to attribute the actions of the animals to their desire for the attainment of their goals, to assume that they perform certain actions as indirect means to the attainment of the goal, that they even construct implements for the sake of, for the purpose of, facilitating the attainment of a goal.[3] And he shows that we cannot properly describe many of their actions without using language which implies such goal-seeking; *e.g.* an animal on successive occasions pushes away a box which obstructs her approach to her goal,

---

[1]*Op. cit.* p. 207.
[2]*Op. cit.* p. 227.
[3]e.g. piling up of boxes to form a platform on which to climb nearer to the goal, and constructing a long stick by fitting two sticks together and even gnawing away the end of one stick in order to make it fit into the cavity of the other.

and on each occasion she handles it in a different manner: the behavior cannot be adequately described by saying that she made such and such movements which, on each occasion resulted in the removal of the box. In order to describe the behavior adequately, we have to say that she removed the obstruction in the course of her efforts to attain her goal.[1]

Professor Koffka[2] also, by a careful analysis of the facts of animal behavior, refutes the theory of learning by association of purely random reflex acts or of reflex acts evoked simply as direct responses to sensory stimuli. He concludes that "the theory of an entirely meaningless learning is simply untenable." He freely realizes the purposive or goal-seeking character of animal behavior; and he does not scruple to use the words 'purpose' and 'intention' and to speak of "what is going on in the phenomenal world of the chimpanzee's mind." He also insists that instinctive process is radically different from the working of a reflex mechanism.

I may add that my own experiments on dogs and rats (briefly reported in my *Outline of Psychology*) illustrate the same facts, the extreme variation of movements in any one *attempt to solve a problem* and in successive struggles with the same problem, movements which nevertheless are all incidents of one process, a striving towards the goal, and which can only be intelligibly described as such. In the same work I have shown in some detail the failure of all the attempts of the S.B. to interpret and explain as mechanical responses to stimuli behavior of two types: first, the simplest possible instances of obtaining food by escape from a maze; secondly, the more complex behavior of returning home, a form of behavior exhibited by a multitude of species some of which are comparatively low in the evolutionary scale.

---

[1] Köhler writes: "Her manner of removing the obstacle was quite different from the first occasion. I wish to stress this point for the enlightenment of students who have not observed chimpanzees carefully. What Chica did this second time was to clear away the cage from the fruit, not to make this or that series of movements." He might well have said that it is necessary to stress this point for the enlightenment of students obsessed and blinded by the mechanistic dogma.
[2] In his "The Growth of the Mind."

CHAPTER XIII

MEN OR ROBOTS?*

By William McDougall

I I

It is necessary to say a few words about the conditioned reflex or conditioned response. I have no desire to belittle the importance of the beautiful experiments of Pavlov and others which have built up a new method of great value for the study of the nervous system. Prof. Burnham of this university has shown us in his book, "The Normal Mind," that the results obtained by this method can be of much value for human psychology, can be incorporated in a sane psychology which does not pretend to ignore the all-important facts of striving, of motivation, of goal-seeking, of incentives and ideals. The experiments on the conditioned response do unquestionably carry us nearer to an understanding of the process of association. And no one denies that association is a process of great importance in our mental life. But all the history of psychology since Locke shows how detrimental to its progress was the overweening faith of the associationist school in the all-sufficiency of its one great explanatory principle. The physiologists of the present time who are enthusiastically exploiting the conception of the conditioned reflex as the one sole and all-sufficient master-key to the secrets of human nature, these physiologists, obstinately blind to the lessons of the past, are repeating the error of the Associationists. James Mill, with a dogmatic confidence which now seems ridiculous, declared that the principle of association of ideas made all our mental processes as obvious as the road from Ludgate Circus to St. Paul's Cathedral. Many of the enthusiasts for the conditioned reflex are making for it the same claim, and are thus repeating his error, with far less excuse. James Mill's error is pardonable in view of the scanty knowledge and insight of his time; but now, when the labors of a multitude of workers throughout well nigh a century have conclusively shown the inadequacy of the association-principle to explain all human activity, there is no excuse for the wilful ignoring of all this improvement of our insight and the repeti-

*Powell Lecture in Psychological Theory at Clark University, December 11, 1925.

tion of the old error in a slightly modified and accentuated form.

The principle of association is valid and important. The mistake of the extreme associationists was to imagine that it rendered all other principles unnecessary, to believe that by a little juggling with words, by the use of such phrases as "the idea of an end or goal," they explained away all the facts of motive, striving, volition, conation, constructive activity. The principle of the conditioned response is equally valid and important; it is the principle of association in an improved form. But the mistake of so many of its exponents is to believe that the demonstration in the laboratory of elementary instances of conditioning of responses proves such responses to be merely mechanical processes that imply no forward striving towards a goal. When Prof. Köhler's ape, Sultan, had learned to reach, with the long rod he had constructed, the banana that lay beyond the reach of a short rod, he may be said to have acquired a conditioned response; just as every instance of the acquisition of skill or knowledge may be so described. The error of the conditioned response enthusiasts is the assumption that Sultan's desire for the banana, his striving towards it, was an irrelevant fact, one which may safely be ignored when we attempt to understand the way in which the new response was acquired and subsequently displayed.

Near Behaviorism

The strict behaviorists do not trouble themselves about the social life of men; they are sufficiently occupied with the self-imposed task of proving that animals and new-born babies are merely machines. But some near-behaviorists have undertaken to write on Social Psychology, basing it on the Watsonian dogma of the absence of all innate endowment other than a limited number of mechanical reflexes. How then do they deal with the complexities of social conduct? There are two pieces of verbal sleight-of-hand on which they chiefly rely in order to conceal from their readers the impossible nature of the tasks they essay, the utter inadequacy of the suppositions with which they set out.

First, they create the false appearance of bringing all social conduct under the stimulus-response formula by aid of a very simple verbal trick, rendered possible by the ambiguity of common speech. The stimulus-response formula of the behaviorist asserts that every action is a response to a stimulus; the word "stimulus" in this formula clearly meaning a physical stimulus applied to a sense-organ or afferent nerve. When, then, they find a man whose conduct is largely governed by his devotion to his country, to an ideal, or to the religion of Christ or Buddha, they describe such things, the country or nation, the ideal, the religion, or the founder of the religion, as a stimulus; and thus all patriotic, or moral, or religious conduct becomes merely a response or series of responses to stimuli.

Secondly, having rejected "instincts," in the interest of the mechanical reflex-theory and on such trivial grounds as Dr. Watson's failure to see evidence of instincts in new-born infants, they introduce the essential notion of a tendency towards an end, an urge towards a goal, surreptitiously by a back door, disguised under all sorts of names chosen to convey as much mechanical implication as may be possible; the favorite terms being *drive, determining tendency, prepotent reflex, prepotent habit, determining set, motor-set.*

Dr. Allport, for example, is not so blind to the facts of nature as Dr. Watson. He sees the plain evidence that maturation of instincts takes place after birth in the young of many animal species; but, seeing also (like Watson) that it is impossible to prove the reality of such maturation in the child by any simple experiment, he concludes: "In view of the uncertainty regarding the maturation hypothesis it seems better to adopt the genetic viewpoint, and beginning at birth with the simple reflexes, which are demonstrably innate, progress with no further assumptions than the well-known facts of the learning process."[1] But, knowing well that human conduct cannot be interpreted in terms of Watson's array of reflexes, Allport very soon introduces and makes great play with the "prepotent reflex." "The human being has inherited a number of prepotent reflexes which are fundamental not only in their original potency, but in the control which they exert over habit formation throughout life. Indomitable restlessness of movement in carrying out prepotent activities in the face of difficulties is universal in the animal kingdom. The imperativeness of the prepotent reflex is Nature's provision that adaptation and survival will be achieved."[2]

Allport, having thus provided himself with something less

---

[1] *Social Psychology*, p. 81.
[2] *Ibid*, p. 57.

sterile than the simple mechanical reflexes, having added to his stock of explanatory principles the "prepotent reflex" which has *a potency for control,* which is *indomitable in the face of difficulties,* and *imperative in its service of the ends of adaptation and survival,* is able to assert: "the intricacies of human conduct arise as modifications of these simple prepotent responses"; and, without arousing the critical tendency of most of his readers, he can introduce such terms as *incentive, end, sanction, drive, urge, desire, motive, wish, selection, choice, means to an end, in order to, struggle, interests, satisfaction, autonomic drives, struggle for satisfaction, settings, attitudes, striving, craving, aims, ideals, values, efforts, success, seeking, conflict* and even *purpose.*

Thus, without gross appearance of inconsistency, he is able to write: "Hunger is the supreme drive of the learning process. Sex is a close rival. Other important factors, such as rivalry, desire for social approval and the like, are incentives derived from these two."[1]   In fact, as the book advances to deal with the actual facts of human life, it falls into the language of good common sense, which everywhere recognizes, implicitly and explicitly, the purposive, the forward striving character of all our activities.

Purposive Behaviorism

We may next examine the procedure of the purposive behaviorist, as exemplified by Professors Perry and Tolman.

Tolman fully recognizes and insists upon the goal-seeking nature of most animal behavior. "Whenever, in merely describing a behavior, it is found *necessary* to include a statement of something either *towards-which* or *from-which* the behavior is directed, there we have purpose. But we may analyze further. Just when is it we find a statement of a 'toward-whichness' or of a 'from-whichness' thus necessary? We find it necessary, whenever, by modifying the various attendant circumstances, we discover that the same goal is still there and still identifying the given response. Thus, when we make minor changes in the position or nature of the *intervening objects* and the behavior readjusts so as to again come to the end-object, the case is one of purpose. Or finally when we remove the goal-object entirely and behavior thereupon ceases, purpose must again have been a descriptive feature. In short, purpose is present, descriptively, whenever a statement of the

---
[1]Social Psychology.

goal-object is necessary to indicate (1) constancy of goal-object in spite of variation in adjustment to intervening obstacles, or (2) variations in final direction corresponding to differing positions of the goal-object, or (3) cessation of activity when a given goal-object is entirely removed." Again: "wherever the purely objective description of either a simple or complex behavior discovers a 'persistence-until' character there we have what behaviorism defines as purpose."

And Prof. Tolman also recognizes that these purposive activities are initiated, guided, and terminated by cognitions, by appreciation of the nature of the goal-object, of the route to be followed for its attainment, and of the new situation which constitutes attainment. In what then does his behaviorism consist? Merely in this—that when we use such terms as purpose, goal-seeking, cognition, knowing, appreciation of, imputing, intents, noetic aspects of behavior, knowledge, desire and purpose, (all of which terms are freely used by Tolman), we must (in order to be scientific and to avoid the dreaded spectre of anthropomorphism) carefully explain that all these words are used in a purely objective sense, that they imply, on the part of the creature whose behavior is described, no experience, no awareness of the goal-object or of the intervening obstacles, no felt impulse or desire for it, no satisfaction on attaining it or coming nearer to it, no dissatisfaction, distress, or urge, on continued failure to attain it.

Now these prohibitions of the behaviorist are intended to apply, not only to descriptions and interpretations of the behavior of animals, but also to all descriptions and interpretations of human behavior. Suppose you see a boy trying to reach an apple on the end of a branch. He reaches up, stands on tiptoe, jumps at it again and again. Then he takes a stick and with it shakes the bough or strikes at the apple; or he runs away, and returns presently with a box or ladder by the aid of which he reaches the apple. Tolman will allow you to say that the boy seeks the apple, that the apple is the goal of his seeking, that the use of the stick or box is a cognitive hunch on the boy's part, that he imputes to the stick the property of extending his reach to the apple, and so on. But if you wish to be scientific, you may not say or imagine that the boy sees the apple and consciously desires to reach and to eat it; still less may you say that he foresees that, by using the stick, he may cause the apple to fall, or that by climbing on the box he may be able to reach it. Nor may you use such language, even if the boy tells you with all the honest naïvety of boy-hood that all these suppositions of yours are true.   To use such language, to allow yourself to suppose that the boy sees and desires and foresees, would be grossly anthropomorphic. The apple stimulates the boy to put out his hand towards it; and when he runs to fetch a stick or a ladder, he is making random movements, or he formerly made such random move-ments and these have become associated, as a conditioned re-flex, with the act of stretching out the arm without subsequent contact with the apple.   And the ray from the apple then in-duces another conditioned reflex, the striking with the stick or the climbing of the ladder.

That or something like it must be the interpretation of the S. B. Prof. Tolman is more lenient. He will allow us to say that it was the purpose of the boy to obtain the apple and that he had a cognitive hunch that the ladder would facilitate his goal seeking; provided that we repudiate all such implica-tion as that the boy sees the apple and foresees its fall.   Even if he gets another boy to shake the branch, and himself stands holding his hands beneath the apple ready to catch it, you still may not say that he foresees its fall.   And Tolman seems in-clined to attach much importance to the fact that by using the words of common speech (such words as *desire, purpose, striving, cognition, perception* and *memory* and *anti-cipation*) you can describe the event and yet can avoid what he calls the 'mentalist' implications, if you carefully explain that you don't mean to use the words in the ordinary sense, but merely as words which are convenient for the description of the objective event you observe.   He assigns to Prof. Perry the credit for pointing out that you can thus describe purposive actions while repudiating one-half of the common meaning of the terms.

If now we turn to Prof. Perry's discussion of behavior, we find that, like Tolman, he freely admits that human and ani-mal action is commonly purposive or goal-seeking and cannot be effectively described in words which do not imply this fun-damental character.   But he would have us interpret these terms as implying, not any foresight of the goal, but only some hypothetical neural arrangement which he calls a "determin-ing tendency."   Perry's behaviorism then is like Tolman's a purposive behaviorism; consisting in so defining the common terms as to repudiate their mentalist implications.

What inducements, then, do Tolman and Perry hold out to us in order to persuade us to use words in this peculiarly mutilated fashion? What advantages do they claim will result from such usage? I must confess that I do not know. So far as I can discover, they do not tell us at all clearly. Perry seems to suggest that the profit or advantage will be the avoidance of all language that implies some difference between mental events and physical events, as all our ordinary speech does. For he is an exponent of a peculiar metaphysic, known as New Realism, which seeks to abolish that distinction. But this is an inducement only for those select few who have accepted that very peculiar philosophy of New Realism. To the majority of us, who regard that philosophy as quite untenable, he offers no inducement. Tolman, so far as I can see, offers us no inducement of any kind. He merely seems to feel that the feat of describing behavior in purely objective terms, terms rendered objective by carefully stripping away their common subjective meaning, is so great an achievement that it is worth doing merely as a display of verbal skill.

Tolman does, however, give one slight cue to his very peculiar attitude in this matter. He remarks: "Although we agree with Professor McDougall in finding his first five marks of behavior characteristic of purpose, we disagree with him in supposing such 'purpose' to be something added on to the mere objective description of the behavior itself." I gather that Tolman means to say that I suppose a purpose to be a peculiar something added to the bodily process.[1] And here, as it seems to me he reveals a difficulty over which many are inclined to boggle, though it arises purely from an unfortunate usage of words; namely, we speak of a purpose as though it were a thing, and then, when we ask what sort of a thing it can be, we can find no intelligible answer.

If, instead of speaking of a purpose, we confine ourselves to the adjective *purposive* and speak merely of purposive action or activity, we avoid this difficulty. *Purposive* is then the adjective which we may use if we wish to describe purely objectively processes of a special kind, namely, the peculiar forms of bodily action we observe in men and animals, the goal-seeking actions. But we may use it, as we do in common speech, to imply also that such actions are accompanied by some fore-

---

[1] Added, not (as Tolman says) to the description, but to the process described.

sight of the goal and some desire to attain it. And the justification for so doing is (1) that, when I myself so act, I know,
if I stop to reflect, that I foresee the goal and desire it; and
(2) that, if I question other intelligent persons, they tell me
that, when they act in this objectively purposive fashion, they
also foresee the goal and desire it. This subjective accompani-
ment of purposive action is so constantly reported that we are
justified in supposing it to be the rule; we can assume it with
a high degree of probability. The question, then, is—Can
we with advantage put aside this knowledge of the subjective aspect of purposive action: can we better understand and control behavior without the aid of this knowledge? I confidently suggest that we cannot; that it is advan-
tageous to use such knowledge, and for the following reasons:

(1) It is surely hazardous and against all scientific principles to put aside any knowledge of an obscure event when we
seek to understand and control it.

(2) When we use this knowledge, we do understand the
event better, we are in a better position to influence or control
it, than if we put it aside. This is true of both human and
animal behavior. We are more familiar with, have much better acquaintance with, foreseeing and desiring, than we have
with hypothetical structures in the nervous system called "determining tendencies" or "motor sets" or what not. And this,
the practical or pragmatic test, is the supreme test of the value
of any assumption. Now I take it, that, in relation to human
behavior, the superior convenience and effectiveness of the
mentalist description and interpretation is beyond dispute.
When the boy fetches a stick and with it knocks down the
apple, we all unhesitatingly interpret his conduct by assuming
that he sees the apple, desires to obtain it, foresees its fall, and
fetches and uses the stick *in order* to obtain it. And, when
the chimpanzee behaves in a very similar manner, fetching and
using a stick to knock down a banana hung above his reach
(Köhler, *op. cit.* p. 146), we all interpret and understand
his behavior in similar mentalist terms. Such interpretation is
not only natural, but it is also profitable; it is far more effective as a guide to our action than any forced unnatural interpretation achieved by disciplining ourselves to repudiate the
mentalist implications of the words we inevitably use. The
man who sympathetically understands animals will manage
them far more effectively than he who interprets their actions

mechanically, even when it is a question of planning and conducting experiments with them.

And this is true not only when we study men and animals under experimental conditions in the laboratory; it is also true and vastly important in the immense experiment which modern industry is making and on the success of which the prosperous development of our civilization depends, namely the experiment of keeping vast numbers of men working at tasks and under conditions that are very unnatural, very different from those to which human nature has become adapted by long ages of development under natural conditions, the conditions of life of the hunter, the warrior and the farmer.

It is just because modern industry has treated the workers as Robots rather than as men that the modern world is so full of strife and unrest, of strikes and lock-outs, and bitter conflicts of all kinds. All these disharmonies and inefficiencies of the industrial world can only be overcome by recognizing far more clearly than has yet been done the complexity of the motives, the desires and the purposes of the workmen, and by delicately adjusting incentives and satisfactions in accordance with these complex desires of every human heart. The theory and practise of modern industry have been vitiated by the tendency to treat men as though the stimulus-response formula of the behaviorist were true. The mechanical arts of industrial production have been developed with astonishing speed and success, by the aid of the magnificent discoveries of the physical sciences; while the art of managing men has remained undeveloped, largely because psychological science, the science of human nature, has remained undeveloped, especially that most important part of it which is concerned, or should be concerned, with human motives and purposes.

Fortunately, many leaders of the industrial world and many students of its problems are now beginning to recognize this truth and are taking thought how to remedy these defects. But they can find no help in any psychology that is not thoroughly and frankly of the purposive type.[1]

---

[1] A most interesting book published only last month (*Mainsprings of Men*, by Whiting Williams) illustrates my point vividly. Mr. Williams, from a rich store of intimate contact with working men, shows the complexity and astonishing power of motives commonly ignored by economists.

I cite a few passages. "No one," he writes, "can expect to secure or maintain his leadership except as he promises fulfillment for the wishes, yearnings, hopings of his workers whose delight is that we

To all this reasoning the mechanist will reply that primitive men interpret inorganic events in the teleological way; that the savage regards the flow of the river, volcanic eruptions and, still more, the working of mechanical contrivances, as purposive activities, and that the advance of science has consisted in progressively getting rid of all such mentalist implications in our dealings with natural processes. And he maintains that, though in dealing with animal and human behavior such extrusion of mentalist implications may be at present difficult and even practically unprofitable, yet we must attempt the task, if we are ever to understand the causation of human and animal actions.

This brings us right up against the fundamental question at issue. The true ground of the behaviorist effort is the belief that animal and human behavior are truly and wholly mechanical, that they are of the same nature as all other processes in nature and that, therefore, the truest, the only true, interpretation of it must be in the terms we use in the inorganic sciences; that, though such interpretation may be difficult and even relatively unprofitable at the present time, yet we must persist in this effort with faith that ultimately it will prove profitable in the long run.

---

are not only workers, but also fathers, worshippers, voters, lovers, —whole men. Even in the factory the hopeful contestant will, accordingly, do well to examine some of those satisfactions which we long for, not because we are workmen, but because we are human beings and persons . . . . let us take a moment's look at the hankerings which appear to bother all of us in the midst of our daily job of just being human."

He finds that "the wish for worth," the desire to be able to feel oneself of real use in the world, is one of the great forces that must be taken account of in any adjustment of the conditions of work that is to secure harmony and efficiency. "The prime influence in all of us today is our wish to enjoy the feeling of our worth as persons among other persons. This feeling can hardly exist without a corresponding recognition, respect on the part of others . . . The connection between this desire and most of the instincts can easily be seen . . . This desire does not require the sense of domination or superiority over others except as such a feeling in certain fields offsets a feeling of inferiority in others.

"First, then, the initial demand within us to be 'worthwhile' and second, the encouraging approval and the opposing disapprovals of others to whom we give attention—these two forces and the constant interplay between them we must understand if we are to know the mainspring of our neighbors and ourselves."

To this the mentalist reply is threefold. First, even if the faith of the mechanist were well grounded and justified, even if we had some impossible, some supernatural, assurance of this, it would still be more profitable now and for a long time to come to make use of the mentalist, the truly purposive, interpretations of behavior; for we are very very far from any adequate mechanical interpretations; and we may hope to arrive at them most rapidly by continuing to use and to improve our mentalist interpretations, to formulate laws of behavior in mentalist terms, postponing the translation of them into terms of mechanism until such time as such interpretation may be a possibility and not merely a misleading pretense, as at present it is.

Secondly, it may be that the faith of the mechanist is altogether ill-based and illusory. To all appearance the life-processes of living things are fundamentally different from inorganic processes; and we have no guarantee, no adequate ground for believing, that this appearance is illusory. And, if we uncritically adopt this mechanistic faith, and under its influence elaborate a picture of the world in mechanistic terms, we inevitably arrive at an absurd position, as the history of thought abundantly shows; we find we have created a picture of the world which leaves out of the picture entirely that mental process, that purposive striving, that creative activity, which has produced the picture; our conscious striving to construct the picture, our conscious appreciation and understanding of it when constructed, remain outside it as something whose reation to the picture is entirely unintelligible. And so we have to start all over again, and strive to "remould it nearer to the heart's desire," the desire to understand man's place in the universe.

Thirdly, the faith of the mechanist implies two assumptions which we must carefully distinguish; for one of them may be false, though the other be true. These two assumptions are (1) that all processes in the world are fundamentally of one kind only (2) that all these processes are of the kind commonly assumed by the physical sciences in their interpretations of inorganic nature; namely mechanistic, or strictly determined and therefore strictly predictable, events.

It may well be, I say, that the former assumption is true, but that the latter is false. And, if we accept the former assumption as a working hypothesis and reject the second, we can hope to avoid the absurdity which, as we have just now seen, inevitably results from accepting both assumptions. At the present time there are indications in various fields of science of a tendency in accordance with this very permissible selection of our fundamental working hypothesis; namely, a tendency to bridge the gap between the organic and the inorganic, not by forcing the organic under the type of strictly mechanistic interpretation that has long been very generally accepted in the physical sciences, but by revising that interpretation in such a way as to render it less rigidly exclusive of and opposed to the purposive interpretation. Physicists are making their assumptions less rigidly deterministic; philosophers and biologists are speculating along these lines. Even Prof. Tolman shows himself hospitable to this possibility. And, when we reflect upon such physical facts as gravitation, chemical affinities, electrical attraction and repulsion, and when we find how varied and how lacking in precision and finality are the physicists interpretations of such phenomena, we cannot refuse to admit that here is an interesting possible line of scientific development.[1]

The most interesting and promising of such efforts is, I venture to think, that of Prof. Köhler, now of this university. With some hesitation and subject to correction, I submit that the essence of his endeavor is to show that some physical phenomena express true tendencies, that they tend towards certain ends. The physical configuration *(or Gestalt)* on which he so strongly insists is something that cannot be adequately described in terms of a spatial collocation: it is something that can only be described in terms of a tendency towards an end or, as he prefers to say, a closure. Thus a soap-bubble has a tendency to assume the spherical form; and that tendency cannot be described or interpreted in terms of its mechanical structure, the spatial arrangement and motions of its parts; the tendency is a dynamic fact which can only be described and interpreted in dynamic terms, in terms of forces; and if you seek to analyze the phenomenon, to reduce it to constituent processes, these again can only be conceived in terms of tendencies.

The mechanist in psychology lightly postulates tendencies, determining tendencies, and implies that in so doing he is providing a mechanical substitute for purposive tendencies and

---

[1] In this connection I refer the reader to Prof. A. W. Whitehead's newly published volume of Lowell Lectures, "Science and The Modern World."

strivings. But, in so doing, he begs the whole question in dispute. He concedes the essence of the purposive psychologists, contention, the contention that human and animal behavior can be understood only in terms of tendencies towards ends of goals; and then he disguises the fact from himself by a mere change of names.

Whether the present highly interesting and promising tendency in science to bridge the gap between the organic and the inorganic, between life and mechanism, by recognizing in the inorganic realms real tendencies, whether this tendency is destined to be successful we cannot yet say. But we can say, I think, that if it should prove successful, it will be by assimilating the inorganic to the organic and by recognizing the source of our understanding of processes and tendencies of all kinds in our own experiences of purposive striving, the most developed and intelligible form of that which we see more obscurely expressed in animal behavior and in the processes of the inorganic realm.

We say, then, to our behaviorist friends—Put aside your ill-founded fear of anthropomorphism. That fear is at the best, premature; and, at the worst, it may drive you far astray, seeking as your goal a mere will-o'-the-wisp. Do not continue to deny yourselves the great advantages of using the mentalist and purposive ways of thinking in your dealings with human and animal behavior. The anthropomorphic way of thinking is highly profitable at present in our sphere; and it may well be that it will prove to be the ultimately profitable way for all science, the only way that leads to a deeper understanding of Nature.

I conclude, then, that at present we stand to gain no advantage by assuming that men are Robots, mere pieces of machinery. Without presuming to assert that men are, or are not, Robots, let us continue to use the working hypothesis that they are not; let us cheerfully go on assuming that men are what they seem to be, namely purposive intelligent agents, striving with some success to improve themselves and the conditions of their life in this strange world. And let us continue to assume that children and animals exhibit in their lower degrees the same principles of action. For that is the profitable way, the way of progress in psychology.

PART V

Reaction Psychology

Knight Dunlap

CHAPTER XIV

THE THEORETICAL ASPECT OF PSYCHOLOGY*

By Knight Dunlap

A discussion of "psychology" at the present time must, of necessity, be prefaced by a careful explanation of the signification in which the term is used; for this is an era of "psychologies," that is, of systems of philosophy, systems of medicine, systems of delusion and systems of graft, each of which assumes the title of "psychology" or of "the new Psychology." The announcement of a new book on *The new psychology and the preacher* might, so far as anyone could predict in advance, be a treatise based on the Freudian or some other psychoanalytic system; it might be an exposition of "new thought" or some other vagary of the Quimby brood; it might be an application of the theories and methods of "intelligence testing"; it might be propaganda for the doctrines and practices of M. Coué; it might be one of the numerous embodiments of phrenology under its more recent name of "character analysis"; it might be a book on psychic research concerning spooks and other magical notions; or it might be one of the less easily nameable nostrums which strut before the public in borrowed plumage, calling themselves "the new psychology."

In spite of all these phantasies, there is a serious and legitimate psychology, which has had a steady growth and development, and which endures and bears fruit in spite of the vicissitudes to which it is subjected by all these pseudo-psychologies, which do, in fact, injure it and retard it, but which are not able to destroy it nor to prevent its growth. And it is this legitimate psychology, which, in its present day developments, well merits the name of *scientific psychology,* that I am about to discuss.

Psychology began in Hellenic days as a study of the conscious processes of the organism, and it is today more adequately described in those terms than in any other way. It belongs, in other words, with the biological sciences, to two of which it is closely related, namely, to biology and anthropology. Biology deals with the fundamental features of the life processes as they appear in animals and plants; anthropology with the concrete results of the life processes in the human being; and psychology with those important manifestations of life in which consciousness appears. No one of these

---

*Powell Lecture in Psychological Theory at Clark University, April 20, 1925.

three sciences includes the others; but each of them necessarily overlaps and combines with the others.

Each of these sciences deals with life from two aspects; those of growth and behavior. The particular aspects of animal growth and behavior with which psychology is concerned are conscious behavior, and the growth or development of the systems of conscious reaction which constitute this conscious behavior. Psychology, like anthropology and biology, has therefore a threefold aspect: general, individual, and genetic; and it has another aspect which perhaps these others also possess, namely: a social aspect. In biology great progress has been made in the study of development. In psychology, however, little progress has been made along the genetic line, and it is chiefly of general psychology that I shall speak today, not excluding references to progress in individual and social psychology.

Whatever may have been the metaphysics of Aristotle on other points, in psychology his position is clear. He was to all intents and purposes a "common sense realist," who assumed as one of the conditions of science, that there is a world of real objects and that we may be really conscious of them. On this basis, it was possible to ask the question: How does the process of perception come about? And the other question: How does that other conscious process, the process of thinking about things, come about? And, Aristotle proceeded to discuss these questions in the light of such information as was then at hand. His discussions, furthermore, assumed these processes to be processes of the organism; and if he dragged in the theory of a psyche, that psyche was no mystical principle, but an energy supposed to reside in the organism; an energy as "physical" as the heat, light and electricity of modern physics. It is true, Aristotle went beyond these practical assumptions, and contrived a theory of the relation of "matter" and "energy" which was mathematical rather than empirical. But in that respect, his method was not far removed from those of modern mathematical physicists, however much he may have erred in his detailed hypotheses. In short: Aristotle, in his psychology, was working along the lines of modern scientific psychology, and this modern science may well be called a return to Aristotle, in spirit if not in detail.

It is doubtful whether, aside from the invention of the name "psychology," any useful contributions were made to psychology during the first 1500 years of the Christian era. I say it is doubtful, because we have no clear knowledge of any such contributions. But the thought of the schoolmen is to-day pretty much a closed book to modern readers and will remain closed until a lot of very bad Latin shall have been translated. Contributions, not evident to us, may have been made through Descartes and others who were instructed in the lore of the philosophers, and who read with ease the bad Latin to which I have referred.

Descartes, who is rated as the first of the modern doctors of psychological theory, built up the subject with his right hand, while with his left hand, perhaps unintentionally, he pulled out the foundations, and gave the structure a decided list to the starboard, which it retained for a long period of further growth. In his *Treatise on the passions of the soul* he laid the cornerstone of physiological psychology, and for the modern reaction theory; although his particular reaction theory has been discarded. In his *Discourse on Method,* however, and in his *Principles,* he weakened the common sense foundation of the subject and prepared the way for the pernicious doctrines of psychophysical parallelism and epistemological dualism which were immediately elaborated by Malebranche, from whom they were taken over by Locke, and which were the architectural plans for the development of psychology for the next three hundred years. These doctrines, in fact, in spite of Huxley and a number of other critics, became gradually adopted by the unscientific world as "common sense," and have been accepted by the world of physical science as good psychology. At the present time, there is an enormous amount of routine teaching—and perfectly futile teaching—of this time-worn philosophy under the guise of psychology; and the most difficult part of the teacher of scientific psychology is to disabuse the student of these notions, and to get him to look at the problems of psychology as they really are. We may put the simple facts of the mental life in scientific (that is, in common sense), form; but the student, trained in this now popular philosophy of Malebranche, misunderstands them in his old familiar terms, and hence fails to grasp the facts at all. More striking direct results of this Malebranchian miasma are the popularly attractive Freudian and other theories of the "unconscious mind," and doctrines of certain schools of less popular psychology which fit in with the popular notion of the mind.

The influence of Locke and his English successors was profoundly felt in Germany; and although the psychology of Herbart and Wundt was presumably founded in the philosophy of Leibnitz, derived from that of Descartes, the Malebranchian influence was really the strongest in the constructions of these and other German psychologists. The German psychology, again, influenced English psychology through Ward and Stout, uniting its influence with that transmitted from Locke through the Scottish school and was passed on to the United States through a number of psychologists of German training. I am justified, therefore, in calling this general current the "Anglo-German Psychology," a name which is sufficiently distinctive, and sufficiently representative of the real history of the current. But, lest my terms should seem to have an ethnological rather than the merely historical reference intended, I shall refer hereafter to this general school of psychological theory as *Malebranchian,* or *introspectional.*

The Malebranchian psychology is characterized by, and limited by, a certain striking conception: the conception of the "mind" as something distinct from, but miraculously related to the body, and as made up out of certain objective elements, which, although in constant flux, are definitely observable. The mind, that is to say, is conceived as made up of *psychic objects,* and the physical world of *physical objects,* made of a different stuff or sort of material from the psychic object.

The relation between the two worlds so conceived has been in the past assumed to be that of "parallelism," illustrated by the likeness to two clocks which keep time together, so that they correspond exactly, but with no influence of one on the other. The further question as to how the two clocks get that way, has either been answered by assuming a divine clockmaker; or else the question has been simply ignored. There has been always, however, a minority group of psychologists who have held the theory of interaction (which was Descartes' real theory), namely: that the two worlds do influence one another, and that the correspondences may therefore be explained causally.

The discussion between the parallelists and the interactionists is now merely of historical interest, and a contribution on the subject would probably be rejected by any of the psychological journals. I think we may safely say that the remaining psychologists of the introspectional school are theoretically parallelists, but practically interactionists; and harmonize their theoretical and practical interests by avoiding the mention of the point at issue. The issue vanishes when the modern viewpoint is adopted.

The general conception or presupposition of the Malebranchian psychology involves several specific minor conceptions, namely: the non-observability of relations; the conception of ideas, sensations and images; and a characteristic conception of introspection. Since the issue between this older psychology and the later scientific psychology has turned on these specific conceptions, I shall briefly outline them.

It may seem strange to say that relations are not observable, since the noting of relations is the most important detail in practical life. But we are forced to the conclusion that the older psychology considered them *psychologically* non-observable, at least, for the orthodox introspectional analysis of the "mind" gave only sensations, images, and feelings. Hence, while the sensational facts of the world were given abundant treatment in the psychological texts, no space was given to relations. If relations were considered, it was merely for the purpose of showing that they turned out to be, on examination, merely sensations; and not even sensations of a distinctive kind. On the other hand, since psychologists were compelled to talk somewhat rationally at times, the perceptibility of relations was implied in the discussion of Weber's law, and in the comparison of pitches, colors and other sense-data. Perhaps the intention was to class relations with physical stimuli, which, although entirely different from sensations, were in a way implied as perceptible. This logical inconsistency, which was never straightened out, was based on an oversight of Malebranche's. Malebranche postulated a mental object for each physical object, but failed to provide a mental relation to correspond to a physical relation. And Malebranche's system was never remodeled.

Malebranche, and Locke after him, assumed that man can never perceive anything except his own mind. Effectively, man was supposed to move in a little world of his own, forever out of perceptual contact, not only with his fellows, but with the physical world. What does he see? Nothing but his own color sensations. What does he hear? Nothing but his own sound sensations. Color, tone, and all the other sensuous qualities, are no features of the real world about us. They are merely parts of our own minds. Physical stimulations falling upon a physical nervous system have no mental nature at all, but, in some mysterious way, sensations in the mind are aroused, and then we can observe those sensations. Leibnitz, in his doctrine of monads, made this doctrine pictorially clear. To many physicists today, this metaphysical theory of four hundred years ago seems perfectly sound.

The philosophers who constructed this remarkable theory saw its obvious difficulty and went further. Man is forever shut off from the physical world, so far as knowledge is concerned: How, then, can we talk seriously about it? How can we talk about other persons? And they found the answer in faith in God. God must have made a "real" world, since we have our little worlds. Therefore, he must have made a real world to agree with our little one, or else he is a deceiver. But the later psychologists have dispensed with God, and kept the faith: a faith, therefore, in nothing whatever!

On this Malebranchian assumption we have a field for psychological study. Physics deals with the big, real world (how, has not been explained, since the physicist can no more perceive the physical world than can the psychologist), and the psychologist should busy himself about his little world, and try to analyse the objects therein. And in this psychic world, the introspectional psychologist found nothing but "sensations," "images," "feelings," and various compounds of these. The study of perception, therefore, turned out to be a study of "sensations"; the study of thought and memory, a study of "images."

We can manage with the concept of "sensations" very well, since we can apply that name to the colors, sounds, tastes, and other sense data which we observe in the world, and can forget the philosophical speculations on which the name is based. By the use of this concept, however, a serious cause of confusion was introduced, since the term "sensation" became slippery, meaning now the sense datum itself, now the process of observing the sense datum. But even that confusion might have been avoided.

"Images" offer a serious difficulty. For the fact has been evident since the time of Aristotle that in thinking of something, we are usually, (and perhaps always), being conscious of something which we perceived at some earlier time. But, according to Malebranche, we never perceive the thing: we observe only our "sensations" in the one case and our "images" in the other. In what sense, therefore, can we say we are thinking of that which we perceived? Where is the identity of the thing perceived and the thing thought of?

The answer is: the "image" must be the "sensation," in another form: changed somewhat, but essentially the same. The nature of the changes the "sensation" underwent in becoming an "image" was a point on which various conflicting views were held; but the fundamental statement was the same on all these theories: the "image" is a *reproduced* "sensation." And the "idea," which is a complex of "images," is, of course, a reproduced percept—the percept being the complex of "sensations" which the human observer foolishly assumes to be an object outside him.

On this basis, the study of images and imagery occupied a considerable part of the older psychological work and their discussion occupied a considerable part of the psychological texts. It was even believed that the determination of imagery-types might be an important matter for pedagogy. But sceptics, (of whom I happened to be one of the worst), appeared, and expressed doubts whether the "image" were anything but a confusion of terms. We recognize quite readily the facts called "sensations" when bits of colored papers are displayed, or a violin is bowed: and we recognize certain facts that might be called either "images" or "sensations" when the eyeball is pressed with the thumb, or an electric current passed through the region of the ear: but the *reproduced* "sensation" is another matter. Can such phenomena really be demonstrated? I came to the conclusion that they could not be. Others have come to the same conclusion.

Now, it must be pointed out, that these sceptical persons, or many of them at least, before they considered the matter carefully, apparently had as vivid "images" as any of those who still held to the image-doctrine; and, by the usual criteria, their imagery could be classified in the usual modal categories. I myself, under the sway of the doctrine originally taught me, had vivid and distinct visual and auditory "images," and "images" of other modes also. It is not probable that my mere change of belief destroyed my "images." The change that occurred was in the critical analysis I made. What I find is, that in "having" a visual "image," I am distinctly thinking of a visual object: that is, an object which, when I perceived it, had light and color. Hence, uncritically, I may still describe my experience as "having a visual image." This is a convenient figure of speech, quite analogous to the speaking of "sunrise," which does not commit me to any theory as to the ultimate nature of the phenomenon. But there is in no sense

"present" anything that could be considered a copy or reproduction of the original object, whether I consider calling that
object a "sensation" or a sense datum. I find also, (and many
others have found the same), that when I am thinking of an
object, such as an automobile, which has both visual and auditory aspects, it is sometimes impossible to decide, on the old
basis, whether the imagery is visual or auditory. This is a
striking fact, since it is not, in general, difficult to discriminate
visual "sensations" from auditory "sensations." Moreover, I
find that in such cases, modal characterization may be effected
by actual muscular activities while thinking: that movements
of the eyes may conduct to the characterization of the thinking as "visual," while certain movements of the head, and contractions of the internal muscles of the ear, conduce to the
characterization as "auditory," although the thinking is not
essentially changed otherwise. From these and other considerations, the conclusion is not far that the "image," as described by the older psychology, is a myth; that is, a name applied to the fact that I think of objects of different modalities,
just as the name "Zeus" or "Thor" applied to the fact that
thunder and lightning occur.

The discarding of the introspectional doctrine of "images"
means the abandoning of the fundamental conception of the
Malebranchian psychology; since without an "image" as an
object of thought-consciousness, the whole mental world,
which is supposed to represent or parallel the real world, goes
to pieces. That the image has been discarded effectively in
American psychology is no secret. The publication of research on imagery has sunk to a negligible stage, and although
certain psychologists still talk in terms of "images," such discussion is largely figurative. A clear indication of the situation is given by the small space given to the discussion of
"images" in even those recent texts which officially follow the
old doctrine. In fact, my own text gives more emphasis to
"images" than do certain of those texts: a matter which has
been extremely puzzling to the introspectionalists. But the
most important indication of a change of viewpoint is the
rapid development of the type of psychology which proceeds
without reference to the philosophy on which the image-doctrine was based.

"Introspection." in the older psychology, meant the observation of "consciousness." But since "consciousness" has been
very generally used in a double sense, this statement needs

supplementation. "Consciousness" means, in popular parlance and in scientific usage also, the *observing* of something. In the Malebranchian psychology, it means the *thing observed*, which, in that psychology, could only be a "sensation," an "image," a "feeling," or a complex of these. It is true that all the older psychologists, and many today, use the term "consciousness" in both ways, and hence commit many logical fallacies, as well as heap up confusions; but when technically exact, the introspectional psychology has meant by "consciousness," the "sensations," "images" and "feelings" as they were defined, namely: as mental objects, to be observed (that is, "sentienda"). But, of course, these mental psychic objects were supposed to be observed; and that observation was called *introspection*.

Now, it might be supposed, on the basis of the principles laid down, that introspection is the only sort of observation possible, since the only thing which can really be observed is "consciousness," that is, the complex of "sensations," "images" and "ideas." Hence, the physicist would use introspection in his work just as much as the psychologist does in his. At this point the Malebranchian psychology undeniably had difficulty, and became correspondingly vague. An early tendency was to admit external observation, as well as internal observation or introspection. Observing the physical world is *external observation;* observing "consciousness" is *introspection.* This admission was fatal, for if the direct observation of the physical world were possible without the intervention of psychical objects, then the whole construction of the world of "images" and "sensations" and "feelings" would be superfluous, and the Malebranchian psychology would commit suicide. Those later psychologists of this school who were troubled by logical scruples, therefore defined "introspection" in another way. It is true, they said, that the physicist, just as much as the psychologist, observes "sensations." (We may omit consideration of "images" and "feelings" since they are not supposed to trouble the physicist.) But he observes them for a different purpose, namely, the purpose of constructing, or at least of referring to, the real (and by hypothesis imperceptible) external world. "Introspection," then, at least so far as it concerns "sensations," was assumed to differ from "external observation" in purpose only: not in the nature of the objects observed, nor in the nature of the observation itself.

There have been, however, other views on the matter of introspection, aside from these orthodox ones I have described. Stout, for example, and a considerable following of his, have meant by "introspection" the direct observing of observing. Assuming, with the rest of the older school, that the things observed in ordinary observation are "sensations," "feelings," and "images," they claimed that by a trick of the mind, the observing itself could be observed. For example: after having observed a "sensation of red," one could observe the preceding observation: this statement not meaning that one could observe the red again, but meaning that one could observe that which was not, at the previous moment, an object, but was the *observing* of an object. The American School of introspectionists, however, have generally repudiated Stout's position, and have never insisted that observing could be observed. In fact, some of them have directly denied that possibility.

The position of Stout and his followers is an important one, and it was against that position that I directed an early paper of mine.[1] Stout's position is not dependent on the Malebranchian assumptions, and is upheld by certain present day philosophers who reject Malebranchism and all its work. Hence, this position is the really critical one, and the attack and defense can by no means be considered ended.

While my own conclusion still is that consciousness, (by which I mean the fact or act of observing), cannot itself be observed, proof to the contrary would not in any wise upset any other conclusion of mine, nor change in any essential way the postulates of scientific psychology.

"Introspection" as the observation of psychic objects: of "sensations," "images," and "feelings"; does not offer much interest in the way of discussion. It is a simple terminological corollary from the general Malebranchian theory, and aside from that theory, merely means that when the psychologist makes an observation, it is to be called "introspection"; and when the physicist makes an observation—perhaps an observation of the same facts the psychologist has observed, it is to be called something else, such as "external observation." The only criticism I should make of this is that it involves the

---

[1]The case against introspection, 1912, *Psychol. Rev.*, XIX, 404-413. This was merely an introduction to another paper, The nature of perceived relations, 1912, *Psychol. Rev.*, XIX, 415-446; which was a thorough discussion of the fundamental points at issue.

waste of a perfectly good term,[2] which ought to be retained for another signification, in which, in our common language, we do use it.

Introspection, as used in every-day language, means literally an inward vision: a paying attention to, or observing of the processes of the organism itself: the feelings, emotions, and organic processes of other kinds—organic sensations, if you want to cling to that term; and in scientific psychology we can most usefully employ the term in practically the same way; to signify the awareness of things inside the body; of feelings, emotions, organic changes, and muscular activities.

I have so far emphasized the inadequacies of the Malbranchian viewpoint in psychology in order to bring out, by contrast, the characteristics of the modern science. On the other hand, it is necessary to point out the continuity of the modern developments with past progress. For it would be a mistake to assume that the scientific psychology of today is a new psychology. Along with the declining influence of the postulates of the Malebranchian metaphysics, there had been, for half a century, a steadily growing experimental psychology whose problems have been less and less formulated in relation to the old viewpoint, and whose interests have gradually been broadening. Many of the results of the early experimental work are invalidated by the postulates which are included in the data from which they were drawn, and many of the data are inadequate because of the bad planning of the work due to the philosophical postulates; but in both Germany and America these conditions steadily improved, and a psychology developed which was independent of the old philosophical bonds, while not formally disowning them. By 1900 an iconoclastic spirit was abroad; an impatience with the restriction of investigation and interests to the examination of an artificial "mind" whose living prototype could not be found. The introduction of experimental methods into the study of animal behavior; the placing of the study of children on the basis of conscious behavior by Binet and Ebbinghaus; and the rise of interest in social psychology; all contributed to the growing tendency of psychology to return to Aristotle and face its problem clearly as the problem *how* we perceive, *how* we think, *how* we act,

---

[2]In another form of this criticism, I would point out that, the assigning of "introspection" as the distinctive method of the psychologist is a needless circle of terms, if "introspection" is defined as merely the method the psychologist uses.

how we feel; instead of the old substitute problem of *what* we perceive, *what* we think of, and *what* we feel; that is, the old analysis of a world of "mental objects." Into this growing movement the notion of mental activity as dependent on, or a part of, not mere action of brain cells, but on reaction, or complete sensori-motor response; a notion whose origins and mode of percolation into psychological thought are still obscure; entered as the great synthetizing factor, and the beginnings of scientific psychology were in existence. This synthesis was made possible by the new conception of the thinking process, first suggested by Max Müller, as dependent on motor activities; a conception which has now become fundamental in scientific psychology.[3]

The result of these changes was apparently a lessening of the emphasis on consciousness; but it was also an increase in the emphasis on consciousness. Consciousness in the Malebranchian sense, (mental objects or mental data or mental stuff) ceased to interest psychologists; and consciousness as the process of observing anything whatever; that awareness which the older psychologists, even James, had refused to admit to psychology, came to its own. It is true, the psychoanalysts have temporarily salvaged the Malebranchian consciousness from the junk heap, and by a continuation of the confusion of the two meanings of the word, have continued Janet's repudiated invention of "unconscious consciousness." But even this revamped form of the old and rusty materials

---

[3] My own pioneering work in the introduction of this conception into the fundamentals of psychology may be traced in *Images and Ideas, Johns Hopkins Circular*, 1914, no. 3, pp. 25-41 (reprinted in part in the Biological Basis of the Association of Ideas, *Psychobiology*, 1920, vol. ii, pp. 29-53); *An Outline of Psychobiology*, 1st edition, 1914, The Johns Hopkins Press, chapter IX, p. 111; Thought Content and Feeling, *Psychological Review*, 1916, vol. xxiii, pp. 49-70; and *Elements of Scientific Psychology*, 1922, the C. V. Mosby Co., chaps. x and xiv. While I had really committed myself to the general position in my *System of Psychology*, 1912, Charles Scribner's Sons, by my treatment of ideas and images, I had not then broken away from the concept of "brain states" as the basis of consciousness, nor from the old doctrine of perception as involving imagination, (which is not the same as *images*).

The conception was of necessity adopted by the behaviorists, and has been of late unduly exaggerated by practically limiting the thought-reaction to the language-reaction, and by assuming that complete reaction is in all cases necessary for thought: neither of these assumptions is as yet justified.

is breaking down, and the spread of the more scientific doctrine is rapidly progressing.

It was not to be expected that this transformation, rapid as it has been, should have been consummated without some off-shoots of a radical sort. The re-emphasis on the study of behavior as the fundamental method of psychology, together with the ejection of consciousness in its Malebranchian meaning, furnished a starting point for behaviorism, which proposed to reduce psychology to mere physical anthropology. But the study of behavior is as old as Aristotle, and the only novelty in behaviorism was what it omitted in its experimental methods; not what it retained. By successive steps to which it has been forced, behaviorism has returned from its meteoric flight, and now differs only verbally from the more conservative schools of psychology, and in the difficulties its verbal inhibitions inflict upon it. In fact, only the acute psychologist can distinguish the behaviorist from the non-behaviorist in these days, except by the labels affixed; and the truth is that some who have labeled themselves have mistaken their own labels. Behaviorism was, a few years ago, a distinctive movement, with unique theories and methods. But it has found itself constrained to abandon its distinctive methods, and its theories, in so far as these are distinctive, are distinctive in terminology only.

We turn now from the survey of the recent past to the consideration of the psychology of today. We have indicated already some of its characteristics, among which the most important is the adherence to the view of the organism as a response mechanism, and the assimilation of the conscious responses to the other responses. This is, in fact, a simplification, rather than an addition, for we have long known that the organism, whatever else it might be, is a response mechanism, and is primarily that. What we have done is merely to extend this necessary biological conception to the psychological field, displacing there the additional hypotheses which had in the past seemed requisite additions. In other words, we have made one well developed hypothesis to grow where several unnecessary ones grew before. This simplification has meant, among other things, a definite break with the phrenological conceptions of brain function which ruled physiological psychology for so long a time, and which the work of Marie and the work of Franz showed to be so inadequate.

The laws of habit, and the laws of heredity have consequently been extended from the biological field to the psychological. This extension has been the easier because the most anciently known laws of habit, the laws of the association of ideas, so-called, were discovered in the psychological field. But with this extension, the problems of mental habit have been vastly simplified, and the knowledge of mental operations have been greatly extended. Ontogenetic psychology has become a possibility; and phylogenetic psychology will also be possible when the subject of genetics has reached a more stable ground.

Another biological concept, specifically a physiological notion, has also been extended to the psychological field as a necessary consequence of the response hypothesis; the conception of *integration,* which is so intimate a part of the modern conception of habit and learning. With the conception of integration, the tendency to look upon the reaction pathways (or arcs) as simple and distinct elements in the neural mechanism, has vanished. The conception of reflexes as merely one variety of reaction, differing from the more complicated responses only in degree; and of the "pure reflex" as only an analytic fiction, non-existent in the normal human animal, although obtainable under abnormal conditions, has been a necessary consequence of the integration conception, and has eliminated a great deal of troublesome theory which had been built up concerning the relation of reflex action to random action, to impulsive action, and to instinctive tendencies.

With the simpler conception of the relation of so-called reflexes and more complicated reactions, new problems open up. It is no longer possible to "explain" instinctive or hereditary reaction tendencies by referring them to a "chain of reflexes" or even by contrasting them sharply with reflexes. All reaction now seems to be of the same essential type, within which the most important variation is in degree of integration. Other variations are too numerous to permit of any simple classification on this basis. The problem of the interrelation of heredity and environment, nature and nurture, instinct and habit, endowment and acquisition, concerns action generally, and perception and thought as well. The older and simpler solution of this problem, by reference to "instincts" has gone by the board, and in its place we have the growing hypothesis that all action is inherited, and all is acquired; that heredity can no longer be contrasted with environment, but that neither has any significance except in terms of the other. It is no longer possible to settle the question as to the future of war by saying that man has a hereditary "pugnacious tendency," or "tendency to conflict." We have to inquire first what this tendency, which may be described as pugnacious in one environmental condition, will be in other environmental conditions. Psychology today bases its conceptions of hereditary tendencies squarely on the biologists' conception of a tendency to react to one stimulus pattern in one way, and to other stimulus patterns in other ways; that is, not as an independent action tendency, but as a response tendency. And we include in the conception of a hereditary tendency a great deal of that which we also call "habit." That is to say, a tendency to react to a certain stimulus pattern in a certain way, is, at the same time, a tendency to react to that pattern in a quite different way after a certain other series of reactions have occurred. If we dub the new-born calf's tendency to suck the cow's nipple or suck your finger, as "instinctive" or "hereditary"; then we must also dub as "instinctive" his tendency to drink milk out of a pail; a tendency which he "acquires" through the reactions of sucking your fingers when you have immersed them and his nose in the milk.

The factors which have contributed to this great and rapid change in the conception of instinct and habit, aside from the fundamental response hypothesis, into harmony with which the conceptions have been brought, have been the growing comprehension of the arbitrariness and unworkableness of the old "instinct" doctrine, and the realization of the fact that *if* the doctrine of the inheritance of complicated reaction tendencies, in magic independence of habit formation, were really true, there would be reason to suspect the inheritance of thinking tendencies too; since the thinking tendencies are reaction tendencies also, and probably not a whit more complicated than the other reaction tendencies which are included under the old category of "instincts." Thus, the Lockian doctrine of *no innate ideas* would go by the board, along with the scholastic doctrine: *nihil est in intellectu quod non fuerit prius in sensu,* which psychology has heretofore so completely accepted.

The most gratifying result of all these changes has been a renewed enthusiasm for experimental research on the problems of mental heredity, including research on the problem raised by Preyer long ago, and later ignored; the problem of the behavior of the embryo *in utero.* The old notion that we can accept the animal at the moment of birth as a machine

prepared entirely through heredity; and assume that the operation of the laws of habit-formation begins to operate only
then, has passed away along with other arbitrary and useless
assumptions.

Another problem on which experimentation has hardly begun, but on which we may definitely expect searching investigation, is the problem of the relative modifiability of the in-
tegratively different grades of reaction. It was assumed once
on a time that there are reflexes which are unmodifiable by the
process of habit formation as ordinarily conceived. Now,
however, there is a tendency to assume that these reflexes are
relatively easily modifiable. But it is admitted that the evidence so far is rather naïve and inconclusive; and the question
of the relative modifiability of so-called reflexes looms as one
of the most important questions bearing on the whole theory
of reactions.

One highly important feature of modern scientific psychology is the emphasis on *patterns*. This emphasis is the result
of many influences, and it is impossible to ascribe it to any
single author or any single preceding development. But it is
an emphasis which would naturally be produced by the conception of integration, and the development of this emphasis
has been, as a matter of fact, a detail in the development of the
integration concept.

James, over thirty years ago, warned us against the treatment of analytical details as actually isolable facts, and the
more scientific treatment he recommended has gradually prevailed. But with the change of psychology from a philosophical to a biological basis, the tendency to treat the analytically discernible reaction pathways as separable elements in
the response mechanism asserted itself, and the tendency to
treat of stimuli as if some restricted detail of stimulation
could of itself bring about this or that specific reaction, was carried over from the earlier psychology. The conceptions of reflexes, in particular, as separable elements in the total responses was one manifestation of this psychological attitude.
The conception of instincts as central forces or plural psyches,
harmonizing and controlling these assumed individual reaction
tendencies, was another manifestation.

The consideration of action as an effective force in the
world, however, calls attention to the enormous significance
of pattern, that is, to the interrelationship, temporally and spa-
tially, of the analytically discriminable details of animal acts.

The fact that seemingly slight changes in the relationships of details may change the practical effects of the whole act is undeniable. A thousand details may be rightly related, but a single detail out of the right relationship may ruin the effect. Obviously, the temporal pattern, or succession of details, is at least as important as the spatial pattern at any moment.

At the other end of the response, the efficacy of stimulation is equally dependent upon pattern. No one reacts to single stimuli, and the analytically distinct detail, such as a descriptively single color stimulus, or single note, may produce, at different times, quite different reactions, depending upon the concurrent and preceding stimulation. Or, rather, these analytical details do not produce the reactions; they are mere details in a total stimulus pattern which, and which only, can be said to initiate the reaction.

Between this stimulus pattern and the resulting action pattern, there is, of course, a neural pattern which is different for each response which differs in action pattern or in stimulus pattern from any other response. Given a stimulus pattern, the action pattern ultimately resulting must be dependent on the neural pattern, or *transit pattern* evoked. The formation of habits is, therefore, essentially the formation of tendencies to integrate the nervous transit activities into certain transit patterns. In the conscious reactions, the type of conscious process depends on the type of transit pattern, and not on mere spatial pattern of brain cell function, as older theories assumed. On this basis, the ontogenetic development of perception is understandable as a building up of reaction patterns so that eventually certain stimulus patterns, or stimulus patterns of a certain type, come to produce more and more specific reaction patterns; and these patterns take on progressively more useful forms, so that the actions and the perceptions involved in them become better and better adapted to the environment. We can see also the reason for the resemblance between the thinking process and the perceiving process; and also the difference between them. If thinking does depend on previous perception, perception must have built up patterns of reaction to external stimuli, and the terminal action patterns are partially repeated later to internal stimuli. But since the stimulus patterns in the two cases are different, the neural patterns are different in spite of the partial identity of the action patterns. Briefly, we can say that the greater or less identity of the perception of anything and the subsequent thinking of the same thing lies in the greater or less identity of the terminal acts of the two reactions; and that the essential difference between the two processes lies in the difference in the stimulation patterns.

Attention, once a formidable problem for psychology, so formidable that it was generally erected into a separate "faculty" of the mind, (the usual way of disposing of something which can not be taken into the general explanatory system), is still a problem. But it is a problem of patterns of integration and future solutions are to be worked out on that basis.

The perception of relations was too hard a nut to crack for the Malebranchian psychology, as I have earlier pointed out. But for the modern scientific psychology it is just one nut among the others, all of which are to be gradually unshelled together. In the little world of mental objects, there were no mental objects provided to represent the actual relations between objects in the big real world. Furthermore, in the phrenological system of the brain there were no "centers" for relations as there were for "sensations." Hence, there was nothing for psychology to do but to soft-pedal the problem of relations and the perception of relations. In modern psychology, however, we have no microcosmic mental world to deal with, and in our psychobiology we have no brain "centers" for the production of mythical mental objects. Relations between external objects we do perceive; and having perceived them, we think of them. That which we perceive is always a pattern, in which relations are always involved; and the selective emphasis on these, or attention to these is a matter of differential integration of the responses, just as is the attention to this or that sense datum. The problems concerning the perception of relation are, therefore, no different from the problems of perceiving sense data, and in so far as the problems of one group is solved the others are *ipso facto* solved.

In what I have called scientific psychology, there can be no reasonable doubt that we have come to a permanent basis for psychology. By permanent, I do not, of course, mean perfect or final. If the science does not die, there must always be progressive improvement in its fundamental conception. But no science can be considered established until it has a basis which is permanent in the sense that whatever further is added, it will remain. Chemistry became an established science with the adoption of the atomic hypothesis, and although the ion and electron theories, and the discoveries of radio activity and of the transformation of elements have vastly extended the basis of the science, and entirely reinterpreted the atomic hypothesis, the hypothesis has not really been superseded. Certain notions as to its finality and sufficiency have been swept away, but in so far as the atomic hypothesis was a useful basis, it still endures. Comparing the atomic hypothesis in chemistry and the Copernican theory in astronomy with the reaction hypothesis in psychology shows significant likenesses in the relations of the three hypotheses to the subject matter of the three sciences in the stage at which they have been introduced. Comprehensive in their scope, leaving nothing out to be a skeleton in the closet; simplifying what previously was excessively complicated; and enormously fertile in regard to further work, these hypotheses are foundations of sciences.

With the responses hypothesis as the basis, the future of experimental psychology is bright. We have our popular psychologists to combat; but the chemists had their alchemists and the astronomers had their astrologers. Perhaps, if we devote ourselves to research as industriously as have the astronomers and the chemists, our character analysts, psychoanalysts and other pseudo-psychologists will be reduced to the same innocuous condition.

Of course, there are many philosophical questions left unsolved by the present psychological position, and the progress of scientific psychology has been rather around them than through them. If I am asked by an acute philosopher: How can you assume the occurrence of consciousness, if you do not assume that consciousness is observable? I have to reply: Well, why not? Consciousness seems to be a fact, and the assumption that it isn't a fact destroys not only psychology but physical science. For it is futile for the physicist to present his observation if he assumes that he hasn't made any observations. On the other hand, I don't think I can observe consciousness; consciousness seems to be always the *observing* of something. If you can prove that consciousness can be observed, then I will accept the proof; but I can't see that that would make any difference in my psychology otherwise. In the meantime, therefore, psychology need not worry over the question.

Furthermore, the ancient epistemological question may still be brought up. I may be asked by the same acute philosopher: How can you possibly observe something outside your mind?

And, again I should answer, Why not? It would seem to me just as difficult to explain how I can observe something inside my mind; and I prefer to let the metaphysical question rest, and stand on the fact that something is observed, and that it frequently is something which is also called the outside world. Further, I should point out that the creation of an internal world to represent the external doesn't solve the problem, for the question remains in the form: How do we get from this microcosm to the macrocosm we are after?

Perhaps the one philosophical question which does directly concern the psychologist's work is the question as to the relation between perceived objects and stimuli. For the practical development of psychological work, even this question is no obstacle, but the psychologist, like all other men, likes to have his logical problems ironed out, even if those problems do not have a practical bearing on his work. The dualistic hypothesis did not solve this problem, although it was precisely the problem that epistemological dualism has contrived to solve. While I have my own solution which is quite satisfactory to me, and which is precisely the solution to which many physical scientists have come, the matter is so far enough detached from the main business of psychology that it is not advisable to drag it into the present discourse.

The philosophical conflict between mechanism and vitalism interests certain psychologists intensely today, but I cannot help feeling that however interesting the problem may be to them personally, it is of no concern to their psychology. The practical solution of this problem is attributed to Lotze, and that solution, although philosophically comic, is really a formulation of a useful practical attitude. Lotze, I believe, taught that before a decision between two alternative courses of action is made, we should regard the future act as free, that is, undetermined; but that in looking back on it, we should regard the course taken as having been rigidly determined.

There is, in short, no conflict between the mechanism which as scientists we all assume, whatever our speculative views, and the effectiveness of purposes which likewise we all assume. What may be the limits of mechanism, and what the limits of purposive effects, is another matter which, it is possible, will some day be of importance to both psychological and physical science, but whose importance is not yet evident. This question, too, we can wisely leave to the philosophers, although among the philosophers we may include ourselves in our leisure moments.

In conclusion, I should like to emphasize again the continuity of psychological progress, and the indebtedness of the viewpoints that seem revolutionary to the viewpoints they supplant. Many, perhaps all, of the positions which we have had to revise have been positions which were true in some fundamental respect, and we have merely made use of them in revised and reinterpreted forms. It is clear that the psychologist has to deal with a world of private content, with which the natural sciences have no dealings directly, just as the Malebranchians assumed. But this world is not the sort of a world they believed it to be. It is merely the world of our own bodies, which we perceive through kinesthesis and organic sensitivity (including feelings and emotions), and which no one else can perceive in that way. This bodily world is the world of actual introspection. Many other conceptions of scientific psychology are reinterpretations of older viewpoints, or directly derived from them. But important as is that which is passed on from previous generations, that which is added by succeeding generations is equally important. The way to our present conclusion has been prepared and made plain by the labor of those who by no means have always agreed to the conclusions to which they have contributed. Acknowledging our indebtedness to them, we cannot but regret that they are sometimes unwilling to consummate their work by advancing with us. And very probably the next generation will be making the same remark about many of us.

CHAPTER XV

THE EXPERIMENTAL METHODS OF PSYCHOLOGY*

By Knight Dunlap

Psychology, in its period of transformation, had apparently an experimental method all its own; the so-called introspective method, which was contrasted with the method of the physical sciences. With the development of psychology into a science on what appears to be a permanent basis, this methodological distinction has passed away. Introspection in the sense of observation of one's own bodily processes remains as a necessary part of experimental method; but, like the observation of external things, it is ruled by more general experimental methods and technique. It might seem, therefore, that the methods of psychology are simply those of natural science in general, and differ from those of biology, chemistry, and physics only in the same way in which the methods of each of these sciences differ from those of the others. It is, of course, obvious that although the methods of science may be general, and apply to all sciences alike, nevertheless they are also particular; and the applications of the general methods in the different sciences will be determined by the specific problems of those sciences.

To a large extent, this conclusion is justified. The fundamental principles of scientific method which rigidly control the physical sciences, control also experimental psychology; and no procedure which does not conform to those general principles is either justifiable or worthy of consideration in psychology.[1]

Obviously, the application of methods and the forms of technique are different in individual psychology as distinguished from general psychology. Animal psychology has its own special techniques, as it has its specific problems. Abnormal psychology and child psychology also have their highly specialized methods or techniques, and the psychologist trained in only one of these various fields is not prepared to enter another until he has become familiar with its peculiar problems and difficulties and mastered its techniques.

*Powell Lecture in Psychological Theory at Clark University, April 21, 1925.
[1]The variations in method which are necessary in psychology may well be described as variations in technique rather than in method; but the delimitation of terms in this precise logical way is not essential.

The fundamental scientific methods of psychology are four-fold. They require, *first*: the recognition of all data as occurring in situations which are describable as observations. That is, its fundamental data are data to consciousness. Data which are not observed data are not data for experimentation. The essential starting point, therefore, for psychological experiment includes the acknowledgment of *consciousness,* and of something *of which* the consciousness is.

Second: the methods require the formation of competent hypotheses derived either from previous experimental work or from less formal observations. Without hypotheses, experimentation is impossible. The competence of the hypotheses depends both on their adaptability for experimental test, and their vital relation to further hypotheses or to applications. Hypotheses are useless unless they are competent.

Third: the hypotheses must be subjected to test, to determine their truth or falsity. Experimentation, in effect, is just the subjection of hypotheses to crucial test, and no other procedure is called by that name. Although the great mass of technical procedure centers about the performance of the test, the test itself is no more vital to experimental work than the formulation of the hypotheses to be tested. Both are requisite, and defects in either may be equally fatal.

Fourth: the proof established by the test must have a specific form, namely, repeatability. The issue of the experiment must be a statement of the hypothesis, the conditions of test, and the results, in such form that another experimenter, from the description alone, may be able to repeat the experiment. Nothing is accepted as proof, in psychology or in any other science, which does not conform to this requirement.

The psychologist must carefully consider these principles of method and view each special technique and application in their light, until they become a part of his habitual method of thought. Only then can he be certain of not applying his time and energy wastefully and of not being caught in eddies and back-currents of experimentation from which there is no progressive issue. What I have to say in the following discourse will, therefore, center about these four fundamentals of scientific method, although I shall not attempt to develop these four principles in a discreet systematic way.

The field of psychology, however, is so broad that it cannot be said that in all of its extensions the principles of natural science are its sufficient chart and guide, although in every province of psychology they are valid and necessary. There is, undoubtedly, a field of educational psychology which will some day be cultivated, and in which already a few slight beginnings have been made. The name, indeed, has long been familiar, but has so far been almost altogether applied to those fragments of general and individual psychology which departments of education have chosen to take over into their curricula; and the fragments have not, so far, been selectively restricted to any particular part of psychology, but cover broadly the whole field.

An examination of the courses offered under the name of "educational psychology" in colleges and universities throughout the United States shows the interesting fact that some of these courses contain one group of psychological topics, some another; and frequently when two courses are compared it will be found that neither contains anything that the other contains. Altogether, these courses scatter over the entire field of psychology, although since the introduction of intelligence tests the courses in educational psychology tend more and more to that topic, and many courses contain nothing but a routine training in the scoring of intelligence tests. In the field of research the same condition obtains. Practically, all of the research articles found in the journals and monographs of educational psychology are, in their scope and topics, such as are common in general and individual psychology.

Yet, a real educational psychology will be developed, and when it is, its methods may be somewhat different from those of the general science. The newly developed subject of social psychology is manifestly waiting for the development of experimental methods of its own, and some of them may be available for educational psychology. Whether racial psychology, when it appears, will have its methods, will determine the possibility of racial psychology being experimental; but in any event, the experimental method of the general science will probably not be sufficient in this field either.

For the present, our greatest concern is with the experimental methods of general psychology, not only because they are fundamental, but also because for all of the special fields of psychology the greatest need is for the application of experimental results from the general field. This is the case, for example, in the psychology of religion, where the interpretation of the data of ancient and savage peoples is, of course, impossible of direct experimental approach, but depends for its interpretation on the experimental data which may be brought to it.

The rapid transformation of psychology in the early part of the 19th century, in its successful attempt to become experimental led to the application to its data of certain mathematical methods taken over directly from physics and astronomy, and which are quite appropriate to physical science, and fruitful therein. These mathematical methods are based on the method of least squares as applied to the theory of probability of errors in observation and chance variations of other sorts; and assume as fundamental the distribution of measurements which are subject to "chance" variation solely, in a form which can be represented by a symmetrical curve which has a definite equation, known as the Gaussian curve, or curve of error. Or more accurately: the distribution approximates the form of the Gaussian curve in proportion as the number of measurements increases, and in proportion as the errors due to other than what is called "chance" are eliminated. For this reason, the Gaussian curve is called the "normal curve" and distributions are said to be "normal" in so far as they approximate reasonably close to the Gaussian form. For the sake of clearness, I shall throughout the following discussion designate the statistical method which depends upon the method of least squares as the *higher* statistical method, (by analogy with the term "higher mathematics"), and certain other statistical methods not depending on Gaussian postulates as the *simpler* statistical methods.

It seemed to many of the nineteenth century psychologists that if the higher mathematical methods, which are useful in physical science, could be applied to psychological data, psychology would *ipso facto* become a science. The methods had been developed in the first place with regard to errors of observation, and are used in physics today, primarily to correct for errors in observation. Psychology deals primarily with observations; and if the variations in observation could be considered as "errors" or chance variations from a true measure, the physicist's methods should be directly applicable.

In that period of psychology, threshold observations and threshold determinations played a relatively more prominent part than they do today; so that it is but natural that the first application of the higher statistical method should have been to the technique of determining thresholds. This application reached its heights in the "Method of Right and Wrong Cases" which occupies a prominent place in the literature of the latter quarter of the 19th century. By mathematical calculation, tables were prepared by which thresholds were computed with great mathematical exactness from relatively few observations. The practical procedure amounted to this: from data obtained by presenting only one, or only a few, stimulus differences, a prediction was made as to what would have happened if a larger series of differences had been presented for observation: and this prediction was named the "threshold."

Fortunately, this practice of giving crude, and often few, data a refined mathematical treatment has practically passed from experimental psychology. In fact, what many students today learn as the "Method of Right and Wrong Cases" is an absolutely different and far simpler method than the original one to which I refer.

The most unfortunate assumption involved in the mathematical threshold methods, was the assumption that the "threshold" is a fixed and definite value, and that the diverse readings obtained in a properly designed series of measurements are of the nature of "errors" or chance variations from the true value which should have been obtained, whereas, as a matter of fact, each of these is as true a threshold as any other. This assumption is embodied in a different form in the assumption that the normal curve of distribution of psychological data, (judgments of difference, in this case), is a "normal" curve in the Gaussian sense; and that the distinctly different forms actually obtained for certain types of data are variations from the true form, and can be corrected for. As a matter of fact, we know that the really normal distributions for many sorts of psychological data are far from Gaussian; and that in these cases an approximation to the Gaussian form would be direct evidence of either gross experimental error, or unjustifiable statistical juggling.

The most serious practical effect of the mathematical method was a lessening of the emphasis on the value of the data itself. Not only were refined calculations made from data too few to be a basis for the simplest mathematical treatment, but the data often were obtained under conditions of planning and execution of the work which were seriously inadequate. Why this effect should have been produced may not be entirely clear, but it manifestly was produced; and with the abandonment of the higher statistical method has come about a great improvement in other respects, principally an increased emphasis on the reliability of the data itself, and increased care in disposing the experimental work to the end of securing data of the maximal quality and adequate quantity. The fundamental difficulties in the way of the application of the higher statistical method to psychological data may be illustrated from reaction-time measurements. Here the normal distribution is distinctly skewed, that is, it is not "normal" at all in the arbitrary Gaussian meaning of the term. Actually, the probability of a positive deviation from the median is greater than the probability of an equal negative deviation, and there is no probable error of the distribution, but two measures which might be called probable errors, namely: the median deviation *above* the average and the median deviation *below* the average. No calculations based on the formula of the Gaussian curve can be made, therefore, unless the difference in the probabilities of the positive and negative deviations can be accurately computed and corresponding corrections introduced in the formulae. Theoretically, this might be done for a given collection of data. But the data required for the purpose would be so copious that there would be no gain in the application of the higher statistical methods, since the results thereof, in so far as valid, would have been already obtained.

But there is still another difficulty which cannot be overcome even in theory. The physical applications of the higher statistical methods depend on the assumption that the conditions of measurement are throughout the same except for the so-called chance variations, that is, the variations which in the long run follow the Gaussian law of error. That which is measured is assumed to have a fixed value, which is independent of the measurements, and is not affected by the measuring process. The length of a bar of steel, for example, at a constant temperature, is assumed to be a fixed definite quantity, and the measurements which the physicist makes are assumed not to affect this length, which is therefore the same throughout the series of measurements. But in psychological measurements the conditions are quite different. That which is measured in the reaction time experiment, for example, is not a fixed quantity, but a variable, and the measurements themselves affect its magnitude. If we obtain a hundred reactions from a given reactor under external conditions as usual as possible, the last measurements differ from the first not merely by chance errors of measurement, but also because that which is measured is itself different. In other words, practice effects are involved, and practice effects continue to manifest themselves even after thousands of reactions have been made. Theoretically, the law of practice effects for a given subject under constant conditions might be computed, and correction made for this: practically, no such corrections would be useful. The higher statistical methods would at this point become so "high" that they would be unwieldy.

The fact is, that after habituation, the reactions become changed in complex ways, involving not only habit formation, but changes in attitudes of the reactor. If we are interested in the type of reactions made in ordinary life, we do not get these after long mechanical practice in a fixed condition. The representative values obtained from higher mathematical treatment of series of reaction times are no more significant at best than the results of the simpler treatment which experimental psychology gives them; and they may be entirely misleading. Similar conclusions obtain for almost all the data of experimental psychology.

At the present time, experimental psychology tends to employ no mathematical methods in the treatment of data beyond simple addition, subtraction and division. In this respect, at least, experimental psychology is distinguished from educational psychology and mental measurements. Averages, medians, and modes as representatives of series of measurements; and mean variations and percentage variations as measures of variation from these representative values, have been established, or are at least accepted, as practically useful and justifiable.[1] Any results and conclusions depending upon more elaborate mathematical treatment of data are under suspicion, and are not accepted unless confirmed by the simpler method. Even the probable error of an average is under the ban, since it really has no significance in most cases, and in every case gives a misleading appearance of a significance which it does not possess.

It was not to be expected, however, that the statistical method would be so easily routed from psychology. It offers an easy method for the obtaining of "results," and the results have an impressive appearance due to the profundity of the mathematical principles involved. The fact that these principles are above the comprehension of the person doing the research, and that the results, therefore, seem to come as gifts

---

[1]This is not intended as a complete list of accepted measures, nor to exclude graphic representation and analysis.

from the gods to the humble turner of the wheel, by no means lessens the impressiveness.   Furthermore, one is enabled to turn out a piece of research which has a considerable magnitude by virtue of the amount of statistical work done on a very little data.   And then, the method is sometimes applicable to problems for which no really experimental methods have been yet devised.

For this reason, the methods of correlation introduced by Pearson and improved by Yule and others, have had a great vogue in individual psychology, and coefficients of correlation are being widely applied, not *to* the solution of various and sundry problems, but applied *as* the solutions; which is quite a different matter.   Now it is true, the correlation method has very important uses, and may have such even in psychology, when applied to a collection of data which really has a Gaussian distribution or whose deviations from this distribution are such as can be corrected.   But I fear that most of those who use the method would not know how to determine whether a given distribution were Gaussian or not, for it is apparent that to many the term "normal distribution" means merely "symmetrical distribution."

The difficulty in the interpretation of a coefficient of correlation is very great; I suppose there is no other representative value obtained from data which offers greater difficulty. The difficulty is strikingly illustrated by a survey of the literature embodying it, in which almost any coefficient is calmly assumed to prove not merely that there is a relation between the arrays correlated, but that the particular relation the seeker hoped to find is there.   In order to avoid what might seem to be personal attack, I shall refrain from the citation of the really humorous cases of this kind which appear in some of our most serious journals.

The disastrous effects of the higher statistical methods on the experimental work of those dazzled by the methods has been apparent in the correlational work, as it was in the earlier psycho-physical investigations.   Much of the data of intelligence testing which has been subjected to mathematical elaboration of this sort has been data so crudely gathered, with so little attention to the principles of scientific method, that it would be worthless for even the simplest statistical treatment.   Illogical as it may seem, the assumption appears to be that data gathered by utterly incompetent persons, sometimes under unknown conditions, sometimes under conditions actually known to be pernicious, is in some miraculous way validated, and made reliable, when the magic method of correlation is applied to it. It must be said, however, that it is not the mental testers alone who have committed these abominations. In the field of vital statistics, so-called, some especially flagrant cases have recently cropped up. However dangerous the higher statistical method may be when applied to data gathered with due experimental precaution and sagacity, it becomes distinctly a public nuisance in the hands of those ignorant or careless of experimental technique.

History repeats itself, occasionally at least. Although we may expect to see the mushroom growth of the higher statistical method as applied to individual psychology shrivel as did its earlier applications to the problems of general psychology, we need not fear that the subject of individual psychology, and its experimental phase in mental measurements, will die with the method. General psychology survived the blow: individual psychology will, too. The vast extension of intelligence testing, which has been largely based on uncritical correlation work, with little actual experimental basis, already shows signs of being a psychological boomerang; but individual psychology will survive even the blow of this back-stroke.

It is interesting to note that the Binet-Simon tests, the forerunners of the later crop of intelligence tests, were not dependent upon the higher statistical methods either for their elaboration or validation. Some of the later group intelligence tests also have had their usefulness for certain purposes established by careful analytical work, quite apart from the method of correlation. Where any test has not been established for a given purpose by other than "correlational" methods, its application is little more than guess work. The establishing of educational and social projects and programs on mere "coefficients" is something which psychology might view merely with compassion, were it not for the fact that such establishment is being made brazenly in the name of psychology; and the public credits the failures to the experimental psychologists who protest against the methods.

The higher statistical method has a place in experimental psychology as a means of preliminary survey, from the results of which indications may be drawn which are helpful in the formulation of problems. It is, in other words, one of the means of prospecting for a problem, and like other means of prospecting its indications may be fallacious. A coefficient of correlation is, in psychology, at the most only the beginning of research; a suggestion for a theory which may be formulated and put to experimental verification. The fallacy which has been committed is considering it the end of a research problem.

Experimental psychology cannot make use of the statistical methods of the physicist and astronomer because its data is not of the sort that makes elaborate mathematical treatment significant, and its problems are not of the sort that receives real illumination from the results of the treatment, even where the treatment is justified. If educational psychology should follow some of the present tendencies in that arbitrarily mapped out field, and become a system based entirely on correlation, it would thereby become a separate field, no longer confused with experimental psychology, at any rate. Individual psychology, which has been carried away by the mathematical fascination, and which has made its mental measurements so largely matters of correlation, can regain its balance and justification by returning to the fold of experimental psychology and profiting by its experiences, disillusionments, and achievements.

So far, we have been discussing those aspects of method which are determined by the treatment of data. The way in which data are to be treated is not merely important in itself; it determines to a large extent the data to be obtained for treatment. No one makes measurements without a consideration of what he will do with the data, in way of treatment, after they are obtained. The actual planning and carrying through of a piece of genuine experimental work must be, and should be, influenced by the treatment which is to be given the data after it is obtained. But there are other considerations of far more importance in the planning and elaboration.

In planning an investigation the most frequent mistake into which experimenters fall is in making the scope of the problem too wide, or including too many problems. This mistake may be made in either of two ways. Often, the program of the research, as laid out, includes so many points that no thorough investigation can be made on any one of them in the time allotted. Not infrequently, a doctoral investigation covering three years or more of work suffers from this sort of planning. As a result, the next investigator must start precisely where the first investigator did, instead of being able to start where he left off. Investigations on reaction times, learning problems, and a great variety of other topics might be instanced as showing this type of work.   In the beginning of investigation on any topic, superficial exploratory work of this character is necessary to uncover the various specific problems involved; and young investigators always find it difficult to restrict themselves to a problem or detail of a problem, so small that it can be actually settled.   But not all of the scattering of labor that comes under this category can be attributed to youth, either of the investigator or of the topic.   In some cases, the scattering is due to lack of grasp on the real problems involved.   Without a sufficient grasp the fundamental small problems which ought to be attacked cannot be determined with clearness.   A great deal of the impulse to scatter is due, however, to the fact that the lengthy and copious working out of a single small point is extremely tedious, and nobody likes tedious work.   The covering of a large topic superficially is much more thrilling.

Another motive to work of insufficient thoroughness is derived from the strong interest we all take in application.   A large part of the research in psychology is necessarily the fashioning and shaping of tools; tools which are then applicable either to practical affairs of life, or else to the shaping and fashioning of still more tools.   In fashioning these tools, it is inevitable that the use or application should be more or less in view, and the urge to hurry on to the application before the tool is really complete is frequently too strong to be withstood.

An illustration which comes to my mind, but which is just one case among many, is the work with the simple and familiar tapping board, the applications of which to the testing of motor functions are practically useful, but which would be much more useful if we really knew more definitely the details of the tapping process itself.   We can even see very clearly the exact problems which have to be worked out in regard to the tapping board; but each of these problems would require several years' work, and demand a high mastery of psychological instrumentation and technique.   Consequently, investigators balk at the problems, and prefer the more entertaining, although far less important, problems of application of the undeveloped tool.

The case of intelligence tests would be just as good on illustration.   Application of tests is interesting and seems urgent, and moreover requires little scientific ability.   On the other hand, the painstaking work of making intelligence tests more worth applying is appalling in its vastness, its lack of thrill, and its requirements of psychological skill.

What we really need in psychology is more of the spirit of Sylvester, who exclaimed, when he had made a discovery in higher mathematics, that he thanked God he had discovered something no one could ever use. What he apparently meant was that he was thankful for the opportunity and ability to work on a problem without reference to the further usefulness of its solution; for that is the way in which great advances in science are really made.

The practical urge to lay hasty foundations and use them prematurely is not entirely the fault of the psychologist. Every psychologist knows how difficult it is to get appropriations and maintenance for purely scientific work, and how much more impressive to the powers that control money is something which is "practical," however flimsy and evanescent its "practicality." The amount of money wasted in practical work which might be saved if more were available for the fundamental scientific work on which eventual practical applications depend, is, of course, enormous, and even in psychology it is relatively large.

In addition to the failure to narrow problems sufficiently in the general planning and laying out of experimental work, there has been a failure to limit sufficiently the specific requirements on the psychological subject or reactor. This failure, however, lies rather in the past, having been peculiar to the introspectional psychology. The essential point of ultimate experimental method as applied to the conditions of the psychological observer himself is, that he shall be required to observe only one point at a time; a point being something which in the ideal case can be reported upon by a "yes" or "no" judgment. Obviously, preliminary work will always be needed; work in which the judgment will be of broader scope; in order that the final experimental conditions may be so arranged that the simpler judgment for final purposes can be obtained. In some cases, even the final conditions will not be ideal; but the nearer they approximate to this ideal, the sounder the work. For this is just the difference between scientific observation and mere testimony, opinion, or guess work: that in scientific observation the conditions are either prearranged or foreseen so that the observer knows what to look for, and the definite time at which to look for it.

A large part of the introspective work reported in the psychological literature of the past flagrantly transgresses this rule. Even when the observer has been introspecting in the sense in which the term is used in modern scientific psychology, that is, has been observing bodily processes, he has been required to cover a large range of observation in a brief period of time, or at least to try to. The result is sometimes distinctly humorous: the observer, after the critical moment of the observation is past, will spend fifteen minutes or more detailing the various things he has observed. Emotions, feelings of pleasure or the reverse, feelings of tension, kinesthetic processes in breast, arms, legs, throat; and sometimes changing details of imagery as well, are solemnly reported as a part of the introspective observation.

The unreliability of such observation, in which the observer, instead of concentrating on a single prearranged point, observes as Charles Dudley Warner shot the bear—by aiming at it generally—has been abundantly demonstrated by the work on the psychology of testimony, and the type of observation is being eliminated, or at least relegated to the limbo of the anecdotal animal psychology and the reports of the society for psychical research. For all types of psychological observation, the principle of concentration is now upheld, regardless of the school of the psychologist.

Perhaps the most important point in psychological method is the formulation of the problem to which research is to be applied. For the evaluation of the importance of problems one against the other there are perhaps certain formal criteria; but over and above these, the final evaluation must be in terms of the experimenter's interests and competence. Certain problems are important because their results are foreseen as determining further research or applications. Certain others are important because of their intimate relation to general hypotheses, which may be either confirmed, modified or extended as the results of the research. But importance in any of these respects is not directly comparable with importance in any other. The relative importance of an investigation into the effects of alcohol on thought processes as compared with the investigation into the detailed features of tapping is to be determined only by the interest and the technical skill the investigator brings to either, and the success in formulating the problems as a distinct hypothesis, the truth or falsity of which the experimenter is to test. Only when this formulation is achieved is the work which follows really experimental. Exploratory work, without distinct hypotheses, is useful at times; but its value is low as compared with experimental work. The most serious obstacle to the extension of knowledge is the difficulty of formulating the hypotheses on which experimental work depends. When the problem is once formulated, the devising of apparatus to suit the problem is possible, and the carrying out of the work itself is largely a matter of industry and careful technique. The formulation of the problem demands scientific imagination, long study of the materials in which the problem is to be found, and general familiarity with the field of psychology in which the materials lie. The present undeveloped state of the psychology of the emotions, for example, is due to the difficulty in the formulation of specific hypotheses capable of experimental test. Broad hypotheses exist, and draw our attention; but these are not capable of experimental test as such. Specific hypotheses, definitely related to the general hypothesis, must be discovered, and these specific hypotheses must not only be such that their confirmation or destruction will throw light on the general problem, but they must be such as can actually be solved. Many specific problems can be formulated, which are not accessible to experimentation. Some hypotheses concerning emotions have been put to the test (*e.g.*, Sherrington's experiment on the dog and Watson's experiments on children). But it turns out in many cases that the hypothesis actually settled has no ascertainable bearing on the larger general conclusions of the experimenter.

For the discovery of vital problems, there are no rules. This part of scientific work is in the same class as the writing of poetry and the creation of paintings. There are principles to which the productions must conform; but these principles do not suffice to make the production possible; they merely differentiate between the successful and unsuccessful productions. Curiously enough, therefore, the starting point of psychological experimentation is not itself a science, but an art; and this is true, of course, of all experimental work. We can lay down rules for the would-be artist to follow in developing his artistic ability; but we cannot create it. By study, direction of interest, and arrangement of circumstances, we can prepare the nest in which the egg is to hatch; but the egg must be supplied to science.

An essential point in experimental method, therefore, is to

be something of an artist: to have a creative imagination along the lines of psychological hypotheses. Having that, and intellectual capacity to discriminate the useful creations from the useless, the materials for these to work upon may be supplied by study of the data and existing hypotheses, by technical training, and by proper emotional application to the problems.

The methods of experimental science all lead to proof or disproof. The progress of any science is the confirmation or rejection of minor hypotheses, one by one. Scientific proof is, in theory, a definite accomplishment; but in practice the limit between probability and certainty can never be exactly set. Proof in science is merely repeatability. The fundamental scientific assumption is of a uniformity in nature, such that what has occurred once under given conditions will occur again if the same conditions are established. Theoretically, therefore, the results of one experiment constitute proof. The famous single experiment of Stratton on the effects of inverted vision may be said to have proved his hypothesis, or disproved the contrary. In fact, in that particular case the results of the single experiment have been accepted, and the former discussion of the causes of correct vision has completely ceased. Yet, in the strict sense of the term, there is as yet no real proof at all. Proof will be accomplished when other experimenters, establishing the condition on which the conclusions are based, find the same phenomena occurring. In this case, we accept the proof partly on faith, on account of our belief in the extreme competence of Stratton, both as an observer and as a technician, and partly because the conclusions fit so perfectly into the general hypotheses of reaction psychology.

The general principle of the uniformity of the laws of nature compel us to assume that if the conditions of Stratton's experiment are repeated, the results obtained must necessarily be obtained again. If this were not true, then no science would be possible. The only question, therefore, concerns the accuracy and completeness of the statement of the conditions and the results. Were the essential conditions those described by him? Were the essential results those described by him? If, in the conditions, some essential point was overlooked, then the results obtained do not apply to the experiment described, but to an actually different experiment, which perhaps may not bear on the hypotheses at issue, or may have an altogether different bearing from that of the purported experiment. If the described results were not the actual results; that is, if the observation was inaccurate, then again, the actual bearing of the results on the hypotheses at issue is different from the purported bearing.

The importance of repetition as a part of proof is, then, due to the necessity, in general, of certifying that the descriptions of conditions and results are accurate to the requisite degree. When another experimenter, setting up the conditions from the description of the first experimenter, obtains results which he describes in the same way as that in which the first experimenter describes his, the presumption of accuracy is enormously increased. Repetition of the experiment by the same experimenter does not have as great demonstrative value because of the possibility that the experimenter in the second experiment may not be actually following his own description, but may be following his first procedure, and therefore may vary from the description in the same way.

There is no assignable limit to the number of repetitions of an experiment which must be made before the results are to be finally accepted. In the case mentioned, no repetitions have been thought necessary. In other cases, many repetitions have been made. In some celebrated instances, the second experimenter has obtained different results because he did not actually repeat the conditions as described by the first experimenter, but performed a different experiment. This was the case when a well-known German psychologist attempted to repeat one of Ebbinghaus' experiments on the relation of the quantity of material learned to the labor learning it. The same experimenter went astray again in attempting to repeat one of Munsterberg's experiments. This persistent bungler finally gave up psychology and went into education. Another psychologist, in attempting to repeat one of my early experiments, obtained different results because he included conditions which I had specifically excluded. Mere failure to obtain the first results by repeating the experiment does not disprove the results; and, likewise, success does not constitute proof, since it is conceivable that two different experimenters might make the same errors. In any case, proof is not begun until the conditions of the experiment, as well as the results, are so accurately described that another person, from the description alone, can repeat the experiment.

The elaborate techniques of the psychological laboratory,

which cannot be reduced to general rules, but which must be learned by actual work in the laboratory upon the problems to which the techniques apply, are devices which are designed to contribute to the certification that the conditions described were the actual conditions of the experiment, and the results described were the actual results. They are vitally important because of the fact that in so far as the descriptions are accurate, the results are conclusive, since the actual results of a single experiment are universally valid for the actual conditions of the experiment.

The experimental work of the psychical researchers is not credited, because of the signal failure of these persons to describe accurately either their conditions or their results. If the results described were obtained under the actual conditions described, they would be conclusive. But every thorough examination of such experiments has shown that the descriptions are vitally inaccurate, or else important conditions are unknown, and every similar experiment under competent psychological direction has failed to show the results claimed.

I come now to a series of distinctions in psychological method which have given rise in the past to serious confusions and striking theories. This series is included under the name of *subjective* and *objective* methods; a pair of terms which designates, unfortunately, not a single distinction, but four quite different distinctions, from the confusion of which endless speculative fallacies have arisen.

In the first place, the terms have been applied to the distinction between the observation of the bodily processes of the observer himself, and the observation of the bodily processes of others. If I may observe my own eye movements, in any way, the observation, on the basis of this distinction, would be said to be *subjective*. If, on the other hand, I observe the eye movements of another man, or of a dog, the observation would be said to be *objective*.

In the second place, the distinction is drawn between observation through the "external" senses and observation through the "internal" senses; that is to say, between observation depending on teleoceptors, on the one hand, and observation depending on interoceptors and proprioceptors on the other. My direct observation of my eye movements would still be subjective; since I can observe my own eye movements only through the so-called muscular sense. (Visual observation of my eye movements, even with the aid of a mirror, happens to be impossible.) The observation of the eye movements of another man may be visual, however, and is therefore objective. I can visually observe the movements of my hand; this would be objective observation. But if I observe my hand movements as I observe my eye movements, that would be subjective observation. My observation of my pains, fatigue, and other feelings, would also be subjective, although from the physiological point of view the type of perceptual reaction is the same in all cases, the only difference being in the classification of receptors.

In the third place, the distinction is made between the direct observation of a process or object, either in myself or another, and the observation of a record mechanically derived from the process. Thus, the observation of my own eye movement or hand movement, and the observation visually of the eye movement of a rabbit or another man, are subjective; but if a motion picture of the eye movement be secured, or, in the case of the rabbit, a kymographic record be secured through the attachment of a writing lever to the rabbit's eyeball, the observation becomes objective.

In the fourth place, those who recognize the possibility of "introspection" as the observation of observation, as Stout does; or as a unique form of observation of any objects whatever, distinguish subjective observation as introspection, objective observation as non-introspective observation. The application of the terms subjective and objective actually commenced in this theoretical distinction, which still largely influences the vague meanings of the terms. Behaviorism had its start in this distinction, and in so far as it retains in any form its original metaphysical basis, it is still a branch of the introspectional or Malebranchian psychology, since without adherence to the older theory of introspection, it has no basis for distinguishing itself from regular psychology. If it abandons the introspectional hypothesis, and if it adopts rigorously the experimental methods which psychology has laboriously evolved, behaviorism becomes scientific psychology and should abandon also the now misleading term "behaviorism."

All forms of self styled "objective" psychology depend for their characterization more or less on this older flavor of the two terms subjective and objective, yet in their illustrations and arguments, they are constantly committing themselves to one or more of the other distinctions. Some "objective" psychologists may, perhaps, be willing to define the terms in this traditional way: none of them would be willing to define them in one of the only other possible ways which I have outlined. All objective psychology, therefore, stands or falls on the acceptance or rejection of Father Malebranche's metaphysics.

When properly analyzed, the distinctions between subjective and objective observation furnish no basis for methodological distinction other than that between what I have called "introspectional" psychology and "scientific" psychology. Yet the first three distinctions do supply us with important side lights on the methods which scientific psychology employs.

There is no question concerning the superiority of mechanically derived records as material for scientific study. The history of experimental psychology during the nineteenth century is a history of persistent and fruitful attempts to obtain "objective" records in place of the observation of the processes themselves. The slow accumulation and adaptation of apparatus during the last fifty years, and the progressive results of scientific imagination in devising new ways in which apparatus can be applied and records obtained, are substantial evidences of the emphasis which psychology has placed on the value of records and the study of records. The store of available apparatus is now being rapidly increased, but the string galvanometer, the motion picture camera, the audion tube, and improved light sources, are no more eagerly welcomed as gifts to our equipment for objective research than were the chronoscope, the spectroscope, and the electric motor by our predecessors in the science. The sudden interest in "objective" psychological methods of experimentation shown by some groups of psychologists and physiologists are, in large measure, nothing more than the effects of a sudden realization that the science had progressed beyond their conceptions; and the commotion they have made is a cloud of dust raised in their belated effort to catch up with the procession.

It would be a mistake, however, to suppose that records have in any sense displaced, or will displace, direct observation of human organic processes. Not merely in the preliminary observations which must be made before records can usefully be made, but also in the obtaining of records, the scientific application of direct observation is imperatively necessary. The records obtained, even in the simple reaction-time experiment, are worthless, unless based on a competent examination of the reactor's behavior: not only observation of the extent to which he is following instructions, but observation of the surrounding conditions which are essential to the interpretation of the records. The employment of mechanical records does not involve a lessening of direct observation, nor a relaxation of the technical care requisite to making such observations effective. "Objective" methods do not even lessen the need and importance of self-observation on the part of the observer or reactor, although the type and form of such observations may be modified. Animal psychology does, indeed, have to proceed without such observations, but that is just what makes the procedure of animal psychology so difficult, and the interpretation of its results so hazardous. Since not all the conditions of the experiment can be specified in animal work, the conclusions are not valid for the conditions which are specified, except on the assumption that unspecified conditions are irrelevant. And this is an assumption difficult to defend in almost every case. Human psychology can, indeed, be reduced to the level of difficulty of animal psychology; but the procedure is analogous to the crippling of a Packard to reduce it to the performance level of a Ford.

In human psychology, the difficulties of experimental observation are maximal in those phases in which the observation is through the internal sense, as determined by the interoceptors and proprioceptors. Here, the obtaining of objective records is less easy. But mere difficulty does not daunt the psychologist. Just as in animal psychology, where he must dispense with the observations of the reactor, he struggles along, under extreme difficulty, but not unprofitably; so in problems of feeling and emotion, where he has mainly the reactor's observation to depend upon, with little help from records, he must struggle along also, and not deny that the problems exist because he has difficulty in solving them. In this field, every step made in the achievement of objective records is of great assistance to the experimental work, but in this field, even more strikingly than in other fields, improvement in the objective method does not lessen the direct observational work, but rather increases it as it makes it more profitable.

Throughout experimental psychology, in short, the dependence on consciousness is definite and marked. Even in the use of objective records, the same observation which is required for the direct study of the processes directly is required for the study of the records. That visual perception is the primary form of observation depended upon in the study of records, does not mean that it is in some mysterious way holy and reliable, whereas auditory, tactual, kinesthetic and organic observation are to be cast out. All forms of observation depend upon the same type of reaction process, and there is nothing about the visual receptors which can give them an exclusive sanctity. If kinesthetic observation is fundamentally unreliable, then visual observation is likewise ineffectual, and no science, psychological or physical, is possible. The reliability of any form of observation depends on the conforming of the observation to the canons of experimental procedure.

Experimental psychology began to shake off the methodological trammels of introspectionalism twenty-five years ago and has practically completed the process. It has now freed itself from the bonds and limitations of behaviorism and other forms of so-called "objective" psychology. It has never adopted the mystical freedom from experimental methods offered by psycho-analysis. It is established on a methodological foundation which is secure and permanent; and its further progress is conditioned by the degree to which psychologists recognize and devote themselves to the established scientific methods of the laboratory, and by the intelligence and industry of psychologists in applying those methods.

CHAPTER XVI

THE APPLICATIONS OF PSYCHOLOGY TO SOCIAL PROBLEMS*

By Knight Dunlap

I have said in my first lecture that social psychology, as a definite field within the larger science, is now established. This claim may be disputed. It may be pointed out that nearly twenty-five years ago the same claim was made; and that looking back from our present orientation we can see clearly that the claim was not valid, and did not become valid for twenty years at least, in spite of the increasing number of text-books and articles appearing under the name of the alleged subject. It is not unreasonable, therefore, to be sceptical still on this point, and to doubt whether the idea of what *ought to be* is not confused with the idea of what *is*. That the mere use of the name, and the collection of miscellaneous materials under the name in texts and college courses does not establish the subject, is to be freely admitted. It is not without importance, in this connection, that so far as college courses are concerned, the greater number of those offered in the past have been offered in departments of education, philosophy, and sociology; and we can now see that the reluctance of psychologists to admit them as a part of psychology was justified. These courses, and the texts on which they were based, may have been good education, or philosophy, or sociology; we may readily leave the experts in those departments to judge of that; but they were not psychology, in spite of their use and misuse of psychological terms and conceptions.

I shall not insist, therefore, on the present changed condition in the alleged subject of social psychology, although my own conviction has been strong enough to impel me to prepare a text and issue it boldly as *Social Psychology*. There are many points of application of scientific psychology to social problems, whether these applications are to be considered as lying in a special department of the science, or as being merely an aspect of psychological application in a general development which it is useless to classify in any technical way.

The social problems to which the application of psychological results, methods and principles is necessary may, for convenience, be grouped under four heads: (1) Problems of the

*Powell Lecture in Psychological Theory at Clark University, April 22, 1925.

sex life and the family organization and functions; (2) Problems of religion and religious organization; (3) Problems of what may be briefly called civic and martial organization; (4) Problems of race and population.

To the solution of the problems gathered under these four heads must be brought in great wealth the results of general and individual psychology; and the main contributions, it seems to me, will be of five general groups. (1) General psychology must contribute information concerning the nature of the sex impulses, and the psychological factors involved in sex relationships; genetic psychology must supply the facts of the development of sex impulses and sex ideas in infancy, childhood, and youth; and individual psychology must contribute adequate information concerning individual differences in the nature and development of these factors. (2) The fundamental nature of religion must be determined with reference to the basis in human capacities, activities, desires, and other feelings on which religion develops. This contribution involves an analysis of the conditions and effects of faith; the psychological foundations and efficacy of ritual; and the nature and significance of symbols. (3) The psychological factors in groups generally must be determined, and also the specific factors or variations in factors peculiar to the different sorts of groups: temporary and permanent groups; groups of low and high organization; groups of greater or less spatial contiguity; and groups of varying temporal extension. We must determine the psychological details of the individual which make these organizations possible; we must determine the forms and varieties of organization; and also the effects which these types of group life have on the individual. (4) The principles and facts of social control must be worked out and systematized. The nature of conventions, of laws, and of standards of taste and of morals must be determined, and the methods of conserving, modifying, and abolishing these important controlling forces must be embodied not only in rules of an art, but also in principles of science. (5) In pursuance of the foregoing objectives, information must be at hand concerning the means of communication between man and man; information of a scientific character concerning language and its extension into culture.

A vast program is therefore mapped out for general, genetic, and individual psychology before anything that could be called social psychology in a final sense can be an actual achievement. Frankly, what we may call social psychology in the immediate future is but a propaedeutic to the real subject: a marshalling of the facts and principles of scientific psychology into new formations, directed towards a specific purpose, namely: their application to social problems. Since, however, the marshalling does have this specific purpose in view, the process and immediate results really belong more to the subject that is to be, than to the topic of general psychology, and it is in this sense that I should claim that social psychology has begun its work, and can be now assigned its name and rank.

A survey of the program I have laid out emphasizes the scarcity of the essential psychological materials for application to social problems. Under all of the five headings I have listed, we have a wealth of speculative opinions contributed by non-psychologists; but scientifically determined facts are few. The labor which experimental psychology has to perform towards the final establishment of social psychology is vast. The reasons for the slow development of the subject are apparent. Not until psychology became really scientific did it begin to accumulate the materials. But the path of development is now open, and the issue depends only on the usual pre-conditions of psychological productiveness: intelligence, industry, material provisions, and the tenacious clinging to scientific psychological methods.

Sex and the Family

The problems of the family constitute a large group of our social problems, and another large group consists of problems which are closely associated with these, and which have their source in those tendencies and characteristics on which the family is based. The family is, and will always be, our most important social institution, and it is also the most highly organized. Although the genetic function of the family has materially diminished with the progress of civilization, and the economic function even has lessened considerably, the psychological functions have increased, and there is every prospect that the family will continue to gain in social importance, whatever the economic and genetic changes of the future. The social problems arising from the family, and the problems surrounding it, become more complicated and more urgent as general social organization increases.

The problems of divorce, of sexual promiscuity, of sex perversions, and of prostitution, (really a form of sex perversion), appear to be the most outstanding in these groups. At the present time divorce occupies the public attention more or less constantly, and we are being subjected to continuous propaganda based on a recognition of the importance of the problems involved, and a total misunderstanding of the nature of these problems. Amazing propositions are made from pulpit and press; propositions for the solution of the problems by the panacea of legislative action, made with entire disregard of the actual conditions of family life and with no knowledge of the actual effects of legislative interference with family and personal life. In past ages, the problems of divorce and marriage may have been largely genetic and economic. Religious attitudes and moral attitudes have, as a matter of fact, been based entirely on genetic and economic grounds. At the present time, the problems are predominantly psychological, and the moral, religious and political considerations which ignore the psychological factors in sex life are not only futile, but distinctly vicious. Economic factors may, by proper efforts, be brought into harmony with psychological facts; but psychological facts cannot be abolished, and the attempt to force them into forms prescribed by unfortunate economic conditions results in perversion. Problems of promiscuity are so essentially bound up with the problems of marriage and divorce that they must be solved with and through the solution of the family problems.

Aside from the family problems which have a legal aspect, there are problems of married life which largely enter into these more obvious problems, but which are hidden from all but the gaze of the specialist who is called upon to adjust domestic disharmonies. These concrete problems, unfortunately, often fall into the hands of persons who have little psychological background, but who try to solve them on the basis of religious prejudices, or pseudo-psychological medical theories. Unfortunately, also, the psychologist who is drawn into these problems is seriously handicapped by the present lack of precise information concerning sexual desires, emotions, and tendencies, of normal human beings, and concerning the way in which these psychological factors are controlled and modified. Sweeping theories concerning sex needs and sex instincts are rife; but the actual facts for the support of these theories are scarce.

In the past, theories have been built on clinical observations, but the attempts to apply these theories have resulted in mis-

fortune and misery.   Today, we recognize that the data on
which dependence has been placed in these thories involves the
pathologist's fallacy throughout.   No one would attempt to
evaluate normal intelligence by the use of data drawn exclusively from the insane.   Yet we have attempted to evaluate normal sex life in terms of data drawn almost exclusively
from the cases of abnormal sex life who come to physicians
for treatment.   Such collections as those made by Havelock
Ellis, for example, are extremely valuable masses of data concerning the pathology of sex life; but tell us very little about
the normal man or woman.

The high organization of the family is based on the complementariness of man and woman; a complementariness which
is not merely physiological, but which is equally striking in the
psychological realm.   Although details are lacking, it is clear
that essential differences of a complementary sort exist not
only in the sexual desires and the emotional processes of an
immediately sexual sort, but also in more general emotional
attitudes of life.   That other differences, not of the complementary sort, exist, is fairly clear; for example, the cyclic
emotional changes which accompany the menstrual cycle in
woman, and from which man is entirely exempt.   Whether
any important sensory or intellectual differences, as such, exist
or not, is not clear; but since the whole process of mental life
is so strongly dependent on the emotional factor, we cannot
expect that woman's total thought processes, or her general
achievement in life will be parallel with man's, whatever her
analytically considered intellectual capacities, since her desires,
her emotions, and her interests are so different.

As an instance of the general unreliability of information
concerning sex differences in the past, we may consider two
rather general comparisons.   It has been widely believed and
taught that woman "matures" sexually a little earlier than
man, and it has also been widely held that man varies more
from his mean than does woman in respect to many characteristics.   On the former assumption, apparently, have been
based our laws and customs regarding age of marriage and age
of citizenship; the latter assumption has been embodied in the
catch phrase that woman is the conservative sex, man the
variable.

With the beginning of exact mental measurements applied
to the problem of sex differences, the first outstanding indication has been that, contrary to the catch phrase, man is less

variable than woman, at least in regard to his mental capacities. While this cannot be considered as finally demonstrated, it has the weight of experimental evidence so far. Consideration of sexual desires and sexual responsiveness shows an even more marked difference in the same direction; and it is now believed that even in physical measurements the same relationship holds. This does not mean, of course, that the *range* of variation is wider for women; we cannot say anything about that as yet; but it does mean that the average variation of a group compared with respect to a given characteristic is greater for women; that men, on the whole, lie closer to the mean.

Further examination of the question of sexual maturity has shown, first, that the term "maturity" is exceedingly vague, and, second, that the comparisons made in the past have been made on quite different kinds of sexual maturity for the two sexes. So far as any really comparable measures are concerned, there is at present no evidence that either sex "matures" earlier than the other, although the surface indications would seem to be that the male "matures" the earlier.

The whole situation clearly shows that conclusions as to sex differences must wait on actual experimental work and upon the results of information collected by scientific methods on points not subject to experimentation. Even on the side of sex behavior, conclusions cannot be drawn until we have further experimental evidence. Even in respect to the final physiological process of coitus, while we may reasonably conclude that there is only one normal type of this specific sex reaction of the male, we do not know at present whether the wide variations shown by the female are pathological, or due to habit, or are based on several distinct normal types of response.

Within the last two or three years it has been shown that the accumulation of precise information on mental sex differences is possible by the methods of experimental psychology. The outstanding difficulty in this field is merely the lack of financial provision for the necessary lengthy labor of determination. Scientifically, the way is prepared; but scientific preparation is not the only essential condition. The most important psychological problems of the family and of sex relations lie now in the experimental field.

There are, however, other points to which the data and methods of psychology must be applied. The general conditions of married life, which are not capable of experimental approach, must be studied. The effects of divorce and divorce laws on the family and on extra-marital sex life must be investigated and given proper statistical treatment. This latter problem, simple as it may seem, offers great difficulty and demands exceptional skill. It is not sufficient to show that the states with the most rigid and mediæval laws on marriage and divorce exhibit also the greatest degrees of family difficulty and the gravest conditions of extra-marital sexual life. These conditions must also be analysed with regard to differences in economic and social conditions of other sorts, and finally, in the light of the experimental evidence concerning the actual psychology of sex, without which no useful conclusions are possible.

Religion and Religious Organization

Religion and the organization growing out of religion present a group of our most serious social problems. Scientifically, we are perhaps too much inclined to look at religion as merely a problem of scientific and social inhibition, that is, as offering serious obstacles to the advancement of science, and to social progress. The recent events in the Southern states undoubtedly have accentuated this view of religion. Some scientists, at least, look upon religion as a malevolent growth upon society, which might be removed with beneficial results, and with no harmful sequellae after the shock of the operation should be over. This view, I think, is unfortunate, and adopted without due consideration of the nature of religion and its relation to general and social psychology.

In the past, the study of religion has taken three general forms: theology, the history of religion (including comparative religion), and the psychology of religion. The psychology of religion, however, has been a rather restricted topic considering mainly the religious experience as it occurs in living man. That is to say, the psychology of religion has been and is a part of general psychology, along with the psychology of music and the psychology of fatigue, and is to be treated as such. The usual experimental methods have not been fully applied, but their applications have been indicated, and there is no doubt that experimental work in this field can and should be carried out. But the results of the preliminary work so far have not been fertile. The topic remains still without vital relations to problems in other fields, and it seems to me evident that it must be fertilized by other than the general psychological methods if it is to bear fruit. What I shall here discuss is, therefore, not the psychology of religion in the accepted significance of the term, but rather what I should call the *social psychology of religion.*

It appears to me that the psychology of religion gives us little information concerning the nature of religion, its foundations in human life and experience, or its relations to our social problems. It is, in short, a subject which is in the same stage as zoölogy prior to the introduction of the hypothesis of evolution, and if we are to obtain useful information concerning the religious motives, tendencies and results, we must add to it the methods of comparative religion and archaeology. From this cross-fertilization, I believe a useful social psychology of religion may be developed.

I am not unmindful of the fact that attempts in this direction have been made. The historical interpretation of religion in terms of sex, for example, has been attempted at various times, and the efforts two generations ago of a group of men among whom Thomas Inman and Payne Knight are perhaps most familiar to American readers, reached its most spectacular point in a system of symbolism which has been bodily adopted and popularized more recently by the psycho-analysts as something new. These early attempts have been of great value, although based on feeble psychology and inadequate archaeology and anthropology. Although the conclusions are discredited and the specific theories must be abandoned, the social psychology of religion is a continuous development from the efforts of these pioneers. Perhaps the greatest damage which the Freudian movement has done has been to inhibit this development somewhat, by fostering old misconceptions and creating new ones. To be specific: while we can no longer hold the theory of Inman and Knight that religion has its basis peculiarly in the sex life, it is a fact that sex plays an important role in the development of religion, as it does in life as a whole; and while the interpretation of religious symbols by these early investigators was superficial and has not stood the test of archaeological facts, the study of symbols is nevertheless a highly important part of the social psychology of religion. When the psychologist begins to consider symbolism and sex in religion, he seems to those ignorant of the historical development, to be adopting Freudian methods and hypotheses, and he is discredited by the absurd developments to which the theories they adopted have been carried.

It is necessary on this point to free ourselves from such prejudices. The analyses and conclusions of Inman, Knight and the other early sex symbolists have not proved correct, but they are nevertheless important and useful, because these authors were making a serious attempt to combine psychology and archaeology, and their attempts must be carried forward. The fact that the Freudians adopted the theoretical conclusions of these men and proceeded to develop them fantastically in disregard of both psychology and archaeology, should not be allowed to dim the lustre of these early workers, nor detract from the usefulness of their work.

Perhaps I may indicate the problems and methodological requirements of psychology in the field of religion by an illustration. It is well known that in the evolution of the conception of divinities, female divinities come first, and that male divinities come next, and sometimes suppress the goddesses. Concerning the reasons for this order of development there are divergent views, two of which are directly opposed, namely: the theory that the elements of religion which have persisted were first developed by women, who would naturally (it is assumed) develop the conception of female divinities; and opposed to this, the theory that the essentials of religion were developed by men, who, (it is assumed) would naturally develop female divinities. Here we have off-hand interpretation running riot.

When we consider religion from the point of view of human desires in general, and not from an arbitrarily exclusive reference to a single type of desire, we find reason to suspect that food would play an enormous part in the development of religious conceptions and religious attitudes. When, further, we examine the historical and archaeological material, we find impressive support for this suspicion. Hereupon, the relation between food and sex that many students of religion have pointed out become deeply significant, and the problem of the female divinity is seen in a new light. When, in this light, we study the development of religion and of religious symbols in Mesopotamia and other regions in which the date palm was of such economic importance, we find both ancient and modern religion brightly illuminated, and begin to see what religion really means in human life.

But even by these discoveries, the problem of male and female divinities is only partly solved. We can see how the female divinities arose; but the crushing out of the goddesses by the gods requires further psychological and archaeological investigation. And the fact that the female divinity does not remain in the discard, but continually reenters religion, requires new consideration of those emotional attitudes and tendencies of men and women to which I earlier referred. These sex differences which are not opposed but complementary seem to throw new light on the goddess problem.

The goddess problem is, however, but one of the many problems which the social psychology of religion faces, and to which it must bring the results and methods of scientific psychology to apply to the data which the archaeologists have provided in increasing measure. No progress in the psychology of religion can be made except through the study of its development in its earliest ascertainable phases, and this development cannot adequately be traced except by psychological applications.

If we divide the phenomena and problems of religion into two groups; those of faith and those of "works" (*i.e.*, ritual), we find a new direction for investigation in which the most important pioneer has been Robertson Smith. Here, again, we may not incontinently accept Smith's conclusion that ritual is the primary factor, and that religious faith develops from it; but nevertheless we have to accept his problem as vital, his method as productive, and his hypotheses as useful steps towards the final development. Here, again, the problem requires the application of all the psychological material we can muster. The desires and tendencies to which ritual appeals today require analysis. The effects of ritual on further psychological processes also requires investigation, if we are to understand the development of the past, and through it the significance of the present.

In the social psychology of religion, as in many other psychological fields, a vast amount of work has already been done by those who are not primarily psychologists. I need only to add to the name of Robertson Smith those of Andrew Lang, Marett Frasier, Jevons, Budge, and Tiele, to suggest at once a whole glorious company who have analyzed data and supplied hypotheses, ideas, and methods of approach which are waiting to be welded into a vital foundation for the subject.

Religion, and especially, organized religion, is important in its effects on all social phenomena. No constructive program in regard to the family, education or any other feature of social organization can be taken up without discovering that the church has to be considered and its influence taken into practical account. But beyond this, religion has a social importance, because it is apparently founded on permanent tendencies of the human mind. It supplies something that man apparently needs. Whether these needs can be supplied better than they are at present; that is, whether religion itself cannot be improved psychologically; or whether, as some think, the needs can be cured, are matters that can be decided only after the real nature of religion has become better understood than it is at present.

General Social Organization

The general principles of social organization are fairly well understood at present. The age of glittering generalities has passed away, and we no longer make the attempt to explain social life by merely classifying activities under such heads as imitation, suggestion, crowd mind, and instincts. Spencer and Schaffle have done their work; and while we avoid their conclusions, we have made use of their methods. As we study the interrelation of details in the animal organization and attempt to arrive at an understanding of its integrative action without falling back on a single magic life principle; so we attempt to study social groups, in which the total activity of the integrated mechanism is understood from the characteristics and potentialities of the component individuals, without falling back on a magic principle in this case either. Without committing the error of considering social groups as exactly analogous to animal organisms, we have not neglected to make use of the partial analogy. We have not been carried away by the doctrine of McDougall that the group is more than the sum of its constituent members, and we recognize no social minds except the minds of individuals in the social groups. In other words, we apply to group psychology the results and principles of general psychology, studying the conscious reactions of the individual to the group environment as we study his reactions to any other environment, and finding in these reactions at least all the complexity we find in his reactions to inanimate objects.

We find grades of social organization corresponding somewhat to grades of organization of animal bodies. We find those in which all the individuals have much the same functions; and we find "higher" forms of organization in which specialization of function brings about greater dependence of one member on the others and greatly increases the efficiency of total action of the group. We find continuous gradations of types from the temporary and fortuitous crowd to the more permanent states, armies, and industrial organizations. I think we may say that the basic principles of group development and group function are well established, and there is left only the vast amount of detailed data to be gathered on the specific action of these principles in specific cases. Here there is plenty of room for the application of psychological principles, but the main interest is in the ascertaining of the way in which these principles work out. And in this field the hasty application of principles without knowing the exact conditions to which they are applied is especially dangerous. I shall illustrate my points here by two examples only.

Group action is controlled in part by conventions, which are in some instances made the basis for laws. I shall not attempt to show the place of a convention in our fundamental scheme of reaction-psychology, into which it fits without difficulty. I shall consider the effects of laws which are broken, that is, which do not represent a convention actually accepted by the individual.

Americans are notoriously a lawbreaking people. Among the vast mass of statutes which we legally adopt and contemptuously disregard, the Volstead act is a mere minor detail. Fish and game laws are notoriously intended for the other fellow. In some states elaborate Sunday laws exist, and are unanimously broken, even publicly broken by many of the individuals who are active in keeping the laws on the statute books. Speed laws are mere joyous scraps of paper, and automobile manufacturers do not hesitate to boost their wares by advertising them as capable of speeds much higher than any state legalizes. Some states have recently passed laws requiring all motor cars to come to a full stop at all railroad crossings; and in those states I have not yet heard of any one who stops if he does not think a constable is in view. Laws against gambling in various forms are common; and are not regarded by anyone who has no conscientious scruples against taking a chance.

All this seems to constitute a serious situation. And it is doubly serious in that many of these dead laws are enforced occasionally on those who are poor and without influence. Negro crap games are raided; but not the bridge and poker games of well-to-do people. Foreigners and poor folks are from time to time arrested and fined for working on Sunday; but not their wealthier or better-class fellow citizens. The occasional speeder arrested is impressed principally by the fact that hundreds of others get away with their joyriding. It may be argued that a contempt for law and for the rights of other people is built up by these laws which are unjustly enforced. But there is another factor in this general lawbreaking which must be considered, even when the attempted enforcement of law is as impartial as possible. Do we form habits of law breaking which are transferred from one law to another? Does the practice of breaking speed laws, game laws, Sunday laws, and numerous other laws, make us more liable to break laws against theft, malicious mischief, and adultery, than we would be if these generally infracted laws did not exist? Certain publicists claim that this transfer of the law-breaking habit actually occurs. But as a matter of fact, this question cannot be so simply settled. We have no basis for the application of simple laws of habit to complicated situations without a comprehensive study of the situation itself, and in regard to this particular situation no study as yet made is sufficient for the validation of the conclusion. Here is really a problem for experimental solution.

Another problem or series of problems is to be found in the field of propaganda. An important part of social control is in the transmission of ideas; in the causing of other men to adopt or accept ideas which are presented to them. This transmission of ideas, or propaganda, is important in the whole field of social relations. It is essential in religious proselyting, political campaigning and commercial advertising. It is the method of modifying conventions, and bringing about the passage of laws. It extends to fashions of dress and moral principles. We know already the general principles underlying propaganda; we know the mental processes in the individual through which the copying and acceptance of ideas are possible; we know the forms in which ideas must be presented; we know the general methods of obtaining the necessary attention to the ideas with the minimal arousal of opposing ideas. We know that logic and reasoning play but minor parts in this whole process. All these factors are reducible to rules as definite as the rules of composition in printing, and the rules can be illustrated point by point from the accepted procedure in advertising. Nevertheless, we do not know the exact extent to which reasoning is effective in propaganda, nor do we know the exact conditions, in relation to other factors, under which reasoning is best applied to the work. Undoubtedly the detailed methods of propaganda which are most effective with certain classes of society are not the most effective with other classes. But precision in planning and application of programs of propaganda to these different classes is not yet possible. Here again are very definite points for experimental and analytical research; research which it is by no means simple to plan and carry out.

But there is another sort of problem of propaganda which has as yet been hardly touched. Under present conditions we are continually subjected to propaganda of a great variety of types. Obviously, the public needs orientation in the methods of withstanding this propaganda. Even commercial advertising has reached the stage of a social nuisance, and is a serious drain on the economics of trade and industry. The application of psychological principles has reached a level of efficiency at which psychologists are scarcely justified in offering courses in the psychology of advertising, but should rather offer courses in how to withstand the appeal of advertisements.

In all social organization, the means of communication between man and man are of the utmost importance. The most important means is, of course, language. Language, as we have seen, is the vehicle of thought as well as of communication, and hence psychology has much to offer on the various problems concerning the use of language. But language is not merely a matter of words with accepted meanings—that is, with standardized reaction patterns to them. Verbal language is a step to culture, and we may with a few words convey richer and more precise meaning to those who share a common culture than we could communicate with a vastly greater verbiage to those who lack the culture. History, art, and literature, are instruments of culture; mediums of communication between man and man, and important solely for that reason. Cultures differ in different levels of society, and culture changes from age to age. Latin and Greek are no longer the cultural topics they once were; chemistry and biology have risen enormously in cultural value. But not all portions of these subjects have the same cultural value, and the determination of the maximal cultural efficiency which can be extracted from them is a serious and worthy problem. Moreover, it is probable that the maximum of cultural efficiency can be attained by certain combinations of these different topics; *which* particular combinations, we ought to determine. College courses and school courses are today largely matters of guesswork, so far as their cultural aspects are concerned, whatever may be the case with their vocational aspects. It should be the business of psychology to make these needed determinations, and psychology ought to be in a position to assume this business, now that it has brought thinking and communication together and illuminated each with the other.

Population

Problems of population have harassed the human race since its earliest history, and it is evident that these problems run back into the legendary period of human development. In the past, these problems were the concern of priests and rulers; but of late they have become a part of the concern of scientific men. The interests of the priesthood are today as active as ever in the original phase of the problem, and ecclesiatical attitudes are by no means a negligible factor in the more recent phases. The church, from the ancient Greek, Roman and Jewish times, has asserted its right to control human sex relations, and has increased rather than diminished its claims in the modern Christian period. In these matters the church is still so powerful in the very quarters where the practical handling of the population problem is most difficult, that it is really one of the major considerations for any program which may be contemplated. The program which succeeds in gaining ecclesiastical approval has the best chance for immediate extension.

Rulers and governmental authorities are as much concerned with population problems as ever they were, and the forms of their problems have become more complex. The operations of governmental agencies in these matters have been so futile; and government itself is so subject to the influence of plain facts, that the civic power offers little obstacle to progress, and much possibility of assistance, except in so far as ecclesiastical power dominates the government, which it still does to a considerable extent.

The problems which may usefully be classed under the general head of problems of population are capable of distribution in two groups, namely: problems of eugenics and problems of over-population. The psychological aspects of these problems are intimately connected with the more general problems of group psychology, and specifically, with racial psychology, and it is the last topic that I propose to discuss first.

Racial psychology is, at the present time, largely a pious wish, and the imposing contributions which have been made to the subject so far are fairly well described by the Freudian cant term: "wish fulfillment." These contributions, we should note, are numerous and extensive. Many of them have been made by sociologists and others, including a few psychologists, under the specific title of race psychology; but vastly more numerous are the contributions which have been made by historians under the plausible caption of history. Reassured by their success in writing psychology under the name of history, some of the historians come out boldly and write more, and worse, under the name of psychology, or the name of some topic drawn from that subject. But any school teacher, doctor, minister, employment manager, novelist, character-analyst, newspaper writer, psycho-analyst, sociologist, spiritualist or real estate agent may confer on himself the title of psychologist in these days, so that it must be understood that the racial psychology I am attempting to discuss is "psychology" only as understood by a relatively small group of persons who are dubbed in derision "Academic" psychologists by the larger group self-styled "psychologists" who occupy a much larger share of the public interest—and who make practically all the profits.

I am not unmindful of the small but growing body of experimental work which has quietly been done by the real psychologists towards the analysis of racial characteristics. I shall not allude specifically to any piece of this, however, since my purpose is a somewhat wider one.

The problems of racial psychology are two-fold. First, we want to know how the minds of the various races actually work. This involves, of course, the examination of the sensory processes, as well as of the thinking processes, feelings and emotions, learning, and motor control. In addition, we want to know the hypotheses or beliefs, and the ideals or standards held by these races, for these are not only results of psychological processes, but actual determiners of those processes.

Some of these facts may be gleaned from the literatures and from the languages themselves, if we can actually subject these data to psychological analysis. For some of the ancient peoples, such as the Greeks and Egyptians, materials for study exist, and may be made use of by the proper combination of psychology, archaeology and philology. For the so-called primitive peoples, who have left no literatures, the materials do not exist.

The other source of information is manifestly the careful observation, measurement, and experimental study of the peoples themselves. For the rapidly vanishing savage races, theoretically this might still be done, although such study would, of course, give us little information, except in the field of anthropometry, of the characteristics of these races before they were so largely modified by the white man; and the observations recorded by explorers, missionaries, and commercial agents of the past, we know are of little real value. But such opportunity as may exist will, in all probability, pass away before any use can be made of it, and we shall probably not know the mental characteristics of even the American Indian, although we may know the worthlessness of the vast amount of junk that has been written about him.

Leaving out the savage and so-called primitive races as hopeless problems, it would seem that we might at least acquire some information about the races which exist in Europe and Asia, and adhere to their own methods of life in spite of contacts with others, and which promise to persist as races for many years to come—perhaps even longer than we shall. But how long it will be before we acquire any useful information, and whether it will be useful by the time we get it, are open questions.

The magnitude of the problem of obtaining an actual comparison of the mentality of two races is almost appalling. Assuming that we had developed measures for the mental factors in which we are interested—and this is a bold and pretentious assumption—the program of applying such measures on a scale comprehensive enough to be of real significance is so great that no organization capable of carrying it out is in existence, nor can the means of bringing it about be foreseen. But let us make another large assumption, and assume that even this obstacle has been overcome. What we would then have would be a comparison of the two races under the conditions of their physical and social environments. We would know, for example, how the French in present day France compare with the English in present day England. An important and interesting stage of information, it is true, but not the information which is most desired. We would not know how these races would compare when subjected to the same physical and cultural environments for a complete generation; and this is what we really want to know for purposes of immigration, of eugenics, and of social progress generally. We would not even know how they would compare physically under such uniform conditions.

It would have been of little use to compare the Romans with the British in the period from 50 B. C. to 50 A. D., unless the total conditions of human development were so well known that it could be predicted what changes would be wrought by changes in food, in other modes of life, and by the absorption of the Roman and Greek cultures by the British. And we can as little tell from the reactions of the French people today what the reactions of their descendants will be when the French modes of life and culture may have been greatly modified.

It would seem, however, that in America there is a chance to study the mental development (and the physical development, too) of diverse races under the same physical and cultural conditions. And perhaps something may be accomplished along this line, if a sufficiently large number of trained workers can be secured, along with sufficiently gigantic sums of money. Theoretically, we should be able to measure the minds of groups of American born and bred of pure Italian, Irish, Scandinavian, Czecho-Slovakian, Greek, Turkish and other blood (in so far as any of these races are pure), who have grown up in sufficiently similar physical and social environments; and so we might arrive at the solution of the question as to what may be accounted for by racial differences alone.

Practically, it would not be possible to do anything of the kind. We know that the peoples of different races in the United States live under essentially different conditions of food, occupation, and culture for several generations; and that as the essential conditions become uniformized these races intermarry, and so the racial "purity" is lost. That the environment of the different races in the United States is different so long as they remain separate races is most clearly shown by reference to the Jews, who are born, reared, and grow old in an essential atmosphere of Jewishness which makes it possible to say that any "Jewish" mental trait, if such can be demonstrated, is racial in the hereditary sense, or merely cultural, that is, hereditary in the social sense only.

Or, take the negroes, on whom several excellent studies of

mentality have been made in a small way. Even if it were possible to make the comprehensive and exact studies we are assuming to be possible, we would have as a result the pattern of the negro's mind as he is: reared, and trained, and his ideals developed, in a physical and social environment distinctly different from that in which the whites are developed. It may perhaps be predicted by some one that at some time in the future it will be possible to study a large body of negroes whose essential environment has, from birth up, been practically the same as that of a large body of whites with whom they may be compared. But it is necessary to bear in mind that if such a condition is realized in any group the "negroes" in the group will not be *negroes;* they will not even be half breeds.

But all this is speculation on the basis of an assumption that requires detailed consideration. Manifestly we have no such measures as those we have been assuming. When will they be developed? I myself am an optimist on this point: I think that we will develop a reasonably adequate battery of such measures relatively soon—perhaps in a hundred years or so. We have a few simple tests now, and these can be extended and added to progressively if we can manage to keep some psychologists on the job of development for a sufficient time. But my optimism begins to rip at the seam when I consider the fact that is hard to keep even a small body of competent investigators at scientific work along this line. The workers who might be laboring in the field are lured away by the siren of application and waste their time and energies in efforts to extend the application of measures which are well enough as clinical expedients, but which should be merely stepping stones to the end in view.

Some people actually seem to think, in short, that the vast problems we face are adequately to be solved by intelligence tests. Now, the intelligence test is all well enough as a means of grading people roughly for certain purposes, when the tests are devised for the specific practical ends to which they are to be applied, and standardized empirically. And the intelligence test might have been a valuable tool with which to carve out other tools of service for the measure of attainments with respect to actual mental standards. What the intelligence test does, when sagaciously applied to a group who have been all trained for a certain purpose (such as banking or entering college), is to measure (very roughly) the extent to which the training for that purpose has been successful. In short, the intelligence test is a trade test, and nothing more, and is most efficient when developed and applied with reference to trades as specific as possible, whether the trade is that of being a college student or a typesetter. But because the intelligence test measures directly only the results of training, and measures with adequacy only training of very specific and limited sorts, its possibilities as an instrument for the solving of problems of racial psychology are very limited, and it can never be more than a minor aid in this work. It seems probable, however, that in the immediate future there will be a considerable flood of supposed contributions on racial differences based on intelligence tests, which will make necessary a painful and dangerous cleaning-up process later.

The problem of psychology, in regard to the field of racial psychology, is not difficult to find, but it hardly lies in that field as yet. We must keep on with the difficult work of developing measures of mental function, and set our faces against the naive and hasty applications of the undeveloped measures as firmly as we set against the conclusions from the simple and uncritical observations with which treatises on racial psychology have hitherto been filled. On a basis of sound experimental work and sound mental measurements, racial psychology may some day be established.

The psychological problems of eugenics and the psychological problems of overpopulation are essentially connected, and both are complicated by the situations we have just discussed.

Eugenics has a positive and a negative program: the promotion of the reproduction of the fit, and the repression of the reproduction of the unfit. But apparently, the positive program is a failure, since no means have been found for the promotion of propagation beyond the rate at which it progresses without encouragement, except the promotion brought about by a reduction of the total population relative to its natural resources and cultural ideals. Propaganda and bonuses, and all other artificial stimulations, are apparently entirely ineffectual. The reasons for this ineffectualness are fairly obvious and we need not pause on them. The relief of the pressure of population, on the other hand, affects all classes, and probably the unfit especially, so that the negative program is doubly important. Moreover, any increase of reproductive rate might be at the present time an evil in itself, since it would add to the present overpopulation.

Since eugenic fitness is a matter of mentality as well as of physique, one problem for the psychologist is outlined: the determination of mental fitness. And here the problem is largely yet to be solved. One class of the unfit, the feeble minded may well be detected by the Binet-Simon tests. But no one could reasonably maintain that the feeble minded are the only mentally unfit from the eugenic point of view. And the determination of the other types, if any, is yet to be made, and the means for their detection developed. It is not merely a matter of the development of measures for emotional and moral deficiency, and for instability, for example: but the determination of the types of deficiency which are fatally hereditary. In this determination the psychologist and the geneticist must work hand in hand, and the psychologist must avoid the genetic use of crude and hastily constructed tests or mere casual observation, such as have, unfortunately, been applied in the genetic field.

At the other end of the scale, the problem is more difficult, if not impossible. The really superior mentality is much more difficult to determine than the really defective. Moreover, if the really superior in some one line is determined, it *may* not be the fittest eugenically: for it *may* carry with it defects in some other line. That we should breed through "genius" is by no means established; perhaps we should breed around it. Happily, this problem of the "fittest" is of no serious consequence eugenically, since the positive program, as I have said before, is impractical.

But having determined, let us assume, the unfit, the matter of their elimination from reproduction is now the question. The lethal method we may consider inapplicable. Sterilization has also turned out to be impracticable, at least in the present social condition. Segregation covers but a fraction of the problem. Prohibition of marrying is merely a form of legal humor, and prohibition of mating can be enforced only on the most unfit and by segregation, sterilization, or death. What, then, is the possibility for an actual eugenic program? Apparently nothing but contraception. And here we run up against psychological problems of a new sort, and of great difficulty.

The problems concerning contraception are of two sorts: those which concern the actual effects of the practice, and those concerning the undoubtedly strong popular feeling against it. The physical problems of the effects of the practice are simple, and the difficulties uncovered by the analysis of the problems are relatively simple also; and there is today no serious doubt that these difficulties could be overcome. On the psychological side the problems are more complicated. The psychological effects of the practice are not definitely known, but are matters still for conjecture and biased belief. This problem is one not to be solved in an easy way, but it must be solved. The question, moreover, as to how different classes of society will react to a fuller knowledge of more efficient and physiologically harmless methods of birth control, is one which must be settled by expert psychological analysis. We know what classes today are practicing family limitation, but we have only theories as to which sections of the classes not practicing it today will practice it to a relatively greater extent than others under conditions of more general extension. We know that among other classes, the feeble minded are not practicing contraception, and will not practice it under present conditions. To what extent they would practice it under improved conditions of cheapness and convenience is the question. I may believe that the eugenically inferior classes will tend to eliminate themselves through contraception, if conditions are made easy for them; but I may be entirely wrong. Actual experimentation would be possible in this field only through embarking blindly on a supposed eugenic problem in order to determine by the results whether it would be actually eugenic, dysgenic, or neither. It is possible, however, that information concerning the reproductive desires of various classes of the population can be obtained in advance of the entering upon such a social program. If so, the information must be gathered by psychologists.

It must be admitted, I think, that the present experimental methods of psychology are inadequate for these problems. As a substitute, the questionary method has been adopted to a certain extent, and I think that some useful material may actually be gathered in this way, although such materials will never be final data, but merely orientational and suggestive. Obviously, some method must be devised that will be of the type which is designated by the vague and misleading term "objective": I have earlier suggested the use of the theatre in such problems, and I think that "objective" material may be gathered which can be statistically treated; but the planning and ordering of the work will require much preliminary analysis. Furthermore, the problem turns on the question of there being a really fundamental distinction between two classes of desires, both sexual in the broad sense, which I have called "reproductive" and "amatory." It does not turn on the question as to the ultimate nature of these or of any other desires.

Another problem, fundamentally involved in the one just outlined, concerns the relation of reproductive desire to stock values. I have an idea that there is a rather definite connection here; that the tendency to reproductive desire is inheritable (in the usual sense of the term); and that the stocks which have the stronger reproductive desire are fundamentally the best stocks in several respects. This, however, is a psychogenetic assumption which must be tested.

The problem of the relation of amatory desire to stock values is a different, but essentially related problem. As I understand it, the notions of some stock breeders are strongly in accord with such an assumption. But among the lower animals, the effective force of reproductive desire is not separable from the effective force of amatory desire; and the same condition largely holds for the human race, so long as contraception is not practiced. But as soon as contraception is introduced, the effects of these desires is dissociated, and the merely amatory desire becomes negligible as a reproductive factor. In fact, it is probable that the reproduction tendency would be lessened, with increasing strength of amatory desire, even if the reproductive desire were not weakened. This possibility introduces a serious eugenic problem, since we do not know whether or not the amatory desire is linked with other tendencies which are of value to the stock, or whether certain valuable tendencies may not even be directly based on the amatory tendencies.

The second group of problems I mentioned above must also be solved if contraception as a eugenic measure is to be seriously considered. The extent and force of the prejudice against contraception are manifestly great. These prejudices would have to be overcome or circumvented, if the practice of contraception were to have eugenic effects. Here, the work of the psychologists would be distinctly in the applied field, and would depend upon an adequate analysis of the causes of the prejudice.

Admittedly, the basis of the prejudices is fear, of two sorts. First: a fear that one's group will be overcome by other groups that reproduce more rapidly; overcome either in war, or else by a more gradual crowding out. This is distinctly a phase of group psychology, dependent on group pride and group feeling of more general sorts. Second: a religious fear of punishment in another world for disobeying a command of the church. The church, however, in promoting this fear, is motived by the same group feelings which are powerful in all other groups. That church whose members reproduce most rapidly has the best chance of survival and growth. This organized opposition of a powerful group which is fighting for its life is admittedly the most serious obstacle to eugenic contraception.

The "will-to-live" of a group (I use this philosophical term with apologies) is a remarkable thing, but is something to be reckoned with. It is manifested in groups of all kinds, and sets the interests of the group above the more strictly individual interests, even where these are in conflict. Aside from the religious groups, its most striking manifestation is in civic groups. The denizens of the modern great cities are proud of their cities' over-growth, and will foster it even at serious individual expense. In spite of the rapid increase in taxes, in rentals and other prices, and the decrease in the general comforts of living which are entailed by overgrowth, the people want it. The inhabitants of Baltimore, for example, outside of a small class of real estate dealers, and speculators whose specific interests are in the exploitation of overgrowth, would benefit very largely if the city should actually shrink a little: yet they are unanimously anxious for rapid growth, and are cast down if their city grows less rapidly than some rival city.

When, to this group mania, you add the religious notion of an other-worldly value in the growth of an organization, the dangerous side of group spirit becomes accentuated. Here is a psychological problem of extreme difficulty, in the face of which one may almost despair.

On the hopeful side, however, we may note that this group tendency has no moral foundation; no basis in the essential necessity of regarding the rights of others, the obligation which binds man to man in all groups above the lowest stage of organization. This is the weak spot in group pride at which the tendency can be attacked.

Every member of the group is anxious for his group to grow, but is perfectly willing that the growth shall be at the expense of other individuals in the group rather than at his own cost. Few opponents of contraception feel a personal duty to reproduce, but feel, rather, a strong desire that other members of the group shall do the reproducing. This fact is strikingly exemplified in the practices of the religious monks and nuns, who, while teaching the sin of non-reproduction, produce no children themselves. Of course, this apparent inconsistency is defended by making a distinction between not marrying, and not marrying reproductively; but this bit of sophistry deceives no one, and general failure of the group-members to mate would exterminate the group as rapidly as would mating contraceptively, and would be as definitely denounced if it threatened.

The same separation of personal practice from group feeling is just as evident outside the church. And inside of the church, as well as out, individuals practice contraception in complete disregard of their group principles and group prejudices. In so far as they are inhibited in the practice they are inhibited by just three things. First: by the individual reproductive desire in its relations to economic status and cultural ideals. Second: by the lack of information, or lack of the means, of contraception. Third: by the personally objectionable features of such means as the individuals may possess.

The prejudices against contraception are therefore more largely to be circumvented than to be overcome, if contraception does turn out to be a commendable eugenic measure. The circumvention is possible through the devising of means of contraception which have not the actual physiological and psychological objections which attach to present day means; and through methods of popular education which are slowly possible in spite of religious prejudices. The first problem must be solved first; but there is no doubt of the success of the experimental work now under way in foreign countries. Even in this problem, the psychological factors are paramount; and the second problem is distinctly one in which applied psychology must play a large role, if the program is really desirable.

All these problems lead to, and in part depend upon, the problem of overpopulation. Years ago, Malthus pointed out the fatal dangers of overpopulation, but his views were shortly discredited through the opening up of vast tracts of land previously unavailable for the support of European peoples. These tracts were opened up by the invention of the steamboat, the locomotive, and modern harvesting and manufacturing machinery. Now that the pressure of population is again acute, and white men are getting a bit squeamish about slaughtering inferior peoples in order to take their lands, and there is clearly no New World to conquer, the importance of Malthus' contribution has been recognized, and the fact, rather than the danger, of overpopulation is admitted. We know that war is caused almost entirely by overpopulation, and that future war is inevitable if the pressure of population is not relieved. We know that our problems of crime and vice are accentuated by overpopulation. We know that while the land may be made to produce vastly more than it does, the labor required for the increase, increases in a much higher ratio than the produce. We know that the culture of a crowded population must decline, even if war is miraculously averted. Specifically, we know that the social problems of the United States would be greatly lessened, and the value of life to the individual inhabitants greatly increased, if the total population could be materially decreased in the next ten years, instead of increased. Worse yet, we know that the available mineral resources of the world are approaching definitely a time of exhaustion, and the soil itself wasted through too extensive cultivation and denuding of forests. And knowing all this, we are beginning to take a tardy interest in the ways and means of reducing population.

The changed methods of warfare which make the prospect of the next war appalling are important influences in determining the new interest in the problems of population: yet I should like to point out that these new methods of warfare are the only means which could delay the final catastrophe, if we do not take other intelligent measures.

In the past, warfare has been necessarily attended by, and based on, vast destruction of natural resources. The destruction of human life has been of little consequence, if any, except to the individuals themselves. But the natural resources destroyed are not replaceable.

When the Assyrians, urged on by over-population of their territories, slaughtered the inhabitants of other lands which they needed, they not only destroyed the buildings and other accumulations of culture, but cut down the vital date palm trees and even the forests. That this was an essential detail of their method of warfare, numerous inscriptions show. Similar methods of destruction were employed by all ancient nations, so that not only the easily replaceable population but also the accumulations of culture were destroyed. And this in many cases was an irreplaceable loss. In the recent conflict, the destruction of mines and machinery and noble specimens of architecture was an essential practical detail of war, and the loss to the world if the Germans had succeeded in demolishing London can hardly be grasped. But still more serious was the irreplaceable loss of metals, especially copper, sunk in the sea and blown into fragments in munitions. This one war took an enormous amount from the steadily shrinking inheritance of our descendants.

But all this will be changed. In another war, by the use of gas, a great city will be taken by the poisoning or asphyxiation of its inhabitants without the injury of a fresco or a linotype machine, and with slight loss of metals. The next war will reduce the pressure of population by mass destruction; but the resources and the accumulations of man will be but slightly diminished. In this respect, chemical warfare will be of incalculable benefit. But on the other hand, war is inevitable so long as the over-population is not alleviated in some other way. The advances of humanitarianism and medical science have but made the conditions worse and accelerated the coming of conflict. Plagues and pestilences, formerly of such service in keeping population down, are being brought under control, and the yellow peril and the perils of all other colors thereby exaggerated. It is a serious question whether the extension of "public hygiene" to Asiatic and African countries is something to be proud of, or another social crime.

I have touched on but a few of the social problems which demand the attention of the psychologist and which depend upon the applications of psychology for their solution. In attacking these problems, we need to make use of the methods and results of general, experimental and individual psychology. In other words, the foundations must be laid in that psychology which is distinctly a biological science. But as we go on towards the solution of our problems we need other conceptions and other methods. The work passes rapidly out of the field of the natural sciences, and becomes more and more affiliated with what are sometimes called the social sciences, and the methods of philology, ethics, political science, and social anthropology become more and more essential. Yet the work is so definitely dependent on its psychological foundations that it still remains psychology. If, in the light of the foregoing discussion, we again ask whether social psychology is a real and distinct subject, the answer, it seems to me, must be in the affirmative. Social psychology is to be distinguished from the more fundamental parts of psychology in that it is a social science, rather than a biological science.

PART VI

Psychologies Called "Structural"

MADISON BENTLEY

CHAPTER XVII

THE PSYCHOLOGIES CALLED "STRUCTURAL": HISTORICAL DERIVATION*

By Madison Bentley

My earliest memory of the newspaper cartoon represents a wide circle of men, all facing outward and each pointing to his neighbor on the right. The cartoonist meant to represent, as I recall, a ring of Tammany politicians surrounding "Boss Tweed." Each is charged with the theft of the city's treasury and each denies his own culpability, pointing to his neighbor as the guilty man. If we ask today who represents the psychology of 'structure,' I doubt whether we shall find anyone to acknowledge that his own brand is of that kind; though the epithet will often be accompanied by a gesture of indication toward a fellow-psychologist. We should all agree that no one in this country has done so much to expound the doctrine as Professor Titchener has; but he has not for some time researched or written under its rubrics and he explicitly remarked some time ago that, in his opinion, "both 'functional' and 'structural,' as qualifications of 'psychology,' are now obsolete terms."[1]

Notwithstanding the fact that the concept of structure, as it has been used to designate a point of view and a method in psychology, is no longer to be regarded as current in our phraseology, the contributions made to the science under its name, as well as the influence which it has exerted upon psychology at large, seem to justify a serious consideration of its meaning and its value. Thus I have accepted your generous invitation to add the psychologies called 'structural' to the other species and varieties which you have already considered in earlier lectures.

In a brilliant essay in 1884[2] the late William James was urging the importance of what he called the *transitive* (as set against the more permanent *substantive*) parts of the stream of consciousness. The transitive parts had been overlooked, as he thought, in the English and German conceptions of the idea

---

*Powell Lecture in Psychological Theory at Clark University, January 5, 1926.
[1] *Amer. J. Psychol.*, 1921, 32, 533.
[2] On some omissions of introspective psychology, *Mind*, 1884, 9, 1-26.

or *Vorstellung*. Instead of gluing ideas together by some out-side force or principle, such as 'reason,' 'intelligence,' 'association' or the 'ego,' James proposed to make the stream real and to complete it by filling in such transitive parts as the feeling of 'and' and the feeling of 'but'; in short, by adding to consciousness something like Herbert Spencer's 'feelings of relation.' "There is no evidence whatsoever (he says) for supposing the pure atomic ideas of red and yellow, and the other elements of mental structure, to exist at all—no one of them is an actual psychic fact." They are only qualities of the outer world; the mental vehicle by which we think them is a "feeling representing a highly complex object, that quality in relation with something else" (p. 9). Instead of separate and discrete elements James proposes to account for the continuity and coherence of our knowledge by a like fluent continuity in the conscious 'stream' or the stream of 'feelings.' Thus he comes to the distinction between the 'subjective constitution' of the 'stream' and the 'cognitive functions' which the 'feelings' subserve (p. 11). The contrast between feeling, on the one hand, and thought or knowledge, on the other, is not a difference between passive sense and creative intellect. The contrast is rather (to quote James's phrase) "between two *aspects,* in which all mental facts without exception may be taken, their structural aspect, as being subjective, and their functional aspect as being cognitions. In the former aspect, the highest as well as the lowest is a feeling, a peculiarly tinged segment. This tingeing is its sensitive body, the *wie ihm zu Muthe ist,* the way it feels whilst passing. In the other aspect, the lowest mental fact as well as the highest may grasp some bit of truth as its content, even though that truth were as relationless a matter as a bare unlocalized and undated quality of pain. From the cognitive point of view (he continues), all mental facts are intellections. From the subjective point of view all are feelings. Once admit that the passing and evanescent are as real parts of the stream as the distinct and comparatively abiding; once allow that fringes and halos, inarticulate perceptions, whereof the objects are as yet unnamed, mere nascencies of cognition, premonitions, awarenesses of direction, are thoughts *sui generis,* as much as articulate imaginings and propositions are; once restore, I say, the *vague* to its psychological rights, and the matter presents no further difficulty.

"And then we see that the current opposition of Feeling to

Knowledge is quite a false issue. If every feeling is at the same time a bit of knowledge, we ought no longer to talk of mental states differing by having more or less of the cognitive quality; they only differ in knowing more or less, in having much fact or little fact for their object. The feeling of a broad scheme of relations is a feeling that knows much; the feeling of a simple quality is a feeling that knows little. But the knowing itself, whether of much or of little, has the same essence, and is as good knowing in the one case as in the other. Concept and image, thus discriminated through their objects, are consubstantial in their inward nature, as modes of feeling. The one, as particular, will no longer be held to be a relatively base sort of entity, to be taken as a matter of course, whilst the other, as universal, is celebrated as a sort of standing miracle, to be adored but not explained. Both concept and image, *qua* subjective, are singular and particular. Both are moments of the stream, which come and in an instant are no more. The word universality has no meaning as applied to their psychic body or structure, which is always finite. It only has a meaning when applied to their use, import, or reference to the kind of object they may reveal" (pp. 18-19, footnote).

It is a curious fact that this *locus classicus* for the psychological distinction between *structure* and *function* should be lodged in a footnote and should be reproduced in the same form in the chapter on Conception in the *Principles of Psychology* of 1890 (vol. i. 478-479). I do not remember that James elsewhere makes use in his psychological writings of the term 'structure'; although his whole descriptive account of 'feelings' and 'thoughts,' of unfringed and fringed segments of consciousness, of the 'psychic body' and its cognitive meaning or function, is logically constitutive of his entire treatment. This neglect of an important pair of terms which he seems to have introduced into our literature, appears to be explained by the fact that his own main interest lay in cognition and in epistemological problems. James excelled, as we all know, in a keen, flashing kind of observation (though continued and consistent scrutiny under experimental conditions irked him); and we owe to him a large amount of inspective information upon the transitive and fleeting aspects of experience. But, even here, the 'feelings' chiefly interest him for the cognitive functions which they carry and much less for their own existential form or, as he puts it, their "substantive mental kernel-of-content," their "psychic body" or "structure." It is also worth noting, as we pass, that the men stamped and impressed by James's teachings have seldom made use of this fundamental distinction and still more rarely have they added to the structure or the existential side of experience. Only Angell, as I recall, has taken seriously the distinction; though he used it, as we shall presently see, in quite a different context.

Now if we turn toward the progress of psychology upon the continent, we shall find still earlier than James a distinction which bears as directly upon our approach to the psychologies called 'structural' as does James. The setting of the two distinctions, however, is different. Instead of the two parallel aspects, structural and functional, we now find psychology taking, at the hands of different psychologists and within the framework of different systems, the two general directions which we might expect from James's distinction. This divergence appears in Brentano's empirical psychology of *act* and Wundt's experimental psychology of *observed process*.[3] Brentano's fundamental facts are, as you know, activities, the activities of ideating, judging and loving-hating. The differentia of these psychical activities is their reference to an object, a relation to a content. This 'immanent objectivity' is never to be found in physical phenomena. Wundt's fundamental facts, on the other hand, are directly drawn from the observation of the processes of life. Physiology views life, so to say, from the outside; but psychology from the inside. The psychical side of life, as it is immediately given, is complex; and the primary function of psychology is therefore to analyse it into its simpler—ultimately into its elementary—parts or processes. So far as logic goes, this psychical side of life is James's existential or structural side; though James was quick to contend that it was no more subject to dismembering by analysis than is the fluent water in the stream. To dismember was, for him, to destroy. At most only moments or phases or coloring could be distinguished as they flash by. For Wundt, on the other hand, observation was able to distinguish sensations, which differed among themselves both in quality and in intensity. In fact, those were the only attributive characteristics of the simple processes. The sensations as so observed and so described made no reference in any direction,

---

[3]Brentano's *Psychologie vom empirischen Standpunkte* and Wundt's *Grundzüge der physiologischen Psychologie* (first edition) both appeared in the year 1874. Cf. E. B. Titchener, *Amer. J. Psychol.*, 1921, 32, 108-120.

neither to the agents and energies of stimulus, nor to the bodily organs themselves, nor to the objects of knowledge or of desire. They were purely existential. Such matters as judgment, conception and emotive attitude toward objects lie outside and beyond this observable region of the mental. Actual experience always contains formations and complexes of the simple processes; but those formations, when existentially regarded, are psychical just as their constituent processes are, and the forms and laws of their construction suggest one of the major problems of psychology. The acts of Brentano, on the other hand, with their immanent objectivity lead us at once to the functional relation of the individual to the objects of apprehension, to the truths and acknowledgments reached in judgment, and to the objects of emotive likes and dislikes, of desire and interest. All this is not to say that Brentano works out his functional view of consciousness as James works out his doctrine of cognition; it is only to say that the same functional aspect of experience as meaning or reference characterizes that side of James's psychology as it does Brentano's.

Neither do I mean to contend that Wundt, on the other side, succeeded, when he came to attention, to action and to thought, in maintaining his existential and descriptive view of mind, which was doubtless suggested, in large measure, by his earlier studies in sense-physiology. But that was his point of departure and it was a view which both led him toward the direct experimental attack upon psychological problems and led his pupils and followers to a more explicit, and possibly more consistent, "structural" view in the Jamesian sense. His psychology, then, with all its frailties and limitations, looks distinctly toward a scientific future of exploration and discovery in the laboratory.[4]

One of the first attempts made by the pupils of Wundt to bring together experimental facts, with as little general theory and philosophical bias as possible, was Külpe's *Grundriss* of 1893. Since this *Grundiss* or Outline was "based upon the results of experimental investigation" we may expect to find in it

---

[4] Of course we must not think of either point of view as originating with these two men. Both are much older. Cf. Titchener, *op. cit.*, p. 119. We need not follow the differences between the non-structural psychologies of function and of act. Titchener has written critically of this distinction in his articles upon Functional psychology and the psychology of act (*Amer. J. Psychol.* 1921, 32, 519-542; 1922 33, 43-83). He is here inclined to read into "function" a biological and teleological sense which does not accord with James's meaning.

a strong emphasis placed upon the analytical observation of experience. By limiting this observation to those properties which are dependent upon the physical organism Külpe followed Wundt to an examination of the elementary processes and of the modes of their interconnection. One of the virtues of Külpe's psychology was the simplicity and the directness of its logic. Another was its success in bringing together in a natural, coherent and empirical way, most of the laboratory studies then extant. Both virtues were destined to exert an influence in later "structural" envisagements of the psychological field.

From Külpe we must turn to Ebbinghaus, who likewise approaches psychology from the controlled observation of the laboratory. The first edition of his *Grundzüge* began to appear (I. Halbband) in 1897. For him the immediate experience of the living being furnishes the materials of psychology. But this material is both extensive and complicated and, like the body, it displays a high degree of unity and integrity. The mental life is organized even as the body is organized. How then is it to be studied and known? We are accustomed, says Ebbinghaus,[5] to approach any complicated set of phenomena from three different directions and thus to regard it in turn from three points of view. First we regard it existentially, for what it is. Here we analyse the complex into simpler parts, work out the structure (*Bau*) and the properties of these parts, and the mode of their combination; secondly, we consider the occurrences and changes to which these parts are subjected, and thirdly, we regard the developmental history of both structure and changes.

These three ways-of-regarding appear, for example, in the sciences of organic nature as (1) morphology, which seeks the laws of structure of living things, (2) physiology, the description of the life-processes, the functions of the organs, and (3) the embryological or racial history of form and function. No one of these modes of approach to natural phenomena is better or more complete than the others. Each is abstract; but each is necessary to the understanding of organic nature. The mental life, too, has its temporal development and transformation. Each aspect must be studied in its place. Mind is, to be sure, unitary and total; but we shall know little about it unless we examine its rich variety, its on-goings and its genetic changes. Our examination must not—of course—

[5]H. Ebbinghaus, *Grundzüge der Psychologie*, 1905, (2nd ed.), vol. i, 176-182.

reduce the totality to a sum or to an aggregate of parts or of separate functions. Thus Ebbinghaus proceeds in his own exposition, first treating his material anatomically or structurally, then advancing to the functional view, and ending with the facts and laws of development. Although the logic of the exposition is by no means so clear-cut as in Külpe, the threefold treatment is sufficiently exemplified. He always keeps within sight, however, of his living organic totality.[6]

In his article of 1897[7] upon *The postulates of a structural psychology* Titchener repeats Ebbinghaus's analogy with the biological sciences, applying the tripartite division also to taxonomy, ecology and phylogeny. The analogy is, as he thinks, complete. "We can represent modern psychology"—so he declares—"as the exact counterpart of modern biology. There are three ways of approaching the one as there are three ways of approaching the other" (450). "The primary aim of the experimental psychologist has been to analyse the structure of mind; to ravel out the elemental processes from the tangle of consciousness. . . . His task is a vivisection. . . . He tries to discover, first of all, what is there and in what quantity, not what it is there for" (450). Mind thus becomes "a complex of processes, shaped and moulded under the conditions of the physical organism" (451).

But "descriptive" psychology—the psychology of memory, recognition, judgment, volition and so on—Titchener discovers to be "chiefly occupied with problems of function" or of "mental physiology." Here there is "much of value"—as he admits; but the functional point of view cannot "lead to results of scientific finality." The revolt from a philosophical treatment of faculties rather leads straight toward a scientific morphology, which is well designed to supply a foundation to the new science. Our author predicts "a long period of analytical research, whose results . . . . shall ultimately serve as basis for the psychology of function" (454). He then goes on to describe the elementary structures in the attributive terms which are familiar to all of you and the complex morphological formations, the structural "organs," in the classes worked out by Wundt and Külpe from the logic of John Stuart

---

[6]See, *e. g.*, his treatment of the *general attributes* of sensation: form, magnitude, interval, movement, identity, similarity, difference, and the like. The recent psychology of the *Gestalt* lies much nearer to this type of psychology than to the systems of Wundt and Külpe.

[7]E. B. Titchener, *Philos. Rev.*, 1898, 7, 449-465.

Mill. He ends by the anticipation that the psychology of function may have "a great future"; but also with the conviction that "the best hope for psychology lies today in a continuance of structural analysis."

In estimating the importance of this paper, which is sometimes referred to as marking the entrance of the structural point of view into psychology, we must observe that its main result was to clarify, as by a refined process of the etcher, the distinction which had already been made. It is very much cleaner-cut than Ebbinghaus, if only because Titchener was throwing up a substantial wall of partition behind which he obviously meant to labor and to give battle; while Ebbinghaus was laying out the wide psychological domains into great fields in which he proposed freely to pass from place to place with only a formal recognition of inside boundaries. However important or trivial we shall find the accomplishments of structuralism to be, we must recognize the gain in clear thinking which accrued to Titchener's sharply drawn distinction between the analytical psychology of structure and the descriptive psychology of mental operation and functional performance.

Within analytical observation itself, he made it clear that much that passes for an introspective photography of mind was a presentation of logical meanings and of ethical and social values; the "unschooled introspection" of the mental "Is-for," he called it, as set against the schooled observation of what consciously "Is" (1899, 291ff). While he tended constantly to speak of the former as the "besetting sin of the descriptive psychologist" and of the latter as the truly psychological method, he does admit a psychology of psychophysical (as distinguished from logical, ethical and social) functions, in which value-to-the-organism shall be the basal concept (1899, 293). Taken as a doctrine and as a fundamental mode of procedure in psychological observation, then, the structural point of view in Titchener seeks to perpetuate and to clarify the contention of James, Wundt, Külpe, Ebbinghaus, and many others, that the ultimate materials of psychology are *Erlebnisse,* not *Erfahrungen*; that is to say, the fluent processes of concrete experiencings, not those crystallized and logicized *ideas* of Hume, Spencer and the Mills, under which he had been reared. In the light of subsequent events in psychology, it is worth noting that so early as 1899 our author had regarded his distinction of structure and function as "no more than a working schema by which one's present knowledge may be temporarily arranged—a schema to be ruthlessly discarded so soon as a better is proposed" (*297*).

Now is is almost a truism that no one understands himself until he understands his opponent. We can hardly expect, therefore, to recover the structural point of view of that time unless we consider the counter doctrine of function against which it contended. Talk as they would in polite terms of parallel advance, dividing the field and complementing each the other, the underlying conviction of each party was that it was itself the main reliance of psychology. Sharpening and narrowing the concept of a dissecting kind of analysis only tended to establish more firmly those who went in for mental functions. We have seen the influence of biology in modeling the newer science of psychology. We must also observe that biology threatened to absorb psychology, as well as to set it models. This threat came through the functionalists. Mind is, so they said, but an organic device. It is one of the means of subsistence and of adjustment to the environment. Perceiving, valuing, appreciating, acting and knowing are devices for survival. They are fuctional resources. Such a view appeared soon after Titchener's article in J. R. Angell's espousal of function.[8] Structure, for him, bore only upon the discernment of complexity in fragments of consciousness. It was not otherwise comparable to the cellular members of a living body or to the physical and chemical elements. Function, on the contrary, was the main aspect of our common experiences. It was the "how" and the "why" of our processes of conscious adjustment; and since it included cognition, conation, affective appreciation, and much besides, it led straight into all the problems of logic, ethics, aesthetics and the other philosophical disciplines.

An interesting variation in the existential or structural treatment appeared in the writings of Münsterberg near the beginning of the century. In his Presidential Address of 1898[9] before the American Psychological Association Münsterberg distinguished psychology from history, contending that psychology, like physics, regards its objects as complexes of elements, while history deals with the will-attitudes and the pur-

---

[8] The relations of structural and functional psychology to philosophy. *Univ. of Chicago Decennial Publ.*, 1903, ser. 1, vol. vi, pt. 2, 55-73; also *Philos. Rev.*, 1903, 12, 243-271. The actual contents of a functional psychology based upon evolutionary conceptions are set forth by Angell in his *Psychology; an introductory study of the structure and function of human consciousness*, 1904.

[9] *Psychol. Rev.*, 1899, 6, 1-31.

poses of a person. But later[10] he came to distinguish within psychology itself both causal and purposive varieties. The first studied consciousness by way of analysis, reducing it to simplest parts, which were then casually explained by reference to neural processes. The second sought to understand in terms of value the purposes of man. Both taken together gave Münsterberg a basis for his psychology of applications. The first appears roughly to represent the structural point of view; but, in reality, it is a mixture of process and function. Sensations and their associated components appear along with such matters of performance as action, perception, and the activities of the social mind. Where, therefore, Münsterberg speaks of "the world of mental processes" (1914, 285), we are not to take the phrase in the sense of Titchener's anatomical description. It soon became the fashion to 'reconcile' structure and function, just as it is now the fashion to reconcile behaviorism and introspection. Among these attempts at reconciliation of the two standpoints may be mentioned the Presidential Address of Professor Calkins before the same Association in 1905.[11] Carrying over George Darwin's distinction between the biologist's functional relationship of the organism to the environment and the physicist's analytic interest in the ultimate structures of matter, Calkins attempted to show that the postulates of a self-psychology could well make use of analysis (which she held to be the essential point of the structuralists) and at the same time make use of the category of function. The self, that is to say, is to be at once structurally analysed and functionally set into relation with the physical and social environment. This view, which regarded with disfavor the biological trend of the times among the functionalists, depended, of course, upon its basal conception of a conscious "self." Its alleged merit is, in this connection, the ackowledgment of an inescapable self, which demands for its description both an analysis into structures and the recognition of outside functional relations.

From the turn of the century, and especially after the rival claims of the structural and the functional psychologies had been set forth by Titchener and Angell, vigorous and widespread discussions upon the distinction sprang up on all sides.[12]

[10]E. g., in *Psychology, general and applied*, 1914.

[11]M. W. Calkins, *Psychol. Rev.*, 1906, 13, 61-81; cf. Psychology as science of selves, *Philos Rev.*, 1900, 9, 490-501.

[12]Among the earliest attacks upon structuralism stand those of W. Caldwell in *Psychol. Rev.*, 1898, 5, 401-408; 1899, 6, 187-191.

Out of these discussions grew a very well marked partisan difference which was destined to play a prominent part in the writings and in the laboratories of American psychology for the next two decades. Let me emphasize the reference to the laboratories, for structuralism has laid great weight upon its own suitability for the experimental attack upon psychological problems. By its contributions to experimental research its value may then fairly be judged. Next time we shall begin here and go on to consider the fruits of the structural view and try to estimate their importance for our subject.

CHAPTER XVIII

THE WORK OF THE STRUCTURALISTS*

By Madison Bentley

A convenient starting-point for our examination of structuralism, as it actually worked itself out in the laboratories, may be set by a summary of the problems of experimental psychology which was made in 1904 by Professor Titchener for the International Congress in St. Louis.

The materials for this summary Titchener gathered, as he tells us,[13] from five representative periodicals, two German one French and two American, and all of them at that time of several years standing.

After drawing a distinction between the "psychological" and the "psychophysical" experiment (the former aiming at an "introspective acquaintance with the processes and formations of a given consciousness"; the latter at a "numerical determination"), the reviewer goes on to give the result of his survey. He finds (1) that the recent course of experimental psychology had been away from psychophysics and toward introspection; (2) that studies upon sensation, attention, perception, memory, association and action had been abundant, and (3) that the trend had been from the simple in mind toward the complex. His counsel for future work lays stress, as we might expect, upon those fields where the structural mode is most at home; first upon sensation, affection and attention, designated as the three fundamental departments of psychology, and afterwards upon the analytical side of memory, association, action and the higher intellectual processes. He is obviously troubled by the functional terms "perception" and "imagination" which he would like to banish or discard. In the one topic he finds "no very pressing problem," and, in the other, experiment "hardly over the threshold." Finally, the conquest of the total consciousness, the "ultimate goal" of experiment, appears to be remote. At the end Titchener considers briefly and with some diffidence the experimental problems of the non-structuralist, the man who is not "enamored of introspection." Though he obviously tries to be non-partisan, he virtually drives the non-structuralist from the study of the normal, human adult. Experiment here "must take the form of introspective analysis."

---

*Powell Lecture in Psychological Theory at Clark University, January 6, 1926.

[13] Amer. J. Psychol., 1905, 16, 208-234.

He has "little sympathy or patience" with others. Their mode is inherently "vicious," and so on. A sort of tolerance is shown for outsiders in animal and child psychology and in the treatment of the abnormal; and the claims made for structural analysis in those domains are decidedly weak.

Here we have, then, twenty years ago, a very fair intimation of what we may expect of a structural psychology, as well as a statement of its past conquests in the experimental field. Now let us turn the page to a later time and look for fulfilment.

When, in the autumn of 1909, Clark University celebrated its twentieth anniversary, Professor Titchener was asked to review the past decade in experimental psychology,[14] a period which was long enough, as he thought, to warrant an inventory. Let us see what the claims of structuralism were at this time. The speaker prefaced his inventory by a high tribute to Ebbinghaus, recently dead, and by an anticipation that only "a small minority" in his audience would adopt his standpoint of unapplied or "pure" science and would accept his conclusions.

By way of review Titchener found heavy inroads of practical interest, mentioning Meumann and pedagogy, Stern and *Aussage,* Jung and diagnosis, Münsterberg and psychotherapy. He hints that such men are casual visitors to psychology, dwelling for a time at the psychological cross-roads and passing on with the gratitude and the "godspeed" of the faithful. In this implied canon of criticism you see now, as some of us saw then, the *parti pris,* the logical *petitio,* and confusion of structural analysis with psychology *ueberhaupt;* and you will be prepared for the standards of criticism by means of which the decade's fruitfulness was judged. Good energy has been "diverted," as we are told, into practical channels which might otherwise have been expended in the service of science, while non-psychological "temperaments," attracted to the laboratory, whether "by curiosity, by mere chance of novelty," or in a "serious mood," have "placed positive hindrances in the way of scientific advance."

The topical review is the same as before. Knowledge of *sensation* has increased, though theory there is still unsatisfactory. The psychophysics of sensation has most strikingly advanced. We well remember that our author has himself, in the meantime, made (especially by way of critical and clarified

14*Amer. J. Psychol.,* 1910, 21, 404-421.

exposition) a very large contribution in his Quantitative Psychology.[15] In *simple feeling* the reviewer found much product but not much gain. The problem is still "upon the regular waiting list," where it remains, as I venture to think, in this year of grace 1926. The subject of *attention* has gained by "many systematic treatises and laboratory studies" upon the measurement of clearness. *Perception* again troubles Titchener as a "field of vast range and uncertain limits." Certain spatial and temporal perceptions have been advanced, notably by Benussi and other members of the Austrian school of Meinong; while biology and motor theories have run riot in America. *Memory* and *association* have profited more in the psychophysical and practical directions than in their pure, analytical problems. Of the four researches mentioned, two authors (Kuhlmann and Whipple) had been connected with your own University. *Action* has taken strides in the way of structural analysis, Ach and Watt making noteworthy contributions. *Imagination* is still "virgin territory." The *emotions* await agreement upon the affective qualities; but the experimental studies of the *thought-processes* have, more than any one line of investigation, "characterized the decennium." You know as well as I the works of Würzburg and of Binet, Bovet, and Woodworth to which reference is made, and you also know the clear-cut exposition of all these works in Titchener's own "Experimental psychology of the thought processes" (1909).

For the extensions of experiment outside these preferred headings of the structuralist, Titchener has time—as before—for "only a word or two." Individual psychology is increasing in importance, while the study of the abnormal has fallen below expectations. The psychology of the animals is growing; but the mental endowment of the animals can be profitably studied "only by men trained in human psychology." Titchener closes his review by the declaration that "to approach the study of mind without analysis would, in fact, be nothing less than ridiculous; and, in fact, no one does it," a statement which would scarcely have been made ten years later.

I have dwelt upon these reviews of 1905 and 1910 less because they represent achievements in the field of psychology at large than because they may fairly be supposed to give a

---

[15]In another connection I have questioned the logic of bringing the psychophysical metric methods under sensation instead of under the rubrics of function. (*The field of psychology*, 1924, 400-413.)

favorable view of structuralism during the years when that form of psychological activity was especially vigorous and productive. In the later review (the earlier is chiefly based upon a general survey of a few of the journals) Titchener cites over 60 articles and books as making contributions to his brand of "pure science." But we must remark that a dozen of these are psychophysical (most of them works on *Methodik*) and of these only two can be said to be chiefly analytical in his sense. Moreover, this whole dozen would appear to be at least as contributive to other brands of psychology; while several of the works can scarcely be called "structural" at all, either in aim or intent.   These include Hering's *Lehre*, Nagel's *Handbuch*, Wundt's *Bemerkungen*, Pillsbury's *Attention*, Dürr's *Aufmerksamkeit*, Woodworth's *Imageless Thought*, and the whole list of Göttingen studies of *Association*.   To be sure many of these works have been found to be useful to men working under what Titchener calls the "temperament" of the structuralist. But all who know the psychological literature of those times will see that, from most of them, the non-structuralist—however "impure" his temperament—has been able to abstract a good deal of comfort.   Nothing could be more useful, for example, to a certain "functional temperament" than G. E. Müller's *Komplex*, Pillsbury's and Dürr's *Attention*, and Messer's and Woodworth's *Gedanken;* while the debt of *Gestaltpsychologie* to Hering and Ebbinghaus is actually as great as it would be if it were frankly acknowledged.

The same selective appropriation from sources common to all psychologies appears in Ruckmick's review in 1915.[16] By counting titles in certain sections[17] of the *Psychological Index* (1905-1915) this historian discovers "roughly two-and-a-half times as many introspective as non-introspective experimental papers."   Again we must make allowance for the outlying provinces of psychology (intensively cultivated during this decade) and also for the fact that "introspective" covers a multitude of meanings and is by no means coincident with the "structural" variety.   The outcome may supply a hard nut for the behaviorist to crack; but I doubt whether anyone, no matter what his "temperament," can extract much consolation from the ratio.

The logical maturity of our doctrine was within sight when

---

[16]C. A. Ruckmick, The last decade of psychology in review, Amer. Psychol. Ass., Dec., 1915, and *Psychol. Bull.*, 1916, 13, 109-120.

[17]Coincident, in the main, with Titchener's range.

Külpe and his pupils approached the citadel of thought by way of the analytical method. Not daunted by Marbe's meagre results with the simpler "judgments" or by Binet's divinatory distinctions in the field of the intellect, Külpe set out upon the direction indicated in Ach's studies of action by the method of "systematic experimental introspection."   We know the general issue of the work. Wundt thought the method employed (*Ausfragemethode*) logically imperfect, and he himself had resorted to the genetic method of the Völkerpsychologie. Titchener, who was presently to undertake these problems in his own laboratory by way of structural analysis, finds[18] in 1909 the "three most tangible things....characteristic and new" in the outcome to be "a specific problem set: a principle of explanation discovered: a volume of untrimmed introspections offered in evidence."

There are many opinions upon the contribution made to thinking by the 'structural' methods.   I doubt, however, whether anyone who has tried to write a coherent psychology of thinking would contend that these methods have either supplied the materials for this difficult chapter or so much as indicated a usable means toward its experimental conquest. We have, to be sure, various raw *Gedankenelemete* and the *processes* of the sensationalists; but, since thinking is a *mode of performance* and not any specific set of processes, the method of structural analysis would appear to be at most a preliminary reconnaissance of new territory and not a means of conquest.

Clark University has played its part in the history of structural examination. The careful and meticulous researches of the late Professor Baird represent, as it seems to me, the most persistent attempt to resolve the subtlest and most refractory problems of experience by the methods of analysis. If they did not succeed in storming the citadels of thinking, they stand, nevertheless, as notable instances of refined scientific procedure in the laboratory, and they have, moreover, produced factual materials with which every student of thought must hereafter acquaint himself.

It is impossible, at this time, to place a final value upon the standpoint which we have been examining. If I set down what seem to me to be its psychological virtues and its limitations, I do this principally by way of an individual opinion when complete objectivity is still out of the question. But

---

[18]*Lectures on the experimental psychology of the thought processes,* 1909, 165.

opinion at least challenges divergent opinion, and it also stands the chance of containing a partial truth.

In the first place, structuralism was timely. It stood for high standards of research when a multitude of new problems appeared for which psychology had no canons and no adequate procedures. Philosophy, physiology, general biology, and the arts of application all stood at the door demanding admittance. By setting off a definite and circumscribed area our doctrine demanded the best empirical tools and means available. It took over, notably from physiology, certain definite problems and these it made really and clearly psychological. The immediate formulation of functionalism and the gradual emergence of an "objective" point of view naturally followed. These proposals had, at the least, something definite against which to protest. Protestantism is never a primary movement in human thought. It presupposes some current doctrine, creed, or method to protest. The more definite and aggressive the entrenched doctrine, the better for the protestants.

In the second place, structuralism had the scientific virtue of reducing logical concepts and of setting free certain problems which demanded an experimental solution. When we examine psychology at the opening of this century we see that this was not a superfluous or merely academic virtue.

In the third place, structuralism set a premium upon historical studies and upon an historical continuity within psychology. Other types of psychology might—but so far as I know no other type does—insist so effectively upon historical coherence. The first generation of psychologists (the generation responsible for the opening of the laboratories and the establishment of academic departments) knew their antecedents. Had they not, I doubt whether they could have made their way with presidents, trustees, and the great public. Such historical knowledge has not been the rule in the succeeding generations. Flagrant instances of ignorance of antecedents, and of present rival doctrines as well, lead one to wonder what mental age would be indicated by an intelligence test applied to psychologists upon their own subject. You will agree, as I think, that no single individual has done so much to cultivate this historical knowledge of psychology as has Professor Titchener.

Again, and finally, the great productivity in certain branches of psychology under the standpoint of structural analysis is acknowledged by everyone who knows the literature of the last quarter-century. Who can here estimate *relative* values? It would be a wise psychologist, much more objective than the most ardent of the "objectivists," who could accord to each school its just due; and, once accorded, what school would be convinced!

Upon certain general points, however, we may, as I think, look for agreement among those who are accustomed to keep the run of psychological production here and abroad.

First, it is obvious that research under the category of "structure" has been most productive in certain limited fields of adult human psychology. These fields include sensation, simple feeling, attention and action. Here description in "process" (or its equivalent) has greatly added to our knowledge. While not inventive or revolutionary the methods here have been— as I should say—sounder and more productive than any other methods in psychology. But wherever the facts and the concepts have called for an account of operation or performance, as in perception, memory and thinking, the structural methods have shown themselves to be inadequate. In the fields of the abnormal, the genetic and the individual, not much has been contributed from this direction.

In the second place, the revival and extension of quantitative problems and procedures owe much to structuralism,—or, at the least, to certain advocates of that doctrine. Titchener's Quantitative Psychology was almost encyclopedic in its proportions. It has greatly advanced what we may call the psychologization of the metric methods. But whether measurement in psychology is really *mental* measurement, as some structuralists have argued, I have had occasion to doubt; for I have thought that what we actually measure by the psychophysical methods is functional output and not anything which can be turned into "process." However that may be, our debt to the strict methodology of the structuralists is here very great; and it will appear greater as the promise of the present is gradually fulfilled.

On the other side of the ledger, too, certain entries must be made. In the first place, structuralism has, to my mind, never justified its dogmatic assertion that first-hand observation of human experience was synomynous with structural observation. Neither has it justified its contention that the main method of science was analysis. It is, as I think, not much less than a caricature of the sciences of nature to say that the physicist, the chemist, and the zoologist are always and only analysing.

Köhler has, as we know, recently given very definite indications to the contrary; but outside the range of this dogma it has, for some time, been generally conceived to be a formal and logical—not a realistic—view of science which has brought into relief the typical chemist or physicist as forever breaking down his substances into constituent elements. Analysis, surely! but not *simply* analysis; and, for many problems, not analysis at all.

Once more. The dogma of the simple has tempted the structuralist to confuse his province with the general range of psychological problems and methods. What this doctrine *can* do has been abundantly shown. Its genius is expressed in the range of its actual accomplishments. But what lies beyond must also be considered. It succeeds best, as it seems to me, in its description of the qualitative variety within experience. There it is very strong where the doctrine of the *Gestalt* is weak. But it needs to be complemented and supplemented by many other characterizations of experience, to say nothing of those problems of organic performance in which experience is only implied. I do not hold with those who believe that a simple verbal formula (*e.g.,* the formula of stimulus-response), with only a general and hypothetical conception of bodily mechanisms, will enable the psychologist to meet the demands both of science and of the various forms of practice from animal training to sociology. That savors of science by the attachment of labels. But I see no reason why all the knowledge we can muster should not be used by those interested in the arts of practice. In reflecting upon the call to administrative duties of your late Professor Sanford, Titchener remarked[19] that experimental results must justify themselves by some sanction, some principle of co-ordination, and that, in experimental psychology, he could see but two sanctions; the first "system, the applied logic of general psychology, and the second application." Surely, if we justify the research of our laboratories by way of these two sanctions, we shall discover not one single experimental road to follow, but many.

There is still another defect which, while it is not peculiar to structuralism alone, deserves to be set down in this list with considerable deliberation. It appears in the assumption that the parts or members of experience run a course parallel to that of excitatory processes in the receptor. In the structural accounts of sensation each element has its own specific

---

[19]*Amer. J. Psychol.*, 1925, 36, 159.

antecedent, and the 'theories' of sensation (visual, auditory, and the rest) attempt to set forth the antecedent term in this invariable sequence. A corollary of this one-to-one relation between sensation and neural process appears in the emphasis laid by the structuralist upon "stimulus."[20] We see, then, how naturally sensationalism has tended toward a peripheral and sensory theory of bodily substrates. Again, in Angell's biological functionalism consciousness confesses its dependence upon physical antecedents within and without the organism. While the one-to-one correlation is less rigidly carried out here, the same principle of determination is evident. Only in the selective powers of attention and volition does consciousness wear the appearance of an originator and director. Nowhere, however, does this principle appear so fundamental to any psychological doctrine as in the stimulus-response hypothesis of behaviorism. There the consequent term is not sensation and not conscious function, but movement. As the organism is stimulated so does it move. Without this one-to-one parallelism behaviorism falls to the ground, or else it becomes (as we now frequently see it becoming) something different, though wearing the same label.

I have spoken of this common tendency as a 'defect.' There is, as I think, enough evidence to sanction the statement. The upholders of the *Gestalt-theorie* have not minimized—as we all know—the deficiencies of this hypothesis of a constant relation of psychological antecedent and consequent (*Konstanz-hypothese*). For them stimulus is not the real determiner of experience. As the latter is always a unitary whole or totality, so does it depend upon a similar kind of total-function in the body. Stimulus is the more or less incidental occasion of the experience, not the model or pattern of its integral characteristics. While an allied tendency to forsake local functions and neuronal tracts in the brain appears in the cerebral studies of Franz, Lashley and others, as well as in much current work among the neurologists *von Fach*. Now the sequences "stimulus-sensation" and "stimulus-movement" rest upon the old conceptions of local excitation and of the reflex-arc as the representative functional unit of the nervous system; conceptions which have, as it seems to many, lost (in spite of their simplicity) most of their former usefulness in psychology. On

---

[20]The study of the affective qualities has always been more difficult. Structural analysis has vacillated between the views of receptors and no-specific receptors for the simple feelings.

the one hand, structuralism and behaviorism have laid too much emphasis upon stimulus and its direct organic effects at the receptor, in the brain, in experience, and in movement. Configurationism, on the other, goes too far in making stimulus and receptor merely incidental to experience. In holding to an intermediate position I should say that stimulus and the integral and functionally tuned body are co-determiners, which must be taken into strict account whether we seek the essential antecedents of experience, of the structural attributes, or of the organic movement.

Thus our adverse criticisms tend rather toward the pretenses and the inherent limitations than toward the actual procedures of structuralism. There is no doubt, moreover, that the criticisms should be tempered by reflection upon the complementary frailties and limitations of competing standpoints. If this creed does ultimately rest upon a certain kind of "temperament," as we have heard that it does, and upon a preference for problems of a certain restricted type, as we have seen that it does, then its claim to supply the one substantial foundation for our subject or to represent a "purer" and more desirable set of scientific principles than others would seem to stand with no more justification than do the similar pretensions of rival doctrines.

In our final estimation of this standpoint we must consider, as we observed at the beginning, that it represents a closed chapter in psychological history.[21] We take the past as it stands. We act foolishly when we try to ignore it; and we proceed with wisdom when we acknowledge the substantial contributions which the doctrine of mental structures has made to the subject of our common study and our common regard.

---

[21]In a remark upon the passing of the structure-function antithesis, Titchener has recently referred to the "radical change wrought over the whole field of the science since it turned to phenomenology" (*Amer. J. Psychol.*, 1925, 36, 323). How emphatically his own envisagement of psychology has been modified is indicated by the catholic range of articles published in the American Journal of Psychology under his competent editorship of the last five years.

CHAPTER XIX

THE PSYCHOLOGICAL ORGANISM*

By Madison Bentley

Within the last three decades the influence of the biological sciences upon our subject has been very great. Especially in America have these disciplines deeply impressed psychology both by way of their general point of view and by way of their methods of procedure. This deep impress of the biological pattern is to be first ascribed, as we may suppose, to the rapid advancement of physiology and of the evolutionary studies of the organism at a time when psychology was forsaking its ancient philosophical allies and seeking an alliance with the sciences of nature. The impress itself is plainly to be seen in the trend of our animal studies, in genetic accounts of the human being, in the adaptive and adjustive types of functionalism, and in various behavioristic writings of the last two decades.

To many this inclination in psychology to merge with the biological group is wholly admirable. Those who encourage the tendency are content to adopt the concepts and the problems of the zoological sciences; though they generally limit themselves to certain problems of anatomy and physiology or to certain phases of the dynamic relations of the animal to its surroundings.

Anyone who is familiar with our current books and periodicals will have observed that this biological point of view has been productive. It has been productive, that is to say, within a fairly limited range of problems; a range which covers many inquiries into neural functions, the movement systems of the body, and the active ecological adjustments of the organism. But we must also observe that many facts of psychological import naturally lie without this range; though they are sometimes forced within it by a strained and illogical inclusion. Such an effort to biologize facts which lie outside the realm of the active body and its functions appears, for example, in the attempts of the behaviorist to write "objectively" of memory, imagination, thinking and the like, in terms of "responsive" adjustments of the body to its environment.

*Powell Lecture in Psychological Theory at Clark University, January 7, 1926.

It is this logical and factual failure of biological concepts and principles within a relatively large part of psychology which suggests the distinction between the biological and the psychological organism; or between what we may more accurately describe as the psychologist's conception as set over against the biologist's conception of the living being. The proposal to start fresh with a new view of the organism is certain to meet with resistance; but with resistance which rests upon nothing more secure, as I venture to believe, than the temporal priority and the scientific prestige of a group of disciplines firmly established in the intellectual life of European and American cultures. We can well conceive that a fundamental and rapid development of psychology fifty or seventy-five years ago, out of which a biological group might gradually have come, would have found us with as strong a contrary bias against a mere anatomy or a mere treatment of bodily functions. At all events it is worth our while to neglect, for the moment, the biological abstractions from the totality of our lives and to encourage a view of the organism which shall be distinctively psychological.

To be sure, such phrases as "the totality of life" or "the total process of living" should be qualified by any form of psychology which hopes to escape the charge that it seeks to embrace the whole round of human life. No one of the sciences treats exhaustively and at large its objects of study. Much is known and written about the surface of the earth which does not fall under geography; much about animals which is not to be found within the zoological treatises, and so with all the others. It is only quite special and restricted views and aspects of objects and processes which fall within the compass of any of the sciences of nature. Psychology orients itself in just the same way. The self-styled psychology of the romantic magazine and of the character analyst may capitalize anything which brings in the "human element" or the "inner life" of man; but any psychology which makes its peace with logic, which is constituted of principles, and which respects facts, must restrict itself to a point of view just as rigorously as do botany, physics, geology, and all the rest.

When we propose the "total" or "psychological" organism as the object of our study and investigation we only mean to psychologize those facts of life which include at once the experiences which we commonly call "thinking," "wishing," "remembering," and the like, and also certain zoological details of the body and its operations. The proposal lays emphasis neither upon a "consciousness" which inhabits or shadows the body nor upon a self-sufficient mechanism of flesh and blood which suffers from and reacts to the agencies of the physical environment and which is only attended by an adventitious and half-real mind or spirit. Instead of two "aspects," then— one of them real and efficacious, the other epiphenomenal—we have one unitary organism, described in part in experiential, and in part in bodily, terms. Thus we advance one step from the abstract, cellular organism of the anatomist, physiologist, and student of genetics, from which all experience has been strained away, toward the concrete creature of our everyday lives. Only one step, for we still abstract, in psychology, from the personal, social, economic and political affairs where value, not description, plays the chief role.

Let us observe how an inquiry into such a *psychological* organism would stand related to some of the conceptions which we find current in our field today.

As regards, first, the behavioristic forms of doctrine we notice a difference with respect to the environment. The basal relation of stimulus to response implies that the environment is primary. The physical *milieu* affects itself by way of the organism, which it essentially controls. Since movement and some other vital activities are ultimately determined by the function of the receptors, and these latter organs by the energies of the stimulus, it follows that, for the behaviorists, the organism is more or less secondary to these physical systems which lie without. In our view, on the other hand, the total organism is central. It is the main object of study. It is no more absolutely independent of other systems than other objects of the universe are; but it is regarded for its own sake and other systems are treated in their relation to it. It is relatively independent.

With respect to the historical doctrine of structuralism our proposal shares the concept of experience. But whereas experience was there regarded as a complex which was to be described first of all by an analysis into elementary processes having assignable properties or attributes, experience is here to be considered as an integral part of the organism, and it is to be described in such subdivisions or aspects as its own nature suggests and to be treated as a part of the activity of the total elementary qualities upon stimulus here gives way to the total organic system. Furthermore, the alleged dependence of the organism, which stands as the real temporal antecedent. One but only one—of the determinants of experience is stimulus, which stands among an entire congeries of physical agents momentarily affecting the organism. Where experience is isolated for its own separate description, both its qualitative variety and patterning and its inherent unities have to be considered: where the organism is to be viewed functionally, experience merges with other factors and moments in the total performance.

From configurationism, taken in the sense of the *Gestalt,* we should chiefly dissent where that doctrine exaggerates the importance of the "total" side of experience, contending for the primacy of the *whole* and subordinating the part, together with its antecedent conditions, to a structure (*Struktur*) which is frequently ambiguous and conspicuously undeterminable. Its neglect of qualitative variety should be replaced by a more empirical and a more catholic description.

While psychoanalysis takes a direction divergent from the psychological view which we here sustain, certain fundamental similarities may be made out. There, too, emphasis is laid upon the integrity, especially the temporal integrity, of the living being. The individual is to be understood, according to the psychoanalyst, only by an inquiry into its past and with a prediction into its future. Whether it is made or marred depends upon its past, and its destiny likewise rests upon its reconstitution and re-organization in course. The divergent path of psychoanalysis begins with the assumption of conflicting psychical forces which are designed to explain the nature of human experience and of human character. Here the mental or the "spiritual" is made primary. Libido, the unconscious, compensation, sublimation, and the like, are causal agents which engender and mould the life-course of the individual and of society. This infringement of the total *psychological* organism and this creation of mental forces stand, of course, against the principles and the point of view here suggested.

These relations and distinctions may be set forth by the aid of the following simple diagram.

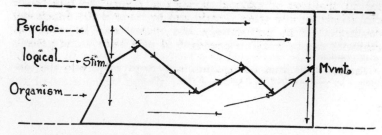

The section of the figure bounded by solid lines is designed schematically to represent the course of events within the psychological organism during a small segment of time. The dotted lines suggest that the segment is to be taken as an artificially limited moment within a continuous course. The zig-zig line from "stim" to "mvmt" stands for the alleged coupling of the behaviorist. Its course suggests that the real connection between a specific stimulus and a certain movement is (a) a continuous and constantly modified series of events, (b) determined in part by a large number of stimulus elements and in part by the total state and functional tendency of the entire psychological organism. The whole figure is meant to emphasize the fact that the organism is for us an integer; *i. e.*, a *relatively* independent system which is, in spite of its constant interplay with other systems, taking its course and making its changeable, but individual, way across its life-span. Here the psychological emphasis is upon the organism; not upon an environment which bounds and determines the organism from the two sides of stimulus and response. As against the structuralist's parallelism formulated between process (or attribute) and stimulus (or property of stimulus) the figure represents the natural coherences of experience and of bodily function as these are decreed by the total antecedent state, the functional trend, and the stimulus-patterns upon many receptors. As set against the psychical agencies which are postulated by the psychoanalyst to explain the "mental" peculiarities of a "physical" organism, the schema proposes a total and integral organism whose functions flow from a long and varied past under the modifying influences of a constantly changing present.

We may, at the end, indicate the way in which the conception of our psychological organism contributes to the solution of the main problems of psychology.[1]

I. *Performance and character of the adult human being.* Description, which is here the primary mode of procedure, takes two directions. The first looks toward the phenomenological depiction of experience, both as regards its qualitative characteristics and other details and as regards the functional description of its performance and operations. In so far as character can be made independent of past history and genetic

---

[1] The problems here distinguished have been more explicitly discussed by the author in *Psychol. Rev.*, 1926, 33, 71-105.

continuity, it becomes, under this heading, the empirical problem of the general and generic features of the individual or "person."

II. *The comparative study of animals.* As in all applications of the comparative method to the sciences, the psychological description of individuals is made as intensive and as exact as possible. Upon the basis of the individual descriptions a legitimate use of inference leads toward a sound comparison of unlike but related organisms. Here the logic of the procedure is exactly the same as it is in astral physics, paleontology and many other natural sciences. The only distinguishing feature of the comparisons here proposed is that the objects compared are psychological organisms and not the organisms of the embryologist and the geneticist.

III. *Psychological history of the individual, of human kind, and of the animal series.* The threefold problem of genesis and development is here wholly determined by the underlying conception of the organism. Zoological histories, whether ontogenetic or phylogenetic, are used only to this end, as are also studies of the behavior of the child, of the cultural levels of man, and of other animals. The primary aim is to establish, by all feasible means and methods, genetic continuities and disjunctions of a psychological kind within the individual and among blood relations.

IV. *Individual, class and racial differences.* Here all the facts and principles derived from the three preceding subdivisions are brought together and made to bear upon the discovery of a differential psychology. The psychological conception of the individual seems to be especially appropriate in this group of problems. For it is plain that neither somatic factors nor mental factors are adequate, when taken alone, to the description of the differentiating characteristics of the individual. The essential similarities and dissimilarities seem, on the contrary, to inhere in the total organism. Even the quantitative distinctions drawn between human beings—as of "intelligence" or of "character"—rest upon functional capabilities which express, not the body alone or the mind alone, but the total organism. Furthermore, the failure of many attempts to typify by a single "measure" these characteristics of the individual suggests that the entire history of the organism must be considered in this branch of psychology. The same necessity for depicting the entire person or individual appears in drawing distinctions between classes, races and ethnic groups.

V. *Psychological deficiencies and disorders.* Those defects, diseases, and abnormalities which the psychologist seeks to describe and to understand rest, for the greater part, upon a disturbance or an eccentricity of functions which express the total organism. The deficiency or disorder appears therefore in memory, perception, understanding, action, emotion, and the like; and these are precisely the functional modes of the psychological individual.

VI. *Social psychology.* Since every empirical psychology has had to reject such fictions as "the social consciousness," "the group mind," "the consciousness of kind," and other like social faculties, the actual realities of socialization itself and the concrete display of socialization in observed human groups and relationships have appeared to be of primary importance in the study of the social life of man and of other animals. And here it appears that man is socialized only as he exercises the functions of the total organism. It is the significance of the object or person perceived, the emotion suffered, the common action undertaken, and so on, that is socialized and that thus socializes the individual and the group. It is not any mysterious instinct or innate power which draws men together. Of course it is necessary in social studies to go behind the actual moment of socialization to its conditions and causes; but here again whatever makes the psychological organism and makes it change and develop underlies the socialized experience and the conduct of the human individual. The integral character of the whole individual likewise suggests an integration of these conditions as well. Hence we have, instead of a bundle of instincts, a dozen springs of human action, or the coercion of "social institutions," the development of the socialized person unfolding as the product (not the sum) of (1) racial stock, (2) the sheer processes of growth, (3) the moulding influence of the physical surroundings, (4) intercourse with other beings, and (5) the impress of institutions, traditions and customs. No one of these factors is to be exalted above the others, and no combination of them is to be regarded as external and merely summative.

We have proposed, in fine, to set out upon the road toward psychological description and explanation under the logical guidance of a *psychologist's organism* or of a *psychological organism;* discounting, on the one hand, the philosopher's notion of an independent mind or consciousness, and, on the other, the biologist's abstraction of an organized and self-sufficient body of flesh and blood. With this approach, our main problems concern those active and experiencing individuals which we ourselves *are* day by day and moment by moment. Only we must leave aside for separate and non-psychological consideration all concerns of "human nature" which are private, valuational and normative. The organism so regarded has seemed to us to offer a promising and suitable approach to the main fields of psychological exposition and research.